INDI
& BANGLAI

a Lonely Planet travel atlas

India

1st edition

Published by
Lonely Planet Publications
Head Office: PO Box 617, Hawthorn, Vic 3122, Australia
Branches: 155 Filbert St, Suite 251, Oakland, CA 94607, USA
               10 Barley Mow Passage, Chiswick, London W4 4PH, UK
               71 bis rue du Cardinal Lemoine, 75005 Paris, France

Cartography by
Steinhart Katzir Publishers Ltd
Fax: 972-3-696 1360, 972-4-624975

Printed by
Colorcraft Ltd, Hong Kong

Photographs by
Greg Elms (GE), Richard I'Anson (RI), Bryn Thomas (BT)

Front cover: Sadhu, Amarnath Cave, Kashmir (GE)
Back cover: Rajasthani women (RI)
Title page: Rupmati's Pavilion, Mandu, Madhya Pradesh (BT)

First Published
April 1995

**Although the authors and publisher have tried to make the information as
accurate as possible, they accept no responsibility for any loss, injury or
inconvenience sustained by any person using this book.**

National Library of Australia Cataloguing in Publication Data

Finlay, Hugh
India travel atlas.

1st ed.
Includes index.
ISBN 0 86442 270 9.

1. India – Maps, Tourist. 2. India – Road Maps. I. Title.
(Series : Lonely Planet travel atlas).

912.54

CONTENTS

Acknowledgements......................4

INDIA

   Locator Maps.........................5-9

   Map Legend...........................10-11

   Maps...................................12-101

Getting Around India

   English 102

   Français..................................103

   Deutsch..................................104-105

   Español 106-107

   日本語 108-109

Index 110-163

Hugh Finlay

After a failed career in engineering, Hugh set off around Australia in the mid '70s, working at everything from parking cars to diamond prospecting in outback South Australia. He spent three years travelling on three continents, all financed by Arab petrobucks earned working on an irrigation project in Saudi Arabia. He finally descended from the ozone in 1985 and joined Lonely Planet soon after.

Hugh has worked on many Lonely Planet books, including guides to north and east Africa, *Malaysia, Singapore & Brunei* and *Australia*. He is also the coordinating author of Lonely Planet's award-winning guide to *India*, as well as serving as the researcher for this pioneering edition of the *India* travel atlas.

About this Atlas

This is the second book to be produced in Lonely Planet's new series of travel atlases. Designed to tie in with the equivalent Lonely Planet guidebook, we hope the India travel atlas helps travellers enjoy their trip even more. As well as detailed, accurate maps, the atlas also contains a multilingual map legend, useful travelling information in five languages, and a comprehensive index to ensure easy location-finding.

The maps were checked out by Hugh Finlay as part of preparation for the next edition of Lonely Planet's *India* guidebook.

From the Publishers

Thanks to Dany Schapiro at Steinhart Katzir Publishers, who researched and drew the maps and prepared the index. At Lonely Planet, the mapping was checked and index finalised by Lou Byrnes and Greg Alford, and by Michelle Stamp, who also prepared the layout, design and cover design. The illustrations were drawn by Tamsin Wilson.

The language sections were coordinated with the assistance of Maria Roca, Keiko Hirata, Megan Fraser, Yoshiharu Abe, Sally Steward, James Jenkin, Arthur Braun, Katie Purvis, Adrienne Costanzo and Zahia Hafs.

Especial thanks to Hugh Finlay for careful and patient map-checking, and for negotiating mysterious whirlpools, mud and the vagaries of the Indian road system.

Request

This atlas is designed to be clear, comprehensive and reliable. We hope you'll find it a worthy addition to your Lonely Planet travel library.

Even if you don't, please let us know! All suggestions and corrections are welcome – write to Lonely Planet and tell us what you think.

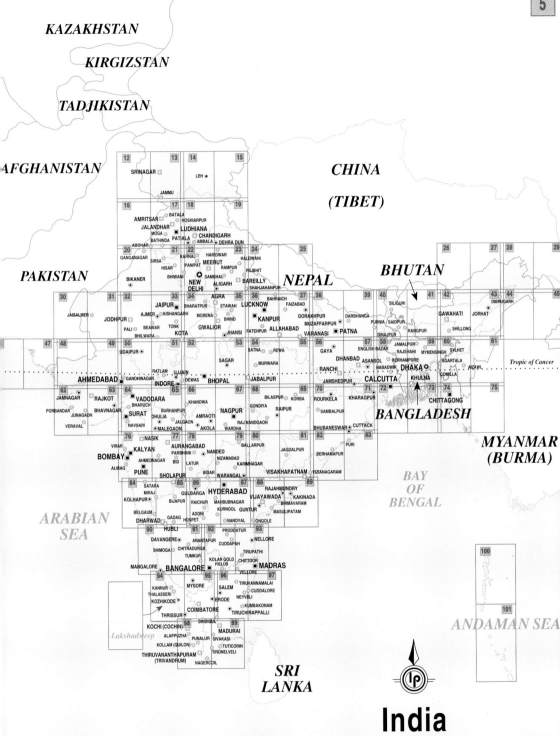

KAZAKHSTAN

KIRGIZSTAN

TADJIKISTAN

AFGHANISTAN

CHINA
(TIBET)

PAKISTAN

NEPAL

BHUTAN

BANGLADESH

MYANMAR
(BURMA)

ARABIAN
SEA

BAY
OF
BENGAL

ANDAMAN SEA

Lakshadweep

SRI
LANKA

INDIAN OCEAN

Tropic of Cancer

India
& Bangladesh

0   300   600 km

The external boundaries
of India in these maps have not been
authenticated and may not be correct

*The external boundaries
of India in these maps have not been
authenticated and may not be correct*

Indus River

PAKISTAN

ARABIAN

SEA

Tropic of Cancer

Narmada River

Grand Trunk Road

Grand Trunk Road

Godavari River

SRINAGAR • LEH

JAMMU

PATHANKOT • DHARAMSALA • MANALI

BATALA

LAHORE • AMRITSAR HOSHIARPUR
JALANDHAR • RAMPUR
SHIMLA
MOGA LUDHIANA
KOT KAPURA CHANDIGARH
ABOHAR AMBALA • DEHRA DUN
BATHINDA PATIALA YAMUNANAGAR
GANGANAGAR SAHARANPUR HARIDWAR
KARNAL RANIKHET
SIRSA MUZAFFARNAGAR
HISAR PANIPAT HALDWANI
BHIWANI ROHTAK SONEPAT MEERUT AMROHA MORADABAD
NEW DELHI HAPUR
GURGAON GHAZIABAD RAMPUR PILIBHIT
FARIDABAD SAMBHAL BAREILLY
BULANDSHAHR BUDAUN
BIKANER ALIGARH SHAHJAHANPUR
ALWAR MATHURA SITAPUR
SIKAR HATHRAS FARRUKHABAD BAHRAICH
JAISALMER BHARATPUR AGRA FIROZABAD HARDOI
JAIPUR ETAWAH LUCKNOW FAIZABAD
JODHPUR AJMER KISHANGARH MORENA UNNAO RAE BARELI
BEAWAR TONK GWALIOR BHIND KANPUR JAUNPUR
PALI FATEHPUR VARA
BHILWARA KOTA JHANSI ALLAHABAD
UDAIPUR MIRZAPUR
SATNA
REWA
SAGAR MURWARA

BHUJ RATLAM
AHMEDABAD GANDHINAGAR UJJAIN BHOPAL JABALPUR
JAMNAGAR WADHWAN NADIAD DEWAS
RAJKOT ANAND GODHRA INDORE
VADODARA BILASPUR
BHAVNAGAR BHARUCH KHANDWA GONDIYA
PORBANDAR JUNAGADH NAGPUR DURG RAIPUR
VERAVAL SURAT BHUSAWAL BURHANPUR AMRAOTI BHILAI
NAVSARI DHULIA JALGAON AKOLA DHAMANGAON RAJ NANDGAON
MALEGAON WARDHA RAJHARA
NASIK YAVATMAL JHARANDALLI
IGATPURI AURANGABAD CHANDRAPUR
VIRAR JALNA BALLARPUR
BHIWANDI AHMEDNAGAR PARBHANI
KALYAN THANE NANDED
BOMBAY BID
ALIBAG CHINCHWAD LATUR NIZAMABAD KARIMNAGAR JAGDALPUR
PUNE NILANGA
SATARA BIDAR WARANGAL KOTTAGUDEM
SHOLAPUR GULBARGA JANGAON
HYDERABAD KHAMMAM

Northern India & Bangladesh

0   150   300 km

*The external boundaries
of India in these maps have not been
authenticated and may not be correct*

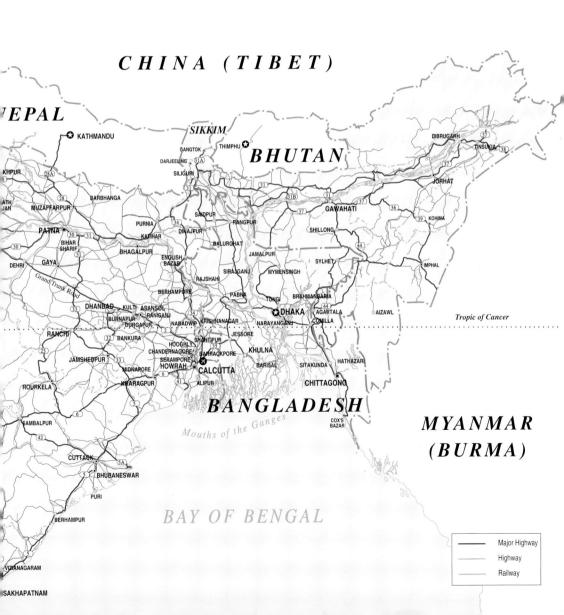

Southern India

BHAVNAGAR
JUNAGADH
VERAVAL
BHARUCH
BHARUCH
SURAT
NAVSARI
DHULIA
MALEGAON
VIRAR
NASIK
IGATPURI
BHIWANDI
KALYAN
BOMBAY
THANE
ALIBAG
CHINCHWAD
PUNE
SATARA
SANGLI
MIRAJ
KOLHAPUR
ICHALKARNJI
BELGAUM
PANAJI
DHARWAD
HUBLI
HARIHAR
SHIMOGA
MANGALORE
MANDYA
KANNUR
THALASSERI
KOZHIKODE
MANJERI
COIMBATORE
PALAKKAD
THRISSUR
KOCHI (COCHIN)
ALAPPUZHA
KOLLAM (QUILON)
NEDUMANGAD
THIRUVANANTHAPURAM
(TRIVANDRUM)

BHUSAWAL
BURHANPUR
JALGAON
AKOLA
AURANGABAD
JALNA
AHMEDNAGAR
PARBHANI
BID
LATUR
NILANGA
SHOLAPUR
BIJAPUR
GULBARGA
GADAG
HOSPET
BELLARY
GUNTAKAL
DAVANGERE
CHITRADURGA
ANANTPUR
TUMKUR
KOLAR GOLD
FIELDS
BANGALORE
MYSORE
COONOOR
BHAVANI
ERODE
TIRUPPUR
POLLACHI
KARUR
VALPARAI
DINDIGUL
MADURAI
RAJAPALAIYAM
SIVAKASI
PUNALUR
TIRUNELVELI
TUTICORIN
PALAYANKOTTAI
NAGERCOIL

KHANDWA
BILASPUR
NAGPUR
GONDIYA
DURG
RAIPUR
BHILAI
AMRAOTI
DAMANGAON
RAJ NANDGAON
WARDHA
YAVATMAL
CHANDRAPUR
BALLARPUR
RAJHARA
JHARANDALLI
NIZAMABAD
KARIMNAGAR
NANDED
JAGDALPUR
WARANGAL
KOTTAGUDEM
BIDAR
JANGAON
HYDERABAD
KHAMMAM
NALGONDA
RAJAHMUNDRY
MAHBUBNAGAR
ELURU
BHIMAVARAM
RAICHUR
VIJAYAWADA
GUDIVADA
KURNOOL
GUNTUR
TENALI
MASULIPATAM
NANDYAL
ADONI
ONGOLE
PRODDATUR
CUDDAPAH
NELLORE
TIRUPATHI
CHITTOOR
ARCOT
MADRAS
VELLORE
KANCHIPURAM
TIRUVANNAMALAI
PONDICHERRY
CUDDALORE
SALEM
NEYVELI
KUMBAKONAM
NAGAPATTINAM
TIRUCHIRAPPALLI
THANJAVUR
PUDUKKOTTAI
KARAIKKUDI
RAMESWARAM

ARABIAN SEA

Lakshadweep

Lakshadweep Sea

Gulf of Mannar

SRI LANKA

INDIAN OCEAN

0   150   300 km

*The external boundaries
of India in these maps have not been
authenticated and may not be correct*

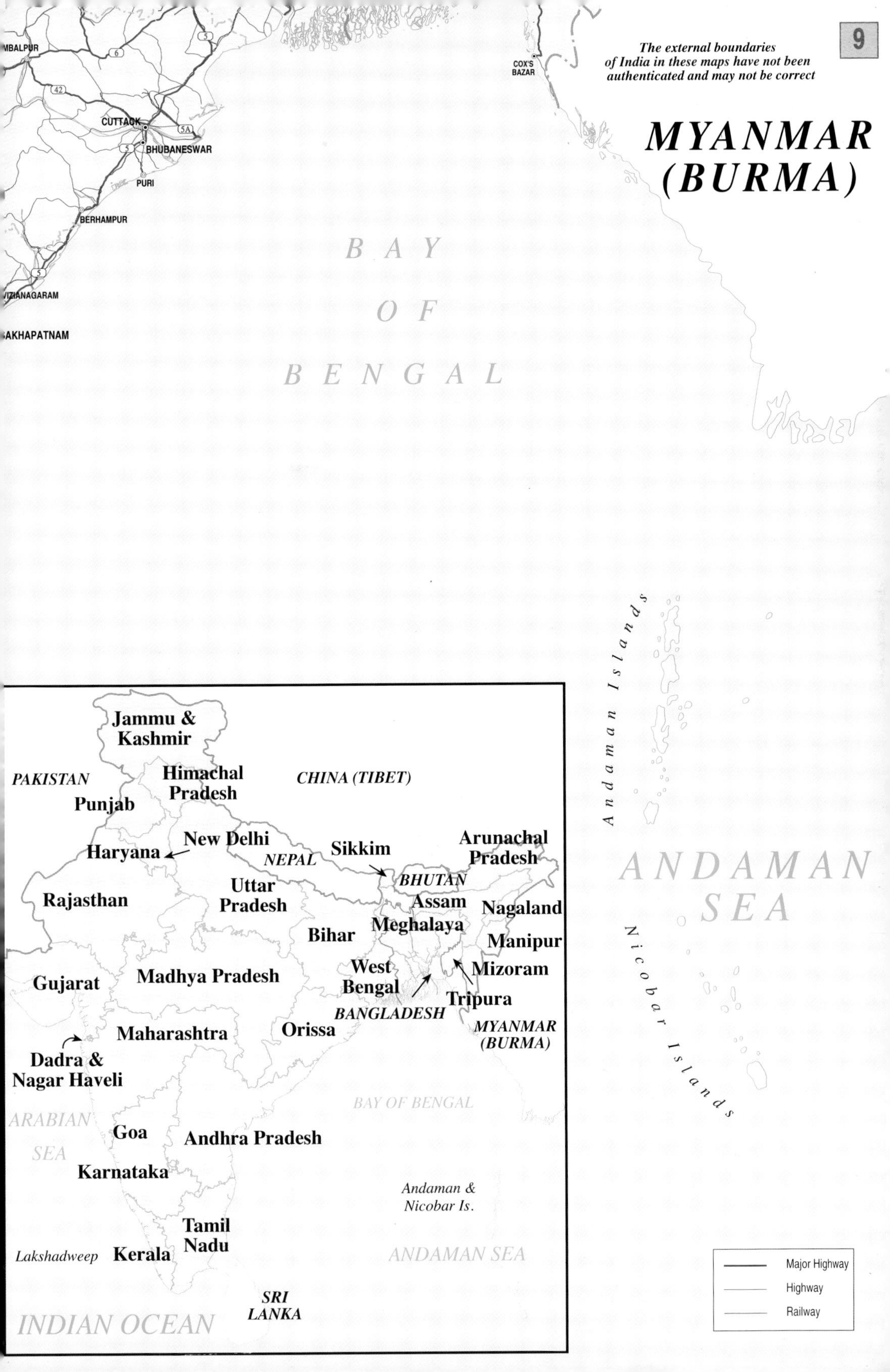

The external boundaries of India in these maps have not been authenticated and may not be correct

MYANMAR (BURMA)

MBALPUR

CUTTACK

BHUBANESWAR

PURI

BERHAMPUR

VIZIANAGARAM

AKHAPATNAM

COX'S BAZAR

B A Y
O F
B E N G A L

Andaman Islands

A N D A M A N
S E A

Nicobar Islands

Jammu & Kashmir

PAKISTAN

Himachal Pradesh

CHINA (TIBET)

Punjab

New Delhi

Haryana

Sikkim

NEPAL

Arunachal Pradesh

Rajasthan

Uttar Pradesh

BHUTAN

Assam

Nagaland

Bihar

Meghalaya

Manipur

Gujarat

Madhya Pradesh

West Bengal

Mizoram

BANGLADESH

Tripura

Maharashtra

Orissa

MYANMAR (BURMA)

Dadra & Nagar Haveli

BAY OF BENGAL

ARABIAN SEA

Goa

Andhra Pradesh

Karnataka

Andaman & Nicobar Is.

ANDAMAN SEA

Tamil Nadu

Lakshadweep

Kerala

INDIAN OCEAN

SRI LANKA

	Major Highway
	Highway
	Railway

MAP LEGEND

Number of Inhabitants:

BOMBAY   > 2,500,000

KALYAN ■ 1,000,000 - 2,500,000

NASIK ☐ 500,000 - 1,000,000

THANE ◉ 250,000 - 500,000

CHINCHWAD ◎ 100,000 - 250,000

KIRKEE ◉ 50,000 - 100,000

Wai ◎ 25,000 - 50,000

TARAPUR ◉ < 25,000

NEW DELHI Capital City
Capitale
Hauptstadt
Capital
首都

✪ Capital City (Locator map)
Capitale (Carte de situation)
Hauptstadt (Orientierungskarte)
Capital (Mapa de Situación)
首都（所在地を表す地図）

BOMBAY State Capital
Capitale d'État
Landeshauptstadt
Capital del Estado
州の中心地

PUNE District Headquarters
Quartier Général du District
Bezirkshauptquartier
Sede Central del Distrito
地区の中心地

IGATPURI Taluk Headquarters
Quartier Général du Taluk
Taluk Hauptquartier
Sede Central del Taluk
タルックの中心地

International Boundary
Limites Internationales
Staatsgrenze
Frontera Internacional
国境

State Boundary
Limites de l'État
Landesgrenze
Frontera del Estado
州の境界線

District Boundary
Limites du District
Bezirksgrenze
Frontera del Distrito
地区の境界線

Major Highway
Route Nationale
Femstraße
Carretera Principal
主要ハイウェー

Highway
Route Principale
Landstraße
Carretera
ハイウェー

Regional Road
Route Régionale
Regionale Fernstraße
Carretera Regional
地方の道路

Secondary Road
Route Secondaire
Nebenstraße
Carretera Secundaria
間道

Railway
Voie de chemin de fer
Eisenbahn
Ferrocarril
鉄道

Route Number
Numérotation Routière
Routenummer
Número de Ruta
幹線道路の番号

Distance in Kilometres
Distance en Kilomètres
Entfernung in Kilometern
Distancia en Kilómetros
距離（km）

International Airport
Aéroport International
Internationaler Flughafen
Aeropuerto Internacional
国際空港

Domestic Airport
Aéroport National
Inlandflughafen
Aeropuerto Interior
国内線専用空港

☒	Hindu/Jain/Sikh Temple	⛴	Seaport	▭	Desert
	Temple Hindouiste/Jaïn/Sikh		Port de Mer		Désert
	Hindu/Jain/Sikh Tempel		Seehafen		Wüste
	Templo Hindú/Jaín/Sikh		Puerto Marítimo		Desierto
	ヒンドゥー教		港町		砂漠

☪	Mosque	⚓	Shipwreck	▭	Reef
	Mosquée		Épave		Falaise
	Moschee		Schiffbruch		Riff
	Mezquita		Naufragio		Arrecife
	モスク		難破船		リーフ

⚛	Buddhist Temple	☼	Beach	▭	Swamp
	Temple Bouddhiste		Plage		Marais
	Buddistischer Tempel		Strand		Sumpf
	Templo Budista		Playa		Pantano
	仏教寺		海水浴場		湿地

✝	Cathedral	◗	Cave	· · · · · · · · · · · · ·	Tropics
	Cathédrale		Grotte		Tropiques
	Kathedrale		Höhle		Tropen
	Catedral		Cueva		Los Trópicos
	大聖堂		洞窟		回帰線

†	Church	Nun ✧ 7135	Mountain
	Église		Montagne
	Kirche		Berg
	Iglesia		Montaña
	教会		山

Ψ	Synagogue	//	Pass
	Synagogue		Col
	Synagoge		Paß
	Sinagoga		Desfiladero
	シナゴーク		峠

✕	Battle Site	🌳	National Park
	Champ de Bataille		Parc National
	Schlachtstelle		Nationalpark
	Campo de Batalla		Parque Nacional
	戦場		国立公園

⛫	Castle/Fort	∿	River
	Château/Château Fort		Fleuve/Rivière
	Burg/Festung		Fluß
	Castillo/Fuerte		Río
	城・砦		川

∴	Ruins	⬭	Lake
	Ruines		Lac
	Ruinen		See
	Ruinas		Lago
	廃墟		湖

☼	Viewpoint	⌒	Spring
	Point de Vue		Source
	Aussicht		Quelle
	Mirador		Manantial
	見学地点		泉

⌂	Lighthouse	⫴	Waterfall
	Phare		Cascades
	Leuchtturm		Wasserfall
	Faro		Catarata
	灯台		滝

Snowline

7000 m
6000 m
5000 m
4500 m
4000 m
3500 m
3000 m
2500 m
2100 m
1800 m
1500 m
1200 m
900 m
600 m
300 m
150 m
0
-150 m
-300 m
-900 m
-3000 m

0   10   20   30   40   50 km

1 : 1 250 000

E   F   G   H   CHENDU 13

The external boundaries
of India in these maps have not been
authenticated and may not be correct

*Under
Administration
of
Pakistan*

1

MOHRI · LILAM · GOZER · SHANKARGARH · DARLI · DAS · CHILAM · CHAUKI · 4969 · Burzil 4199 · BURAIL · *Deosai Basin* · 5058 · DHAPPA · 4872 · KHARTAKSHO · PAPALDO · 5270

GUN · KEL · SURJANWALA · KALAPANI · 5069 Bhigar · KARBOS · TOHUROWAS · DUMGUL · 5287

DHAKKI · FOLOWAI · Kamri 4705 · MINIMARG · PASHWARI · Deosai 3765 · MATIYAL

DAPPAL · TAOBAT · KAMRI · CHORWAN · GULTARI · SOWARAN · FARANSHAT · DALUNAG · KHARAL

MUHRI · DUDI · BAGTOR · KORAGBAL GURIAS · *Drass Basin* · KUNAR · KAKSHAR · 23

ALHOM · KULIGAM · KANZALWANO · **Line of Actual Control** · KHARBU · GRANTUNAG · 5168

KHURHOM · LALPUR · SOGAM · MUQAM · BANDIPUR · KASHMIR NORTH · KUTHPATHRI · BADOAB · ABDULLUN · 5353 · TASGAM · DRASS · *Zanskar Range* · KUNORE

WARA · Tragbal 3531 · TRAGBAL · ATHWATOO · SEMATHAN · *Jammu and Kashmir* · GREAT HIMALAYA · MUSK · SUKTIYAL · PHARONA

HANDWARA · WATLAB · KUDOR · Haramukh 4876 · WANGAT · SANGAM · NICHINAI · MATAYAN · Umba II 5412 · UMBA · SANKO · KARTSE

Sopur · *Wular Lake* · GURUR · AJAS · MANGOM · NARA NAG · 4371 · Zoji La 3529 · SONAMARG · BALTAL · THAMO · 5461 · PARKUTSA

mula · NAIDHAL · SAFAPUR · KANGAN · 4345 · GUND · KULAN · *Kolahoi Glacier* 5007 · Amarnath Cave · SURU · 5971

JL · SANGROM · SUMBAL · GANDERBAL · NAGBAL · SUMBAL · *Kolahoi* 5425 · LADAKH · PARKARYAN · Nun 7135 / 135

JR · KRAR · PATTAN · BADAMIBAGH CANTONMENT · Mahadev 3966 · 3428 · ARU · 4687 · TANIN · SHESHNAG · HAMPET · PARKARYAN · TONGUL · FARIABAD

SRINAGAR · 2682 · PANDRETHAN · KHREUH · SOTUR · *KASHMIR SOUTH* · CHANDANWARI · 4638 · SOKHNIZ

ulmarg · TANGMARG · BEDGOM · PAMPORE · PASTON · PAHALGAM · RIKINWAS · SHUPKANJAN

SOTIPURA · YECHAGAM · ARIGAM · AVANTIPUR · TRAL 3454 · BATAKUT · 4407 · 14

DRANG · RENGAZABAL · TASRAR SHARIF · PULWAMA · SETHAR · VIDAI · AISH MUQAM · 4426 · APHIT

CH · DANNA · CHHANZ · *Kashmir Valley* · BIJBIHAR · SALI · INSHAN · 4374

YUSMARG · MONU · SANGARWAIN · 1660 · MARTAND · LIHINWAN · METWAN

NAGABAL · KHANABAL · ANANTNAG · CHHATTARGUL · GAORAN · YUROD

CHANOWALI · SEDAN · SHUPIYAN · KULGAM · **Achabal** · QASBA NAUBUG · DAKSUM · NAPAZ · ANYAR

Pir Panjal II · ALIABAD · MANZGOM · KOKARNAG · 4299 · BARYINNAR · HANZAL

BARAMGALA · MAHI NAG · DOB DABYAN · KOTAMARG · BAINMUL · QAZIGUND · DORU · RASOOL · WANGOM · HAWAL

THANNA MANDI · NAKAWAS · MUNDA · VERINAG · KARBUDURUN · Sinthan Pass · 4321

Budil Pir II · *Pir Panjal Range* · BANIHAL II Banihal 2832 · AHLAN · SINGPUR · CHATRU · SONDAR

THANNAMANG · **RIASI** · GUND · HINGPUR · 4429 · IKHALE · Neran

KOT BAINKA · DHARAR · BUDHAL · MALI KOT · SHADAUL · MANGAT · MUGHAL MAIDAN · PUSHAL · 3783 · GALHAR · SHAZAL

RAJAURI · 4552 · *Shiwalik Range* · RAMSU · 3971 · DRUBIL · KWAR · KISHTWAR · GULABGARH

KALAKOTE · SAMOT · DAMNI · DIGDAUL · **UDHAMPUR** · THANA · KESHWAN · *Pir Panjal Range* · KITHAR

DILHORI · DHALAN · NAR KOT · RAMKANDU · KUND · GUJARARU · MALAN · 4072 · BHART · KUTAL · 4039 · 4587

HINGAS · SIAL SUI · KHORBANI · GUL · RAMBAN · BATOTE · GANIKA · UDINPUR · JANGALWAR · DEVIGOL

OSHERA · ARNAS · 3018 · TANGAR · SANASAR · PATNITOP · DODA · BHELA · THATRI · 2653 · JAUTA · MANO · 4410

DHARMSALA · BHARAK · RIASI · VAISHNO DEVI · *Daman Koh Plain* · TOTI · KHALEM · DRANGA · BHARGI · BALHAR · KITHAR

PAONI · BAGOT · KATRA · 34 · KUD · PARBAL · 3389 · BHADARWAH

KALDABI · DAGER · BARDHAL · CHANAS · DRAMTHAL · NARSU · SUD MAHADEV 3048 · THANALA · BHANDEL

LOT · GARH · TIKRI · DOMEL · 2487 · CHAPAR · DUDU · LANGERA · 3917 · KUNDOLU · THANEL

JAKHAR · KALIT · KOT · DAMI · KACHHAPIND · **Udhampur** · JINGHANU · 4341 · SARTAL · KILLAR

BARNALA · NARIANA · CHAK BOWAL · KARLUP · JINDRAH · RAMNAGAR · BASANTGARH · LOANG · SANU KOTHI

CHHAMB · MUNNAWAR · NAGROTA · SURUIN · THALORA · **KATHUA** · KILOR · TISA · TUNGUNA

AWALA · NAWANSHAHR · **JAMMU** · PARMANDAL · BABNEGARH · 2201 · 2531 · SHERPUR

LAPUR · Kotli Loharan · TANDA · PUL BAJUAN · GIGRIAL · **Bari Brahmana** · 17 · BISHNAH · RAMKOT · SAMBA · BILAUR · BHUD · DALHOUSIE · LAHRI · BHAGOT

2

3

4

5

6

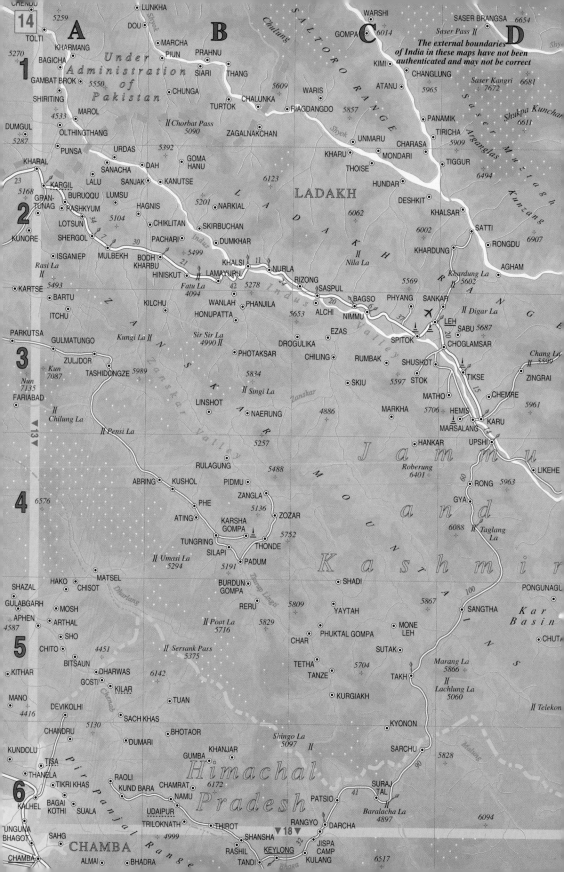

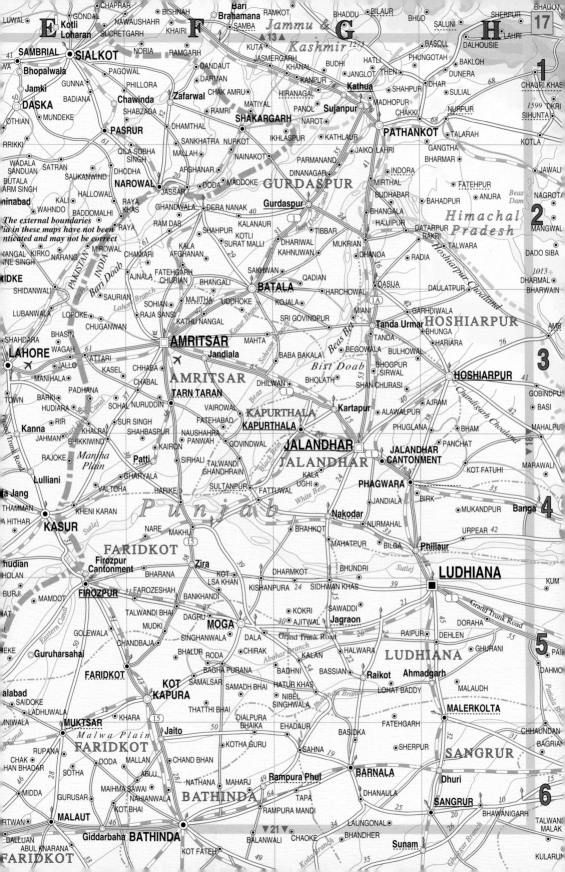

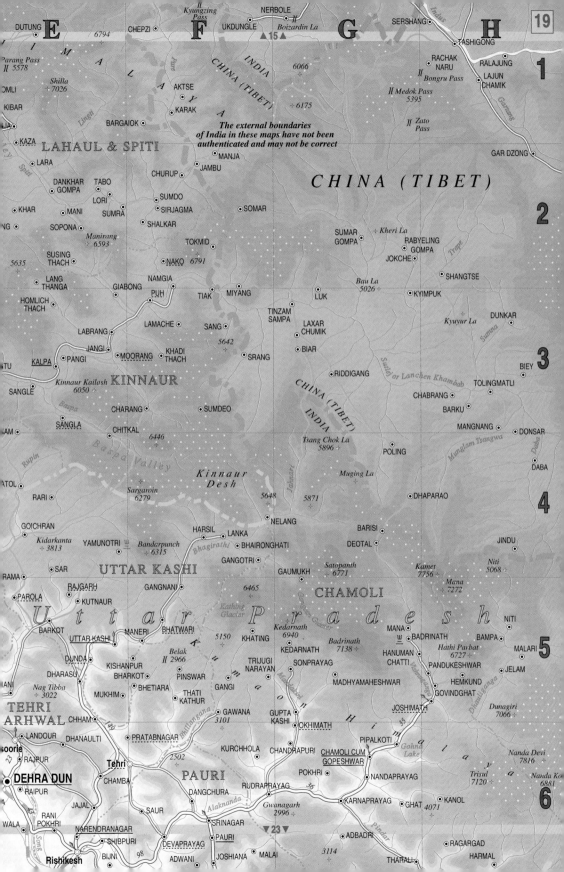

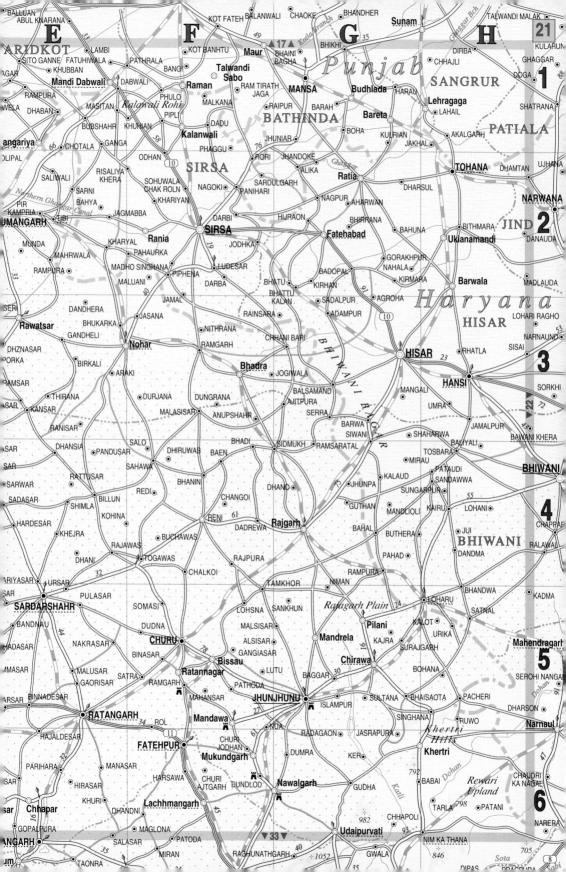

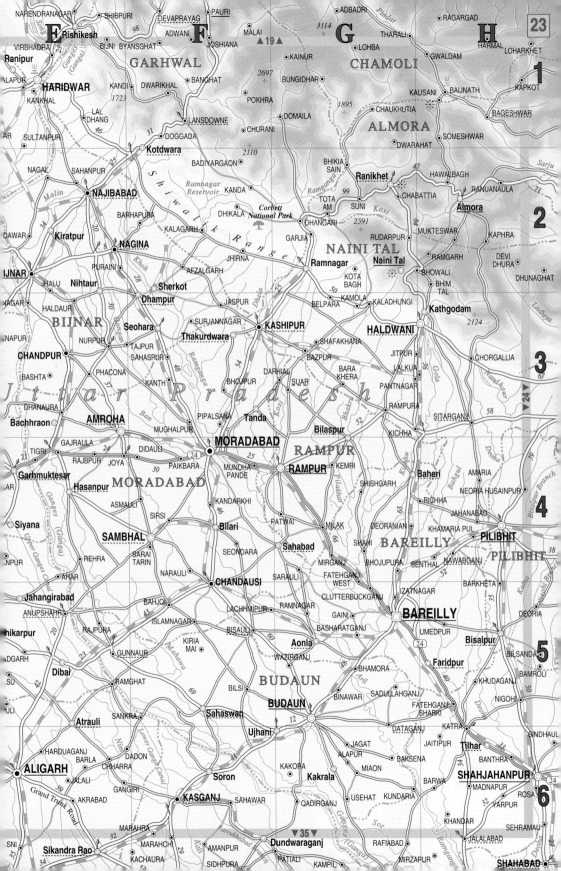

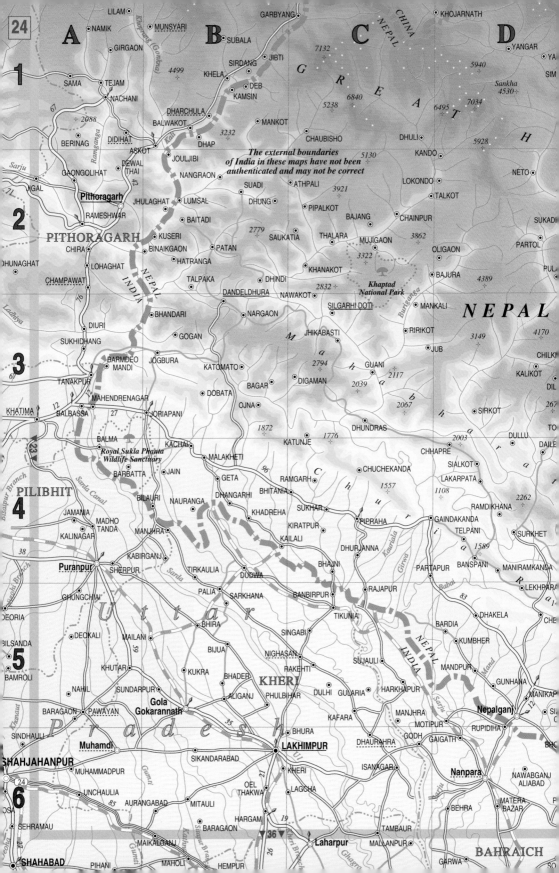

E   F   G   H

1

2

3

4

5

6

6715
6147
Kyang
PARYANG   4578
TRUKSUM
5410
Brahmaputra
1777   5157
DONGBA

Namja 4944
CHINA (TIBET)
NEPAL
NAMLA
NAGOR

BRO
Margor ☆ 4057
NEPKA
6597
6092
MUGU
6855
3658
6491   6562   6546
5726

UNAPANI
DARMA
DAURA ☆6373
Khung 5974 ☆
6170

M
SORUKOT
MANGRI
DALPHU
Mugu Karnali
5791
PHOPAGAON
Chungphari Tal

A
RARA GUM
2989
Rara Daha
7043
PHIJORGAON
LURIGAON 6439
NISALGAON   5974
SIMENGAON

L
Rara National Park   CHAUTHA
SINJA
SALDANGGAON
6187

A
BISTBARA
LAMRI
JUMLA
6860
Shey - Phoksundo National Park
SYA GOMPA
TINGJEGAON
6645

BHOLI
2324
R
SALDANGGAON

Y
LUNISHERA
DHITA
MINIGAON
A
TIBRIKOT
6401
Mohala   6582

A
LITAKOT
TOPLA
Chakhure 4081
RIMI
Sehula 6974
Chhala 6127
TUKOTIGAON

Samla 4677
N
PARA

Thari Patan ☆4543
5459
LUNH
4214
Phokswmdo Tal
6157
TARENGGAON

G
BARIKOT
RASI
Mukut Himal
SYANG

KOT
SHIBKHOLA
AULGURTA
DURGAON
TARAKOT
E
6582

KHURPA
Hiunchuli Patan 5922
Toridwari 5272
TAJIPALI GOMPA
Dhaulagiri 8172 ☆

BARABAN
DHALI
PASANDHARA
Churen Himal 7363
7639
Kali or Krishna Gandaki

JAJARKOT
Bheri
BARGAON
GONGRALI
MAIKOT
LETA

NEPA
BHURCHAUR
PHUGRU
JIBU
Sani Bheri
3926
GURJAKHANA
DANA

LABU
THANDAR
RUKUMKOT
Royal Dhorpatan Hunting Reserve
LUNTSUM
NARCHENG

BURIALI
ULEJULA
SUBAKONE
4021
PADMI   4044
DHORPATAN   3786

2639
GAIRAGAON
3585
DAREGAUNRA
RANIPAUWA
3661

SALLYANA
SIMAGAON
UWAGAON
3638
BURTIBANG
Mayangdi
BENI

SITALPATI
2830
2499
3297
KUTHARPEKOT
BAGLUNG

2412
LAWAMJULA
LIBANGGAON
SEULABANG
3168
GALKOT
KUSMA

MDWALI
PHALABANG
KAPARKOT
DABAN
2446
MANUNG
MUSIKOT
BANSKOT
JEMIR GHAT

TULSIPUR
2152
DAKHAKOT
KOROPANI
PURTI GHAT

1256
BIJAURI
SWARGDWAR
PIUTHAN
2574

BALAPUR
GHORAI
KUMALTAR
2148
ARGHAKOT
GULMIKOT
BALKOT

92
1811
Mahabharat
BIRI BAZAR
Kali Gandaki

BHAWANIPUR
870
REAR
NAMAI
DEBIKAT
2277
PALPA
TANSING

KATKUIYAN   BHOWA
BILASPUR
NEPAL
INDIA
Churia
THARAKOT
1895
1850

ANGAHA
KHANGRA
Dundwa Range
Rapti
39
Range
NAWAKOT

BHINGA
BANKATWA
BHADWAR
KOILABAS
Gaurloir Baba Pass
CHANDANPUR
37
BHAGWANPUR
65
PANBARI
BUTWAL
SOMNATH

Rapti
GUGAULI
JARWA
BHARTABAS

The external boundaries of India in these maps have not been authenticated and may not be correct

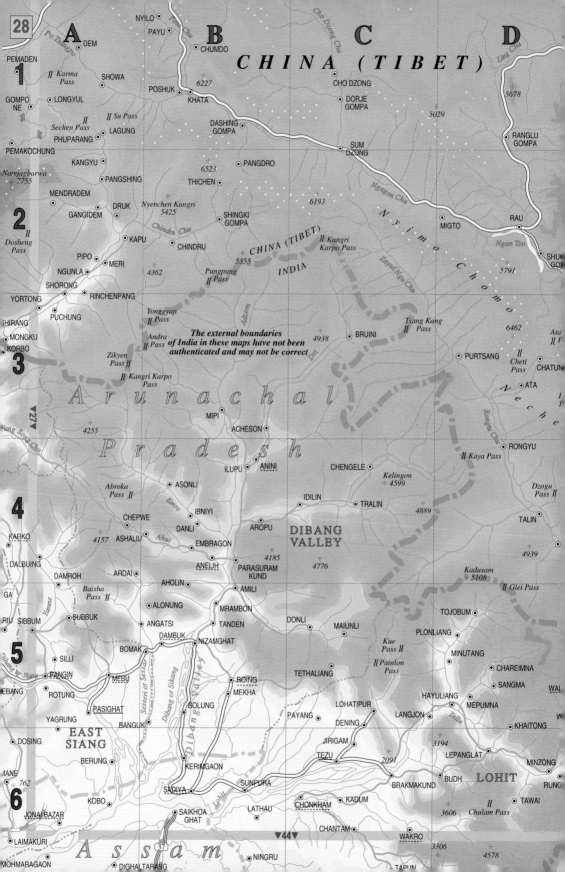

A B C D

CHINA (TIBET)

1

PEMADEN
DEM
NYILO
PAYU
CHUMDO
CHO DZONG
6227
Po Thangoo
Cho Dzong Chu
Ling Chu
5678

II Karma Pass
SHOWA
POSHUK
KHATA
DORJE GOMPA
5029

GOMPO NE
LONGYUL
Su Pass
DASHING GOMPA
SUM DZONG

Sechen Pass
LAGUNG
PANGDRO
RANGLU GOMPA

PHUPARANG
KANGYU
THICHEN
6523
6193

PEMAKOCHUNG
PANGSHING
SHINGKI GOMPA
RAU

Namjagbarwa
7755
MENDRADEM
DRUK
Nyenchen Kangri
5425
MIGTO

2

GANGIDEM
KAPU
Chindru Chu
CHINDRU
Kangri Karpo Pass
Ngagon Chu
Ngan Tso

Dosheng Pass
PIPO
MERI
5355
CHINA (TIBET)
SHU GO
5791

NGUNLA
SHORONG
4362
Pungpung II Pass
INDIA
Zayul Ngu Chu

YORTONG
PUCHUNG
RINCHENPANG
Tsang Kang II Pass
6462
Ata

SHIRANG
Yonggyap II Pass
BRUINI
4938
PURTSANG
Cheti Pass
CHATUN

MONGKU
Andra Pass
Dri
ATA

3

KORBO
Zikyen Pass II
The external boundaries of India in these maps have not been authenticated and may not be correct
Neche

II Kangri Karpo Pass
RONGYU

Arunachal
MIPI
4255
ACHESON
II Kaya Pass

Pradesh
ILUPU
ANINI
CHENGELE
Kelingon
4599
Dzogu Pass II

Kang Sang Chu
ABROKA Pass II
ASONLI
IDILIN
TRALIN
4889
TALIN

4

KARKO
CHEPWE
Emra
IBNIYI
AROPU
DIBANG VALLEY
4185

DALBUING
4157
ASHALIU
DANLI
EMBRAGON
4776
Kadusam
5108
4939

GA
ARDAI
Ahui
ANELIH
PARASURAM KUND
II Glei Pass

RIU
DAMROH
AHOLIN
AMILI
TOJOBUM

SIBBUM
Baisha Pass II
SUBBUK
ALONUNG
MRAMBON
DONLI
MAIUNLI
PLONLIANG

Yamne
ANGATSI
TANDEN
Kue Pass II
MINUTANG

5

SILLI
DAMBUK
NIZAMGHAT
II Painlon Pass
CHAREIMNA

BOMAK
Dihang or Siang
Sessen or Sessar
ROING
TETHALIANG
HAYULIANG
SANGMA
WAL

EBANG
PANGIN
MEBU
MEKHA
LOHATIPUR
LANGJON
Tellu

ROTUNG
PASIGHAT
BOLUNG
Dibang Valley
PAYANG
DENING
MEPUMNA

YAGRUNG
BANGUK
JIRIGAM
KHAITONG

EAST SIANG
BERUNG
KERIMGAON
TEZU
2091
3194
LEPANGLAT
MINZONG

6

MANE
762
KOBO
SADIYA
SUNPURA
LATHAU
BRAKMAKUND
LOHIT
BUDH
RUNG

JONAI BAZAR
SAIKHOA GHAT
Lohit
CHONKHAM
KADUM
3606
Chulam Pass
TAWAI

LAIMAKURI
Assam
DIGHALTARANG
NINGRU
CHANTAM
WAKRO
3306
3578

MOHMARAGAON
37
44
TAPLIN

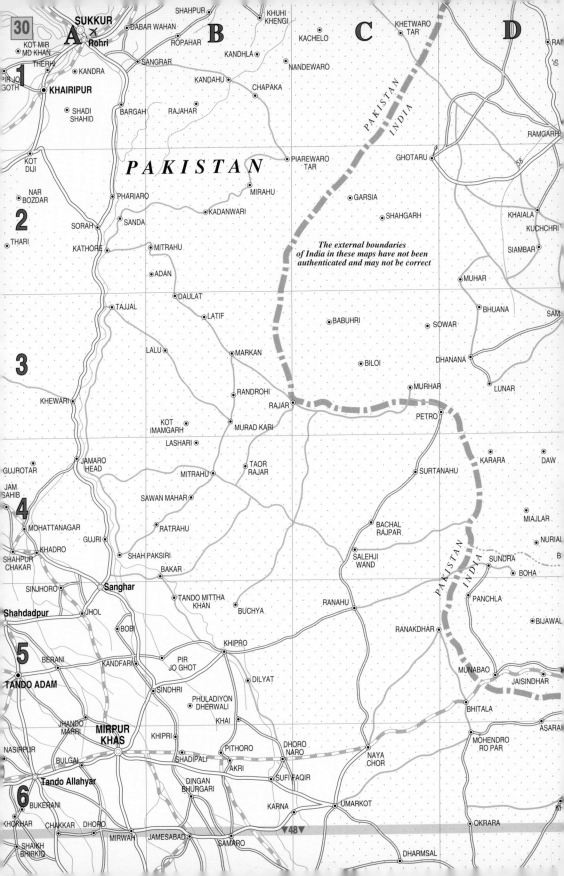

30

A   B   C   D

SUKKUR
Rohri
KOT MIR
MD KHAN
THERHI
PIR JO
GOTH
KHAIRIPUR
KANDRA
SHADI SHAHID
BARGAH
KOT DIJI
NAR BOZDAR
PHARIARO
THARI
SORAH
SANDA
KATHORE
MITRAHU
ADAN
TAJJAL
DAULAT
LALU
LATIF
MARKAN
KHEWARI
RANDROHI
RAJAR
KOT IMAMGARH
MURAD KARI
LASHARI
GUJROTAR
JAMARO HEAD
MITRAHU
TAOR RAJAR
JAM. SAHIB
SAWAN MAHAR
RATRAHU
MOHATTANAGAR
GUJRI
KHADRO
SHAH PAKSIRI
SHAHPUR CHAKAR
BAKAR
SINJHORO
Sanghar
Shahdadpur
JHOL
BOBI
BERANI
KANDFARI
PIR JO GHOT
TANDO ADAM
SINDHRI
DILYAT
PHULADIYON DHERWALI
JHANDO MARRI
MIRPUR KHAS
KHIPRI
KHAI
NASIRPUR
BULGAI
SHADIPALI
AKRI
Tando Allahyar
DINGAN BHURGARI
PITHORO
SUFI FAQIR
BUKERANI
KHOKHAR
CHAKKAR
DHORO
MIRWAH
JAMESABAD
SAMARO
SHAIKH BHIRKIO
KARNA
DHARMSAL

SHAHPUR
DABAR WAHAN
ROPAHAR
SANGRAR
KANDHLA
KANDAHU
CHAPAKA
RAJAHAR

KHUHI KHENGI
NANDEWARO
KACHELO

KHETWARO TAR

PAKISTAN
INDIA

RAMGARH

PIAREWARO TAR
MIRAHU
KADANWARI
GHOTARU

GARSIA
SHAHGARH

KHAIALA
KUCHCHRI
SIAMBAR

The external boundaries of India in these maps have not been authenticated and may not be correct

MUHAR
BHUANA
SAM

BABUHRI
SOWAR

BILOI
MURHAR
DHANANA
LUNAR

PETRO
KARARA
DAW

SURTANAHU

MIAJLAR
NURIAL

BACHAL RAJPAR
SALEHJI WAND
SUNDRA
BOHA
B

TANDO MITTHA KHAN
BUCHYA
RANAHU
PANCHLA

KHIPRO
RANAKDHAR
BIJAWAL

MUNABAO
JAISINDHAR

BHITALA
ASARA

DHORO NARO
NAYA CHOR
MOHENDRO RO PAR

UMARKOT
OKRARA
KI

PAKISTAN

▼48▼

E · SARKARI TARA · F · G · H

BALAN · BHAREWALA · CHINNU · BORANA

HUTTEWALA · SARKARI TARA · NOKH

1

SADHAN · DIGAH · GHANTIALI · NACHNA · *Indira Gandhi Canal* · KANASAR · BAP

KHINYAN · MANDA · ASKANDRA · BARA · DEDASRI · SHEKAPUR

RIWAT · SRI · TADANA · DIDU · CHHAIN · SIRDON · MALHAR

KANDIALA · DEWA · MOHANGARH · BALANA · KERU · AJASAR · **Pholodi**

MOKAL · KATHORI · KANOD · AINTA · JAISALMER · TEKRA · MOKHERI · KHICHAN

2

HADASAR · BIRAMSAR · JESURANA · SRI BHADRIA · KHETOLAI · RAMDEORA · KHARA

UPSI · HAMIRA · SODAKOR · 15 · 42 · ODANIA · 59 · KOLU

Jaisalmer · CHANDHAN · DHOLIA · POKARAN · LAWAN · MARLA

DAMADARA · BARAGAON · DHAISAR · THAT · UJLAN · DHOLESAR · DECHU · THADIA

HA · DEDHA · NIRAUN · SANAWARA · RASLA · SANKRA · LUNA · BANIANA · RATRIA · SHETRAWA

KOTRI · KURI · DEVIKOT · LAKHMANA · BHAINSARA · DHASANIA · DERO · SULKIA TALA

3

SATANGAR · RAMA · 15 · DANGRI · RAJAMATHAI · BHIKORAI JUNI · 48 · SHERGARH

DEORA · MANDAI · BINJORAI · ARANG · PHALSUND · SOINTHRA

EJRAWA · RAJRAYAL · BHIYAR · UNDU · HARWA · KHARRA · SEMARKHIA

JINJHINIALI · BIAU · KANASAN · MUKHAB · PATODI

4

LAKHA · GUNGA · SHIV · KHINSAR · LAPUNDRA · THOB

DAROR · JHINKALI · BALASAR · BATARU · UTARNI · PACHPADRA

GIRAB · BHADKA · KOHI · AKDARA · TILWARA · **Balotra**

HARSANI · BALEWA · DUDABERI · CHHITAR KA PAR · BAETU · CHANDESRA · NAGAR MEWA · JASOL · ASOTRA · MUTHLI

RANASAR · BADANA · BISALA · SAR KA PAR · SAMESRA · SINLI · TAPRA · SIWANA

ADRA ROAD · RAMSAR · **BARMER** · RAWATSAR · SANYA MANJI · DAKHAN · INDRANA

5

BUKAR · SHEOKAR · BHUKAN · PADRU

USAR · AKORA · UDKA · SARLI · HODU · SINDARI · SADHU KI DHANI · *Siwana Hills* · 975

RATTASAR · CHOHTAN · RAMDERIA · **BARMER** · NOKHRA · SARANA · *Chhapanka Pahar* 834 · GOL

KELNOR · ALAMSAR · SANAWARA · *Lower Luni Plain* · BAUTRA · SAILA

BAMNOR · ROHLA · KHUNDALA · JESAWAS · MEGALWA · SURANA · PUNAWAS · BAKRA

6

USAR · RABASAR · 15 · BHANIA · DHORINIANA · GURA · NAGAR KHAS · NANDIA · BAGORA · PANTHERI

The external boundaries of India in these maps have not been authenticated and may not be correct

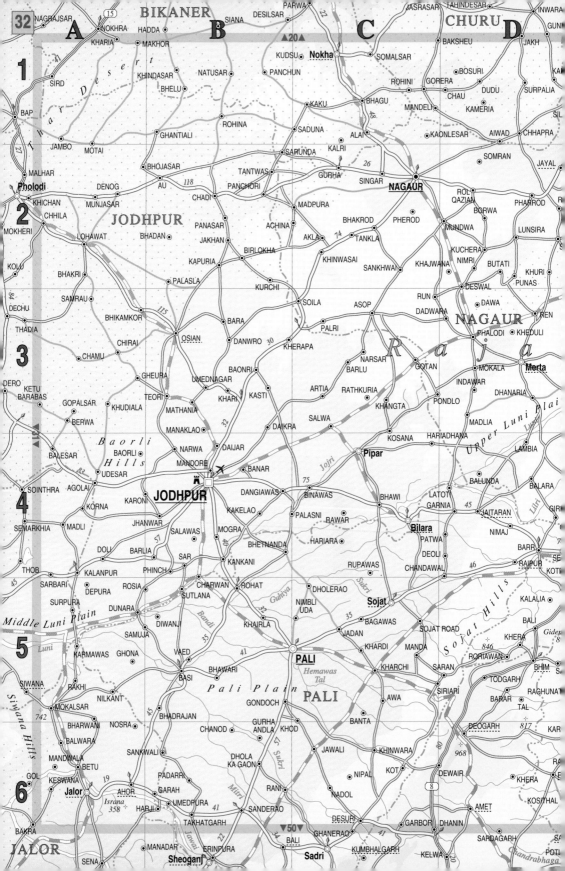

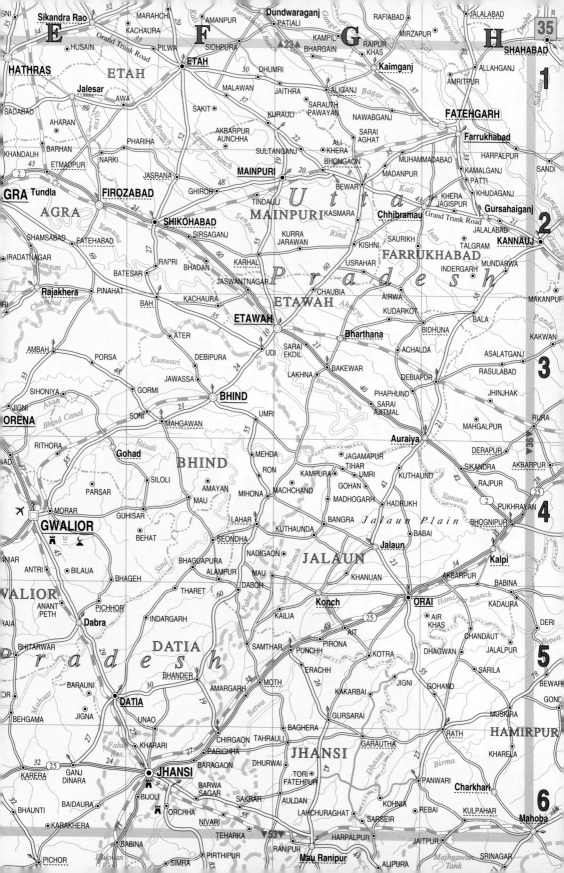

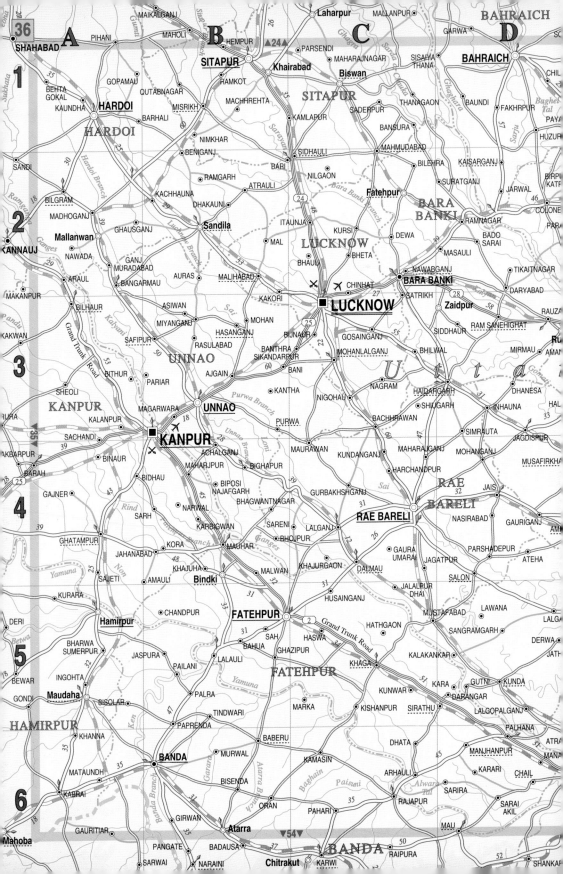

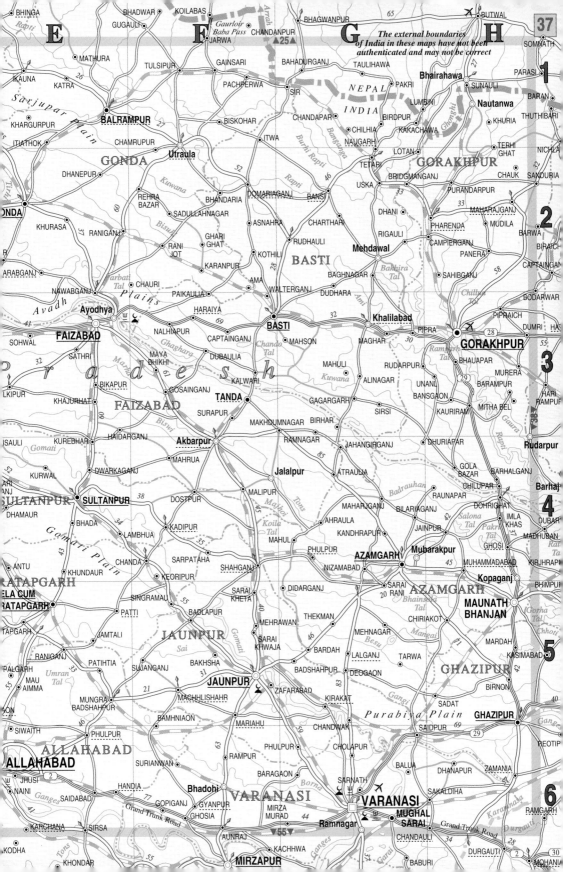

E   F   G   H

The external boundaries of India in these maps have not been authenticated and may not be correct

BHINGA, BHADWAR, KOILABAS, BHAGWANPUR, 65, BUTWAL, SOMNATH
GUGAULI, Gaurloir Baba Pass, CHANDANPUR, ▲25▲, NEPAL, INDIA, PARASI
MATHURA, JARWA, BAHADURGANJ, TAULIHAWA, Bhairahawa, SUNAULI
IKAUNA, KATRA, 26, TULSIPUR, GAINSARI, PACHPERWA, SIR, PAKRI, LUMBINI, Nautanwa, BARAN, THUTHIBARI
BALRAMPUR, 27, BISKOHAR, CHANDAPAR, CHILHIA, BIRDPUR, NAUGARH, KAKACHAWA, Ghonghi, KHURIA
KHARGURPUR, Sarjupar Plain, CHAMRUPUR, Utraula, ITWA, Burhi Rapti, Banganga, NICHLA
ITIATHOK, GONDA, DHANEPUR, 52, DOMARIAGANJ, BANSI, Rapti, 46, USKA, TETARI, BRIDGMANGANJ, CHAUK, SANDURIA
GONDA, KHURASA, 37, RANIGANJ, REHRA BAZAR, SADULLAHNAGAR, BHANDARIA, ASNAHRA, CHARTHARI, RUDHAULI, DHANI, RIGAULI, PURANDARPUR, MAHARAJGANJ, MUDILA
ARABGANJ, RANI JOT, GHARI GHAT, KOTHILI, Mehdawal, CAMPIERGANJ, PHARENDA, PANERA, BARWA, BIRAICH
NAWABGANJ, Parbati Tal, CHAURI, KARANPUR, AMA, WALTERGANJ, BAGHNAGAR, DUDHARA, Bakhira Tal, SAHIBGANJ, 58, CAPTAINGAN
Avadh, Plains, Ayodhya, PAIKAULIA, HARAIYA, 69, 32, Khalilabad, PIPRA, Chilua Tal, BODARWAR
FAIZABAD, NALHIAPUR, CAPTAINGANJ, BASTI, MAHSON, MAGHAR, 30, GORAKHPUR, 28, DUMRI, HA
SOHWAL, SATHRI, MAYA BHIKHI, DUBAULIA, Chando Tal, MAHULI, RUDARPUR, Ramgarh Tal, BHAUAPAR, 55
BIKAPUR, GOSAINGANJ, KALWARI, ALINAGAR, UNANL, MURERA, HARI RAMPUR
LKIPUR, KHAJURHAT, FAIZABAD, TANDA, SURAPUR, Kuwana, BANSGAON, KAURIRAM, MITHA BEL, BARAMPUR
ISAULI, KUREBHAR, HAIDARGANJ, MAKHDUMNAGAR, BIRHAR, SIRSI, DHURIAPAR, Gaura, Rudarpur
Gomati, DWARKAGANJ, Akbarpur, RAMNAGAR, 85, JAHANGIRGANJ, GOLA BAZAR, CHILUPAR, BARHALGANJ, Barhaj
KURWAL, MAHRUA, Jalalpur, ATRAULIA, RAUNAPAR, DOHRIGHAT, IMLA KHAS, DUBAR
SULTANPUR, SULTANPUR, 38, DOSTPUR, MALIPUR, Majhoi, Tons, MAHARJGANJ, BILARIAGANJ, JAINPUR, GHOSI, MADHUBAN
DHAMAUR, BHADA, LAMBHUA, KADIPUR, Koila Tal, AHRAULA, KANDHRAPUR, Salona Tal, Pakri Tal, 37
Gomati Plain, CHANDA, SARPATAHA, MAHUL, PHULPUR, AZAMGARH, Mubarakpur, 45, MUHAMMADABAD, KIRJHRAPI
ANTU, KHUNDAUR, KEORIPUR, SHAHGANJ, NIZAMABAD, SARAI RANI, AZAMGARH, Rat Ta
RATAPGARH, SINGRAMAU, 55, SARAI KHETA, DIDARGANJ, 20, Bhainsala Tal, MAUNATH BHANJAN, Gorha Tal, Chhoti
ELA CUM RATAPGARH, PATTI, BADLAPUR, 40, THEKMAN, CHIRIAKOT, MARDAH, KASIMABAD
TAPGARH, JAMTALI, MEHRAWAN, MEHNAGAR, Besu, Mangai, GHAZIPUR
PALGARH, RANIGANJ, PATIHTIA, SUJANGANJ, BAKHSHA, SARAI KHWAJA, BARDAH, LALGANJ, TARWA, BIRNON
MAU, AIMMA, Umran Tal, 33, 31, BADSHAHPUR, DEOGAON, 83, SADAT, GHAZIPUR
MUNGRA BADSHAHPUR, MACHHLISHAHR, JAUNPUR, ZAFARABAD, KIRAKAT, Purabiya Plain, SAIDPUR, 69, 29, Ganga
AON, SIWAITH, BAMHNIAON, Sai, MARIAHU, CHANDWAK, CHOLAPUR, BALUA, REOTIP
ALLAHABAD, PHULPUR, Gomati, RAMPUR, PHULPUR, 39, DHANAPUR, ZAMANIA
ALLAHABAD, SURIANWAN, BARAGAON, Borna, SARNATH, SAKALDIHA, Karamnasa
JHUSI, 2, HANDIA, 77, Bhadohi, VARANASI, MIRZA MURAD, 44, VARANASI, Durgauti, RAMGARH
NAINI, SAIDABAD, GOPIGANJ, GYANPUR, GHOSIA, Ramnagar, MUGHAL SARAI, Grand Trunk Road, 2, 30
KARCHANA, SIRSA, Grand Trunk Road, ▼55▼, Ganges, CHANDAULI, DURGAUTI, MOHANI
KODHA, KHONDAR, Tons, AUNRAJ, KACHHWA, Garai, BABURI, 28
MIRZAPUR

A
B
C
D
1
2
3
4
5
6
KATHMANDU
LALITPUR
BHAKTA
PHARPING
CHISPANI GARHI
GODAWARI
LELE
DHUL
2960
BHIMPHEDI
MAKWANPUR GARHI
HITAURA
HARDIA CHAUKI
HARIHARPUR GARHI
PAHR
BELANI
MARUWA GHAT
NARAYARGADH
BHARATPUR
KANDRAN GARHI
PADRIYA
CHHANAUTIYA
PATLAHARA
ANDRAULI
JHAWANI
DEBICHAUR
NANDPUR
OMNATH
ARASI
DIBNI
TRIBENI GHAT
BARAN
HUTHIBARI
BHAGAURA
Royal Chitwan National Park
HARTA
GARDI
BHIKMA THORI
NICHLAUL
HARNATANR
GOBARDHANA
BHATA
AMLEKHGANJ
PASCHIM-CHAMPARAM
GAWNAHA
SANDURIA
SIDHAW
RAMPUR
NIJGARH
PATHALIA
SISWA BAZAR
KHADA
CHHITAUNI
SUKHBAN
RAMNAGAR
SIMRA
JURIBELA
SHIKARPUR
Nakartiaganj
MAINATANR
RAMNAGAR
Bayaha
NIBUA RAIGANJ
NEPAL
INDIA
Birganj
KALAIYA
BAIRA
HARP
ARWA
BIRAICHA
BHAUNRA
SIKTA
MADHUBANI
LAURIYA MANDANGARH
BATRA
PACHGACHHIY
APTAINGANJ
RAMKOLA
KHAIRA TELA
CHANPATIA
Raxaul
The external boundaries of India in these maps have not been authenticated and may not be correct
MALANG
Padrauna
JOGAPATTI
CHAMPAPUR
ODARWAR
Majhwalia
NARKATIA
GHORASAHAN
HAJMINIA
SONB
DEORIA
BISHUNPURA
BETTIAH
KADARBANA
KUSHINAGAR
MAHUA
Sagauli
PURBA
HATA
KASIA
TURKAULIA
LAKHAURA
CHAMPARAM
Bairagnia
MAJORGA
Uttar
TAMKUHI
TARIA SUJAN
HARSIDHI
MOTIHARI
CHAIRAIYA
DHAKA
BATHNA
TARKULWA
RIGA
RAMPUR
TURKAULIYA
PATAHI
SITAMARHI
HARI AMPUR
PATHARDEWA
PAHARPUR
PIPARIYA
PAKRIDAYAL
Pradesh
KUCHAI KOT
SASAMUSA
KATEA
SHEOHAR
DEORIA
BIJAIPUR
GOPALGANJ
ARERAJ
PIPRA
Gopalganj
SANGRAMPUR
BELSAND
BHORE
UCHKAGAON
SALIMPUR
KALYANPUR
CHAKIA
MADHUBAN
SITAMARHI
BHAWANIPUR
MANJHAGARH
Barauli
RAJPUR
CHHAPRA
KHAMPAR
HATHWA
MIRGANJ
KESARIYA
MEBSI
Barhaj
MAJHAULI
SHAHIBGANJ
HALIMPU
PAINA
SALIMPUR
BARHARIA
BAIKUNTHPUR
MINAPUR
KANDAULI
SIWAN
PARURAJ
DUBARI
Lar
MAIRWA
TITARA
SISAI
GOREAKOTHI
DEORIA
KANTAI
MADHUBAN
SIWAN
BASANTPUR
MUZAFFARPUR
BOCHAHA
GOTHINI
HUSSAINGANJ
HARDI
Ratoi Tal
ANDAR
MUZAFFARPUR
DAB
BILTHAR
ASAON
MAHARAJGANJ
JHRAPUR
NAWANAGAR
DARAULI
DURAUNDHA
MASRAKH
TARAIA
TURKI
TAJPUR
SIKANDARPUR
RAGHUNATHPUR
BAGAURA
BISHUNPURA
VAISHALI
BAKHRA
SILA
BHIMPURA
AMNAUR
KURHANI
MANIAR
EKMA
BANIAPUR
MAKER
KESRAWANDIH
NAGRA
KHAJURI
DAUDNAGAR
GANGAPUR SISWAN
DAUDPUR
SARAN
MARHAURA
GORAUL
SONE
RATSANR
BARAGAON
TAJPUR
BHELDI
VAISHALI
Bisnali Tal
Ghaghara
NAGRA
KHAIRA
KUMAR BAZIDPU
BANSDIH
Suraha Tal
GARKHA
Lalganj
RASRA
REOTI
MANJHI
SARIA
Revelganj
CHAPRA
SARAI
CHIT FROZEPUR
SAHATWAR
BALLIA
DARIAPUR
MAHUWA
KASIMABAD
BALLIA
BARHRA
DIGHWARA
HAZRAT JANDAHA
BISHAMBHARPUR
Ganges
DOMGANJ
Sonepur
HAJIPUR
KARIMUDDINPUR
GHAZIPUR
SEMARIYA
DANAPUR
SAHDAR
Muhammadabad
NEAZIPUR
BARHAMPUR
SHAHPUR
KOELWAR
Maner
PATNA
NARAINPUR
BHOJPUR
ARRAH
Khagaul
BIDUPUR
Mahnar Bazar
SHERPUR
BUXAR
BIHTA
PHULWARI
RAGHOPUR
REOTIPUR
Dumraon
RAGHUNATPUR
Fatwa
Gahmar
CHAUSA
UDAWANTNAGAR
NAUBATPUR
PUNPUN
KURAN SARAI
CHAUGAIN
BIKRAM
JAITIPUR
NOAWAN
JAGDISPUR
BAKHTIYARPUR
RAJPUR
BHOJPUR
NAWANAGAR
GARHANI
PATNA
DANIAWAN
CHARPOKHRI
SANDES
HARNAUT
DHANSOI
AGIAON
Masaurhi
CHANDI
BABHNOUL
Hilsa
RAMGARH
KOATH
PIRO
PALIGANJ
NADAUL
DAWATH
SAHAR
NUR SARAI
KOCHAS
DINARA
ARWAL
JEHANABAD
KAKO
EKANGAR SARAI
BIHAR SHARIF
BIKRAMGANJ
TARARI
SAJHAULI
KARAKAT
GHOSI
DIPNAGAR
56

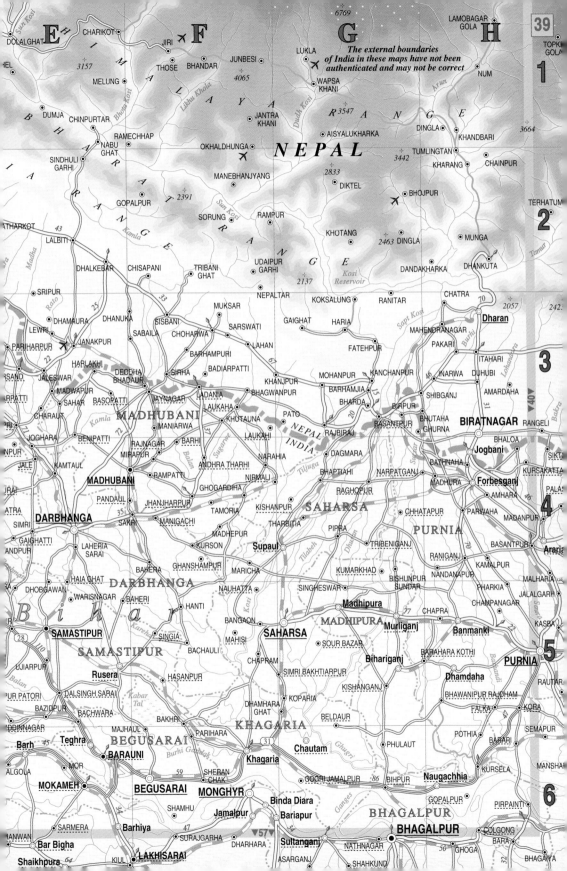

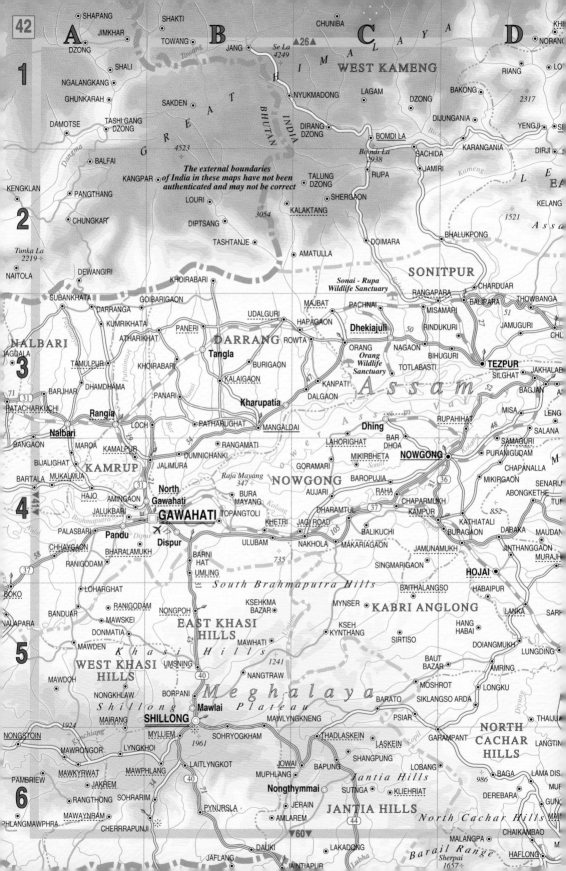

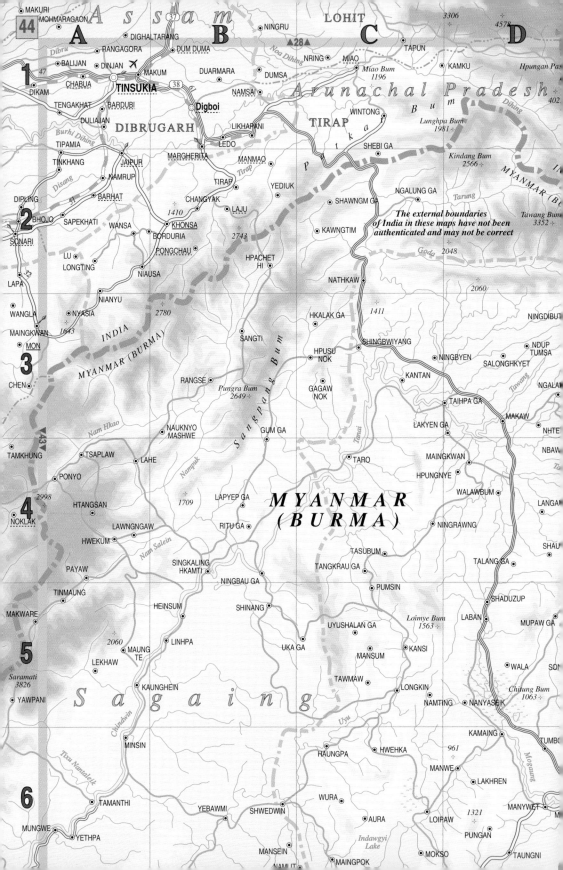

44

A   B   C   D

1

2

3

4

5

6

Assam   LOHIT   3306   4578

MAKURI
MOHMARAGAON   NINGRU   ▲28▲
DIGHALTARANG
RANGAGORA   DUM DUMA   NRING   MIAO   TAPUN   KAMKU
Dibru   Noa Dihing   Miao Bum   Hpungan Pas
BALIJAN   DINJAN   MAKUM   DUARMARA   DUMSA   1196
47
DIKAM   CHABUA   **TINSUKIA**   NAMSAI   Arunachal Pradesh   402
38
TENGAKHAT   BARDUBI   **Digboi**   WINTONG   B u m
DULIAJAN   LIKHAPANI   **TIRAP**   Lunghpa Bum
DIBRUGARH   LEDO   1981
Burhi Dihing   SHEBI GA   Kindang Bum   MYANMAR (B
TIPAMIA   MARGHERITA   MANMAO   2566
TINKHANG   JAIPUR   P   NGALUNG GA   Dihing
NAMRUP   TIRAP   YEDIUK   a   Tarung   Tawang Bum
Disang   Tirap   t   3352
DIPLING   BARHAT   CHANGYAK   i   SHAWNGM GA
51   1410   LAJU   k
BHOJO   SAPEKHATI   WANSA   KHONSA   a   *The external boundaries*
SONARI   BORDURIA   2743   KAWNGTIM   *of India in these maps have not been*
LU   PONGCHAU   HPACHET   *authenticated and may not be correct*
LONGTING   HI   Goda   2048
LAPA   NIAUSA   NATHKAW   2060
NIANYU   2060
WANGLA   NYASIA   2780   SANGTI   HKALAK GA   1411   NINGDIBUT
1643   INDIA   SHINGBWIYANG
MAINGKWAN   HPUSU   NDUP
MON   MYANMAR (BURMA)   NOK   NINGBYEN   TUMSA
RANGSE   GAGAW   KANTAN   SALONGHKYET
CHEN   Pungra Bum   NOK   NGALA
2649   Tawang
Nam Hkao   TAIHPA GA
NAUKNYO   GUM GA   LAKYEN GA   MAKAW
43   MASHWE   NHTE
TAMKHUNG   TSAPLAW   LAHE   TARO   MAINGKWAN   NBAW
PONYO   Nampuk   HPUNGNYE   Ta
2998   1709   LAPYEP GA   **M Y A N M A R**   WALAWBUM   LANGA
NOKLAK   HTANGSAN   RITU GA   **(B U R M A)**   SHAU
LAWNGNGAW   NINGRAWNG
HWEKUM   Nam Salein   TASUBUM   TALANG GA
PAYAW   SINGKALING   TANGKRAU GA
HKAMTI   NINGBAU GA   PUMSIN   SHADUZUP
TINMAUNG   HEINSUM   SHINANG   Laimye Bum   LABAN   MUPAW GA
MAKWARE   UYUSHALAN GA   1563
2060   LINHPA   UKA GA   KANSI   WALA   SON
LEKHAW   MAUNG   MANSUM
Saramati   TE   TAWMAW   LONGKIN   Chitung Bum
3826   KAUNGHEIN   NAMTING   NANYASEIK   1063
YAWPANI   S a g a i n g   Uyu   KAMAING
Chindwin   961   TUMBO
Tixu Namtaleik   MINSIN   HAUNGPA   HWEHKA   MANWE   Mogaung
MUNGWE   TAMANTHI   YEBAWMI   SHWEDWIN   WURA   AURA   LAKHREN   1321   MANYWET
YETHPA   MANSEIN   Indawgyi   LOIPAW   M
NAMI IT   Lake   MAINGPOK   MOKSO   PUNGAN   TAUNGNI

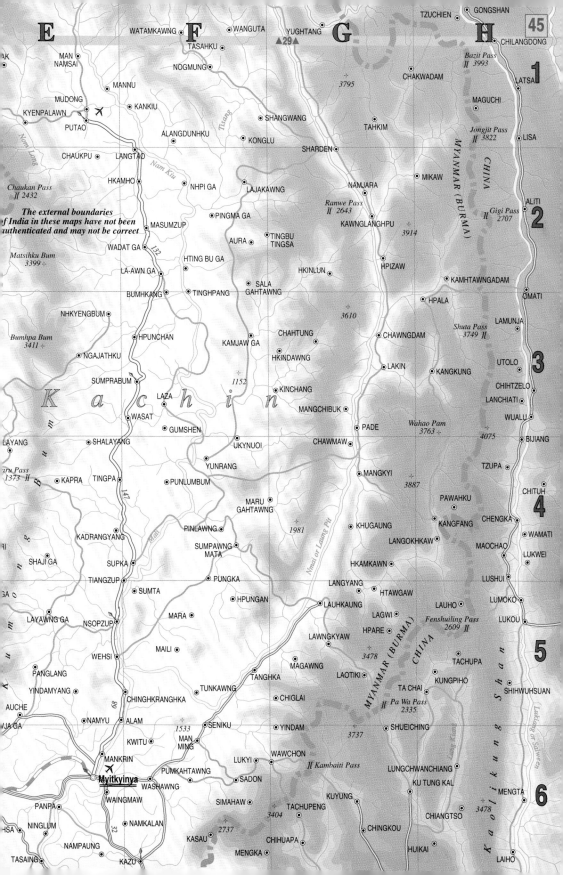

46

A	B	C	D

1

GOT
MUH

GHULAM WAD

Churma I.

HAJI DARYA
KHAN

*Ras Muari
(Cape Monze,*

2

3

4

A R A B I A N

5

6

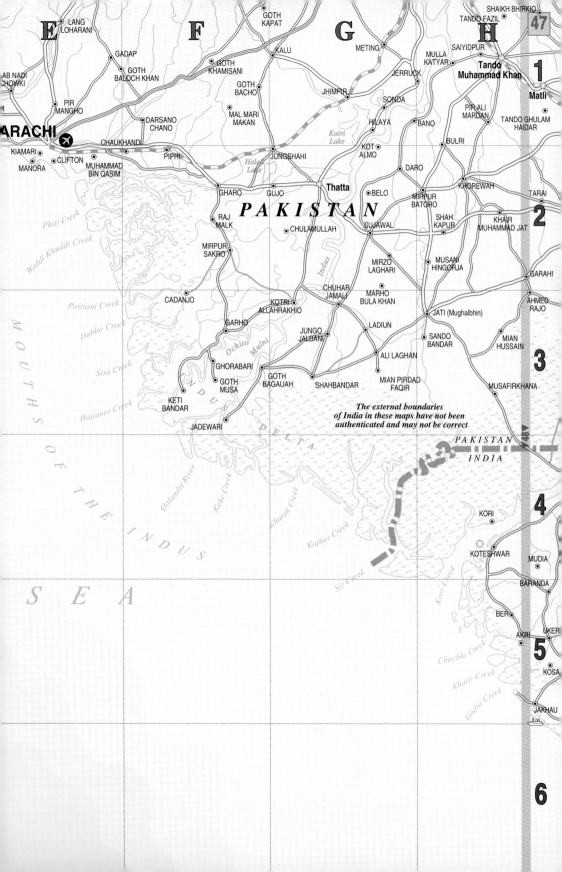

E F G H

1

SHAIKH BHIRKIO
TANDO FAZIL
LANG LOHARANI
GADAP
GOTH KAPAT
SAIYIDPUR
GOTH BALOCH KHAN
GOTH KHAMISANI
KALU
METING
MULLA KATYAR
Tando Muhammad Khan
Matli
AB NADI HOWKI
PIR MANGHO
GOTH BACHO
JHIMPIR
JERRUCK
GOTH KHAMISANI
DARSANO CHANO
MAL MARI MAKAN
SONDA
PIR ALI MARDAN
TANDO GHULAM HAIDAR
ARACHI
HILAYA
BANO
KIAMARI
CHAUKHANDI
PIPRI
Kairi Lake
KOT ALMO
BULRI
CLIFTON
Halar Lake
JUNGSHAHI
DARO
MANORA
MUHAMMAD BIN QASIM
GHARO
GUJO
Thatta
BELO
MIRPUR BATORO
KHOREWAH

2

TARAI
PAKISTAN
RAJ MALK
CHULAMULLAH
SUJAWAL
SHAH KAPUR
KHAIR MUHAMMAD JAT
Phiti Creek
Waddi Khuddi Creek
MIRPUR SAKRO
MIRZO LAGHARI
MUSANI HINGORJA
GARAHI

3

CADANJO
KOTRI ALLAHRAKHIO
CHUHAR JAMALI
MARHO BULA KHAN
JATI (Mughalbhin)
AHMED RAJO
Paitiani Creek
GARHO
JUNGO JALBANI
LADIUN
SANDO BANDAR
MIAN HUSSAIN
Dubbo Creek
Ochito
Mulni
ALI LAGHAN
Sisa Creek
GHORABARI
GOTH MUSA
GOTH BAGAUAH
SHAHBANDAR
MIAN PIRDAD FAQIR
MUSAFIRKHANA
Hajamro Creek
KETI BANDAR
INDUS DELTA
JADEWARI

M O U T H S

The external boundaries of India in these maps have not been authenticated and may not be correct

4

O F

Qalandri River
Kohr Creek
Kharak Creek
PAKISTAN
INDIA
T H E
Kajhar Creek
KORI
Sir Creek
KOTESHWAR
MUDIA

I N D U S

BARANDA

5

S E A
Chachla Creek
Kari Creek
BER
AKRI
UKER
Kharo Creek
KOSA
Godia Creek
JAKHAU

6

48

A   B   C   D

1

SHAIKH BHIRKIO JAMESABAD SAMARO
KHACHHAR DUMBALO DIGRI KUNRI ▲30▲ DHARMSAL
  TANDO GHULAM ALI TANDO JAN MUHAMMAD MALUK SINGH DARELO CHACHRO MITH TAR
Matli RAJO KHANANI SARMAST LIGHARI NABISAR ROAD NABISAR DHARINDHARO
  TANDO GHULAM HAIDAR TALHAR KHADARO JHUDO SAID KHAN LIGHARI NOHTUN JO GOTH CHAILAN BHORILA DHAKIA
  Jamali KHARIPUR NAUKOT **PAKISTAN** LUNHYAR
  PUNHO CHANDIA MUKAM DALFUR SINGHARA

2

TARAI DATO Badin NINDO SHAHR PANGRI JURYAR MITHI
  LUWARI WANGO KALOHI PILORO JEHPOYO ISLAMKOT KHARIO LU
  SIRAN KHARUK BHADUR CHOWPANI BORLI GOF
  KADHAN PABUHAR KARKASUR
AHMED RAJO SHADMAN LUND BHADMI GAJAWARI GALAU DIPLO WADAN *The external boundaries*
  MITHI RAHIM HI BAZAR SARAI JO GOTH BUNDRA LUS NAHISAR *of India in these maps have not* PAKISTAN
  SALT CHAUKI KANJAR KOT BALHARI *authenticated and may not be c* INDIA

3

PAKISTAN INDIA VINGUR
  Biar Bet *Bawaria Bet* *Maruda Takkar*
  Gainda Bet *Sindai Bet*
  R A N N *Kara Dongar* O F K
  465 ✢

4

LAKHPAT KHAVDA *Pachham I.* DHOLAVIRA GADHADA
  KUNRIA *Khadir I.* JANAN
PANADRA *Lakhpat Hills* LUNA G u j a
MUDIA UMIA JARA HODKA JHO 24 BHERANDIALA KUTCH SUVI
BARANDA 79 RAMWAO
  MATANOMADH RAWAPUR *Dhinodhar* BEBAR NIRUNA 40 CHOBARI KAN Ve L
UKER BHADRA NETRA 388 ✢ *Jhura* JHURA LODAI ADHOI

5

WADSAR RAMPUR BANDIA KHOMBHADI VIRANI 316 ✢ KUNRIA JHURAN LA
KOSA TERA NAKHTARANA *Varar* *Habo Hills* DUDHAI WONDH
  NALIYA MAJAL 344 *Chaduva Katrol Range* NANGOR 82 BHACHAU 17 SAM
JAKHAU MOTHALA ROHA 55 **BHUJ** KUKMA BHIMASAR 43
  WADAPADHAR MAGWANA MANKUWA REHA RATNAL SAMPARDA 8A Ja
  KOTHARA VINJHAN SISAGADH *Dhola Range* DAISARA BHARAPAR **Anjar** **GANDHIDHAM**
SOTHRI DUMRA KOTADI KHOJACHORA KERA KHEDOI KHARI ROBAR Ve

6

  SANDHAN NANGARECHA ASAMBIA BERAJA RATADIA TUNA **Kandala** VE
  SABHRAI 41 BAET GODRA *Kanta Plain* WADALA *Tekra I.* AMR
  BADA LAEJA KODAE BIDADA BHUJPUR FARADI BHADRESWAR *Nakri Creek* BEL
  Mandvi BHADIA ▼62▼ MUNDRA *Hansthal Creek* JODIYA BANDAR BALAMBA BHM
  MUNDRA BANDAR

GULF OF KUTCH

E   F   G   H

BARMER

Rajasthan

JALOR

BANAS KANTHA

The external boundaries
dia in these maps have not been
enticated and may not be correct

INDIA
PAKISTAN

Karunjhar Hills

USAR
RABASAR
BHANIA
DHORINIANA
GURA
MORAIM
NAGAR KHAS
NANDIA
BAGORA
NARSANA
PANTHERI
Suki
Sogi

BAORI
SIRWA
KABULI
PURASA
BERI
GANDAP
JHAB
DUDA
PUNAS
DUNGARWATAL
Bhinmal
GAJIPURA

TIDERA
JATON KI DHANI
GANGHASARA
AGRAWA
SANTA KUNI
HARIYALI
KARWARA
BILAR
SELWASAN
Jaswantpura

CHOTAL
DUTHWA
CHITALWANA
SEWARA
MALWARA

SAMI VERI
BAKHASAR
JANVI
AMLI
SANCHOR
RIWARA
RANIWARA
BARGAON
Sunda 991
Hills

ILU
BHAWATRA
LELAVA
GARH ANAPUR
KHEMAT
MANDAR

GADRO CHARAN
KUDALIA
KARBAN
RAHA
DHANERA
PATHAVADA

VIRAWAH
BHOROL
DUVA
RAMSAN
DANTIVADA

NAGAR PARKAR
VETAWA
DHIMA
DAIDARDA
KHERALA
JHERDA
BHARAT
VAGROL

ADIGAON
KASBO
KUWALA
Bordia Bet
Parbatana Bet
VAV
THARAD
KOTADA
DAMA
DEESA
CHANDISAR

Nara Bet
ASARA
MADKA
LAKHNI
BHILARI
OLD DISA
PALANPUR

Khijadiawala Bet
BHARDUVA
MAKDALA
VATAM
MARANGADH
SAMOU MOTAWAS
KANODAR
KODRAM

SUIGAM
VAJAPUR
DIYODAR
MUDETHA
RANER
KAKOSHI

BHABBAR
KHODA
SIHORI
MORPA
WAGROD
SIDHPUR

WARSARA
TERVADA
SAMPRA
SUJNIPUR
UNJHA
MEHERVARA

JHAJHAM
THARA
SANKRA
PATAN
ARIA
GOKALPURA
CHANASMA
BHANDU

KORDA
RHILOT
Radhanpur
MANDVI
JAMANPUR
HARIJ
DHINOJ

BELA
MOUANA
BAKUTRA
VARAHI
SATUN
VED
SAINI
MODHERA
MAHESANA

JATAWADA
SANTALPUR
GOKHATAR
GOTARKA
DUDKHA
CHANDRORA
MAHESANA

GEDI
FATEHGADH
PIPRALA
ANTARNES
RAPHU
KUWAR
MANJPUR
SANKESHWAR
KATOSAN
JAGUDAN

SELARI
ADESAR
VED
ADRIANA
PANCHASAR
SITAPUR
VITNALAPUR
NANDASAN
LANGHNAJ

BHIMASAR
VARAU WANDH
PALIANAWA
WARGAM
VANOD
MITHAPUR
DETROJ

KIDIANAGRU
KUTCH
JHINJHUVADA
DASADA
Kadi
KALOL

HIROD
WISAWARI
ZAINABAD
MANDAL
DASLANA
KHAWAD

DHIA
LITTLE
TIKAR
KUDA
OORU
PATDI
GORIA
VIRAMGAM
THOL

RANN
Little Rann of Kutch
Wildlife Sanctuary
Kharagoda Tank
BAJANA
THALA
KARAKTHAL
Sanand
SARKHEJ

MALIYA
KAKREJI
GHANTILA
MAYARNAGAR
KUWA
VITHALGADH
KARAKTHAL
RUPAWATI

SARWAD
JETPUR SHAPUR
DEOLIA
HALVAD
GHANSHYAMPUR
DHRANGADHRA
METHAN
VANA
LAKHTAR
BHALALA
AHMADABAD
BAVIA

SARA
RANGPUR
BELA
CHARADVA
SURENDRANAGAR
RAJSITAPUR
DEVLIA
TALSANA
Nal Sarovar Bird Sanctuary
DHOLKA

MORVI
GHOTA
MATHAK
KODH
ANKEVALIA
KHODU
RAJPUR
DEDADRA
Nal Lake

Bamshan Plain
SARA
SARLA
DIGSAR
Surendranagar
WADHWAN
RANAGADH

CH

Bela I.
Hills

Phulka
East Kathiawar Plains
Banas
Rupen
Saraswati

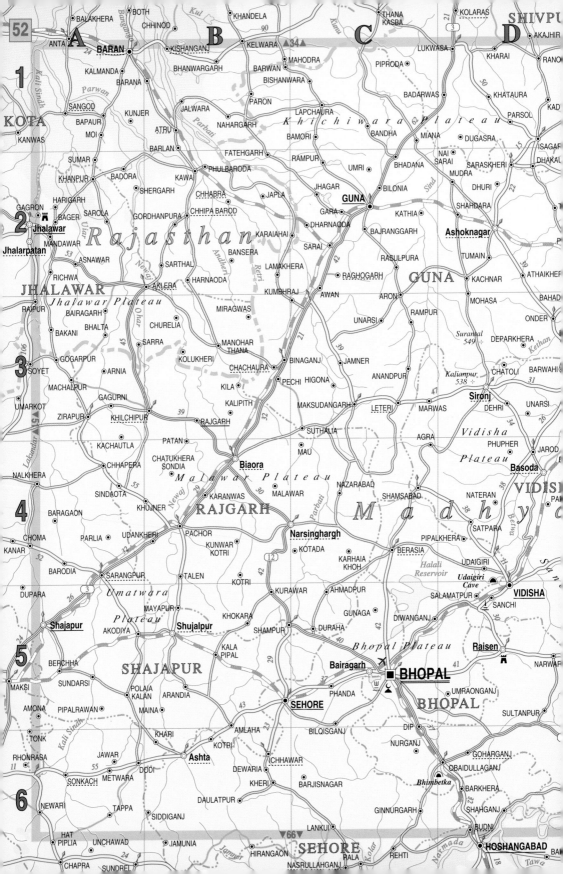

E F G H

1
2
3
4
5
6

Uttar Pradesh

PICHOR
BABINA
PIRTHIPUR
RANIPUR
JAITPUR
SRINAGAR
Urmal
Majhgawan Tank
SIMRA
Mau Ranipur
ALIPURA
85
BASAI
BAMORI
LUGASI
MALAHAR
KHANIADHANA
CHANDERA
GARRAULI
NOWGONG
MAHARJPUR
Dharm Sagar
Jagat Sagar
31
LADHAURA
JATARA
PALERA
CHATARPUR
GATHAURA
RAJNAGAR
BIJROTHA
PARON
MOHANGARH
DIGAURA
TIKAMGARH
ISANAGAR
CHAUKA
33
KHAJURAHO
26
BANSL
KELGAWAN
MAJNA
BHELSI
CHANDERI
BASARI
GHURA
34
KELWARA
BANPUR
TIKAMGARH
BALDEOGARH
RAGAULI
CHATARPUR
RAJGARH
SILON
LALITPUR
19
Dhasan
75
GULGANJ
Bijawar
NONANPANJI
AMRONIA
Gangau Res.
LALITPUR
MAHRONI
SOJNA
MALEHRA
JAKHLAUN
Govind Sagar
35
Bijawar Hills
SHAHGARH
KISHANGARH
SERAI
BIRDHA
GHAURA
DEOGARH
PALI
PATHA
KAKARWAO
DARGAWAN
Vindhyan Scarpland
Sonar
68
DHAURA
39
GIRAR
HIRAPUR
MARIAD
GAISABAD
MUNGAOLI
GONA
MADAORA
Dhasan
BAKSWAHO
40
MADANPUR
BARAITHA
47
SHAHGARH
FATEHPUR
MOHDRA
KANJIA
KARONDA
RURAWAN
BATIAGARH
73
Hatta
RANEH
39
BARODIA
DELPATPUR
KERBANA
38
BANGAON
JUDPUR
KHINLASA
Bina Etawa
Bina Plateau
74
BANDRI
BEHROL
Banda
BHADRANA
SATPARA
NARSINGHGARH
PATERA
KUMHARI
RAIPURA
54
KHURAI
KARRAPUR
PATHARIA
HINDORIA
DALPATPUR
JERUWAKHERA
33
32
Bewas
SHAHPUR
48
PARHARI
NARVAULI
SAGAR
Kopra
DAMOH
GHATERA
JHILLA
JALANDHAR
38
DHANA
HARDOT
GARHAKOTA
32
Bearma
SAGONI
RAHATGAR
41
20
BHURI
ABHANA
NOHTA
Damoh Plateau
BAKAI
Sonar
radesh
Sagar Plateau
691
SURKHI
SAGAR
Rehli
BALEH
TEJGARH
Mala Tank
40
JABERA
GYARASPUR
MUHAMMADGARH
JAISINGHNAGAR
BILEHRA
752
GOURJHAMAR
DAMOH
752
GUBRA
NAWAB BASODA
BEGAMGANJ
JAITPUR
KUDPURA
TENDUKHEDA
KATANGI
MAJHOL
HARDOTE
KESHLI
Dehori
TARADEHI
22
KAIMORI
PATAN
BELKHARU
GHAIRATGANJ
721
SODARPUR
SAHAJPUR
39
MAHARAJPUR
Hiran
60
JABALPUR
DEHGAON
SILVANI
JAITHARI
TENDUKHEDA
BHERAGHAT
GARHA
12
Hills
BAMHORI
DEORI
SUATALA
KERPANI
BELKHERA
63
SHAHPURA
22
GUWARGHAT
AISEN
UDAIPURA
95
SANKAL
26
Tendoni
Sindikar
BRAHMAND
NAYAGAON
CHHOTA CHHINDWARA
BARELI
Narmada
PALOHA
KHULRI
28
Shen
SINGHPUR
SRINAGAR
BARGI
SAINKHEDA
Narsinghpur
BILKHERI
HULKI
DEMRA
SANDIA
Gadarwara
16
Narmad
GAKHERA
BABAI
KARAPGAON
35
Kareli
AMGAON
NARSINGHPUR
MUNGWANI
SOBHAPUR
57
Chitarewa
Dudhi
Shakkar
SHIKARA
SOHAGPUR
Pipariya
BANKHERI
GOTITORIA
KOTRA
KUNDALI
68
DHANKAKRI
DHUMA
67
24
Temur
26
Macharewa

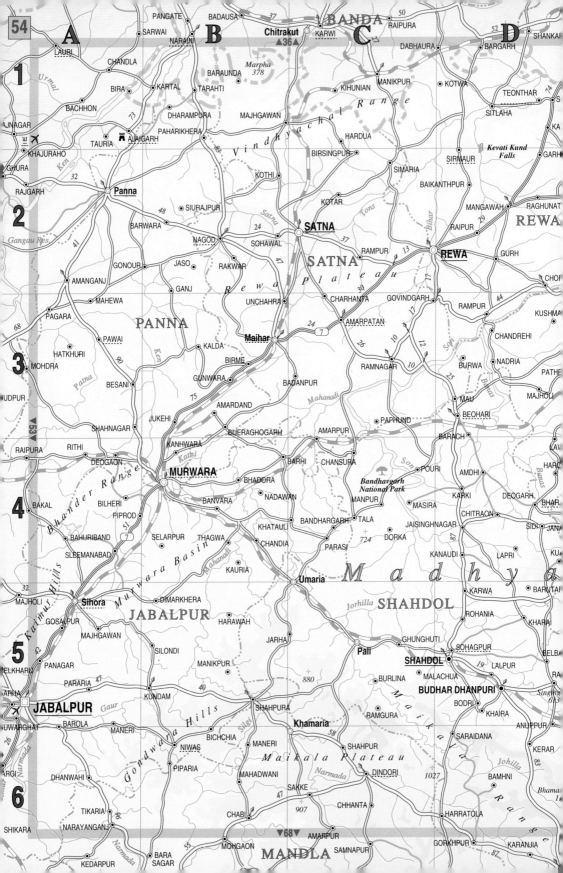

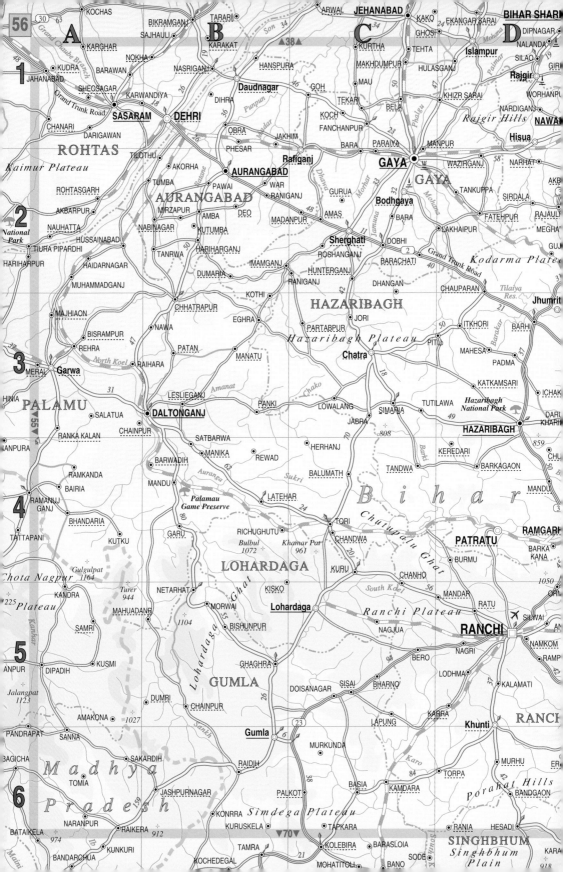

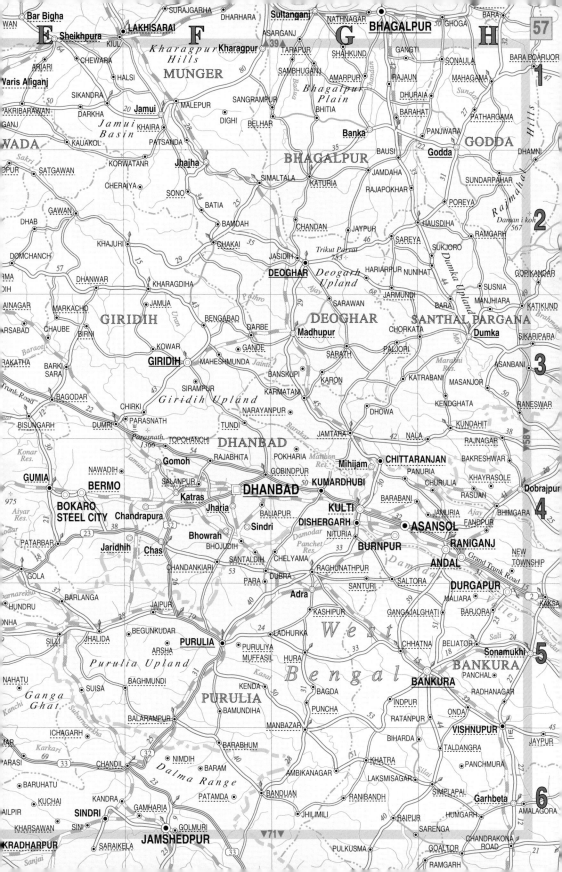

E   F   G   H

PARA · BHARATKHALI · RAJENDRAGANJ · DALU · INDIA · BAGHMARA · RONGARA · PANIKUNDA

JUMABARI · DIWANGANJ · NALITABARI · 52 · ▲41 · BANGLADESH · DURGAPUR · MANTALA · Rauar

ISLAMPUR · The external boundaries of India in these maps have not been authenticated and may not be correct · HALUAGHAT · MUNSHI HAT · KALUMA KANDA · CHHANBARI · SUKHAIR · SACHNA

MELANDAHA · SHERPUR · DURAIL · PHULPUR · GUATALA · GHAGRA · JARIA JHANJAIL · RAIPUR · DHRMAPASHA

JAMALPUR · RAUHA · MYMENSINGH · PURBBA DHALA · Kangsa

GABARGAON · GUNERBARI · NARUNDI · TARAKANDA · MAILAKANDA · Netrakona · BARHATTA · MOHANGANJ · SYLHET

CHANDANBAISA · BANGALI · MUKTAGACHA · GOURIPUR · NANDIKHILA · MENDIPUR · GABINDASTI · KANDIGAON

UNAT · SARISHABARI · DIGPAIT · BASURI · MYMENSINGH · ISWARGANJ · AKHASRI · KHALIAJURI · Kalni

R · SONAMUKHI · PINGNA · HASNAI · DHANBARI · PHULBARIA · NANDAIL · ATHARIBARI · KENDUA · TARAIL · BADLA · AJMIRIGANJ · SIBPASA

IPUR · BAGBARI · SIRIGANJ · Gopalpur · MADHUPUR · BAGA · TRISAL · KARIMGANJ · ITNA · BITANGAL

ILA · Jamuna · NAGARBARI · DEOPARA · ALAHARI · BISHNUPUR · GHAFARGAON · HUSAINPUR · KISHORGANJ · MITAMAIN · MADUA

HHI · 98 · KAMARKHANDA · SALAP · MAGRA · BHALUKA · MASAKHALI · Brahmaputra · Baulai

APARA · BELKUCHI · BALLA · TANGAIL · CHHOTA GAJARA · ASTAGRAM · LAKHAI

BNA · BETIL · SITHAL · Tangail · BASAIL · ULUSARA · KATIADI · BAJITPUR · CHATALPAR

JR · Shahzadpur · MATESWAR · JAMURKI · HATAIA · SRIPUR · MANOHARDI · CHONTA · NASIRNAGAR · 60

ATHPUR · DULAI · PACHH ELASIN · DELDUAR · BANGLADESH · KAPASIA · SIBPUR · BHAIRAB BAZAR · ASHUGANJ · MADHABPUR

BERA · KASINATHPUR · MIRZAPUR · KALIAKAIN · DAKAHIN SIMULEA · JOYDEVPUR · DHAKA · BRAHMANBARIA · CHANDURA

SUJANAGAR · NAGARPUR · DAULATPUR · BALIATI · SATURIA · DHAMRAI · DHIRASRAM · RAIPURA · GOKARNA · BAMUTIA

NAGARBARI · ARICHA GHAT · GHIOR · DHAUKORA · SAVAR · TONGI · PUBAIL · ARIKHOLA · NARSINGDI · BIDYAKOT · PAGHACHANG · SINGARBIL

BARKHANPUR · SIBALAY · Manikganj · SINGAIR · BIRABA · RUPGANJ · ARAIHAZAR · NABINAGAR · NARAYANPUR · AGARTALA

Padma · GOALUNDO · BANKHARI · MIRPUR · TEZGAON · NASIRABAD · GANGASAGAR · BINAUTI

Rajbari · HARIRAMPUR · ROHITPUR · DHAKA · BANCHHARAMPUR · KUT · KASHA · MADHUPUR

BAHARPUR · 28 · NAWABGANJ · Burhi Ganga · BAIDYA BAZAR · HOMNA · BAKHRABAD · CHANDLA · BISALGAR

LIAKANDI · JHENIDA · DOHAR · NARAYANGANJ · SONARGAON · MURADNAGAR · SUBIL · SIBNAGAR

FARIDPUR · CHAR BHADRASAN · SRINAGAR · SERAJDIKHAN · Munshiganj · DEBIDWAR · RAJAPUR · BURICHANG · INDIA

KUNAIPUR · SADARPUR · BHAGYAKUL · TANGIBARI · DAUDKANDI · ELLIOTGANJ · JAFARGANJ · MAINAMATI · SONAMURA

49 · BINODEPUR · NAGARKUNDA · MATBARAR CHAR · LOHAGANJ · RAJBARI · COMILLA · CHANDINA · RAMMOHAN · 50 · COMILLA

UHAMMADPUR · BHUSHANA · BHANGA · SIBCHAR · JANJIRA · MOHANPUR · KHIDIRPUR · BARURA · BHATPARA

NAHATA · ALFADANGA · KALAMRIDA · NARIA · ASIKHATI · KACHUA · BAGHMARA · GALIMPUR · 26 · KASHINAGAR

ERPARA · FARIDPUR · KHANDARPARA · CHIKANDI · MAHISAR · HAJGANJ · 71 · Laksham · CHAUDDAGRAM

ARAL · BHATIAPARA · RAJAIR · PALANG · BHEDARGANJ · CHANDPUR · CHITOSI · 59

LOHAGARA · MADARIPUR · NARASINHAPUR · FARIDGANJ · NATHERPETNA · GUNABAT

SRIDHARPUR · GOPALGANJ · KALKINI · GOSAIRHAT · CHAR HAIM · RAMGANJ · BIPULASHAR · BAKSHGANJ

ARA · PHULTALA · KAJALIA · MEDAKUL · BADARTUNI · RAIPUR · JOYAG · SONAIMURI · RAJAPU

RPARA · GAURNADI · CHAR BANSI · NOAKHALI · SENBAG · 35

TPUR · TERAKHADA · MOLLAHAT · SAFIPUR · GAILA · HIJLA · KALIKAPUR · DAGANBHUIYA

KHULNA · MATIBHANGA · BATAJOR · BARISAL · MULAD · DADPAR · Lakshmipur · Begamganj · MAIDJI · BASHAR HA

IULNA · ILUHAR · WAZIRPUR · MEHANDIGANJ · FARASHGANJ · CHAR MATUA · NOAKHALI · RAMNIA

ATTAKI · JATRAPUR · NAZIRPUR · BANARIPARA · KAZIR CHAR · 73 · CHAR JAGABANDHU · MIAR HAT

AURAMBHA · SWARUPKATI · BARISAL · BHOLA · Shahbazpur · CHAUDHURI HAT · CHAR ALEXANDER · KHASER HAT

A   **B** ▲48▲   **C**   **D**

1

2

3

4

5

6

GULF OF KUTCH

MUNDRA BANDAR

Pirotan I.

JODIYA BANDAR

JODIYA

BH BALAM

Nora I.

Karumbhar I.

HARIANA

JAMBURA

BEDI

DHROL

OKHA

Island of Bet

Baida I.

SIKA

BED

PHALA

37

JAMNAGAR

WANTHALI

JALIA

PA

MITHAPUR ARANTA

Gandhia I.

PADANA

BERAJA

73

MATWA

KHANDERA

KHIJARIYA

GADECHI

PANTRA

Jar I.

Panera I.

Salaya

ARIK

LALPUR

KALIANA

SISANC

LALOI

Dwarka

Gomti Creek

WARWALA

GORGAT

ASOTA

Khambhaliya

JAMNAGAR

KHARBA

Kalavad

CHATAR

MULILA

BHATIA

MOVAN

VARTHARA

BHANGOR

GUNRA

SARMANA

TORA

KHAF

MADHI

GADHKA

BHADTHAR

75

GUNDA

WADALA

UMRALA

SATODAD

BAKURI

DRAFA

WADALI

DWARKA COAST

BHOGAT

KALYANPUR

RAWAL

ADWANA

BHANVAD

BAWALA

Jamjodhpur

PANELI

JAMKANDORNA

82

Wartu

RANPUR

Venu 637

MORPUR

SIDSAR

BHAYAVADAR

LAMBA

MISNI

KILESHWAR

Alech Hills

DHANK

KOLKI

DHORAJ

Meda Creek

MODHWARA

KHAMBHODAR

Barda Hills

WANSJALIA

KHAGASARI

AMRAPUR

UPLETA

MARAD

JETA

BAKHARIA

DEORA

33

GANOD

Osam 314

Ubon

Chowpatty Beach

RANAVAV

27

KANDORNA

8B

Kutiyana

MARMAT

SARDAGARH

KALANA

Gor

PORBANDAR

MOKAL

18

JUNAGADH

ADODAR

Bhadar

Manavadar

12

Girnar 346

BHAD

BANTVA

VANTHLI

SHAPUR

KHARI

MYARI

MANDODRA

27

PORBANDAR COAST

NAVIBANDAR

Ojat

22

AGATRAI

BALAGAM

KADACH

28

Kanara 326

KESHOD

MENDA

MESWAN

AJAB

MADHAVPUR

22

SHERGAD

CHANDAW

Megal

SA

SIL

48

MALIA

Mangrol

BHANDURI

JUNAGA

CHORWAD

BHOLAWAT

Chorwad Beach

VERAVAL

Somna

SUTRAPARA

ARABIAN

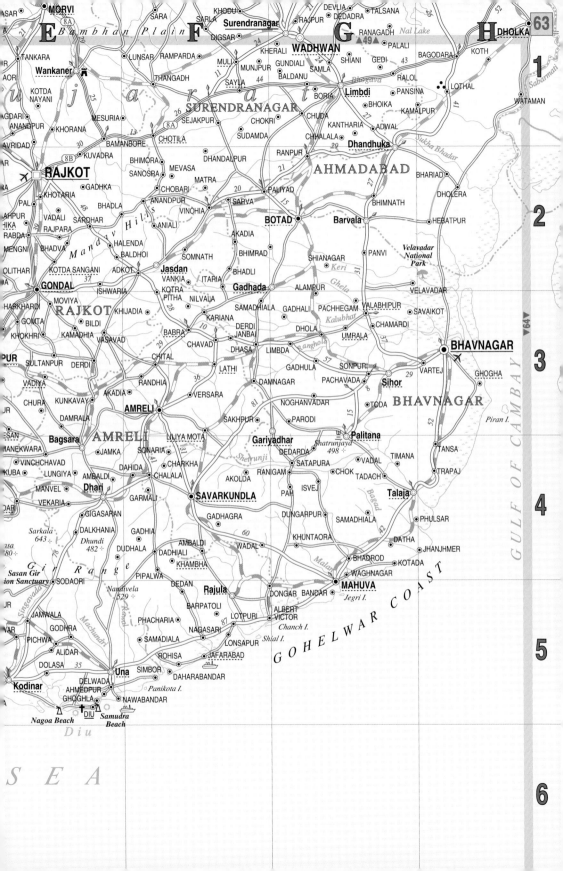

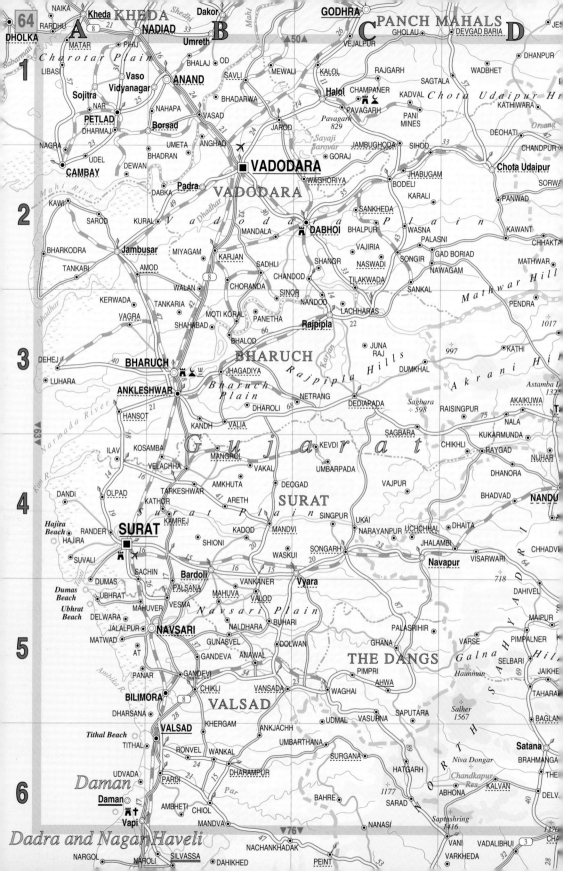

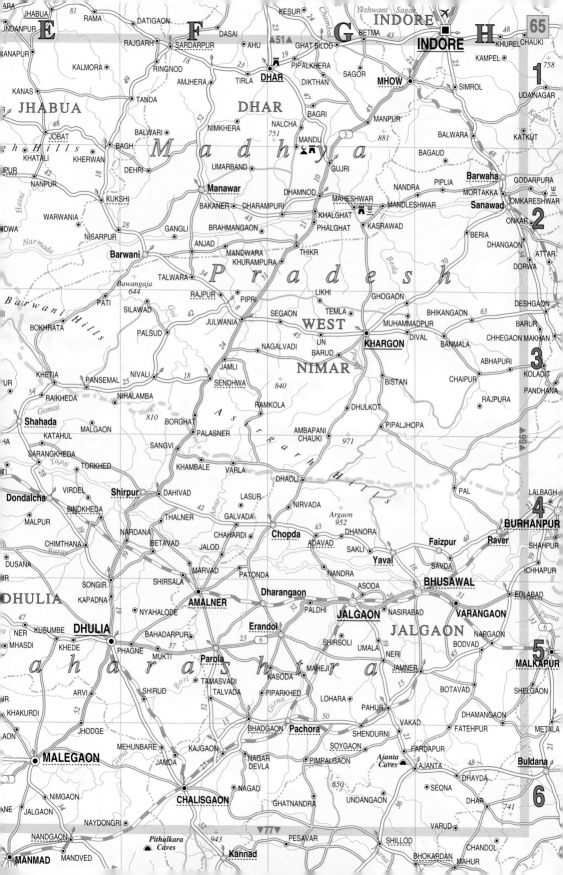

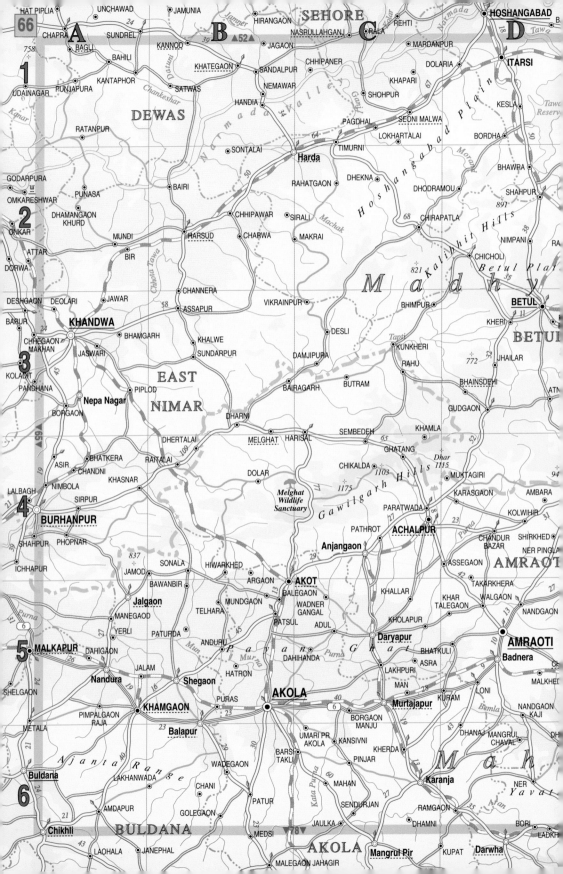

E F G H

PENDRA *Pendra Plateau* 1

PENDRA · EGHAGRA · AHIRPARA · *Tan* · MATIN · KENDAI · BHAKURMA · JALDEGA · PIDIKALO · CHANDAGAR

KHODRI · NAGAI · ▲55▲ · LEMRU · 990 · *Chhuri* · SIANG · BAJPAR · PATHALGAON · *Udaipur*

KENDA · KATGHORA · 988 · SATRENGA · 989 · *Hills* · LABAID · DHARMJAYGARH · 35 · BAKARAMA · BOGUDEGA · *Hills*

BELGAHNA · CHAITMA · 56 · MADANPUR · PHULSARI · SITHRA · BOTURAKACHAR · BULDEGA

821 · PONDI · PALI · **KORBA** · KARKOMA · KARTALA · MUNUND · 806 · GHARGHODA · KAMPARA · TOLONGA · KUNGJARA

KOTA · RATANPUR · *Kurung Tank* · BHELAI · *Korba* *Basin* · DHONDHATARAI · 19 · KHAMAR · SAMARUMA · **RAIGARH** · KOSDOL · MILUPARA

GANIARI · GHUTKU · 807 · NARGORA · BURGAHAN · SOHAGPUR · KHAMAR · 74 · 2

50 · 24 · BALODA · JARWE · SAKTI · GURDA · *Raigarh* · TAPARIA

KHATPUR · **BILASPUR** · AKALTARA · 42 · **Champa** · SAKTI · GURDA · *Basin* · KOSDOL

BILASPUR · **Janjgir** · SARAGAON · KHARSIA · **RAIGARH**

r a d e s h · BELHA · MASTURI · BAMNIDIHI · ADBHAR · KOTRA · KOTARLIA · ⑦0

Seonath · MALHAR · PAMGARH · 47 · MALKHURDA · 47 · 28 · MAHADEOPALI · 3

LPUR · NIPANIA · 23 · JAIJAIPUR · DABRA · PADIGAON · DHOLUNDA

HAT · LOHARSI · SON · HASAUD · JASPUR · CHANDARPUR · 22 · SARIA · AMBABHONA · *Hiraku*

Bhatapara · SEORINARAYAN · 24 · BHATGAON · 29 · BARAMKELA · *Mahanadi* · SAMARDARHA

HERA · BALODA BAZAR · KASDOL · BILAIGARH · SARSIWA · SARANGARH · *Basin* · BHATLI

NEORA · HIRMI · SEMRADIH · MADHUBAN · RAMTEK · JIKHIPALI · 4

Kumhari · PALARI · ARJUNI · 40 · **BARGARH**

Tank · SASHA · NAWAGAON · *734* · KEDUA · BARPALI

KHARORA · TALA · JAGDISHPUR · 38 · SARAIPALI · 68 · SOHELA · BIJEPUR

31 · SIRPUR · 16 · SANKRA · SINGHORA · GHENS

SAMODA · PATEWA · BASNA · *Surangi* · 31 · BALODA · 5

TUMGAON · ⑥ · 56 · PITHORA · PARASWANI · JAGDALPUR · MELCHHAMUNDA · AGALPUR · DUNGRIPALI

9 · **RAIPUR** · KHALARI · BHURKUNJ · BADIKATA · LAKHAMARA · *Parbat* · SALEBHATTA · LOCHIPUR

ARANG · BELAHONDA · 57 · MAHASAMUND · BAGBAHARA · **SAMBALPUR** · PADAMPUR · DOMKIPALI · LOISINGHA

s i n · CHAPAJHAR · BELTIKRI · PALSADA · 822 · SILATPALI · LORMA

GOBRA NAWAPARA · FINJESHWAR · KHAMHARIA · SUARMAR · MAROSILE · *O r i s s a*

KHADMA · CHHURA · SIRGIRI · KHARIAR ROAD · DHANDAMUNDA · BOLANGIR · TARBH

THIDIH · NAWAPARA · PATNAGARH · **BOLANGIR** · ATGAON

67 · DHARAMBANDHA · 69 · LATHOR · DEOGAON · GHANTAPAF

MOHERA · GARIABAND · *Pairi* · RASELA · **KALAHANDI** · TARBOR · BELAPARA · BUDABAL · 32 · 6

DEOGAON · LITIPARA · *Sonabera* · **BOLANGIR** · SAINTALA

ABAKRA · SONABERA · KOMHA · TUREKELA · KANTABANJI · TIKARPARA · RANIPUR · SIRUBAL

ILLI · BINDRA NAWAGARH · *Plateau* · 38 · JHARIAL · GUMSAR

NAGRI · 929 · DHAWALPUR · JARANDH · AMAMORA · 38 · *Lan*

SANKRA · BARDULA · MANPUR KHURD · PATDARHA · ▼81▼ · BORAN · KHARIAR · BANGOMUNDA · SRIRAM · **Titlagarh** · LEGARA · 889

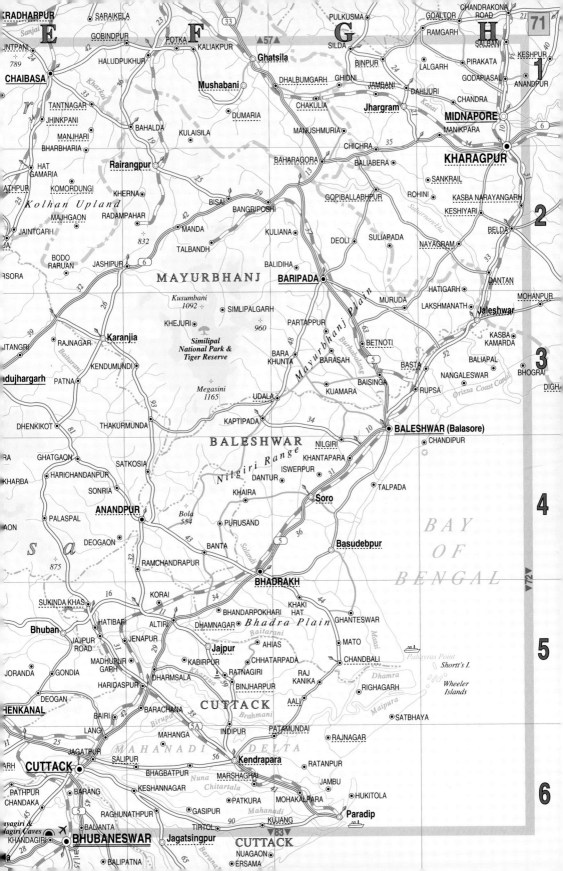

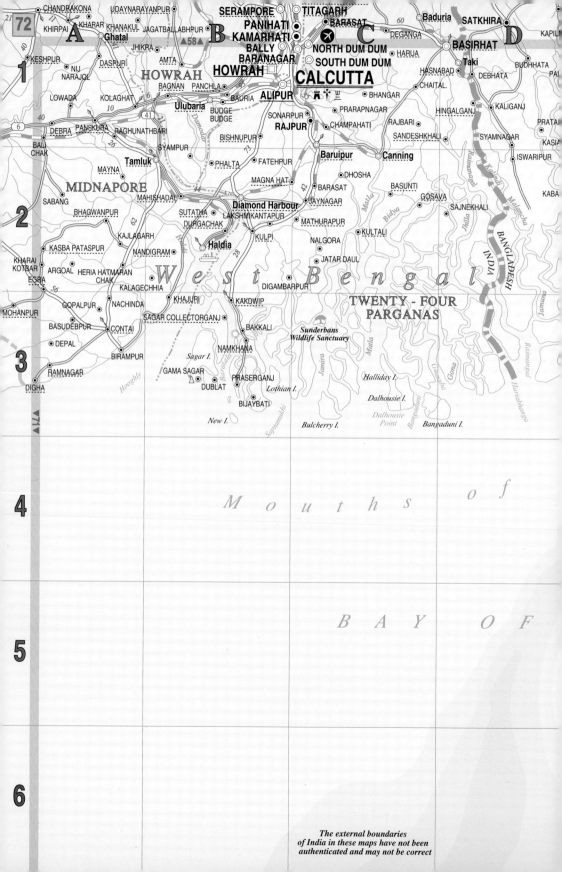

A   **B**   **C**   **D**

CHANDRAKONA
UDAYNARAYANPUR
KHIRPAI
KHARAR KHANAKUL JAGATBALLABHPUR
JHIKRA
SERAMPORE
TITAGARH
PANIHATI
BARASAT
Baduria
SATKHIRA
DEGANGA
KAPIL
KESHPUR
Ghatal
▲58▲
KAMARHATI
BALLY
✈
NORTH DUM DUM
HARUA
BASIRHAT
Taki
BUDHHATA
PAI
NIJ NARAJOL
DASPUR
AMTA
BARANAGOUR
HOWRAH
HOWRAH □
SOUTH DUM DUM
CALCUTTA
HASNABAD
DEBHATA
HOWRAH
BAGNAN PANCHLA
BAURIA
ALIPUR
CHAITAL.
HINGALGANJ
KALIGANJ
PRATA
LOWADA
KOLAGHAT
6
10
Uluberia
BUDGE BUDGE
BHANGAR
PRARAPNAGAR
SONARPUR
RAJPUR
CHAMPAHATI
RAJBARI
SANDESHKHALI
SYAMNAGAR
KASIA
DEBRA PANSKURA RAGHUNATHBARI
41
BISHNUPUR
Baruipur
Canning
ISWARIPUR
BALI CHAK
40
SYAMPUR
26
73
DHOSHA
BASUNTI
KABA
Tamluk
MAYNA
PHALTA FATEHPUR
Magna Hat
BARASAT
JAYNAGAR
GOSAVA
SAJNEKHALI
MIDNAPORE
MAHISHADAL
Diamond Harbour
LAKSHMIKANTAPUR
MATHURAPUR
KULTALI
SABANG
BHAGWANPUR
SUTATHA DURGACHAK
Haldia
KULPI
NALGORA
KAJLAGARH
14
KASBA PATASPUR
NANDIGRAM
28
JATAR DAUL
KHARAI KOTBAR
ARGOAL HERIA HATMARAN CHAK
West Bengal
EGRA
56
KALAGECHHIA
DIGAMBARPUR
MOHANPUR
GOPALPUR
NACHINDA
KHAJURI
KAKDWIP
TWENTY - FOUR PARGANAS
BASUDEBPUR
CONTAI
SAGAR COLLECTORGANJ
BAKKALI
Sunderbans Wildlife Sanctuary
DEPAL
BIRAMPUR
NAMKHANA
RAMNAGAR
Sagar I.
GAMA SAGAR
PRASERGANJ
Halliday I.
DIGHA
DUBLAT
Lothian I.
BIJAYBATI
Dalhousie I.
New I.
Bulcherry I.
Dalhousie Point
Bangaduni I.

M o u t h s   o f

B A Y   O F

BANGLADESH
INDIA

The external boundaries of India in these maps have not been authenticated and may not be correct

E ... **F** ... **G** ... **H**

NAZIRPUR
JATRAPUR
SWARUPKATI
BARISAL
CHAR JAGABANDHU
MIAR HAT
CHAUDHURI HAT

AURAMBHA
Bagherhat
KACHUA
Jhalakati
NALCHITI
▲59▲
CHARAMADDI
BHOLA
DAULATHKAU
CHAR ALEXANDER
KHASER HAT

AKUPI
RAMPAL
Pirojpur
UMEDPUR
BAKARGANJ
DAULIA
JAYNAGAR
North Hatia I.
CHAR GAZI
NOAKHALI
HARNI

1

K h u l n a
MORRELGANJ
BETAGI
MIRZAGANJ
BAGA
BAUPHAL
BARAHANUDDIN
Dakhin
TAZUMUDDIN
HARNI
BARISAL
KALAIA

TUSHKADI
KATHALIA
PATUAKHALI
Shahbazpur I.
CHANCHRA
SUKHCHARER HAT

Mongla
SARANKHOLA
MATBARI
BAMNA
DASMINA
CHAR LALMOHAN
CHAR MANPURA
South Hatia I.

KHULNA
PHULJHURI
PATUAKHALI
Manpura I.
CHENGAR CHAR

BARGUNA
GALCHIPA
ULARIA
SAGARIA

DOANI
AMTALI
LONDA

2

PATHARGHATA
Burishwar
CHHOTA BAISDIA
Donmanick Is.

KELAPARA
Rabnabad Is.

Sunderbans National Park
TETULBARIA
LALNA

Kunga
BARAPARA
DHULASAR

Hiron Point (Nilkamal)
Bangra
t h e   *G a n g e s*

3

B E N G A L

4

5

6

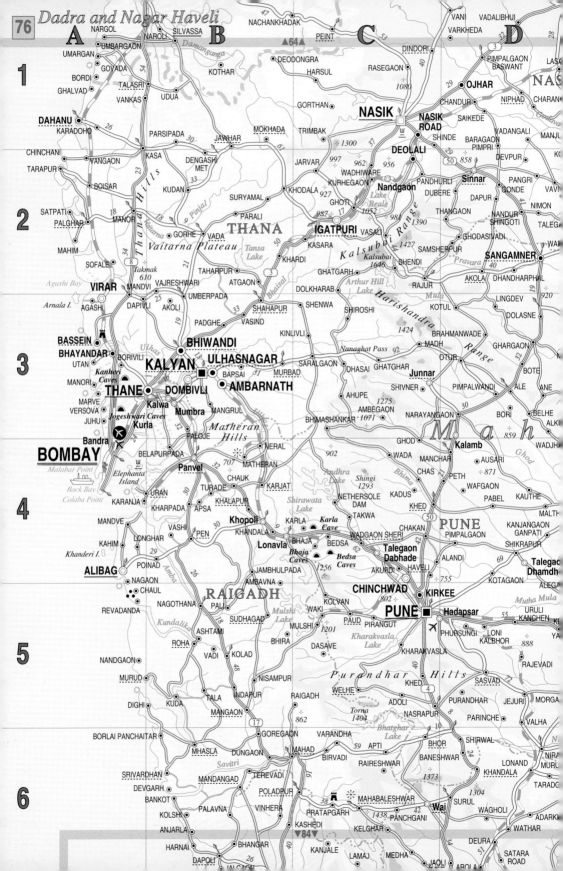

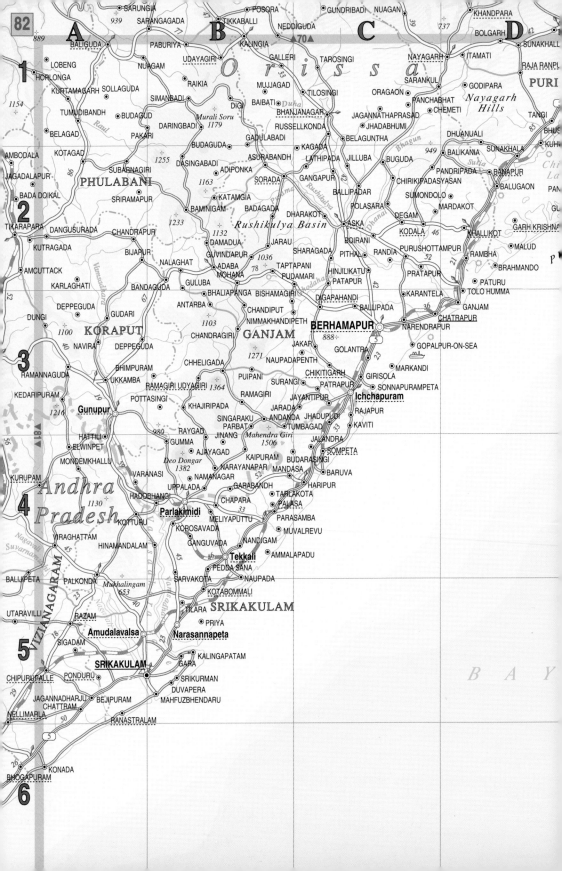

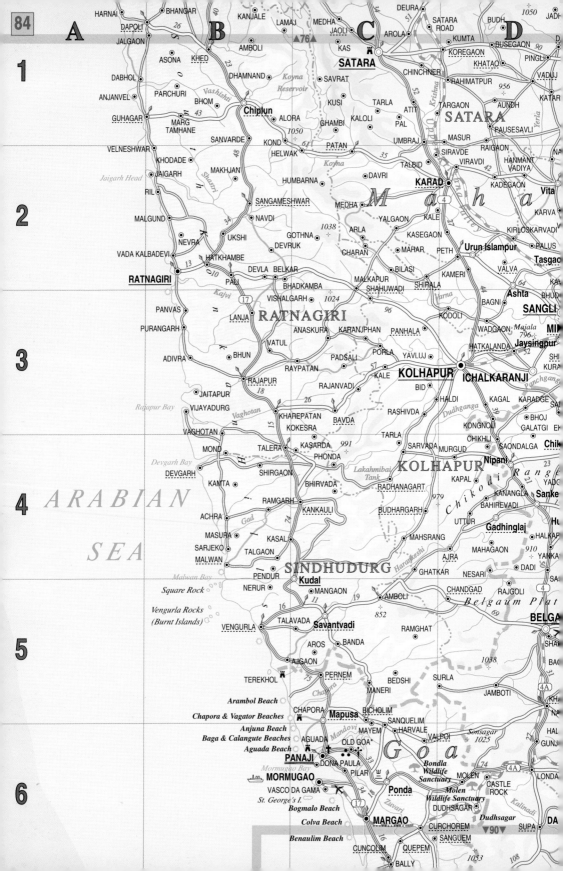

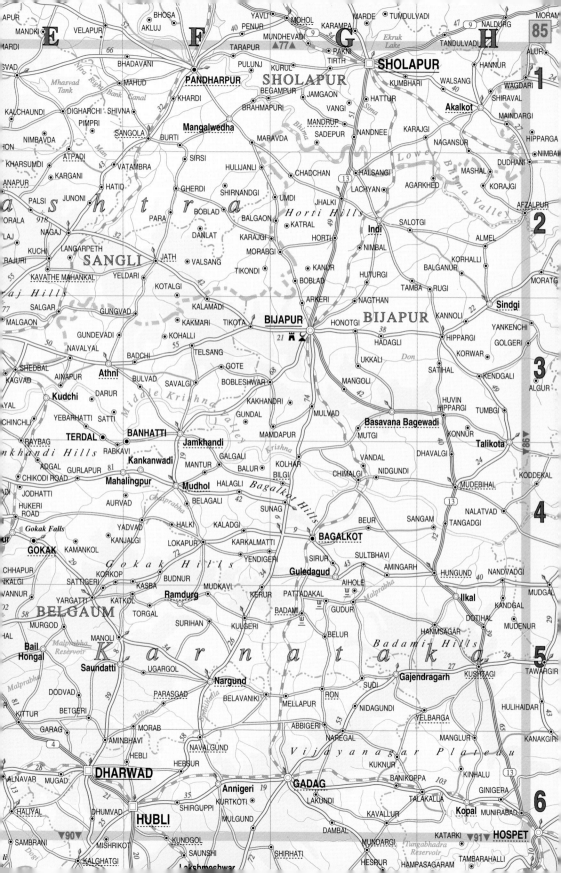

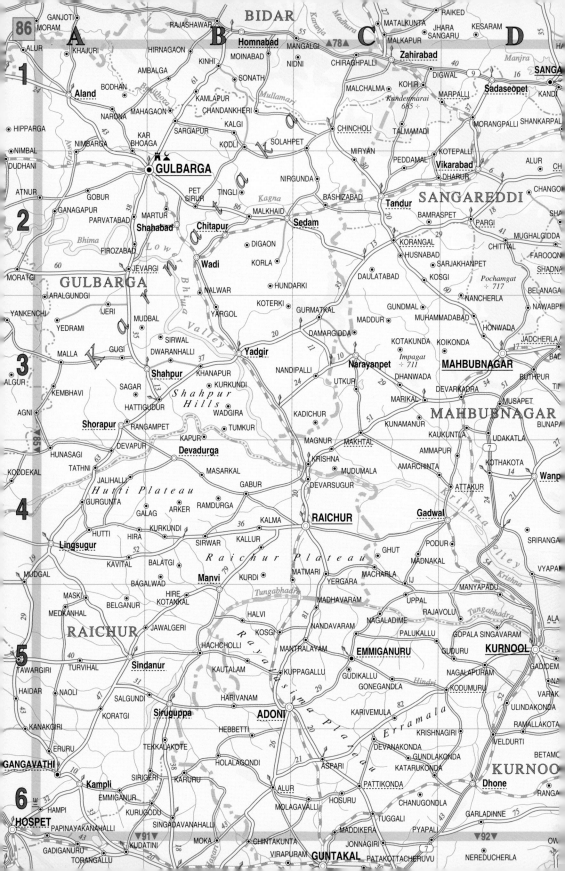

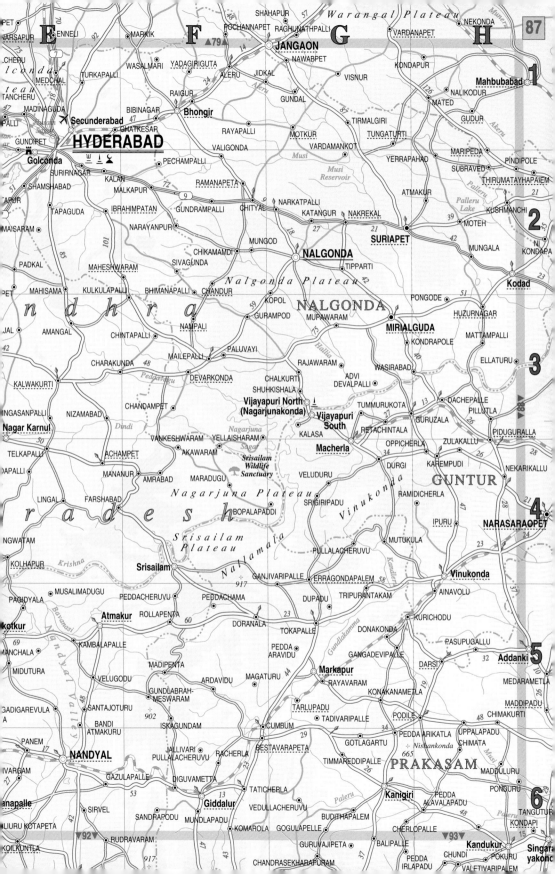

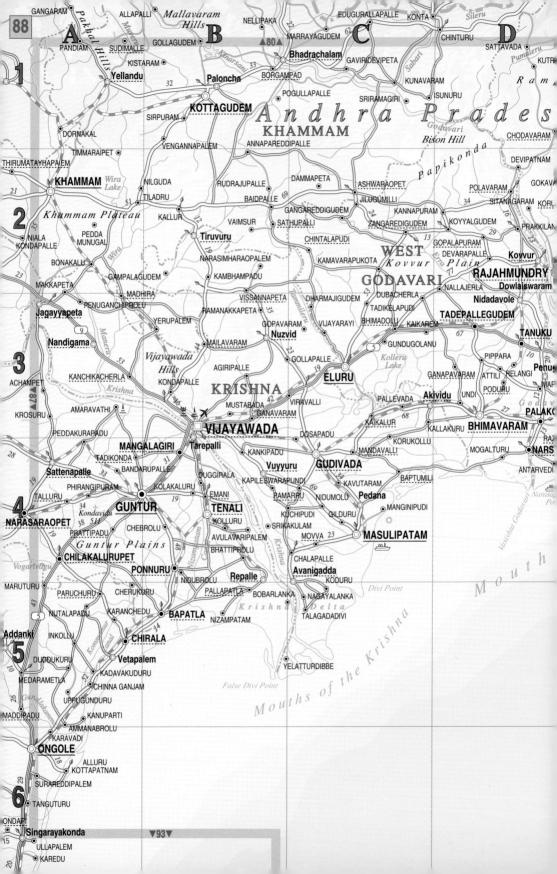

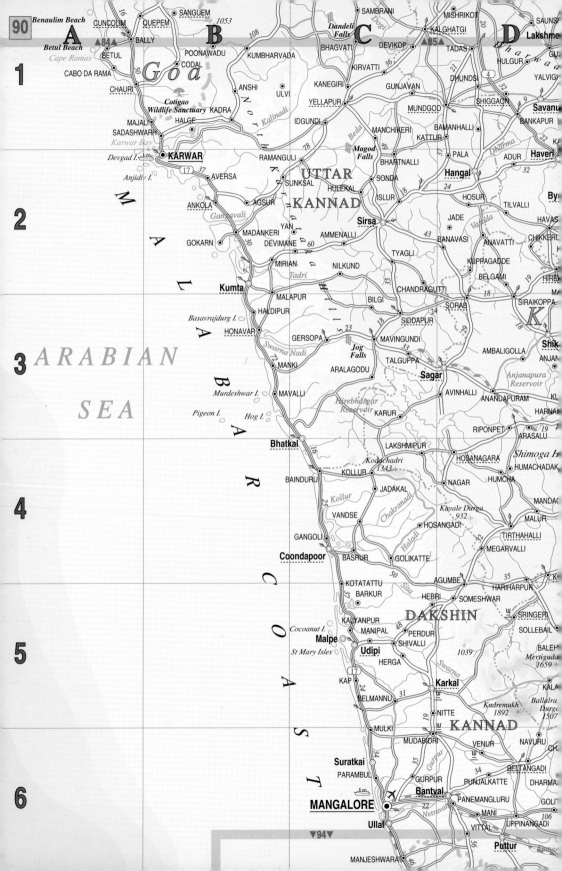

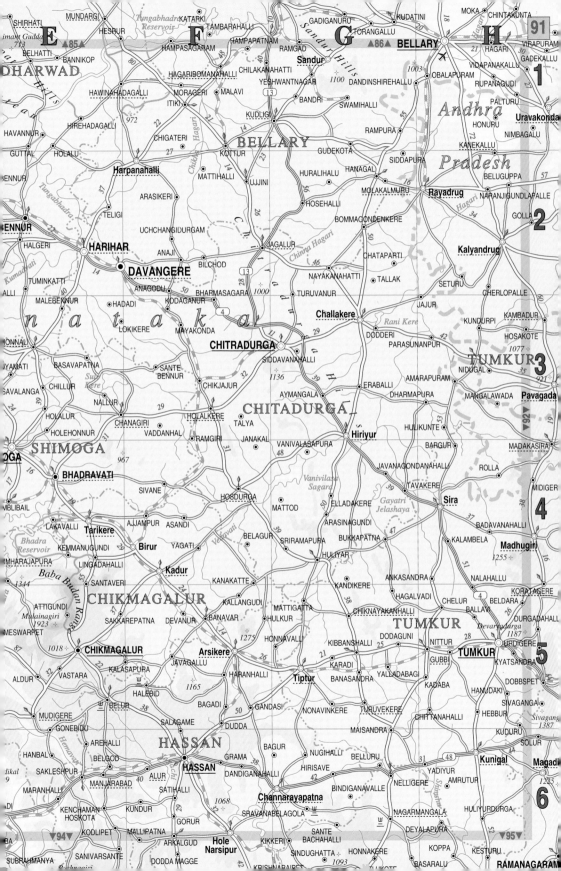

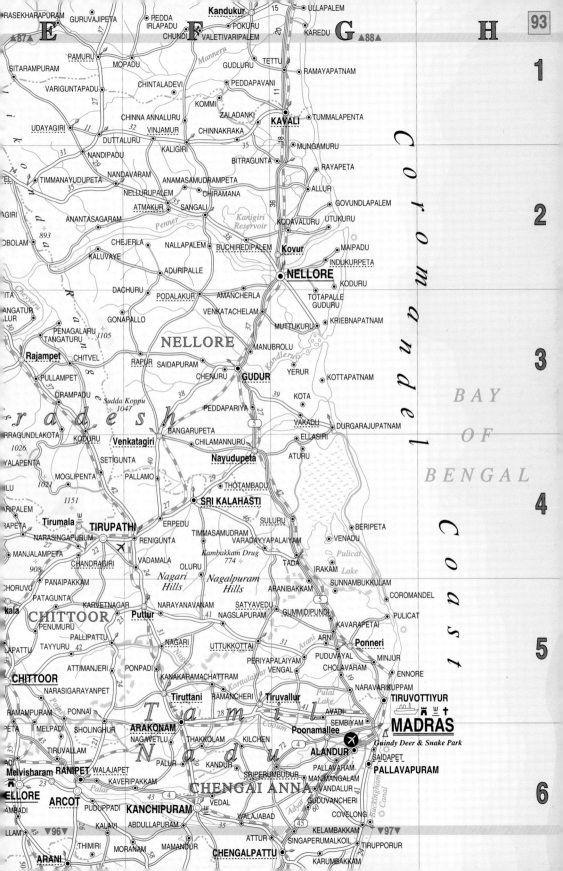

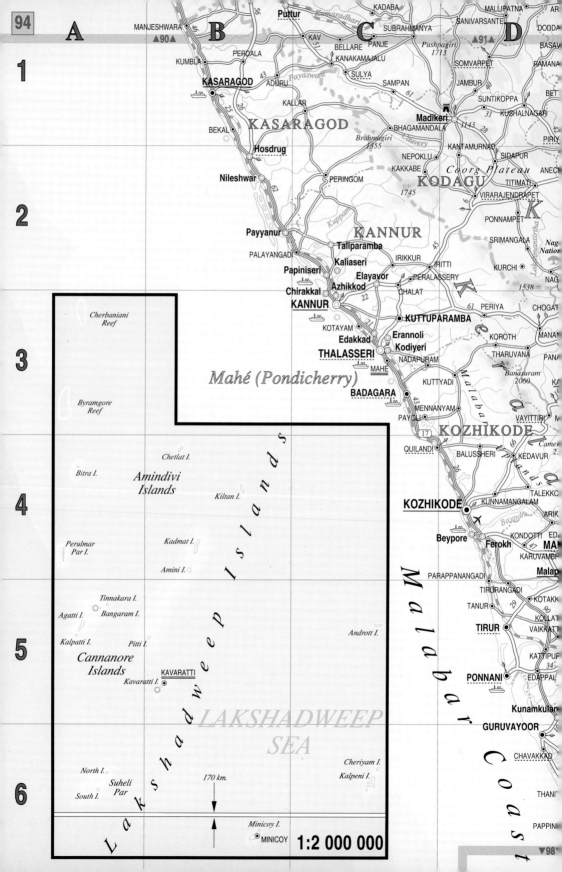

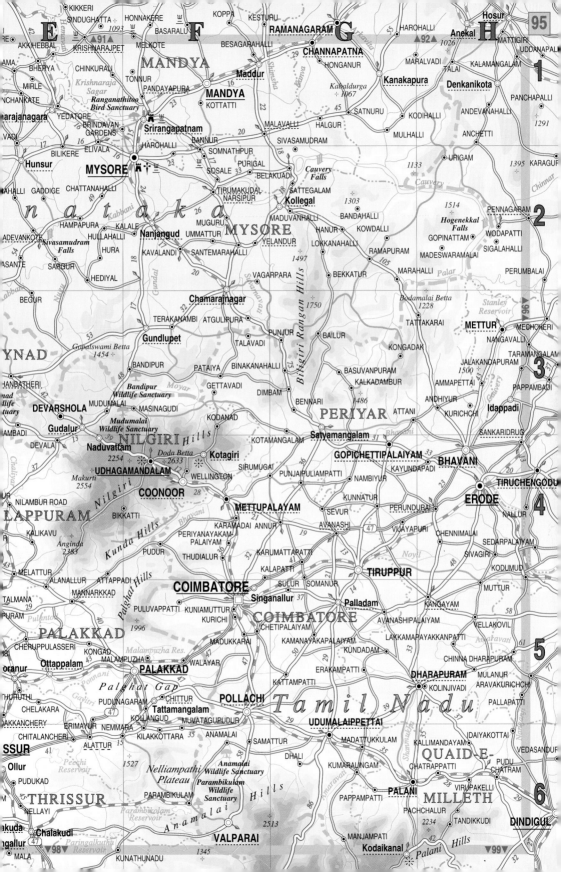

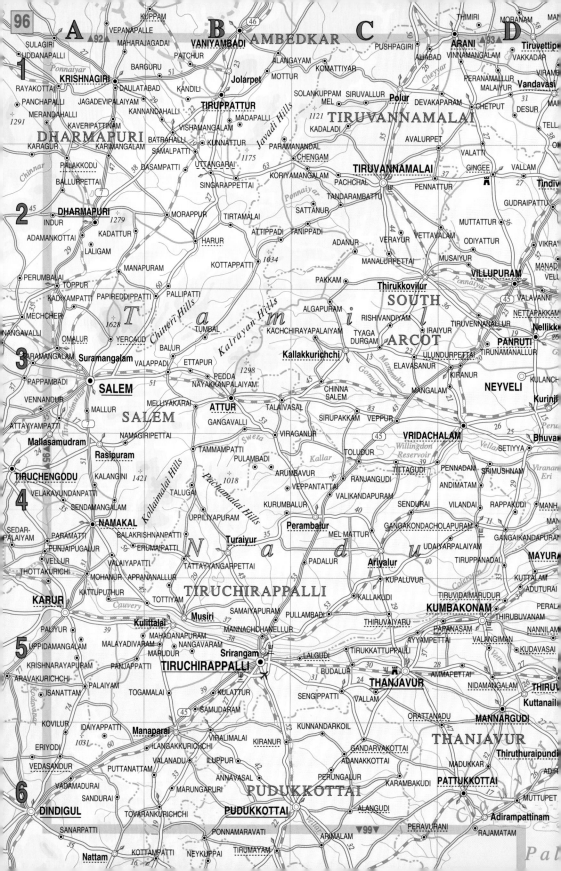

ATTUR **CHENGALPATTU** TIRUPPORUR
KARUMBAKKAM
ORAGADAM ▲93▲ 31
PADALAM MAHABALIPURAM
erur TIRUKKALIKKUNRAM
tangal KARUNGULI SADRAS
Sanctuary
Madurantakam
PAKKAM KOVATTUR
CHITTAMUR
HEHA-
AKKAM CHEYYUR
AMBER

GUR CHUNAMPETTAI
ATTUR
MARAKKANAM

Kaliveli
Tank
KALAPETTAI

arai
AUROVILLE
PONDICHERRY
ARIANKUPPAM 22
OUR

CUDDALORE

AKKAM

orto Novo
arangippettai)

PICHAVARAM

DAMBARAM

ARANCHATTRAM

zhi TIRUMULLAIVASAL

SVARANKOIL
TIRUVENGADU
POOMPUHAR
TIRUKKADAIYUR
AR TRANQUEBAR
KOTTUCHERY
ADU
KARAIKAL *Karaikal (Pondicherry)*

ALAIRAYAN PATTINAM
NAGORE
NAGAPATTINAM
AL
VELANGANNI

TIRUPPUNDI

TALAINAYAR
AGRAHARAM

TOPPUTTURAI

Vedaranniyam
Calimere
Sanctuary
KODIKKARAI
Point Calimere
trait

Coast
Coromandel Coast
Pondicherry

BAY
OF
BENGAL

1

2

3

4

5

6

A B C D

1

**BAY
OF
BENGAL**

Table I.
Great Coco I.
Alexandra Channel

Little Coco I.

MYANMAR (BURMA)
INDIA

Coco Channel

2

Landfall I.   East I.
West I.   Cleugh Passage
White Cliff I.   Cape Price
Reef I.

Paget I.   Table Is.
195
Point Stuart
SHYAMNAGAR
NORTH   LAKSHMIPUR   Smith I.
PHAIAPONG   Port Cornwallis
Casuarina Bay
ANDAMAN   338   RAMKRISHNAGRAM

Snark I.
NABAGRAM   Saddle Peak
738

N Reef I.   RAMNAGAR   *Taralai Bay*

Stewart I.
AUSTEN
Austen   Bacon   Sound I.
Harbour   Bay

Interview I.   MAYABANDAR   *Seaword Bay*
PUDUMADURAI   PAHLAGAON
TUGAPUR   *Paikat Bay*
226

Anderson I.   Mt. Diavolo
515
Roberts Bay   *Cuthbert Bay*

SANTIPUR
438   DHARMAPUR
RONGAT   AMKUNJ
MIDDLE   438
Flat I.   SABRI   *Rongat Bay*
ANDAMAN   310   Beshive Hill
171

4

*Middle Coral
Reef*

Parlob I.   Long I.
North
Button I.
Spike I.   North   *Outram Harbour*
UTTARA   Passage I.
Cape Bluff   KADAMTALA   Colebrooke I.   Outram I.
Baratang I.
Wilson I.   Henry Lawrence I.

*South Coral
Reef*   Nicholson I.   **Ritchie's**
Peel I.   John Lawrence I.
PORT MEADOWS   **Archipelago**
Defence I.   Petman I.
Jatang   Kyd I.
213
354   Havelock I.
460
Neill I.
Sandy I.   243   322
WRIGHTMYO
HERBERTAHAD   365   Sir Hugh Rose I.

Constance Bay   **Port Blair**
SIPPIGHAT   BEADONABAD
**Wandoor National
Marine Park**   CALICUT
Tarmugli I.   WANDOOR   MANGLUTAN
North   Boat I.   265
Sentinel I.   CHIRIYA TAPU
Rutland I.   435
Woodmason Bay
Twins Is.

6   Cinque Is.

Manners Strait

Passage I.
The Sisters
Duncan Passage

*West Coral
Reef*

**SOUTH
ANDAMAN**

Narcone
71

I   s   l   a   n   d   s

Barren I.
355

ANDAMAN

SEA

A   n   d   a   m   a   n

1:1 500 000

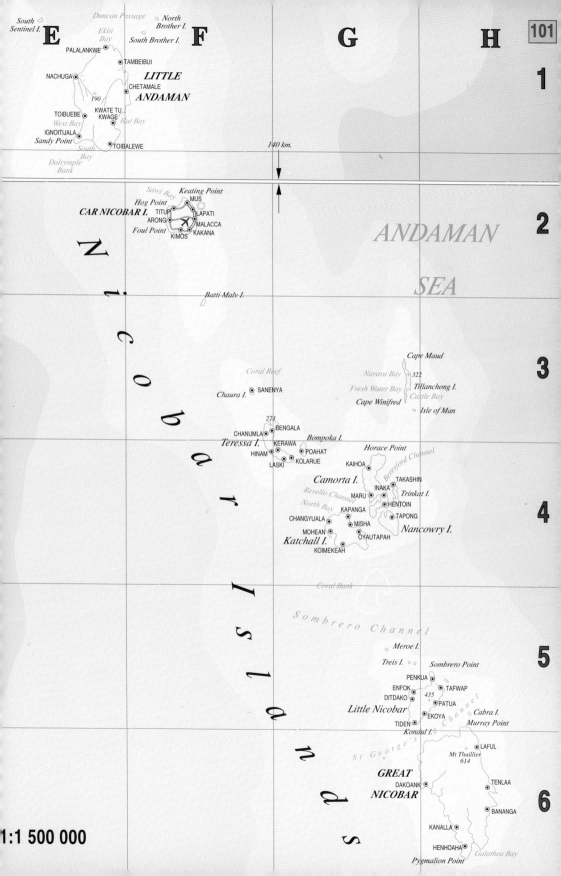

GETTING AROUND INDIA

Train

The Indian railway system has attained almost legendary status for travellers. It's the world's fourth-largest system, with over 11,000 trains running every day, connecting 7000 stations and carrying over nine million passengers. It employs a staggering 1.6 million people! Travellers will find the 100-page *Trains at a Glance* or the more comprehensive *Indian Bradshaw* indispensable for navigating this vast network.

There are three track gauges in India – most travellers will find the trains they want on broad guage lines. These trains are much faster than those that travel on metre and narrow guage lines. Additionally, travellers are faced with the choice of going on a mail, express or passenger train. The first two are preferable, as they are much faster and (mostly) more comfortable and don't stop at every little station. Finally, travellers have the choice of 1st or 2nd class; these categories are often subdivided according to whether air-con and sleepers are offered.

Fares are based on distance and are very affordable for Western travellers. Reservations cost little extra money, but you can often spend hours of your time waiting to make them. Thus the Indrail Pass, which covers a variety of periods ranging from 7 to 90 days, is popular. It's probably not worth it in strictly financial terms, but it certainly saves much of the hassle involved in queueing for regular tickets.

Bus

In many parts of India, especially those covered only by metre or narrow guage rail track, it's better to travel by bus. In many places buses offer a parallel service to trains, and can be quicker than the equivalent train service.

Ordinary buses are usually crowded, slow and uncomfortable – and sometimes dangerous. However, you certainly get a good picture of life on the road in India. Some states have 'deluxe' or express buses which are much quicker and more comfortable. On virtually all buses, however, travellers have to contend with local pop music blasting out at maximum decibels. Some overnight express buses have videos, which are also played at full volume.

Most buses don't require reservations and fares are pretty cheap. In most areas a state-owned bus company travels nearly all routes, often in competition with some private companies. Travellers need to keep watch over their luggage, especially if it's tied up on the roof.

Road

The Indian road system is very extensive and you can get almost anywhere if you have wheels. However, since few people come overland from Europe anymore, as rental usually means hiring car and driver, and since cars are expensive to buy, few foreigners tour India by car these days.

Motorbike tours, however, are popular with an increasing number of travellers. India has a range of Japanese and locally-made bikes, with the 250cc Enfield Bullet being probably the most popular brand for foreigners. On the whole, it's better to bring your own helmet, gear and tools – spare parts for locally sold models are readily available throughout the country.

Petrol is relatively expensive and road signs are often inadequate or absent altogether.

Roads are often of poor standard, and routes like the Grand Trunk Road can be crowded and dangerous, with a plethora of vehicles – from lumbering oxcarts to huge trucks travelling at breakneck speed. At night, plenty of vehicles are not illuminated. Take care!

Bicycle

Perhaps a slower, gentler way to travel is by bicycle. If you bring your own bike, make sure you have all the spares and tools you'll need, as it's unlikely you'll find what you need in India. Alternatively, you can buy a local clunker – they're heavy but cheap and sturdy, and parts are available everywhere.

Big cities are very hazardous for bicycles, but you can put your bike on a train or bus to cover long distances between major points. Major trunk roads should be avoided also. In the countryside, however, not only is life on a bike much more pleasant but you can be guaranteed of meeting many of the locals – whether you want to or not!

Bikes should be locked up carefully overnight; some foreigners even take them into the hotel room with them! Direction-finding can be difficult and persistence is necessary; however, you'll certainly get an intimate picture of local village life.

Boat

Since the demise of the Goa to Bombay ferry, the only real options for travellers are the backwater trips from Kollam to Aluppuzha in Kerala. There are occasional ferries from the mainland to the Andaman Islands, but space on board is limited.

COMMENT CIRCULER EN INDE

FRANÇAIS
Train

Indian Railways a acquis une réputation quasi légendaire auprès des voyageurs.

C'est le quatrième réseau ferré au monde. Chaque jour, plus de 11 000 trains sont en circulation, transportant quelque neuf millions de passagers dans 7 000 gares. C'est aussi le plus gros employeur du monde avec 1,6 million d'employés.

Pour se repérer, il est indispensable de se procurer le guide *Trains at a Glance* (100 pages) ou l'*Indian Bradshaw*, encore plus complet.

Il existe trois écartements de voies en Inde. La plupart des voyageurs optent pour les lignes à voies larges. Les trains y sont plus rapides que sur les voies à écartement plus étroit (un mètre et moins). De même, les voyageurs ont le choix entre le train postal, l'express ou le train de passagers. Les deux premiers sont préférables car plus rapides, plus confortables et ils ne s'arrêtent pas à toutes les gares. Enfin, il existe deux classes, la première et la seconde. Ces deux catégories sont subdivisées selon qu'elles offrent l'air conditionné ou des couchettes.

Les prix sont calculés en fonction de la distance. Ils sont tout à fait abordables pour les Occidentaux. Le coût des réservations est dérisoire mais le temps qu'il faut y consacrer peut être démesurément long.

L'Indrail Pass, très populaire, est un forfait dont la validité peut aller de 7 à 90 jours. Ce n'est pas vraiment un moyen de faire des économies mais plutôt un bon achat pour des raisons de commodités et de simplicité.

Bus

Bus et train sont souvent en concurrence sur une même ligne mais, dans nombre de régions, le bus est plus pratique et plus rapide notamment lorsque les trains roulent sur des voies étroites.

En règle générale, les bus sont bondés, lents, inconfortables et parfois même dangereux. Toutefois, le voyage par la route donne un bon aperçu de l'Inde. Dans certains États, on trouve des bus de luxe ou express, rapides et plus confortables. Quelle que soit la catégorie, il faut s'attendre à de la pop music hindi totalement assourdissante. Quelques bus disposent de vidéos dont le son est toujours mis au maximum.

Il est rarement nécessaire de réserver son billet et les prix sont relativement bon marché.

La plupart des États possèdent leur propre compagnie publique de bus auxquelles s'ajoutent les bus privés, circulant sur quelques lignes.

Concernant les bagages, il est conseillé de prendre quelques précautions surtout lorsqu'ils sont hissés sur le toit.

Conduire

Le réseau routier indien, très étendu, permet de se déplacer quasiment n'importe où sur deux ou quatres roues. Toutefois, les étrangers circulent rarement dans leur propre véhicule. En effet, peu de gens s'embarrassent de leur voiture pour se rendre en Inde, le plus souvent la location sans chauffeur n'est pas autorisée et l'achat d'un véhicule revient très cher.

Ces dernières années, la moto est devenue un moyen populaire de voyager en Inde. On trouve facilement des motos japonaises ou indiennes dont l'Enfield Bullet, la plus répandue de toutes. Il est conseillé de prendre avec soi son propre casque et ses outils. On peut se procurer assez facilement et un peu partout les pièces détachées.

L'essence est assez chère et la signalisation sur les routes souvent indadéquate voire inexistante.

Bien souvent, l'état des routes est médiocre, c'est le cas de la Grand Trunk Road surchargée et dangereuse. Toute sorte de véhicules y compris d'énormes camions circulent jour et nuit à toute vitesse et de préférence tous phares éteints la nuit. La prudence s'impose !

A bicyclette

C'est sans doute le moyen le plus lent et le plus tranquille pour voyager en Inde. Si vous emportez votre propre vélo, veillez à prendre également les pièces détachées et les outils dont vous pourriez avoir besoin. Sinon, vous pouvez toujours acheter une bicyclette en Inde. Elles sont lourdes mais bon marché et l'on peut trouver des pièces partout.

Circuler à vélo dans les grandes villes représentent un véritable défi. Pour couvrir de longues distances, vous pourrez toujours transporter votre deux roues dans le bus ou dans le train. Mieux vaut éviter les grands axes à forte circulation.

En revanche, le cyclotourisme est bien plus agréable à la campagne où l'on est sûr de rencontrer nombre de gens – que l'on veuille ou non d'ailleurs ! – et de vraiment découvrir l'atmosphère qui règne dans les petits villages.

Bateau

Depuis la disparition de la ligne de ferry entre Bombay et Goa, la seule occasion pour les voyageurs de faire du bateau consiste à naviguer sur les canaux d'Alappuzha à Kollam dans le Kerala. Il existe quelques ferries en direction des Iles Andaman, bien que la place à bord soit limitée.

REISEN IN INDIEN

 ## Per Zug

Das indische Eisenbahnnetz hat für Reisende eine beinahe sagenhafte Berühmtheit erlangt. Es ist das viertgrößte Netz der Welt mit mehr als 11 000 Zügen pro Tag, die 7000 Bahnhöfe verbinden und über 9 Millionen Fahrgäste befördern. Es beschäftigt die verblüffende Anzahl von 1,6 Millionen Angestellten! Um sich in diesem Riesennetz zurechtzufinden ist für Reisende das 100-seitige Trains at a Glance oder das umfassendere Indian Bradshaw unentbehrlich.

Es gibt drei Spurweiten in Indien – die meisten Reisenden werden die von ihnen benötigten Züge auf Breitspurlinien finden. Diese Züge sind bedeutend schneller als die, welche auf Normal- oder Schmalspur fahren. Außerdem haben Reisende die Wahl zwischen einem Mail-, Express- oder Passenger-Zug. Die ersten beiden sind vorzuziehen, weil sie viel schneller und (meistens) bequemer sind und nicht auf jedem kleinen Bahnhof anhalten. Schließlich müssen Reisende entweder 1. oder 2. Klasse wählen; diese unterteilen sich

noch danach, ob sie Klimaanlage und Schlafwagen bieten.

Die Fahrpreise werden nach Entfernung berechnet und sind für westliche Reisende gut erschwinglich. Reservierungen kosten nur wenig mehr Geld. Aber Sie können oft Stunden damit verbingen, solche zu machen. Folglich ist der Indrail Pass, der eine Anzahl von Zeitspannen von 7 bis zu 90 Tagen umfaßt, beliebt. Er ist zwar nicht unbedingt preiswert, aber erspart sicherlich viel Ärger beim Anstehen nach normalen Fahrkarten.

Per Bus

In vielen Teilen Indiens, besonders in solchen, die nur vom Normal- oder Schmalspurnetz erfaßt werden, ist es besser per Bus zu reisen. Vielerorts fahren Busse im Parallelverkehr mit Zügen und können schneller sein als die entsprechenden Züge.

Die normalen Busse sind gewöhnlich überfüllt, langsam und unbequem – und manchmal unsicher. Andererseits erhalten Sie auf Indiens Straßen gewiß einen hervorragenden Einblick in das tägliche Leben.

In einigen Staaten Indiens gibt es "Deluxe" oder Express Busse, die wesentlich schneller und bequemer sind. Aber auf praktisch allen Bussen müssen sich Reisende mit der in höchster Lautstärke geschmetterten lokalen Popmusik abfinden. Einige Nachtbusse haben Videoanlagen, die ebenfalls auf voller Lautstärke laufen.

Für die meisten Busse ist keine Vorbestellung nötig, und Fahrpreise sind ziemlich billig. In den meisten Gegenden fährt eine staatliche Busgesellschaft auf beinahe allen Strecken, oft in Konkurrenz mit einigen privaten Busgesellschaften. Reisende müssen auf ihr Gepäck aufpassen, besonders wenn es auf dem Dach verladen ist.

Straßen

Das indische Straßennetz ist sehr ausgedehnt, und Sie können beinahe überall per Achse hinkommen. Da aber heute nur wenige Reisende von Europa über Land kommen, das Mieten eines Autos gewöhnlich den Fahrer mit einschließt und der Erwerb eines Wagens teuer ist, bereisen nicht viele Ausländer Indien mit dem Wagen.

Anderseits erfreuen sich Motorradtouren zunehmender Beliebtheit bei Reisenden. Indien hat eine Auswahl von japanischen und lokal hergestellten Motorrädern, von denen das 250cc Enfield Bullet wohl das bei Reisenden beliebteste Modell ist. Im übrigen bringt man besser seinen eigenen Helm, eigene Kleidung und Werkzeuge mit – Ersatzteile für die örtlich verkauften Modelle sind überall im Lande leicht erhältlich.

Treibstoff ist verhältnismäßig teuer, und Straßenzeichen sind oft ungenügend oder fehlen ganz. Der Straßenzustand ist vielfach

Elephant, Kanha National Park (BT)

schlecht, und Fernstraßen wie die Grand Trunk Road können überlaufen und unsicher sein mit einer Überfülle von Fuhrwerken – vom schwerfälligen Ochsenkarren bis zu riesigen, mit halsbrecherischer – Geschwindigkeit fahrenden Fernlastern. Nachts sind viele Fahrzeuge unbeleuchtet. Daher Vorsicht!

Per Fahrrad

Eine langsamere und sanftere Art zu reisen ist vielleicht per Fahrrad. Wenn Sie Ihr eigenes Rad mitbringen wollen, müssen Sie unbedingt alle erforderlichen Ersatzteile und Werkzeuge dabei haben, denn es ist unwahrscheinlich, daß Sie diese in Indien auftreiben können. Sonst kaufen Sie sich eine indische Drahtziege – die sind schwer, aber billig und stabil, und Ersatzteile sind überall zu haben.

Die großen Städte sind sehr riskant für Fahrräder; aber Sie können Ihr Fahrrad mit dem Zug oder Bus befördern um große Entfernungen zwischen den Hauptattraktionen zu überbrücken. Die Fernverkehrsstraßen sollte man ebenfalls meiden. Auf dem Lande dagegen ist das Leben auf dem Fahrrad nicht nur angenehmer, sondern Sie werden unter Garantie mit vielen Einheimischen in Kontakt kommen – ob Sie es wollen oder nicht!

Räder sollte man sorgfältig über Nacht einschliessen; einige Ausländer nehmen sie sogar mit ins Hotelzimmer! Manchmal ist es schwierig, den richtigen Weg zu finden, und Ausdauer ist nötig. Aber Sie bekommen mit Sicherheit einen guten Einblick in das örtliche Dorfleben.

Per Schiff

Nach dem Ausfall der Fähre von Goa nach Bombay, bleiben als einzige reelle Wahl für Reisende nur Fahrten auf den Binnengewässern von Kollam nach Aluppuzha in Kerala. Es gibt gelegentlich Fähren vom Festland zu den Andamanen Inseln; jedoch ist Platz an Bord begrenzt.

Top Left: Jolly Buoy Island, Andaman Islands (BT)
Bottom Left: Villagers at the base of Konke La, Ladakh, Jammu & Kashmir (RI)
Right: Sheshnag Lake, Kashmir (GE)

VIAJANDO POR INDIA

Tren

El sistema ferroviario de la India ha adquirido una reputación casi legendaria entre los viajeros. Es el cuarto sistema ferroviario más largo en el mundo, con 11.000 trenes que recorriendo diariamente conectan 7.000 estaciones y transportan más de 9 millones de pasajeros. Los ferrocarriles emplean la asombrosa cantidad de un ¡millón seiscientas mil personas! Un libro de 100 páginas que los viajeros encontrarán muy indispensable es "Trains at a Glance", u otro más comprensible "Indian Bradshaw" para poder trasladarse a través de la vasta red nacional de ferrocarriles.

Existen tres diferentes clases de trochas ferroviarias, la mayoría de los viajeros encontrarán que los trenes que desean usar son de trocha ancha. Estos trenes son más rápidos que los de trocha de un metro y que los trenes de trocha aún más angosta. Se puede escoger entre los trenes que llevan el correo, los expresos y los trenes de pasajeros. Los dos priméros son preferibles, ya que son mucho más rápidos y (generalmente) más cómodos, además de no parar en cada pequeña estación. También los pasajeros tienen la oportunidad de escoger entre primera y segunda clase; estas clases o categorías están subdividas frecuentemente, dependiendo en que los compartimientos cuenten con aire acondicionado y coches-cama.

El precio de los viajes está basado en la distáncia de los mismos, precio que está al alcance de los turistas occidentales. Las reservaciones del los billetes no cuestan mucho, pero suele representar una pérdida de tiempo el conseguirlas. El "Indrail Pass", que tiene una validez que varía entre 7 a 90 días, es muy popular. Probablemente este medio de viajar, financieramente, es el menos aconsejable, pero indudablemente ahorra mucho tiempo, así como los problemas que acompañan a la compra de los billetes o pasajes regulares.

Autobús

En muchas regiones de la India, especialmente en aquellas en que solamente existe el ferrocarril de trocha de un metro o de trocha más angosta, es mejor viajar por autobús. En muchos lugares los autobuses ofrecen un servicio paralelo al del tren, este servicio resulta con frecuencia ser más rápido que el de los trenes.

Los autobuses regulares por lo general van siempre repletos, son lentos e incómodos y algunas veces hasta peligrosos. Sin embargo viajando por este medio de transporte se puede apreciar verdaderamente el ritmo de vida en la India. Algunos estados tienen autobuses "Deluxe" o expresos que son mas rápidos y cómodos, no obstante, casi en todos los autobuses los viajeros tienen que soportar el ruido de las radios tocando música local "pop" a todo volumen. Algunos autobuses nocturnos tienen servicio de videos, los cuales igualmente, son mostrados a todo volumen.

Para la mayoría de los

All aboard!

autobuses no se requiere hacer reservaciones y el costo de los billetes o pasajes es bastante barato. En casi todas las regiones existen compañías estatales de autobuses que cubren muchas de las rutas, y por lo general éstas están en competencía con compañías privadas. Es indispensable que todos los viajeros tengan cuidado con su equipaje, especialmente si éste va amarrado en el techo de autobús.

Carreteras

El sisteme de carreteras en la India es muy vasto y siempre que se cuente con un cocho, se puede llegar casi a cualquier localidad. Sin embargo, últimamente poca gente de Europa víaja a la India por carretera; arrendar un coche usualmente significa alquilar uno juntamente con un chófer, y como comprar un coche resultaría demasiado caro, actualmente muy pocos extranjeros hacen turismo en coche por la India.

El turismo en motocicletas es muy popular, con la cantidad de motociclistas en aumento. En la India se usa una gran variedad de motocicletas japonesas, así como otras fabricadas localmente, siendo la "250cc Enfield Bullet" la marca preferida entre los extranjeros. En general es aconsejable llevar consigo su própio casco y caja de herramientas – los repuestos para las motocicletas fabricadas localmente se encuentran fácilmente a través del pais.

La gasolina es relativamente cara, y las señales de tráfico en las carreteras son inadecuadas o prácticamente no existen. Las carreteras por lo general están en malas condiciones; rutas como la "Gran Trunk Road" suclen estar congestionadas, representando un gran pelígro con el exceso de vehículos que varía desde enormes carretas tiradas por bueyes, hasta vehículos pesados, los cuales viajan a increíbles velocidades. Por la noche muchos automóviles carecen de iluminación en sus faros. ¡Tenga cuidado!

Bicicletas

Tal véz, un medio más lento y placentro de viajar es en bicicleta. Si usted lleva su propia bicicleta, lleve también consigo repuestos y herramientas que pudiera necesitar ya que es muy dificil conseguir repuestos en India. Alernativamente, se puede comprar bicicletas rudimentarias hechas localmente, las cuales son pesadas pero baratas y resistentes, además, se pueden encontrar los respuestos necesarios en caso de emergencia.

Montar en bicicleta en ciudades grandes es muy peligroso, pero se puede llevar la bicicleta en tren o autobús para cubrir distancias largas entre los lugares importantes. Se debe evadir carreteras transitadas por vehículos pesados; viajar por el campo, no es solamente más agradable, sino que ciertamente, durante el recorrido se encuentra mucha gente local.

Toda bicicleta debe guardarse bajo llave por la noche, algunos extranjeros inclusive guardan sus bicicletas en sus piezas del hotel. Para encontrar direcciones se tiene que ser muy persistente, ya que algunas veces resulta muy dificil conseguir éstas, sin embargo por este medio de transporte se disfruta intensamente de las costumbres locales de los pueblos.

Barco

Desde la desaparición del transporte en barco desde Goa a Bombay, la única opción para los turistas son los viajes a través de los remansos desde Kollam a Aluppuzha in Kerala. Se usan ocasionalmente pequeños botes para cruzar desde los puertos principales hasta las islas de Andamán; lamentablemente conseguir espacio en estas embarcaciones es muy dificil.

Camels in the Thar Desert, Jaisalmer, Rajasthan (RI)

インドの旅

日本語

鉄道

インドを訪れる旅行者にとって、鉄道は有意義で必要不可欠な交通機関です。路線の全長は世界で４番目に長く、一日総計１万1,000台を超える電車が走っています。電車の駅は7,000以上あり、鉄道の利用者は一日900万人にものぼり、鉄道の職員総数は、160万人にもなります。インドの鉄道は広範囲に渡って伸びていますので、鉄道案内書を利用することをお薦めします。100ページからなる「一目でわかる鉄道（Trains at a Glance）」案内書と、「インドのブラッドショー鉄道旅行案内（Indian Bradshaw）」の２種類があります。後者の方が、より総合的な鉄道案内書になっています。

　　インドの鉄道は、広軌、標準軌間、狭軌の３種類の軌間（ゲージ）に分けられます。海外からの旅行者には、広軌鉄道が一番便利です。広軌鉄道を走る列車は、標準軌間及び狭軌鉄道よりもずっとスピードが出ます。また、電車の種類としては、郵便の運搬を兼ねる列車、急行列車、乗客専用列車があります。郵便列車と急行列車の方がスピードがあり快適な上、小さな駅には停車しないので目的地に早く到着します。列車の客室には一等室と二等室があります。更に、エアコン付きか、寝台付きかによって区分されています。

　　運賃は距離によって違いますが、一般にそれほど高くはありません。座席を事前に予約しようとすると多少、予約料金がかかりますし、予約をするためにかなりの時間待つこともあります。７日間から最高９０日間までの期間を選択できるインドレールパスがありますので、これを利用すると便利です。インドレールパスは料金を大幅に節約することにはなりませんが、行く先々で切符を買うために長い列に並ぶ手間を省くことができます。

バス

インドでは、地域によっては電車よりもバスを利用した方が便利なところもあります。特に標準軌間や狭軌鉄道しか通っていない地域ではバスの利用をお薦めします。ほとんどの地域ではバスは電車の路線と平行に運行していますので、バスの方が電車よりも早く目的地に着くことがあります。

　　一般のバスは車内がかなり混んでいて、スピードも遅く乗り心地はそれほど良くありませんし、危ないこともあります。しかし、道路周辺の景色を楽しんだり、地元の人々の生活に直接触れることができるという利点があります。デラックスバスや急行バスが走っている州もあり、これらのバスは早くて快適です。バスの車中では、大きな音量でインドの流行歌をかけていることがありますので、これに耐える心構えが必要です。夜行の急行バスでも、同様に大きな音量でビデオをつけていることもあります。

　　バスはほとんどの場合、予約なしで乗れますし、運賃もそれほど高くありません。地域によっては、州が経営する公営バスと私営バスが同じ路線を運行し、バス会社の間で競争し合っているところもあります。また、バスに乗る時は、持ち物や

荷物に注意を払う必要があります。荷物をバスの屋根上にくくりつけてある場合は絶えず気をつけるようにして下さい。

道路

インドでは広範囲に渡って道路が整備されていますので、車があれば国内、いろいろなところに行けます。しかし、大陸を横断してヨーロッパから車を運転してインドに来る人は皆無に近く、インドでレンタカーを借りるとなると、ドライバー付きの車ということになり、車の購入は高価につくので、海外からの旅行者でインドを車で回る人はあまり見られません。

インドをオートバイで旅行する人の数は、最近増加しつつあります。インドには、いろいろな種類の日本製、国産のオートバイがあります。中でも、250ccのエンフィールド・ブレット (Enfield Bullet) が外国からの旅行者に一番人気があるようです。ヘルメットや修理道具、その他の必需品は持参した方が無難でしょう。国産のオートバイの部品は、国内どこでも手に入ります。

ガソリンはかなり高く、道路には交通標識がなかったり、あっても標識が不親切なところもあります。道路事情はあまりよくないところが多く、グランド幹線道路 (Grand Trunk Road)は、混雑していて危険極まる道路の一つです。ここでは、牛が引く荷車から大きなトラックを屋根に積んで猛スピードで突っ走る車に至るまで、さまざまな種類の車が路上に溢れています。夜間でも、ヘッドライトなしで走る車がたくさんありますので、十分な注意が必要です。

自転車

時間をかけて安全に各地を回りたい方には、自転車旅行をお薦めします。自分の自転車を持ってくる場合は、部品や修理道具を必ず持参するようにして下さい。国産以外の自転車の部品の入手は、インドではなかなか難しいようです。インドで中古の自転車を買うこともできます。かなり重量のある自転車ですが、安くて頑丈な上に部品は国内どこでも手に入ります。

交通量の多い都会を自転車で回るのは危険ですが、都会を避けて目的地まで電車あるいはバスに自転車を載せて旅行することもできます。主要な幹線道路を自転車で走るのは避けた方が無難です。いなかの方に行くと、快適な自転車の旅が楽しめると同時に、地元の人たちと知り合うことができるでしょう。

夜は自転車に必ず鍵をかけるようにして下さい。ホテルに宿泊する場合は、ホテルの部屋に自転車を持ち込むことができることもあります。目的地までの道や方角探しはかなり大変で根気が必要ですが、地方の生活を体験できる絶好のチャンスです。

ボート

ゴアとボンベイ間のフェリーが運航中止になって以来、船の旅と言えば、ケララ州のコラムからアルプザまでの船しかなくなりました。本土からアンダマン島へ行くフェリーが時折運航していますが、いつも混雑しているようです。

INDEX

Note: to find Beaches; Capes & Headlands; Caves; Forts & Havelis; Islands; Mosques; Mountains & Passes; National Parks & Wildlife Sanctuaries; Rivers, Lakes & Bays; Ruins; Temples; Valleys; and Waterfalls see the alphabetical listings under each heading at the end of the general index.

GENERAL INDEX
All places are in India, except:

Ba = Bangladesh
B = Bhutan
C = China
M = Myanmar
N = Nepal
P = Pakistan

For duplicate names in India, the state abbreviations are:

AI = Andaman Islands
And = Andhra Pradesh
Aru = Arunachal Pradesh
Ass = Assam
Bih = Bihar
Del = Delhi
Goa = Goa
Guj = Gujarat
Har = Haryana
Him = Himachal Pradesh
J&K = Jammu & Kashmir
Kar = Karnataka
Ker = Kerala
Mad = Madhya Pradesh
Mah = Maharashtra
Meg = Meghalaya
Miz = Mizoram
Ori = Orissa
Pun = Punjab
Raj = Rajasthan
Tam = Tamil Nadu
Tri = Tripura
Wbg = West Bengal
UT = Union Territories
Utt = Uttar Pradesh
* = J&K; between Line of Actual Control and Official Indo-Pakistani border

Aali 71 G5
Abbigeri 85 G5
Abbottabad (P) 12 B3
Abdullapuram 93 F6
Abdullun 13 G2
Abdulpur (Ba) 58 C3
Abhaipur 43 G2
Abhana 53 G4
Abhanpur 68 H5
Abhapuri 65 H3
Abhayapuri 41 G4
Abhona 64 D6
Abiramam 99 F2
Ablu 17 F6
Abohar 16 D6
Abongkethe 42 D4
Abring 14 A4

Abu Road 50 A2
Abul Knarana 17 E6
Achabal 13 F4
Achalda 35 G3
Achalganj 36 B4
Achalpur 66 C4
Achampet 87 E4
Achanakmar 69 E1
Ache (C) 26 A3
Acheharapakkam Peramber 97 E1
Acheson 28 B3
Achhnera 34 D2
Achina (Har) 22 A4
Achina (Raj) 32 B2
Achra 84 B4
Ada (P) 16 A4
Adaba 82 B2
Adalaj 50 A5
Adamankottai 96 A2
Adampur 21 G3
Adamwala Keta 20 B3
Adan (P) 30 B2
Adankkottai 96 C6
Adanpur (Ba) 60 B3
Adanur 96 C2
Adarki 76 D6
Adas 77 H4
Adasa 67 F4
Adavad 65 G4
Adbadri 19 G6
Adbhar 69 G3
Addanki 87 H5
Addatigala 89 E1
Adegaon 67 G1
Adesar 49 E5
Adgal 85 E4
Adhaura 55 H2
Adhonigarh 70 B6
Adhunagar (Ba) 74 B2
Adiala (P) 12 B4
Adigaon (P) 49 E3
Adilabad 79 F2
Adinath Bazar (Ba) 74 B3
Adiponka 82 B2
Adirampattinam 96 D6
Adirangam 96 D6
Adivra 84 B3
Adkot 63 E2
Adodar 62 B3
Adoli 76 C5
Adoli Kekatumar 78 B1
Adoni 86 B3
Adra 57 G5
Adriana 49 G5
Adugiri 41 F6
Adul (Mah) 66 C5
Adul (Mah) 77 G2
Adung Long (M) 29 F5
Adur (Kar) 90 D2
Adur (Ker) 98 C3
Aduripalle 93 F2
Aduru 94 B1
Aduturai 96 D5
Advi Devalpalli 87 G3
Adwal 63 G1
Adwana 62 B3
Adwani 19 F6
Adyal 67 H5
Afghanar (P) 17 F2
Afridian (P) 16 A5
Afzalgarh 23 F2
Afzalpur 85 H2

Agalpur 69 H5
Agamani 41 E4
Agar 51 H4
Agaram 92 D6
Agarkhed 85 G2
Agartala 60 A4
Agashi 76 A3
Agasode 53 E3
Agastiswaram 98 D5
Agatrai 62 D4
Agaundh 22 A1
Agham 14 D2
Aghar 18 A3
Agia 41 G4
Agiaon 38 C6
Agiripalle 88 B3
Agni 85 H3
Agolai 32 A4
Agori 55 G2
Agra (Utt) 35 E2
Agra (Mad) 52 C3
Agral 51 E6
Agrawa 49 F1
Agroha 21 G3
Agrong 41 G3
Agsur 90 B2
Aguada 84 B6
Agumbe 90 D4
Ahal (P) 12 B2
Ahar 23 E4
Aharan 35 E1
Aharwan 21 G2
Ahat 50 C2
Ahatagiri 43 F2
Ahias 71 F5
Ahiri 80 A3
Ahirpara 55 F6
Ahiwara 68 D4
Ahlan 13 G4
Ahmadabad (P) 16 A1
Ahmadgarh (Pun) 17 G5
Ahmadgarh (Utt) 23 E5
Ahmadpur (Mad) 52 C5
Ahmadpur (Wbg) 58 A4
Ahmadpur (Mah) 78 B4
Ahmdal (P) 12 A5
Ahmed Rajo (P) 47 H3
Ahmedabad 50 A6
Ahmednagar 77 E3
Ahmedpur 63 E5
Ahobilam 92 D1
Aholin 28 B4
Ahor 32 A6
Ahraura 55 G1
Ahu 65 F1
Ahupe 76 C3
Ahwa 64 C5
Aichisagami 43 G4
Aihole 85 G5
Aiju 18 B2
Ainak 75 E1
Ainapur 85 E3
Ainavolu 87 H5
Ainggyi (M) 75 G4
Aingma (M) 75 G2
Ainta 31 F2
Air Khas 35 H5
Airwa 35 G2
Aish Muqam 13 G3
Aisyalukharka (N) 39 G1
Ait 35 G5
Aiwad 32 D1
Aizawl 60 D1
Ajab 62 D4

Ajaigarh 54 A1
Ajanta 65 H6
Ajas 13 E2
Ajasar 31 G2
Ajayagad 82 B4
Ajgain 36 B3
Ajgaon 84 C5
Ajgarhbura 55 F4
Ajita 33 H6
Ajitpura 21 G3
Ajitwal 17 G5
Ajjampur 91 F4
Ajmer 33 E3
Ajmiriganj (Ba) 59 H2
Ajnala (P) 16 B2
Ajnala 17 F2
Ajnianwala (P) 16 C2
Ajodhya Bazar (Ba) 60 B6
Ajra 84 D4
Ajram 17 H3
Akadia (Guj) 63 E3
Akadia (Guj) 63 F2
Akaikuwa 64 D3
Akajhiri 34 D6
Akalgarh (P) 16 C1
Akalgarh (*) 12 C5
Akalgarh (Pun) 21 H1
Akalkot 85 H1
Akalsia 18 C6
Akaltara 69 F2
Akatse (C) 19 F1
Akawaram 87 F4
Akbarpur 22 D6, 34 A1 (Raj)
Akbarpur (Utt) 35 H4
Akbarpur (Utt) 37F4
Akbarpur (Bih) 56 A2
Akbarpur (Bih) 56 D2
Akbarpur Aunchha 35 F1
Akdara 31 G5
Akhar Hat (Ba) 74 A1
Akhasri (Ba) 59 H2
Akhegwo 43 G5
Akhnoor 13 F6
Akhori (P) 12 A4
Akividu 88 C3
Akkelpur (Ba) 58 D1
Akkihebbal 95 E1
Akla 32 C2
Aklera 52 B2
Akluj 77 E6
Akmewala (P) 16 A3
Akodha 37 E6
Akodra 52 A5
Akola (Raj) 50 D2
Akola (Mah) 66 B5
Akola (Mah) 76 D2
Akola (Mah) 79 E1
Akolda 63 F4
Akoli 76 B3
Akora 31 F6
Akorha 56 B2
Akoria 33 F4
Akot 66 B5
Akrabad 23 E6
Akrani 64 D3
Akri (P) 30 B6
Akri 47 H5
Aksapur 79 H2
Akuke (P) 20 B1
Akurdi 76 C4
Alagarkoil 99 F1
Alagiri 92 D4
Alahari (Ba) 59 F2

Alai 32 C1
Alam (M) 45 F5
Alamanda 81 H4
Alamdanga (Ba) 58 D4
Alamgarh (P) 12 D6
Alampur (Ba) 58 D4
Alampur (Mad) 35 F4
Alampur (Guj) 63 G2
Alampur (And) 86 D5
Alamsar 31 E6
Alamuru 89 E3
Alanallur 95 E4
Aland 86 A1
Alandur 93 F6
Alanganallur 99 E1
Alangayam 96 B1
Alangdunkhu (M) 45 F1
Alangudi 96 C6
Alappakkam 97 E3
Alappuzha 98 A2
Alapur 23 G6
Alattur (Ker) 95 E6
Alattur (Tam) 97 E2
Alawalpur 17 G3
Albaka 80 B5
Albert Victor 63 G5
Alchi 14 C3
Aldur 91 E5
Ale 76 D3
Alegaon 76 D5
Alegyun (M) 74 D5
Aleru 87 F1
Alet Kyaungdaung (M) 74 D6
Alethangyaw (M) 74 C5
Alewah 22 A2
Alewahi 67 H6
Alfadanga (Ba) 59 E5
Algapuram 96 C3
Algur 85 H3
Ali Akbardeil (Ba) 74 B3
Ali Khera 35 G1
Ali Laghan (P) 47 G3
Aliabad * 12 D3
Aliabad (J&K) 13 E4
Aliabad (Tam) 96 C1
Alibag 76 A4
Alidar 63 E5
Aliganj (Utt) 24 B5
Aliganj (Utt) 35 G1
Aligarh (Utt) 23 E6
Aligarh (Raj) 33 H5
Alika 21 G2
Alikhen 78 C6
Alinagar 37 G3
Alipur (Del) 22 C4
Alipur (Mah) 67 F6
Alipur (Wbg) 72 B1
Alipur Duar 41 E3
Alipura 35 G6
Alirajpur 65 E2
Alishahbad (Ba) 60 A3
Aliti (C) 45 H2
Alkuti 76 D3
Allagada 92 C1
Allahabad 37 E6
Allahdurg 78 D6
Allahganj 35 H1
Alland 77 G1
Allapalli 80 B6
Allapallai 80 A3
Allur 93 G2
Alluru Kottapatnam 88 A6
Almai 14 A6

Almel 85 H2
Almora 23 H2
Alnar 81 E3
Alnavar 85 E6
Alniawas 33 E3
Alon (M) 75 H2
Along 27 H5
Alonung 28 B5
Alora 84 B1
Alot 51 G4
Alsindhi 18 B4
Alsisar 21 F5
Altiri 71 F5
Alur (Kar) 85 H1, 86 A1
Alur (And) 86 B6
Alur (And) 86 D2
Alur (Kar) 91 F6
Aluva 98 B1
Alwar 34 A1
Alwar Tirunagari 99 E4
Alwarkurichi 98 D4
Ama (B) 41 E1
Ama 37 F2
Amabera 80 C1
Amadi (Ba) 72 D1
Amakona 56 A5
Amala Cantonment 18 B6
Amalagora 57 H6
Amalapuram 89 E3
Amalner (Mah) 65 F5
Amalner (Mah) 77 G4
Amamora 69 F6
Amancherla 93 F3
Amangal 87 E3
Amanganj 54 A2
Amaniganj 36 D3
Amanpur 23 F6
Amarapuram 91 G3
Amaravathi 88 A3
Amaravati 99 G1
Amarchinta 86 C4
Amardaha (N) 39 H3
Amardand 54 B3
Amargarh (Raj) 34 B4
Amargarh (Mad) 35 F5
Amaria 23 H4
Amarkantak 68 D1
Amarpatan 54 C3
Amarpur (Mad) 54 C3
Amarpur (Mad) 54 C6
Amarpur (Tri) 60 A5
Amarpura 20 B5
Amarsar 33 G1
Amarwara 67 G2
Amas 56 C2
Amatulla 42 C2
Amauli 36 B4
Amayan 35 F4
Amb 17 H3
Amb Darband (P) 12 B2
Amba (Bih) 56 B2
Amba (Mah) 77 G3
Ambabhona 69 H3
Ambad 77 H2
Ambadiha 58 A2
Ambagarh Chauki 68 B5
Ambah 35 E3
Ambahta 22 C1
Ambahta Sheikha 22 C2
Ambajogai 78 A4
Ambala 18 B6
Ambala Sadar 18 B6
Ambalapulai 98 A2
Ambalga (Mah) 78 B6
Ambalga (Kar) 86 A1
Ambaligolla 90 D3
Ambaltek 78 A4
Ambapani 51 E3

Ambapani Chauki 65 G3
Ambara (Mah) 66 D4
Ambara (Mad) 67 E3
Ambarnath 76 B3
Ambarpet 79 G4
Ambasa 60 B4
Ambasamudram 98 D4
Ambavna 76 B4
Ambegaon 76 C3
Ambela (P) 12 A2
Amber 33 H2
Ambheti 64 B6
Ambikanagar 57 G6
Ambikapur 55 G5
Amboa 18 D5
Ambodala 81 H2
Amboli (Mah) 84 B1
Amboli (Mah) 84 C5
Ambowari 77 F2
Ambur 92 D6
Amdabad 40 A6
Amdapur 66 A6
Amdhi 54 D4
Amet 32 D6
Amethi 36 D4
Amgaon (Mad) 53 F6
Amgaon (Mah) 68 B4
Amgura Bazar 41 G3
Amguri (Ass) 42 D3
Amguri (Ass) 43 G3
Amhara 39 H4
Amili 28 B5
Amin 22 B1
Aminbhavi 85 E6
Amingaon 42 A4
Amingarh 85 G4
Amirpura (P) 16 B5
Amjhera 65 F1
Amkhuta 64 B4
Amkunj 100 B4
Amla (Ba) 58 D4
Amla 67 E3
Amlaha 52 B6
Amlakhi 43 E5
Amlarem 42 B6
Amlekhganj (N) 38 C2
Amli (Raj) 33 F5
Amli (Raj) 49 G2
Amlia 55 F3
Amlipadar 81 F1
Amliyara 50 B5
Amloh 18 A5
Ammalapadu 82 B4
Ammanabrolu 88 A6
Ammapettai (Tam) 95 H3
Ammapettai (Tam) 96 D5
Ammapur 86 C4
Ammenalli 90 C2
Amnaur 38 C5
Amnura (Ba) 58 C2
Amod 64 A2
Amoi Patha 34 D6
Amola 34 D6
Amona 52 A5
Amour 40 A4
Ampani 81 E2
Ampi Bazar 60 A4
Ampur (P) 16 A3
Amra 55 F5
Amrabad 87 F4
Amran 48 D6
Amraoti 66 D5
Amrapara 57 H2
Amrapur 62 C3
Amrati 81 E2
Amreli 63 F3
Amring 42 D5
Amritpur 35 H1

Amritsar 17 F3
Amroha 23 E3
Amronia 53 H2
Amrui 12 D2
Amruka (P) 16 D6
Amrutur 91 H6
Amta 72 B1
Amtali (Ba) 73 F2
Amtika 41 G3
Amudalavalsa 82 A5
Anagodu 91 F2
Anaji 91 F2
Anakapalle 89 G1
Anamalai 95 F6
Anamasamudrampeta
    93 F2
Anand 64 B1
Anandapuram 90 D3
Anandgarh 20 B4
Anandpur (Mad) 52 C3
Anandpur (Guj) 63 E1
Anandpur (Guj) 63 F2
Anandpur (Ori) 71 E4
Anandpur (Wbg) 71 H1
Anandpur Sahib 18 B4
Anant Peth 35 E5
Anantagiri 81 G5
Anantapur 92 A2
Anantaram 79 F5
Anantasagaram 93 E2
Anantnag 13 F4
Anaskura 84 C3
Anauk Myinhlut (M) 74 C5
Anavatti 90 D2
Anawal 64 B5
Anchal 98 C4
Anchetti 95 H1
Andal 57 H4
Andanda 82 B3
Andar 38 B4
Andarsul 77 E1
Andevanahalli 95 H1
Andharketha 58 C3
Andhiyur 95 H3
Andhori 78 B4
Andhra Tharhi 39 F4
Andimatam 96 D4
Andipattijakkampatti 99 E1
Andol 79 E6
Andori 67 E6
Andra 50 A2
Andrauli (N) 38 B1
Andulbaria (Ba) 58 D5
Andur 78 C6
Anduru 66 B5
Ane 76 D3
Anechaukur 94 D2
Anekal 92 B6
Anelih 28 B4
Angadipuram 95 E5
Angai 34 C3
Angara 56 D5
Angatsi 28 B5
Anghad 64 B1
Angnac 20 A5
Angneu 20 A5
Angul 70 D5
Ani 18 C3
Aniali 63 F2
Anikkaranchattram 97 E4
Anini 28 B4
Anjad 65 F2
Anjanapura 90 D3
Anjangaon 66 C4
Anjania 68 B1
Anjanvel 84 A1
Anjar 48 C6
Anjarla 76 B6

Anjenjo 98 B4
Anji 67 F5
Ankai 77 E1
Ankalgi 85 E4
Ankasandra 91 G4
Ankevalia 49 F6
Ankisha 80 A4
Ankjachh 64 B6
Ankleshwar 64 A3
Ankli 85 E3
Ankola 90 B2
Annapareddipalle 88 B1
Annavaram 89 E2
Annavasal 96 B6
Annigeri 85 F6
Annur 95 F4
Anshi 90 B1
Anshing 78 C1
Anta 34 A6, 52 A1
Antagarh 80 C1
Antaram 78 D5
Antarasante 95 E2
Antarba 82 B3
Antarda 33 H5
Antarnes 49 F4
Antarvedipalem 88 D4
Antri (Mad) 35 E4
Antri (Raj) 50 C4
Antu 37 E4
Anupgarh 20 B3
Anuppur 54 D5
Anupshahr (Raj) 21 F3
Anupshahr (Utt) 23 E5
Anura 17 H2
Anwalkhera 51 E1
Anwara (Ba) 74 B2
Anyaban (M) 75 G3
Anyar 13 G4
Aonla 23 G5
Apaukwa (M) 74 D5
Aphen 13 H5
Aphit 13 G3
Appananallur 96 A4
Apsa 76 B4
Apti 76 C6
Ara (P) 12 C6
Araidanga 40 B6
Araihazar (Ba) 59 G4
Arain 33 F4
Arajkund 68 B5
Araki 21 E3
Arakonam 93 F6
Arakot 18 D4
Araku 81 G5
Aralagodu 90 C3
Aralgundi 86 A2
Aramba 68 A3
Arambagh 58 A6
Aramboli 98 D5
Aran 77 F6
Arandia 52 B5
Arandkhera 51 H1
Arang (Raj) 31 F3
Arang (Mad) 69 E4
Arangaon 77 F4
Arani 93 E6
Aranibakkam 93 G5
Aranta 62 A1
Araria 39 H4
Arasalu 90 D3
Arasikeri 91 F2
Arasinagundi 91 G4
Araul 36 A2
Arauti (P) 16 A5
Aravakurichchi 95 H5
Arcot 93 E6
Ardai 28 A4
Ardavidu 87 F5

Ardharpur 78 C3
Aregaon 67 F5
Arehalli 91 E6
Areraj 38 C3
Areth 64 B4
Argaon (Mah) 66 B4
Argaon (Mah) 78 B2
Arghakot (N) 25 G5
Argi 15 E4
Argoal 72 A2
Arhauli 36 C6
Ari 67 H2
Aria 49 G4
Ariankuppam 97 E3
Ariari 57 E1
Arifwala (P) 16 B6
Arigam 13 E3
Arik 62 C2
Arikhola (Ba) 59 G4
Arikkod 94 D4
Arimalam 96 C6
Ariyalur 96 C4
Arja (P) 12 C3
Arjunda 68 C5
Arjuni (Mah) 68 A5
Arjuni (Mad) 69 F4
Arkalgud 91 F6
Arkar 68 D5
Arker 86 B4
Arkeri 85 G3
Arki 18 B4
Arla 84 C2
Arli 79 E2
Armori 68 A6
Armur 79 E4
Arnas 13 F5
Arnaud 51 F4
Arnauli 18 A6
Arnetha 33 H6
Arni (Mah) 78 D1
Arni (Tam) 93 G5
Arnia (Utt) 22 D5
Arnia (Mad) 52 A3
Arnoda 51 F2
Arola 76 D6, 84 C1
Aron (Mad) 34 D5
Aron (Mad) 52 C3
Arong 101 F2
Aropu 28 B4
Aros 84 C5
Arrah 38 B5
Arsha 57 F5
Arsikere 91 F5
Arthal 14 A5
Arthuna 50 D5
Artia 32 C3
Aru 13 G3
Arukuti 98 B1
Arumbavur 96 B4
Arumuganeri 99 F4
Aruppukkottai 99 E2
Aruri (P) 16 A2
Arvi (Mah) 65 E5
Arvi (Mah) 77 E5
Arwal 38 C6
Arwi 77 G3
Asalatganj 35 H3
Asambia 48 B6
Asanad 79 H4
Asananggiri 41 F5
Asanbani 57 H3
Asandh 22 A2
Asandi 91 F4
Asansol 57 G4
Asaon 38 B4
Asara 49 F3
Asaralia (P) 30 D6
Asarganj 39 G6

Asenyewang (C) 29 G1
Ashaliu 28 A4
Ashoknagar (Mad) 52 D2
Ashoknagar (And) 80 A6
Ashta (Mah) 52 B6
Ashta (Mah) 64 D4
Ashta (Mah) 84 D3
Ashtal 77 G6
Ashtami 76 B5
Ashti (Mah) 67 E4
Ashti (Mah) 77 F4
Ashti (Mah) 77 H3, 78 A3
Ashuganj (Ba) 59 H3
Ashwaraopet 88 C2
Ashwi 76 D2
Asifabad 79 G3
Asikhati (Ba) 59 G5
Asind 33 E5
Asir 66 A4
Asiragarh Hills 65 F3
Asiwan 36 B3
Aska 82 C2
Askandra 31 G1
Askot 24 A2
Aslaoda 51 G5
Asmauli 23 E4
Asnahra 37 F2
Asnawar 52 A2
Asoda 65 G5
Asona 84 B1
Asonli 28 B4
Asop 32 C3
Asota 62 B2
Asotra 31 H5
Aspari 86 C6
Aspur 50 D4
Asra 66 C5
Assaspur 66 B3
Assegaon 66 D4
Assundi 80 A2
Astagram (Ba) 59 H3
Asthanwan 39 E6
Astrang 83 F1
Asudah Todran 22 B4
Asurabandh 82 B2
At 64 A5
Ata 28 D3
Atamkur 79 H6
Atangulam 98 D4
Atanu 14 C1
Ataraumba 50 A6
Atari (P) 16 D5
Atarra 36 B6
Ateha 36 D4
Ater 35 F3
Atgaon (Ori) 69 H6
Atgaon (Mah) 76 B2
Atgulipura 95 F3
Athaikhera 52 D2
Atharibari (Ba) 59 G2
Atharikhat 42 A3
Athgarh 71 E6
Athmalgola 39 E6
Athmallik 70 B5
Athmauza (N) 40 A3
Athni 85 E3
Athpali (N) 24 C2
Athwatoo 13 F2
Ating 14 B4
Atit 84 C1
Atmakur (And) 79 F4
Atmakur (And) 87 E5
Atmakur (And) 87 H2
Atmakur (And) 93 F2
Atmakuru 92 A2
Atner 66 D3
Atnur 85 H2
Atpadi 85 E2

Atrampur 36 D6
Atraula 37 G4
Atrauli (Utt) 23 E5
Atrauli (Utt) 36 B2
Atraulia 37 G4
Atru 52 B1
Attabira 70 A4
Attaki (Ba) 59 E6
Attakur 86 D4
Attani 95 G3
Attappadi 95 E4
Attar 65 H2
Attari 17 E3
Attayyampatti 96 A3
Attigam 81 F3
Attigundi 91 E5
Attili 88 D3
Attimanjeri 93 E5
Attingal 98 C4
Attippadi 96 B2
Attock (P) 12 A3
Attur (Tam) 93 F6
Attur (Tam) 96 B3
Atura (Ba) 58 C1
Aturu 93 G4
Atwari (Ba) 40 C4
Au 32 B2
Auche (M) 45 E5
Aujari 42 C4
Auktaung (M) 61 G3
Auldan 35 G6
Aulgurta (N) 25 F3
Aundah 78 B2
Aundh 84 D1
Aungsaik (M) 74 D5
Aungywa (M) 75 F6
Auniati 43 F2
Aunraj 37 F6
Aunwa 33 G5
Aura (M) 44 C6
Aura (M) 45 F2
Aurad 78 C5
Aurad Shahjahani 78 B6
Aurai 39 E4
Auraiya 35 G3
Aurangabad (Har) 22 C6
Aurangabad (Utt) 24 B6
Aurangabad (Bih) 38 D5
Aurangabad (Mah) 77 F2
Aurangabad Saiyid 22 D4
Auras 36 B2
Auroville 97 E2
Aurvad 85 E4
Ausa 78 A5
Ausari 76 A4
Ausgram 58 A5
Ausia (P) 12 C3
Austen 100 B3
Avadaiyarkovil 99 H1
Avadi 93 G5
Avalurpet 96 C1
Avanashi 95 G4
Avanashipaliyam 95 G5
Avaniapuram 99 E1
Avanigadda 88 C4
Avantipur 13 F3
Avati 77 G5
Aversa 90 B2
Avinhalli 90 D3
Avulavaripalem 88 B4
Avupalli 80 C5
Awa (Raj) 20 B4
Awa (Raj) 34 B5
Awa (Utt) 35 E1
Awan 52 C2
Awar 51 H3
Ayanur 90 D3
Ayirala 92 D5

Aymangala 91 G3
Ayodhya 37 E3
Ayur 98 C4
Ayyampettai 96 C5
Azamgarh 37 G4
Azamnagar 40 A6
Azhikkod 94 C2
Azimabad 20 D1
Azimganj 58 B3

Baba Bakala 17 G3
Babai (Raj) 21 H6
Babai (Utt) 35 G4
Babai (Mad) 52 D6, 66D1
Babai (Mad) 53 F6
Babain 22 B1
Babalwara 50 C3
Baberu 36 B6
Babhaleshwar 77 E2
Babhnoul 38 B6
Babina (Utt) 35 E6, 53 E1
Babina (Utt) 35 H4
Babnegarh 13 F6
Babra (Guj) 63 F3
Babra (Mah) 77 G1
Babuchara (Ba) 60 B5
Babugarh 22 D4
Babuhri 30 C3
Babulgaon (Mah) 67 E6
Babulgaon (Mah) 78 A3
Babupet 79 G1
Baburi 37 G6
Bachagaon 43 F2
Bachap (B) 41 E2
Bachasar 20 B6
Bachauli 39 F5
Bachhon 54 A1
Bachhraon 23 E3
Bachhrawan 36 C3
Bachial Rajpar (P) 30 C4
Bachun 33 G3
Bachwara 39 E5
Bada 48 A6
Bada Barabil 70 D2
Bada Doikal 81 H2
Bada Gowah (P) 12 C6
Badagada 82 B2
Badagara 94 C3
Badahahpur 22 C5
Badalgachhi (Ba) 58 C1
Badami 85 G5
Badamibagh Cantonment
  13 F3
Badana 31 E5
Badanpur 54 B3
Badarkhali (Ba) 74 B3
Badarpur (Del) 22 C4
Badarpur (Ass) 60 C1
Badartuni (Ba) 59 G6
Badarwas 52 C1
Badausa 36 B6
Badavanahalli 91 H4
Badchi 85 F3
Baddomalhi (P) 17 E2
Badepalli 86 D3
Badgaon (Ba) 60 B2
Badhal 33 G2
Badhauli 18 C6
Badhni 17 G5
Badhurpara 60 B4
Badhwana 21 H4
Badiana (P) 17 E1
Badiarpatti (N) 39 F3
Badikata 69 G5
Badimpur 40 C6
Badin (P) 48 A2
Badkulla 58 C5

Badla (Ba) 59 H2
Badla 50 C2
Badlapur 37 F5
Badli (Har) 22 B4
Badli (Del) 22 C4
Badmor 23 E5
Badnapur 77 G2
Badnawar 51 F6
Badnera 66 D5
Badno 20 C6
Bado Sarai 36 D2
Badoab 13 F2
Badopal 21 G2
Badora 52 A2
Badrinath 19 G5
Badshahibagh 18 D6
Badupi (M) 75 E3
Baduria 58 C6
Badvel 93 E2
Baen 21 F4
Baer 15 H4
Baet 48 B6
Baetu 31 G5
Baffa (P) 12 B2
Baga (Ba) 59 F2
Baga (Ba) 73 G1
Baga 42 D6
Bagadi 91 F5
Bagai Kothi 14 A6
Bagalkot 85 G4
Bagalur 92 B6
Bagalwad 86 A4
Bagana 51 H6
Bagar (N) 24 B3
Bagar Meo 34 B1
Bagathala 49 E6
Bagaud 65 H2
Bagaura 38 B4
Bagawas 32 C5
Bagbahara 69 F5
Bagbari (Ba) 59 E2
Bagbor 41 H4
Bagchini 34 D3
Bagda 57 G5
Bagdaha 58 D5
Bagdapalli 79 G4
Bagdogra 40 B3
Bagepalli 92 B5
Bager 52 A2
Bageshwar 23 H1
Bagewadi (Kar) 84 D5
Bagewadi (Kar) 85 E4
Baggar 21 G5
Bagh (P) 16 A4
Bagh (*)12 C3
Bagh (Mad) 65 E2
Bagha Purana 17 F5
Bagham (P) 12 C5
Baghdarra (P) 12 A3
Baghera (Raj) 33 G4
Baghera (Utt) 35 G5
Bagherhat (Ba) 73 E1
Bagherpara (Ba) 59 E5
Baghiapara 70 B5
Baghmara (Ba) 59 H5
Baghmara 41 G6
Baghmundi 57 F5
Baghnagar 37 G2
Baghpat 22 C3
Baghra 22 C2
Bagi 18 C4
Bagicha (P) 14 A1
Bagicha 55 H6
Bagjan 42 D3
Baglan 64 D5
Bagli 66 A1
Baglung (N) 25 H5
Bagmara (Ba) 58 C2

Bagnan 72 B1
Bagni 84 D3
Bagodar 57 E3
Bagora 31 G6
Bagot 13 E5
Bagra (P) 12 A2
Bagrakasa 68 B4
Bagraudih 55 F4
Bagri 65 G1
Bagrian 17 H6
Bagribari 41 F4
Bagru 33 G3
Bagsara 63 E4
Bagso 14 C3
Bagtor 13 E2
Bagula 58 C5
Baguliaghat 43 E4
Bagur 91 F6
Bah 35 F3
Bahadarpur 65 F5
Bahadpur 17 H2
Bahadurganj (N) 37 G1
Bahadurganj 40 A4
Bahadurgarh 22 B4
Bahadurpur (Raj) 34 B4
Bahadurpur (Mad) 52 D3
Bahal 21 G4
Bahalda 71 F1
Bahamniwala 17 E5
Baharagora 71 G2
Baharpur (Ba) 59 E4
Bahawainagar (P) 20 B1
Bahela 68 B4
Bahera 39 F4
Baheri (Utt) 23 G4
Baheri (Bih) 39 E5
Bahili 66 A1
Bahin (M) 75 G3
Bahirevadi 84 D4
Bahjoi 23 F5
Bahli (P) 16 B6
Bahmni 67 G5
Bahora 22 B5
Bahour 97 E3
Bahraich 36 D1
Bahre 64 C6
Bahsunta 22 D3
Bahtar (P) 12 A4
Bahu 22 A4
Bahua 36 B5
Bahubal (Ba) 60 A3
Bahuna 21 G2
Bahuriband 54 A4
Bahya 21 E2
Baibati 82 B1
Baichhata (Ba) 74 B2
Baidaura 35 E6
Baideswar 70 D6
Baidpalle 88 B2
Baidya Bazar (Ba) 59 G4
Baidyapur 58 B5
Baihar 68 B2
Baihatola 55 E5
Baijnath 18 B2
Baikanthpur 54 D2
Baikunthapur 55 F1
Baikunthpur 38 C4
Bail Hongal 85 E5
Bailur 95 G3
Bainai 22 A3
Bainduru 90 B4
Bainmul 13 F4
Baira (N) 38 D2
Baira 56 A4
Bairagarh (Raj) 52 A3
Bairagarh (Mad) 52 C5
Bairagarh (Mah) 66 B3
Bairagnia 38 D3

Bairat 33 H1
Baireddipalle 92 D6
Bairi (Mad) 66 B2
Bairi (Ori) 71 E5
Baisi 40 A5
Baisinga 71 G3
Baitadi (N) 24 B2
Baitalpur 69 E3
Baithalangso 42 C5
Bajag 68 D1
Bajalia (Ba) 74 B2
Bajana 49 G6
Bajang (N) 24 C2
Bajaura 18 B2
Bajkatta (P) 12 A2
Bajna (Utt) 22 D6
Bajna (Mad) 51 E5
Bajnath 23 H1
Bajoli 18 B1
Bajpar 69 H1
Bajrakot 70 C4
Bajranggarh 52 C2
Bajtipur (Ba) 59 H3
Bajura (N) 24 D2
Bakal 53 H4, 54 A4
Bakalo 55 F6
Bakaner 65 F2
Bakani 52 A3
Bakar (P) 30 B4
Bakarama 69 H1
Bakarganj (Ba) 73 G1
Bakewar 35 G3
Bakhar (P) 30 B4
Bakhaasar 49 F2
Bakhra 38 D4
Bakhrabad (Ba) 59 H4
Bakhri 39 F5
Bakhtiyarpur 38 D6
Bakisha 37 F5
Bakkali 72 B3
Bakloh 17 H1
Bakong 42 D1
Bakor 50 C5
Bakra 31 H6
Bakreshwar 57 H4
Baksar 23 E4
Baksena 23 G6
Baksheu 32 D1
Bakshganj (Ba) 59 H6
Bakshpur (Ba) 60 A2
Bakswaho 53 G3
Baktuni 51 G2
Bakudi 58 A1
Bakuri 62 B2
Bakutra 49 E4
Bala 35 H3
Balachor 18 A4
Balagam 62 C4
Balaganj (Ba) 60 B2
Balagarh 58 B5
Balaghat 68 A3
Balaing (M) 74 D3
Balakhera 34 A6
Balakot (P) 12 B2
Balakrishnanpatti 96 A4
Balam Takli 77 G3
Balam Yelim 77 G3
Balamba 48 D6
Balana (Har) 18 B6
Balana (Raj) 31 F2
Balanga 83 E1
Balanwali 17 F6
Balapanuru 92 B2
Balapur (N) 25 E5
Balapur 66 B6
Balara 32 D4
Balarampur (Wbg) 41 E4
Balarampur (Wbg) 57 F5

Balarampuram 98 C5
Balasar (Raj) 31 F4
Balasar (Guj) 49 E4
Balatgi 86 B4
Balbassa 24 A3
Balbil (M) 61 F4
Balcha 18 D4
Baldanu 63 G1
Baldeo 34 D1
Baldeogarh (Raj) 34 A2
Baldeogarh (Mad) 53 G2
Baldher (P) 12 B3
Baldhoi 63 E2
Balegaon 66 B5
Baleh 53 G4
Balehonnur 90 D5
Balesar 32 A4
Baleshwar (Balasore)
  71 G3
Balewa 31 E5
Balfai (B) 42 A2
Balganur 85 H2
Balgaon 85 F2
Balgiran 12 C2
Balhar 13 H5
Balhari (P) 48 B3
Balhom 13 H2
Bali (Raj) 32 B6, 50 B1
Bali (Raj) 32 D5
Bali Chak 72 A1
Bali Chowki 18 C3
Balia (Raj) 51 H3
Balia (Dri) 70 C3
Baliabera 71 G2
Baliakandi (Ba) 59 E4
Balianta 71 E6
Baliapal 71 H3
Baliapur 57 F4
Baliati (Ba) 59 F3
Balidiha 71 F2
Baliguda 82 A1
Balijan 44 A1
Balijipeta 81 H4
Balikanai (P) 12 B1
Balikania 82 D2
Balikuchi 42 C4
Balikuda 83 F1
Balil 18 B3
Balimila 81 E5
Balipalle 87 G6
Balipara 42 D3
Balipatna 71 E6
Balitha 58 A6
Baliyali 21 H3
Baljod 70 C2
Balkassar (P) 12 A6
Balkonda 79 E4
Balkot (N) 25 H6
Balla (Ba) 59 F3
Ballabgarh 22 C5
Ballarpur 79 G2
Ballavi 91 H5
Ballia 38 B5
Balliar 20 A5
Ballipada 82 C3
Ballipatar 82 C2
Balloki (P) 16 C4
Balluan 17 E6
Ballurpettai 96 A2
Bally (Wbg) 72 B1
Bally (Goa) 84 C6
Balma (N) 24 A3
Balochia 20 C3
Balod 68 C5
Baloda (Mad) 69 F2
Baloda (Mad) 69 G4
Baloda Bazar 69 E3
Balotra 31 H5

Balrampur 37 E1
Balsamand 21 G3
Balta 17 H2
Baltal 13 G3
Balu 22 A2
Balua 37 G6
Balugaon 82 D2
Balumath 56 C4
Balunda 32 D4
Balur (Kar) 85 F4
Balur (Tam) 96 B3
Balurghat 40 C6
Balussheri 94 D4
Balwakot 24 B1
Balwara (Raj) 32 A6
Balwara (Mad) 65 H1
Balwari 65 F1
Baman Hat 41 E4
Bamanbore 63 E1
Bamangaon 33 H5
Bamangola 40 B6
Bamanhalli 90 D1
Bamanpalli 80 B3
Bamanwas 34 A3
Bamdah 57 F2
Bamhni (Mad) 54 D6
Bamhni (Mad) 68 B1
Bamhniaon 37 F5
Bamho 43 G4
Bamhor 33 H4
Bamhori 53 E5
Bamini 80 D2
Baminigam 82 B2
Bamna (Ba) 73 F2
Bamni 78 A2
Bamnia 51 E6
Bamnidihi 69 F3
Bamnikhera 22 C5
Bamnor 31 F6
Bamor 53 E1
Bamora (Raj) 50 D2
Bamora (Mad) 53 E3
Bamori (Mad) 52 C1
Bamori (Mad) 53 G1
Bampa 19 H5
Bamraspet 86 C2
Bamroli 23 H5
Bamundiha 57 F5
Bamur 70 B5
Bamutia (Ba) 59 H3
Ban (P) 12 C4
Banakhok 33 H3
Bananga 101 H6
Banapur 82 D2
Banar 32 B4
Banarhat 40 D3
Banaripara (Ba) 59 F6
Banasandra 91 G5
Banat 22 C2
Banavar 91 F5
Banavasi 90 D2
Banbarad 68 D4
Banbirpur 24 C5
Banchharampur (Ba) 59 G4
Banda (Utt) 36 B6
Banda (Mad) 53 F3
Banda (Mah) 84 C5
Bandaguda 82 A2
Bandahalli 95 G2
Bandai (P) 12 A1
Bandamurlanka 89 E4
Bandanwara 33 E4
Bandapal 80 D2
Bandar (Ba) 74 B2
Bandar (Mad) 55 F6
Bandar (Guj) 63 G5
Bandarban (Ba) 74 C2

Bandarian Balagra (P)
  12 C4
Bandarupalle 88 A4
Bandgaon 56 D6
Bandha 52 C1
Bandhargarh 54 C4
Bandi 12 C2
Bandi Atmakuru 87 E5
Bandi Dhundan (P) 12 C2
Bandia 48 A5
Bandipur (J&K) 13 E2
Bandipur (Kar) 95 F3
Bandnau 21 E5
Bandra 76 A4
Bandri (Mad) 53 F3
Bandri (Kar) 91 G1
Banduan 57 F6
Banduar 42 A5
Bandugam 81 H4
Banehwala (P) 20 A4
Banera 33 E6
Baneshwar 76 C6
Banethi 18 C5
Banga 17 H4
Bangahari (Ba) 58 B1
Bangarapet 92 C6
Bangalhalia (Ba) 74 C1
Bangali (Ba) 59 E2
Bangalore 92 B6
Bangaluda 81 G3
Bangana 18 A3
Banganapalle 87 E6
Bangaon (Bih) 39 F5
Bangaon (Mad) 53 H3
Bangaon (Wbg) 58 C6
Bangarmau 36 A2
Bangarupalam 92 D5
Bangarupeta 93 F3
Banghat 23 F1
Bangi 21 F1
Bangomunda 69 G6
Bangra 35 G4
Bangrakot 40 C2
Bangriposhi 71 F2
Bangrod 71 F5
Bangsi 41 G5
Banguk 28 A5
Banhatti 85 F4
Bania 55 E6
Baniagaon 80 D1
Baniana 31 G3
Baniapur 38 C5
Banigochha 70 B6
Banigratri (Ba) 74 B2
Banihal 13 F4
Banikoppa 85 G6
Baniyachung (Ba) 60 A2
Banjar 18 C3
Banjarewla (P) 16 A6
Banka 57 G1
Bankacha 34 B5
Bankapur 90 D1
Bankatwa 25 E6
Bankhandi 17 F5
Bankhari (Ba) 59 F4
Bankheri 53 F6
Banki 70 C2
Bankigarh 70 D6
Bankora 50 D4
Bankot 76 B6
Bankura 57 G5
Banmala 65 H3
Banmanki 39 H5
Bannikop 91 E1
Bannur 95 F3
Bano (P) 47 H1
Bano 56 C6
Banola 79 E4

Banor 70 C4
Banpur (Utt) 53 F2
Banpur (Guj) 63 E3
Bansberia 58 B6
Bansdih 38 B5
Bansera 52 B2
Bansgaon 37 G3
Bansi (Utt) 37 G2
Bansi (Utt) 51 E3
Bansi (Utt) 53 E1
Bansihari 40 B6
Bansiwara 50 B2
Banskandi 60 D2
Banskot (N) 25 H5
Banskot 81 E1
Banskupi 57 F3
Banspani (N) 24 D4
Bansrai 34 C3
Bansur 22 A6
Bansura 36 C1
Banswada 78 D5
Banswara 51 E5
Banta (Raj) 32 C5
Banta (Ori) 71 F4
Bantala 70 D5
Banthra 23 H6
Banthra Sikandarpur 36 B3
Bantva 62 C4
Bantval 90 C6
Banupratappur 68 C6
Banur 18 B5
Banvara 54 B4
Banwara 33 G4
Baonli 34 A4
Baonri 32 B3
Baori 49 E1
Baorli 32 A4
Bap 31 H1
Bapatla 88 B5
Bapauli 22 B3
Bapaur 52 A1
Bapeo 20 D6
Bapsai 76 B3
Baptumil 88 C4
Bapunda 33 F4
Bapung 42 C6
Bar Bigha 39 E6
Bar Dhoa 42 C3
Bar Kotkai (P) 12 A1
Bara (Raj) 31 G2
Bara (Raj) 32 B3
Bara (Mad) 34 D5
Bara (Bih) 39 H6
Bara (Bih) 56 C1
Bara (Bih) 56 C2
Bara (Bih) 57 H3
Bara Bangahal 18 B1
Bara Banki 36 C2
Bara Bazan 60 C2
Bara Boarijor 57 H1
Bara Dahai 60 C2
Bara Delana 20 C4
Bara Digar 43 E6
Bara Gali (P) 12 C3
Bara Khera 23 G3
Bara Khunta 71 G3
Bara Sagar 54 B6
Barabakunda (Ba) 74 A1
Baraban (N) 25 E4
Barabani 57 G4
Barabhum 57 F6
Barach 54 D3
Barachana 71 F5
Barachati 56 C2
Barad 78 C3
Baradarga (Ba) 40 D6
Baragaon (Him) 18 C4
Baragaon (Utt) 24 A5

Baragaon (Utt) 24 B6
Baragaon (Raj) 31 F3
Baragaon (Utt) 35 F6
Baragaon (Utt) 37 F6
Baragaon (Utt) 38 B5
Baragaon (Mad) 52 A4
Baragaon Nandur 77 E3
Baragaon Pimpri 76 D1
Baraghar (P) 16 C4
Baraghop (Ba) 74 B3
Barah (Pun) 21 G1
Barah 35 H4, 36 A4
Barahanuddin (Ba) 73 G1
Barahara Kothi 39 H5
Barahat 57 G1
Barai 13 E1
Baraigram (Ba) 58 D3
Baraitha 53 F3
Barakatha 57 E3
Barakhola 60 D1
Barakot 70 C3
Baram 57 F6
Baramati 77 E6
Baramba 70 D6
Baramgala 13 E4
Baramkela 69 H3
Barampur 37 H3
Baramsar 21 E3
Baramula 13 E3
Baran (N) 37 H1
Baran 52 A1
Barana (P) 16 A2
Barana 52 A1
Baranagar 72 B1
Baranda (Har) 22 B3
Baranda (Guj) 47 H5
Barang 71 E6
Barania (Ba) 74 B2
Barapara (Ba) 73 F2
Barar 32 D5
Barara 18 B6
Barari 39 H6
Baras 22 B2
Barasah 71 G3
Barasat (Wbg) 58 C6, 72 C1
Barasat (Wbg) 72 C2
Barasi 55 E4
Barasloia 56 C6
Baratla 12 D5
Barato 42 C5
Barauda 51 F4
Barauli (Utt) 23 E5
Barauli (Utt) 34 D1
Barauli (Bih) 38 C4
Baraunda 54 B1
Baraundha 55 F1
Barauni (Mad) 35 E5
Barauni (Bih) 39 E6
Baraut 22 C3
Barawan 56 A1
Barawarda 51 E3
Barbaru 43 H1
Barbaspur 55 F5
Barbatta (N) 24 A4
Bardah 37 G5
Bardhal 13 E5
Bardia (N) 24 D5
Bardoli 64 B4
Bardubi 44 A1
Bardula 69 E6, 81 E1
Bareguda 80 B4
Bareilly 23 G5
Bareja 49 H6
Barel 34 B4
Bareli 53 E6
Barenda 55 F4
Barengapara 41 F6

Barer 34 C5
Bareta 21 G1
Bareth 52 D4
Bargah (P) 30 A1
Bargaior 19 E1
Bargana 22 C6
Bargaon (N) 25 F4
Bargaon (Raj) 49 H2
Bargaon (Mad) 55 E4
Bargaon (Ori) 70 B2
Bargarh (Utt) 54 D1
Bargarh (Ori) 69 H4, 70 A4
Bargawan 34 B5
Barghat 67 H2
Barguna (Ba) 73 F2
Bargur 91 H4
Barguru 96 A1
Barh 39 E6
Barhaj 37 H4
Barhalganj 37 H4
Barhali 36 B1
Barhamjia (N) 39 G3
Barhampur 38 B5
Barhampuri (N) 39 F3
Barhampuri 78 B3
Barhan 35 E1
Barharia 38 B4
Barharwa 58 A1
Barhat 44 A2
Barhatta (Ba) 59 G1
Barheli 68 C6
Barhi (Bih) 39 F4
Barhi (Mad) 54 C4
Barhi (Bih) 56 D3
Barhi (Mad) 68 D6
Barhiya 39 E6
Barhra 38 B5
Bari (Raj) 34 D3
Bari (Utt) 36 B2
Bari (Mad) 53 E6
Bari Brahamana 13 F6
Bari Sadri 51 E2
Bariapur 39 G6
Barikai 92 B6
Barikot (N) 25 F3
Barikot (P) 12 A2
Baripada 71 G2
Barisal (Ba) 59 G6, 73 G1
Barisi 19 G4
Barjala 60 A4
Barjhar 42 A3
Barjisnagar 52 C6
Barjora 57 H5
Barka Kana 56 D4
Barkagaon 56 D4
Barkal (Ba) 60 C6
Barkhanpur (Ba) 59 E4
Barkhera 52 D6
Barkheta 23 H5
Barki (P) 17 E3
Barki Sara 57 E3
Barkot 19 E5
Barku (C) 19 H3
Barkuhi 67 F2
Barkur 90 C5
Barla 23 E6
Barlan 52 B1
Barlanga 57 E5
Barli 33 E5
Barlia 32 A4
Barlias 33 F6
Barlu 32 C3
Barmdeo Mandi (N) 24 A3
Barmer 31 F5
Barnagar 51 G6
Barnala (P) 16 B3
Barnala (*) 13 E6

Barnala (Pun) 17 G6
Barni Hat 42 B4
Barod 51 H4
Baroda (Raj) 34 B1
Baroda (Mad) 34 B6
Barodia (Mad) 52 A4
Barodia (Mad) 53 F3
Baroknar 55 E1
Barola 54 A5
Baroli 51 E2
Baroni 33 H4
Baropal 20 D2
Baropujia 42 C4
Barpali 69 H4
Barpara (Ba) 74 C2
Barpathar 43 F4
Barpatoli 63 F5
Barpatti 39 E3
Barpeta 41 H4
Barpeta Road 41 G3
Barr 32 D4
Barrackpore 58 C6
Barria 51 F3
Barridand 55 E6
Barsar 18 A3
Barshong (B) 41 E1
Barsi 77 G5
Barsi Takli 66 B6
Barsoi 40 A5
Barsur 80 D3
Bartala 41 H4
Barthi 55 H4
Bartu 14 A3
Baruagaon 43 F3
Baruapara 40 C3
Barud 65 G3
Baruhatu 57 E6
Baruipur 72 C2
Barundhan 33 G6
Barur 65 H3
Barura (Ba) 59 H5
Barutara 54 D5
Baruva 82 C4
Barvala 63 G2
Barwa (Har) 21 G3
Barwa (Utt) 23 H6
Barwa (Utt) 37 H2, 38 A2
Barwa Sagar 35 F6
Barwadih 56 B4
Barwadili 55 G2
Barwaha 65 H2
Barwahi 52 D3
Barwala 21 H2
Barwan (Mad) 52 B1
Barwan (Wbg) 58 A4
Barwani 65 E2
Barwara 54 A2
Basagude 80 C5
Basai 53 E1
Basail (Ba) 59 F3
Basal (P) 12 A4
Basantgarh 13 G6
Basantpur (Him) 18 C4
Basantpur (Bih) 38 C4
Basantpur (N) 39 G3
Basantpur (Bih) 39 H4
Basanwahi 81 E1
Basar (Aru) 27 H6
Basar (Mah) 78 D4
Basarulu 91 G6
Basari 53 H2
Basavakalyan 78 B6
Basavana Bagewadi 85 G3
Basavapatna (Kar) 91 E3
Basavapatna (Kar) 94 D1
Basbari 41 F4
Basdarra (P) 12 A2
Baseri 34 C3

Basetihalli 92 B4
Bashar Hat (Ba) 59 H6
Basharatganj 23 G5
Bashizabad 86 C2
Bashta 23 E3
Basi (Pun) 17 H3
Basi (Har) 18 B5
Basi (Raj) 32 B5
Basi (Raj) 33 H2
Basi (Raj) 51 E1
Basia 56 C6
Basidka 17 G6
Basirhat 72 D1
Basirpur (P) 16 D5
Basmath 78 B3
Basna 69 G4
Basnamba 78 C2
Basoda 52 D4
Basoli (Him) 17 H1
Basoli (Him) 18 A3
Basopatti 39 E3
Basrur 90 C4
Bassein 76 A3
Bassi Pathana 18 A5
Bassian 17 G5
Basta 71 G3
Bastam 22 D2
Bastar 81 E3
Basti 37 F3
Basti Qasn (P) 16 A4
Basudebpur (Ba) 58 C2
Basudebpur (Ori) 71 G4
Basudebpur (Wbg) 72 A3
Basugaon 41 G3
Basunti 72 C2
Basuri (Ba) 59 F2
Basuvanpuram 95 G3
Baswa 34 A2
Bataikela 55 H6, 56 A6
Batajor (Ba) 59 F6
Batakut 13 G3
Batal 18 C1
Batala 17 F2
Batang (C) 29 H1
Batara (P) 12 A2
Bataru 31 F4
Batesar 35 E2
Bathad 18 C3
Bathgaon 68 D4
Bathinda 17 F6
Bathnaha (Bih) 38 D3
Bathnaha (Bih) 39 H4
Batia 57 F2
Batiagarh 53 G3
Batka 58 B5
Batote 13 G5
Batra (N) 38 D2
Batrahalli 96 B1
Batrel 68 D6
Battaknndi (P) 12 C1
Battal (P) 12 B2
Battulapalle 92 B2
Batwa 50 A6
Baudh Raj 70 B5
Baudikui 34 B2
Bauna (Ba) 40 D6
Baund 22 A4
Baundi 36 D1
Bauphal (Ba) 73 G1
Baura (Ba) 40 D4
Baura 77 F6
Bauria 72 B1
Bausi 57 G2
Baut Bazar 42 C5
Bautra 31 H6
Bavanipet 79 E5
Bavda 84 C3
Bavia 49 H6

Bawal 22 B5
Bawala 62 C3
Bawana (Har) 22 A5
Bawana (Del) 22 B4
Bawanasi 87 E5
Bawanbir 66 B5
Bawani Khera 21 H3
Bawanni (P) 16 B5
Bawli Bazar (M) 74 C4
Bayad 50 B5
Bayaha 38 A2
Bayana 34 C2
Bayinnar 13 G4
Bazargaon 67 F4
Bazidpur 39 E5
Bazpur 23 G3
Beadonabad 100 B5
Beawar 33 E4
Bebar 48 B5
Bebejia 43 G2
Bechiwara 50 C4
Bed 62 C1
Bedawal ki Pal 50 D3
Bedgom 13 E3
Bedi 62 C1
Bedsa 76 C4
Bedshi 84 C5
Begamabad 22 D4
Begamganj 53 E4
Begamganj (Ba) 59 H6
Begampur 85 F1
Begodra 63 H1
Begowa (P) 17 E1
Begowala 17 G3
Begun 51 F1
Begunia 70 D6
Begunkudar 57 F5
Begur 95 E3
Begusarai 39 F6
Behali 43 E3
Behat (Utt)18 D6, 22 D1
Behat (Mad) 35 F4
Behgama 23 E5
Behra 24 D6
Behraj 67 H2
Behraonda 34 A5
Behrar 34 C5
Behrol 53 F3
Behror 22 A6
Behta Gokal 36 A1
Bejipuram 82 A5
Bejjangivada 81 E6
Bekal 94 B1
Bekkatur 95 G2
Bel Pimpalgaon 77 E2
Bela (Pun) 18 A4
Bela (Guj) 48 D6
Bela (Guj) 49 E4
Bela (Guj) 49 E6
Bela (Bih) 56 C1
Bela (Mah) 67 G5
Bela (And) 79 F2
Bela cum Pratapgarh 37 E5
Belagad 82 A1
Belagali 85 F4
Belagam 81 H4
Belaguntha 82 C1
Belagur 91 F4
Belahonda 69 E4
Belaichhari (Ba) 74 C1
Belakoba 40 C3
Belakuadi 95 F2
Belanagar 86 D2
Belani (N) 38 A1
Belapara 69 G6
Belapur 77 E2
Belapurpada 76 A4
Belavaniki 85 F5

Belbahara 54 D5
Belda 71 H2
Beldanga 58 B3
Beldara 91 H5
Beldaur 39 G5
Belgachhi 40 A5
Belgahna 69 E1
Belgami 90 D2
Belganur 86 A5
Belgaon 68 B3
Belgaum 84 D5
Belgod 91 E6
Belha 69 E3
Belhar 57 F1
Belhatti 91 E1
Belhe 76 D3
Beliator 57 H5
Belkar 84 B2
Belkharu 53 H5
Belkhera 53 G5
Belkuchi (Ba) 59 E3
Bellala 79 F3
Bellampalli 79 H4
Bellare 94 C1
Bellary 91 H1
Belluru 91 G6
Belma 80 D1
Belmannu 90 C5
Belo (P) 47 G2
Belonia 60 A5
Belpara 23 G3
Belsand 38 D3
Belshakarga 78 B5
Beltangadi 90 D6
Beltikri 69 F5
Beluguppa 91 H2
Belur (Kar) 85 G5
Belur (Kar) 91 E5
Belura 78 B6
Belvandi 77 E4
Bembal 79 H1
Bembla 77 F6
Bemetara 68 D3
Bemli 77 H6
Bengabad 57 F3
Bengala 101 G3
Beni (N) 25 H5
Beniganj 36 B2
Benipatti 39 E3
Bennari 95 G3
Benoda 67 E4
Benura 81 E2
Beohari 54 D3
Ber 47 H5
Bera (Ba) 59 E3
Bera 50 B1
Beraja (Guj) 48 B6
Beraja (Guj) 62 C1
Berani (P) 30 A5
Berasia 52 C4
Berchha 52 A5
Bergaon 68 B5
Berhait 58 A1
Berhamapore 58 B3
Berhampur 82 C3
Beri (Har) 22 A4
Beri (Raj) 49 G1
Beria 65 H2
Berinag 24 A1
Beripeta 93 G4
Beriwala 20 A4
Berjan 43 H3
Berla 68 D3
Bermo 57 E4
Bero 56 C5
Bersi 30 D4
Berung 28 A6
Berwa 32 A3

Besagarahalli 95 F1
Besal (P) 12 D1
Besani 54 A3
Besham Qalla (P) 12 B1
Besroli 33 E2
Bestavarapeta 87 F6
Beswan 22 D6
Betagi (Ba) 73 F1
Betamcherla 86 D6
Betavad 65 F4
Betgeri 85 E5
Bethia 80 B2
Bethuadari 58 B4
Betia 55 H2
Betil (Ba) 59 E3
Betma 51 G6
Betmangala 92 C6
Betmogra 78 C4
Betnoti 71 G3
Bettadpur 94 D1
Bettiah 38 B3
Betu 32 A6
Betul (Mad) 66 D3
Betul (Goa) 90 A1
Betul Bazar 66 D3
Beur 85 G4
Bewal (P) 12 C5
Bewar (Utt) 35 G2
Bewar (Utt) 35 H5
Beypore 94 C4
Bhabbar 49 F3
Bhabhru 33 H1
Bhabra 64 D1
Bhabua 55 H1
Bhachau 48 D5
Bhad 62 C4
Bhada (Utt) 37 E4
Bhada (Mah) 78 A5
Bhadan (Raj) 32 B2
Bhadan (Utt) 35 F2
Bhadana 52 C2
Bhadaria 56 A4
Bhadarwa 64 B1
Bhadarwah 13 G6
Bhadas 22 B6
Bhadasar (Raj) 21 E5
Bhadasar (Raj) 31 E2
Bhadaura 51 E2
Bhadavani 85 F1
Bhadde (P) 16 D2
Bhaddi 18 A4
Bhaddu 13 G6
Bhader 24 B5
Bhadera 20 C4
Bhadesar 51 E2
Bhadgaon 65 F6
Bhadi 21 F4
Bhadiaranwala Khuh (P)
    20 A3
Bhadka 31 F4
Bhadkamba 84 B2
Bhadla 63 E2
Bhadli 63 F2
Bhadmi (P) 48 A3
Bhadohi 37 F6
Bhadora 54 B4
Bhadoti 34 A4
Bhadra (Him) 14 A6
Bhadra (Raj) 21 F3
Bhadra (Guj) 48 A5
Bhadrachalam 88 C1
Bhadrajan 32 B5
Bhadrakh 71 F5
Bhadran 64 B2
Bhadrana 53 G3
Bhadrapur (N) 40 B3
Bhadravati 91 E4
Bhadreswar (Guj) 48 C6

Bhadreswar (Wbg) 58 B6
Bhadrod 63 G4
Bhadson (Pun)18 A5
Bhadson (Har) 22 B1
Bhadthar 62 B2
Bhadur (P) 48 C2
Bhaduria (Ba) 40 D6
Bhadva 63 E2
Bhadvad 64 D4
Bhadwar 25 E6
Bhagaiya 39 H6
Bhagalpur 39 G6
Bhagamandala 94 C1
Bhagat (P) 16 A5
Bhagatanwala (P) 16 B2
Bhagaura (N) 38 B1
Bhagbatpur 71 F6
Bhageh 35 E4
Bhagiratpur 58 C3
Bhagnanpur 58 B2
Bhagor 51 E6
Bhagot 13 H6
Bhagthal (P) 12 A6
Bhagu (Pun) 21 E1
Bhagu (Raj) 32 C1
Bhaguapura 35 F4
Bhagvati 90 C1
Bhagwal (P) 12 A5
Bhagwangola 58 B3
Bhagwanpur (N) 25 G6
Bhagwanpur (N) 39 F3
Bhagwanpur (Utt) 22 D1
Bhagwanpur (Bih) 55 H1
Bhagwanpur (Wbg) 72 A2
Bhagwanpura 33 E6
Bhagwantnagar 36 B4
Bhagyakul (Ba) 59 F5
Bhahkot 17 G4
Bhahra (P) 16 B1
Bhai Pheru (P) 16 D4
Bhailal 22 C2
Bhainawa 34 B3
Bhaini Bagha 21 G1
Bhainsa 78 D3
Bhainsara 31 F3
Bhainsdehi 66 D3
Bhainskuchi 41 E4
Bhainsrorgarh 51 G1
Bhairab Bazar (Ba) 59 H3
Bhairahawa (N) 37 H1
Bhairamgarh 80 C4
Bhairon 34 C6
Bhaironghati 19 F4
Bhairowal (P) 16 C1
Bhaisaota 21 G5
Bhaislana 33 F2
Bhaiswahi 55 E4
Bhaja 76 C4
Bhajaola 20 D3
Bhajni (N) 24 C4
Bhakarapeta 93 E4
Bhakri (Raj) 32 A2
Bhakri (Raj) 33 E3
Bhakrod 32 C2
Bhaktapur (N) 38 D1
Bhakurma 55 G6
Bhal (P) 12 B5
Bhalaj 64 B1
Bhalala 49 G6
Bhalan 18 A4
Bhaliapanga 82 B3
Bhalki 78 C6
Bhaloa 39 H4
Bhalod 64 B3
Bhalpur 64 C2
Bhalta 52 A3
Bhaluka (Ba) 59 F2
Bhaluka 40 A6

Bhalukpong 42 D2
Bhalur 17 F5
Bhalwal (P) 16 B1
Bhalwani 77 F5
Bham 17 H3
Bhamaragarh 80 B3
Bhamgarh 66 A3
Bhamora 23 G5
Bhanas Hivre 77 F2
Bhandak 79 G1
Bhandar (N) 39 F1
Bhandara 67 H4
Bhandara Road 67 H4
Bhandarej 34 A3
Bhandari (N) 24 B3
Bhandari 43 F4
Bhandaria 37 F2
Bhandarpokhari 71 F5
Bhandel 13 H6
Bhander 35 F5
Bhandher 17 G6
Bhandu 49 H4
Bhanduri 62 D4
Bhandwa 21 H5
Bhanga (Ba) 59 F5
Bhanga 60 C1
Bhangaha 25 E6
Bhangala 17 G2
Bhangali 17 F2
Bhangali Gujar (P) 12 B5
Bhangar (Wbg) 72 C1
Bhangar (Mah)76 B6,
    84 B1
Bhangbarai (B) 41 F1
Bhangor 62 C2
Bhania 31 F6
Bhanin 21 F4
Bhanjanagar 82 B1
Bhanpura 51 H2
Bhanpuri 68 C4
Bhanur 20 C1
Bhanvad 62 C3
Bhanwargarh 52 B1
Bhaogarh 51 F4
Bhaptiahi 39 G4
Bharai 33 G5
Bharak 13 E5
Bharalmukh 42 A4
Bharana 17 F4
Bharapar 48 C6
Bharat 49 H3
Bharatkhali (Ba) 41 E6
Bharatpur (N) 38 B1
Bharatpur (Raj) 34 C2
Bharatpur (Mad) 54 D4
Bharatpur (Wbg) 58 B4
Bharawas 22 A5
Bharbharia 71 E1
Bharda (N) 39 G3
Bharduva 49 F3
Bhargain 35 G1
Bhargi 13 H5
Bhariad 63 H2
Bharkao (P) 12 B4
Bharkodra 64 A2
Bharkot 19 E5
Bharmar 17 H2
Bharmasagara 91 F2
Bharno 56 C5
Bharpur (P) 12 A6
Bharro 20 B5
Bhart 13 G5
Bhartabas (N) 25 G6
Bharthana 35 G3
Bhartnalli 90 C2
Bharuch 64 B3
Bharunda 33 E3
Bharwa Sumerpur 36 A5

Bharwain 17 H2
Bharwani 32 A6
Bhasawar 34 B2
Bhasin (P) 17 E3
Bhasma 70 A2
Bhastara 58 B6
Bhata (N) 38 C1
Bhatagli 78 A6
Bhatana 50 A2
Bhatapara 69 E3
Bhatar 58 A5
Bhatea (P) 12 C4
Bhatewar 50 D2
Bhatgaon 69 G3
Bhatia 62 B2
Bhatiapara (Ba) 59 E5
Bhatiot (P) 12 A4
Bhatkal 90 B4
Bhatkera 66 A4
Bhatkheri 51 F2
Bhatkuli 66 C1
Bhatli 69 H4
Bhatnawar 34 C5
Bhatpara (Ba) 59 H5
Bhatpara 58 C6
Bhatrari (Ba) 74 A1
Bhattigam 81 F3
Bhattiprolu 88 B4
Bhattu Kalan 21 F2
Bhatu 21 F2
Bhatumra 78 C6
Bhatwari 19 F5
Bhauapar 37 H3
Bhaudi 77 E4
Bhauli 36 C2
Bhaun (P) 12 B6
Bhaunathpur 55 H2
Bhaunra 38 B2
Bhaunti 35 E6
Bhaurasa 50 D2
Bhavani 95 H4
Bhavnagar 63 H3
Bhawana (P) 16 A3
Bhawani Pangri 77 G1
Bhawanigarh 17 H6
Bhawanipatna 81 H1
Bhawanipur (Ba) 59 E2
Bhawanipur (N) 25 E6
Bhawanipur (Utt) 38 B4
Bhawanipur (Ass) 41 H3
Bhawanipur Rajdham
    39 H5
Bhawari 32 B5
Bhawatra 49 F2
Bhawi 32 C4
Bhawra 66 D2
Bhayandar 76 A3
Bhayavadar 62 D3
Bhedarganj (Ba) 59 G5
Bheemunipatnam 81 H6
Bhela (J&K) 13 G5
Bhela (Mad) 34 B5
Bhelai 69 F2
Bheldi 38 C5
Bhelsi 53 G2
Bhelu 32 B1
Bhera (P) 16 B1
Bheraghat 53 H5
Bheramara (Ba) 58 C3
Bherandiala 48 C4
Bherya 95 E1
Bhesan 63 E3
Bhesawa 33 G2
Bhesola 51 F5
Bheta 36 C2
Bhetiara 19 F5
Bhetnanda 32 B4
Bhichor 51 F1

Bhigvan 77 E5
Bhikamkor 32 A3
Bhikangaon 65 H3
Bhikhi 17 G6
Bhikia Sain 23 G2
Bhikkiwind 17 E4
Bhikma Thori (N) 38 C1
Bhikorai Juni 31 G3
Bhila Hithar (P) 17 E4
Bhilai 68 D4
Bhilari 49 G3
Bhilka 62 D4
Bhiloda 50 B4
Bhilori 34 C5
Bhilwal 36 C3
Bhilwara 33 E6
Bhim 32 D5
Bhim Tal 23 H2
Bhimadevarpalli 79 G6
Bhimadolu 88 C3
Bhimanapalli 87 F2
Bhimasar (Guj) 48 D5
Bhimasar (Guj) 49 E5
Bhimashankar 76 C3
Bhimavaram 88 D3
Bhimgara 57 H4
Bhimgarh 67 H2
Bhimkatta 48 D6
Bhimnath 63 G2
Bhimora 63 F2
Bhimphedi (N) 38 C1
Bhimpur 66 C3
Bhimpura 37 H5
Bhimpuram 82 A3
Bhimrad 63 F2
Bhina 33 E4
Bhind 35 F3
Bhindar 50 D2
Bhindosi 22 B6
Bhinga 25 E6
Bhinmal 49 H1
Bhira (Utt) 24 B5
Bhira (Mah) 76 B5
Bhiragaon 80 C1
Bhirnbar 12 D5
Bhirrana 21 G2
Bhirvada 84 C4
Bhisi 67 G6
Bhitala (P) 30 D5
Bhitania (N) 24 B4
Bhitarwar 35 E5
Bhitia 57 G1
Bhiv Dhanora 77 F2
Bhiwandi 76 B3
Bhiwani 21 H4
Bhiwani Mandi 51 G2
Bhiwapur 67 G5
Bhiyar 31 F4
Bho Asal (P) 16 D4
Bhogapuram 81 H6
Bhogarmang (P) 12 C2
Bhogat 62 B2
Bhognipur 35 H4
Bhogpur Sirwal 17 G3
Bhograi 71 H3
Bhogriwala 18 C6
Bhoika 63 G1
Bhoj 84 D3
Bhojasar 32 B2
Bhojo 43 H2
Bhojpur (N) 24 D6, 39 G2
Bhojpur (Utt) 23 F3
Bhojpur (Utt) 36 B4
Bhojpur (Bih) 38 A5
Bhojpur (Ori) 70 B3
Bhojudih 57 F4
Bhojupura 23 G4
Bhokar 78 D3

Bhokardan 65 H6
Bhola (Ba) 59 G6
Bhola 22 C3
Bhola Hat (Ba) 58 B1
Bholath 17 G3
Bholawat 62 D5
Bholi (N) 25 E2
Bhom 84 B1
Bhoman Shah (P) 16 C5
Bhondiapara 68 C6
Bhongaon 35 G2
Bhongir 87 F1
Bhongra 51 E4
Bhonkani (P) 16 B2
Bhopa 22 D2
Bhopal 52 C5
Bhopalpatnam 80 B4
Bhopalwala (P) 17 E1
Bhor 76 C6
Bhoranj 18 B3
Bhore 38 A4
Bhorila (P) 48 D1
Bhorol 49 F2
Bhorvadi 77 E3
Bhos 77 G2
Bhosa 77 F6
Bhotaor 14 B6
Bhotemari (Ba) 40 D4
Bhowa (N) 25 E6
Bhowali 23 H2
Bhowrah 57 F4
Bhuana 30 D3
Bhuban 71 E5
Bhubaneswar 71 E6, 83 E1
Bhuchal (P) 12 A6
Bhud 13 G6
Bhudgaon 84 D3
Bhuj 48 C5
Bhujpur 48 B6
Bhukan 31 H5
Bhukarheri 22 D2
Bhum 77 G5
Bhun 84 B3
Bhunanahalli 95 E2
Bhunarheri 18 A6
Bhundri 17 G4
Bhundsi 22 B5
Bhunga 17 H3
Bhuntar 18 B2
Bhura 24 C6
Bhurchaur (N) 25 E4
Bhurgaon 41 G2
Bhuri 53 G4
Bhurkarka 21 E3
Bhurkunj 69 F4
Bhusandpur 82 D1
Bhusawal 65 G5
Bhushana (Ba) 59 E5
Bhutaha (N) 39 H3
Bhutapandi 98 D5
Bhuttewala 31 E1
Bhuvanagiri 96 D4
Biadola 40 B5
Biaora 52 B4
Biar (C) 19 G3
Biarai (P) 12 B1
Biarasar 21 E4
Biau 31 F4
Bibinagar 87 F1
Bibipet 79 F5
Bicaneri 20 A5
Bichchia 54 B6
Bichhia 68 B1
Bichhua 67 G3
Bichkurda 78 D5
Bicholim 84 C5
Bid (Mah) 77 G4
Bid (Mah) 84 C3

Bidada 48 B6
Bidar 78 D6
Bidasar 21 E6
Bidauli 22 B2
Bidhau 36 A4
Bidhuna 35 H3
Bidi 85 E6
Bidkingaon 77 G2
Bidsangri 77 F4
Bidupur 38 D5
Bidwal 51 F6
Bidyakot (Ba) 59 H4
Biey (C) 19 H3
Bigga 20 D5
Bighapur 36 B4
Bigod 33 F6
Biha (P) 12 A1
Bihali (P) 12 B3
Biharda 57 G6
Bihariganj 39 G5
Biharigarh 18 D6
Biharpur 55 F5
Bihar Sharif 38 D6, 56 D1
Bihpur 39 G6
Bihpuriagaon 43 F2
Bihta 38 C6
Bihuguri 42 C3
Bijainagar 33 E5
Bijaipur (Mad) 34 C4
Bijaipur (Utt) 38 A3
Bijalighat 42 A4
Bijamal 69 H6
Bijapur (Raj) 50 B1
Bijapur (Mad) 80 C4
Bijapur (Ori) 82 A2
Bijapur (Kar) 85 G3
Bijauri (N) 25 F5
Bijawal 30 D5
Bijawar 53 H2
Bijaybati 72 B3
Bijbihar 13 F4
Bijepur (Ori) 69 H4
Bijepur (Ori) 81 H2
Bijeraghogarh 54 B3
Bijiang (C) 45 H4
Bijnapalli 86 D3
Bijnar 23 E2
Bijnaur 36 B3
Bijni (Utt) 19 E6, 23 E1
Bijni (Ass) 41 G3
Bijoli 35 F6
Bijolia 33 G6
Bijrotha 53 E1
Bijsipur 55 F1
Bijua 24 B5
Bikaner (N) 20 B5
Bikaner (Har) 22 B5
Bikapur 37 E3
Bikarni 50 B2
Bikkatti 95 E4
Biknur 79 E5
Bikram 38 C6
Bikramganj 38 B6
Bilaigarh 69 F3
Bilar 49 H1
Bilara 32 C4
Bilari 23 F4
Bilariaganj 37 G4
Bilasi 84 C2
Bilaspur (Him) 18 B4
Bilaspur (Har) 18 C6
Bilaspur (Utt) 22 D5
Bilaspur (Utt) 23 G3
Bilaspur (Utt) 25 E6
Bilaspur (Mad) 69 E2
Bilaua 35 E4
Bilaur 13 G6

Bilauri (N) 24 A4
Bilchod 91 F2
Bildi 63 E3
Bilehra 36 C2
Bilga 17 G4
Bilgaon 34 D4
Bilgi (Kar) 85 G4
Bilgi (Kar) 90 C3
Bilgram 36 A2
Bilhaur 36 A3
Bilheri 54 A4
Bilimora 64 A5
Bilkhawtlir 60 D3
Bilkheri 53 G6
Billun 21 E4
Biloi 30 C3
Biloli 78 D4
Bilona 34 A3
Biloni 34 C3
Bilonia 52 C2
Bilqisganj 52 C6
Bilsanda 23 H5
Bilsar 37 E2
Bilsawar 34 D1
Bilsi 23 F5
Bilthar 38 A4
Bimbala 70 D4
Bimgal 79 E4
Bina Etawa 53 E3
Binaganj 52 B3
Binaikgaon (N) 24 B2
Binakanahalli 95 F3
Binasar 21 F5
Binauli 22 C3
Binaur 36 A4
Binauti (Ba) 59 H4
Binawar 23 G5
Binawas 32 C4
Binda Diara 39 F6
Bindiganavalle 91 G6
Bindki 36 B4
Bindra Nawagarh 69 E6
Bindula 27 F6
Binewal 18 A4
Bini 27 G6
Binjasar 20 C5
Binjbaila 20 C2
Binjharpur 71 F5
Binjorai 31 F3
Binka 70 A5
Binnadesar 21 E5
Binodepur (Ba) 59 E5
Binota 51 E2
Binpur 71 G1
Binur 80 D2
Binusuli 81 F3
Biposi Najafgarh 36 B4
Bipulashar (Ba) 59 H6
Bir (P) 12 B3
Bir (Him) 18 B2
Bir (Raj) 33 E4
Bir (Mad) 66 A2
Bira 54 A1
Biraba (Ba) 59 G4
Biraicha 37 H2
Birampur 72 A3
Biramsar 31 E2
Biratnagar (N) 39 H3
Birdha 53 E2
Birdpur 37 G1
Birganj (Ba) 40 C5
Birganj (N) 38 C2
Birgudi 69 E6
Birhar 37 G3
Biri Bazar (N) 25 H6
Birjnagar 55 G4
Birk 17 G4

Birkali 21 E3
Birkera 70 C2
Birkur 78 D3
Birlokha 32 B2
Birmaharaipur 70 A5
Birmana 20 C3
Birme 54 B3
Birmitrapur 70 B1
Birnagar 58 C5
Birni 57 E3
Biron 37 H5
Birpara 40 D3
Birpur (Mad) 34 C4
Birpur (Bih) 39 G3
Birpur Katra 36 D2
Birsingpur 54 C2
Birur 91 F4
Birvada 76 C6
Bisai 71 F2
Bisala 31 F5
Bisalpur 23 H5
Bisambharpur 55 H5
Bisauli 23 F5
Bisenda 36 B6
Bishamagiri 82 B3
Bishambharpur 38 A5
Bishanwara 52 B1
Bishenpur 61 E2
Bishnah 13 F6
Bishnath 43 E3
Bishnupur (Ba) 59 G2
Bishnupur 72 1B
Bishrampur 55 G5
Bishunpur (Bih) 40 A5
Bishunpur (Bih) 56 B5
Bishunpur Sundar 39 G4
Bishunpura 38 A3
Biskohar 37 F1
Bisra 70 C2
Bisrampur 56 A3
Bissamcuttack 81 H2
Bissau 21 F5
Bistan 65 G3
Bistbara (N) 25 E2
Bisungarh 57 E3
Biswan 36 C1
Biswanath (Ba) 60 A1
Bitangal (Ba) 59 H2
Bitargaon 78 D2
Bithli 68 B3
Bithmara 21 H2
Bithnok 20 A6
Bithur 36 A3
Bitragunta 93 F2
Bitsaun 14 A5
Bizang (N) 61 F4
Boath 79 E3
Bobarlanka 88 B5
Bobbili 81 H4
Bobi (P) 30 A5
Boblad (Mah) 85 F2
Boblad (Kar) 85 G2
Bobleshwar 85 F3
Bochaha 38 D4
Bochegaon 77 H2
Boda (Ba) 40 C4
Bodal Dayaka (P) 16 D5
Bodarwar 37 H3
Bodeli 64 C2
Bodhgaya 56 C2
Bodh Kharbu 14 A2
Bodhan (And) 78 D4
Bodhan (Kar) 86 A1
Bodhegaon 77 F3
Bodinayakkanur 98 D1
Bodo Raruan 71 E2
Bodri 54 D5

Bodvad 65 H5
Boge (C) 29 G3
Bogra (Ba) 58 D1
Bogudega 69 H1
Boha (Pun) 21 G1
Boha (Raj) 30 D5
Bohana 21 H5
Bohar 22 B3
Boipariguda 81 F4
Boirani 82 C2
Boisar 76 A2
Bokajan 43 F4
Bokakhat 43 E3
Bokaro Steel City 57 E4
Bokhrata 65 E3
Boko 41 H5
Bokri 48 D6
Bolangir 69 H5
Bolba 70 B1
Bolgarh 70 D6
Bolia 51 H3
Boljang 61 G2
Bolkheraghat 51 G4
Bolpur 58 A4
Bolthan 77 F1
Bolung 28 B5
Bomak 28 A5
Bombal (M) 43 H6
Bombay 76 A3-4
Bomdi La 42 C1
Bomdo 27 H4
Bommagondenkere 91 G2
Bonaigarh 70 C3
Bonakalu 88 A2
Bong (M) 75 F4
Bongaigon 41 G3
Bongbal Khulen 61 G2
Bopalapaddi 87 F4
Borabas 51 G1
Borai 81 E1
Boran 69 F6
Boratal (P) 16 A6
Bordehi 67 E2
Bordha 66 D1
Bordi 76 A1
Bordoloni 43 G1
Borduria 44 B2
Borduttighat 43 F2
Boren (P) 20 A4
Borgampad 88 B1
Borgaon (Mad) 66 A3
Borgaon (Mah) 67 F5
Borgaon (Mah) 77 H4
Borgaon Manju 66 C5
Borghat 65 F3
Bori (Mah) 66 D6
Bori (Mah) 67 G5
Bori (Mah) 76 D3
Bori (Mah) 78 B2
Bori (Mah) 78 B5
Bori (Mah) 79 F2
Boria 63 G1
Boria Tibhu 68 C6
Borigumma 81 F3
Borivili 76 A3
Borjhar 65 E1
Borkhedi 67 F5
Borla 68 C2
Borlai Panchaitar 76 A6
Borli (P) 48 D2
Borpani 42 B5
Borsad 64 B1
Borsi 68 D5
Bortalao 68 B4
Boru 27 G5
Borwa 32 D2
Bosana 33 F1
Bosun 32 D1

Botad 63 F2
Botavad 65 H5
Bote 76 D3
Both 34 A6
Bothidih 69 E5
Boturakachar 69 H1
Brahmagiri 83 E2
Brahmanbaria (Ba) 59 H3
Brahmand 53 G6
Brahmando 82 D2
Brahmangaon (Mah) 64 D6
Brahmangaon (Mad) 65 F2
Brahmanwade 76 C3
Brahmapuri 85 F1
Brahmaur 18 A1
Brakmakund 28 C6
Bramhapari 67 H6
Bridgmanganj 37 G2
Brikutsa (Ba) 58 C2
Brindavan Gardens 95 E1
Bruini 28 C3
Bualpui 60 D3
Buanlung (M) 75 E1
Buarpui 60 C5
Bubshahr 21 E1
Buchawas 21 F4
Bucheke (P) 16 C4
Buchiana (P) 16 C3
Buchiredipalem 93 F2
Buchya (P) 30 B5
Bud Bud 58 A5
Budabal 69 G6
Budagud 82 A1
Budaguda 82 B1
Budal (P) 12 A2
Budalur 96 C5
Budarasingi 82 B4
Budaun 23 F5
Budge Budge 72 B1
Budh (Aru) 28 D6
Budh (Mah) 76 D6, 84 D1
Budha Khera 22 A2
Budhabar 17 G2
Budhal 13 E4
Budhar Dhanpuri 54 C5
Budhargarh 84 C4
Budhbare (N) 40 A2
Budhhata (Ba) 72 D1
Budhi 17 G1
Budhlada 21 G1
Budikote 92 C6
Budithapalem 87 G6
Budni 52 D6
Budnur 85 F4
Bugga (P) 16 A1
Bugian 20 C2
Buguda 82 C2
Bugwah (Ba) 41 E5
Buhari 64 B5
Buhlewal (P) 16 C5
Buj 51 G2
Bukar 31 E5
Bukerani (P) 30 A6
Bukhari (P) 16 A3
Bukkapatna 91 G4
Bukkapatnam 92 B3
Bukpui 60 D5
Bulandshahr 22 D5
Buldana 65 H6
Buldega 69 H1
Bulgai (P) 30 A6
Bulhowal 17 G3
Bulri (P) 47 H1
Bulvad 85 F3
Bumhkang (M) 45 F2
Bunar 81 G2
Bundi 33 G6
Bundra 30 D4

Bundra Lus (P) 48 C3
Bundu 57 E5
Bunga Hayit (P) 16 C5
Bungidhar 23 G1
Bungilang 74 D1
Buni 23 E1
Bupania 22 B4
Bura Mayang 42 B4
Buragaon 42 D4
Burail 13 F1
Burakek 43 E4
Burawal (P) 12 D1
Burdapur 78 A5
Burdeli 68 C3
Burdun Gompa 14 B5
Burera 34 B5
Burgahan 69 F2
Burgam 80 D5
Burghat (Ba) 60 B6
Burhana 22 C3
Burhanpur 66 A4
Buri Bazar 61 F2
Buri Khamar 41 G3
Buriali (N) 25 E4
Burichang (Ba) 59 H4
Burigaon 42 B3
Burighat (Ba) 60 B6
Buriya 18 C6
Burlina 54 C5
Burmu 56 D4
Burnpur 57 G4
Burrakayakalota 92 C4
Bursu 33 E2
Burti 85 F1
Burtibang (N) 25 G5
Buruqqu 14 A2
Burwa 54 D3
Burwan (Barddhaman)
    58 A5
Busal (P) 16 C1
Busana 22 A4
Busegaon 84 D1
Butala Sharm Singh (P)
    17 E2
Butana 22 B3
Butati 32 D2
Butewala (P) 16 B3
Buthera 21 G4
Buthidaung (M) 74 C5
Buthpur 86 D3
Butram 66 C3
Buttayyagudem 80 A5
Butwal (N) 25 H6
Buxa Duar (B) 41 E3
Buxar 38 A6
Buzo (M) 75 F6
Bwechaung (M) 75 F6
Byadgi 90 D2
Byakar Dzong (B) 41 G1
Byansghat 23 F1

Cabo da Rama 90 A1
Cadanjo (P) 47 F3
Calcutta 72 B-C1
Calicut (Ker) see Kozhi-
    kode
Calicut 100 B6
Cambay 64 A2
Campierganj 37 H2
Canning 72 C2
Captainganj (Utt) 37 F3
Captainganj (Utt) 37 H2,
    38 B2
Castle Rock 84 D6
Chabal 17 F3
Chabattia 23 G2
Chabi 54 B6
Chabiana (P) 16 C6

Chabiana (P) 20 C1
Chabrang (C) 19 H3
Chabua 44 A1
Chachar (P) 16 A1
Chachar 55 F3
Chachauda 51 G3
Chachaura 52 B3
Chachiorten (C) 29 G2
Chachor 51 G2
Chachot 18 B3
Chachro (P) 48 D1
Chadchan 85 G2
Chadi 32 B2
Chagalamarri 92 D1
Chagaon 79 G4
Chahardi 65 F4
Chahtung (M) 45 G3
Chaibasa 71 E1
Chaikambao 42 D6
Chail (Him) 18 C4
Chail (Utt) 36 D6
Chailai Pathan (P) 12 B1
Chailan (P) 48 C1
Chaingtso (C) 45 H6
Chainpur (N) 24 C2
Chainpur (N) 39 H2
Chainpur (Utt) 55 H1
Chainpur (Bih) 56 B5
Chainpur (Bih) 56 A3
Chaipur 65 H3
Chairaiya 38 C3
Chaital 72 C1
Chaitma 69 F1
Chaitrori 31 E5
Chak (P) 20 A2
Chak Amru 17 F1
Chak Beli (P) 12 B5
Chak Bowal 13 F6
Chak Chaddhri (P) 16 C2
Chak Mahan Bhadar 17 E6
Chak Paddar 12 D3
Chak Sana 34 D2
Chak Swari 12 D5
Chakai (P) 12 B1
Chakai 57 F2
Chakalia 43 H2
Chakan 76 C4
Chakavel 92 B4
Chakchoka 41 E3
Chakdaha 58 C5
Chakesar (P) 12 A1
Chakhla 67 F1
Chakia (Bih) 38 C4
Chakia (Utt) 55 G1
Chakkar (P) 30 A6
Chakki 17 G1
Chakothi 12 C3
Chakpikarong 61 F3
Chakradharpur 57 E6
Chakrata 18 D5
Chakri (P) 12 B5
Chakri (P) 12 C6
Chaksu 33 H3
Chakur (Mah) 78 B5
Chakur (Mah) 78 B6
Chakwadam (M) 45 G1
Chakwal (P) 12 B6
Chalakudi 95 E6
Chalala 63 F4
Chalapalle 88 C4
Chalat 94 C2
Chalisgaon 65 F6
Chalkoi 21 F4
Chalkuri 87 G3
Challakere 91 G3
Chalong 61 F3
Chalunka (P) 14 B1
Chamakpur 70 D2

Chamarajnagar 95 F3
Chamarchi (B) 40 D2
Chamardi 63 G3
Chamba 19 E6
Chambi 13 F6
Chamiari 17 F2
Chamkor 18 A5
Chamoli cum Gopeshwar
    19 G6
Champa 69 F2
Champadanga 58 A6
Champahati 72 C1
Champai 61 E5
Champanagar 39 H5
Champaner 64 C1
Champaneri 33 F5
Champapur 38 C2
Champawat 24 A2
Champua 71 E2
Chamrat 14 B6
Chamrupur 37 E1
Chamu 32 A3
Chamursi 79 H1
Chamutong (C) 29 G5
Chanagiri 91 E3
Chanarh 79 E2
Chanari 56 A1
Chanarthal 18 A6
Chanas 13 F5
Chanasma 49 G4
Chanchra (Ba) 73 H1
Chand (Bih) 55 H1
Chand (Mah) 67 G2
Chanda 37 E4
Chandaka 71 E6
Chandampet 87 F3
Chandan 57 G2
Chandanbaisa (Ba) 59 E2
Chandankheri 86 B1
Chandankiari 57 F4
Chandanpur 25 F6
Chandapar 37 G1
Chandarni 50 B4
Chandarpur 69 G3
Chandas 78 B1
Chandauli 37 G6
Chandaus 22 D5
Chandausi 23 F4
Chandaut 35 H5
Chandawal 32 C4
Chandawari 62 D4
Chandbaja 17 F5
Chandbali 71 G5
Chand Bhan 17 F6
Chandel 61 F3
Chandera 53 G1
Chanderi (Mad) 53 E2
Chanderi (Utt) 53 G2
Chandernagore 58 B6
Chandesra 31 G5
Chand Ghat (Ba) 60 B1
Chandha 55 F4
Chandhan 31 F2
Chandi (Bih) 38 D6
Chandi (Mah) 77 F3
Chandia 54 B4
Chandigarh 18 B5
Chandil 57 E6
Chandina (Ba) 59 H5
Chandio 33 H2
Chandipur 71 H4
Chandiput 82 B3
Chandisar 49 H3
Chandla (Ba) 59 H4
Chandla 54 A1
Chandli 62 D2
Chandma 33 G3

Chandni (Raj) 20 B6
Chandni (Mad) 66 A4
Chandod 64 B2
Chandol 65 H6
Chandpara 58 C6
Chandpur (Ba) 59 G5
Chandpur (Ba) 74 B2
Chandpur (Utt) 23 E3
Chandpur (Utt) 36 B5
Chandpur (Mad) 64 D2
Chandpur (Ori) 70 D4
Chandra 71 H1
Chandragadi (N) 40 A3
Chandraghona (Ba) 74 B1
Chandragiri (Ori) 81 G3
Chandragiri (Ori) 82 B3
Chandragiri (And) 93 E4
Chandragutti 90 C2
Chandrakona 57 H6
Chandrakona Road 57 H6
Chandrala 50 A5
Chandrapur (Mah) 79 G1
Chandrapur (Ori) 82 A2
Chandrapura 57 E4
Chandrapuri 19 F6
Chandrasadhubari 60 A4
Chandrasekharapuram
    87 F6
Chandrehi 54 D3
Chandrora 49 G4
Chandru 14 A6
Chandrupatla 80 B5
Chandsain 33 G4
Chandui 55 H2
Chandupura 34 D4
Chandur (Mah) 76 D1
Chandur (Mah) 79 G2
Chandur (And) 87 F2
Chandur (Mah) 66 D5
Chandur Bazar 66 D4
Chandura (Ba) 59 H3
Chanduria 58 D6
Chandvad 64 D6
Chandwa 56 C4
Chandwaji 33 H2
Chandwak 37 G6
Chandwasa 51 G3
Chang (C) 27 E3
Chang 22 A3
Changanassery 98 B2
Changannur 98 B3
Changla Gali (P) 12 B3
Changlung 14 C1
Changoi 21 F4
Changomal 86 D2
Changrabadha 40 C4
Changtrong (C) 27 E3
Changtsu (C) 26 A2
Changyak 44 B2
Changyuala 101 G4
Chanho 56 C4
Chani 66 B6
Channapatana 95 G1
Channarayapatna 91 F6
Channera 66 B2
Chanod 32 B6
Chanowali 13 E4
Chanpa 67 G5
Chanpatia 38 B2
Chansura 54 C4
Chantam 28 C6
Chanthang 40 C1
Chantongia 43 H3
Chanugondla 86 C6
Chanumla 101 F3
Chao (C) 27 E1
Chaoke 17 G6
Chaorokiagaon 43 G2

Chapadgaon 77 F3
Chapajhar 69 E5
Chapaka (P) 30 B1
Chapanalla 42 D4
Chapar (J&K) 13 G6
Chapar (Ass) 41 G4
Chapara 82 B4
Chaparmukh 42 C4
Chapora 84 C5
Chappar (P) 12 C4
Chapra (Bih) 38 C5
Chapra (Bih) 39 H5
Chapra (Mad) 52 A6, 66 A1
Chapra (Wbg) 58 C4
Chapram 39 F5
Chaprar (P) 13 E6
Chaprar 21 H4
Char (J&K) 14 C5
Char (Him) 18 A1
Char Alexander (Ba) 73 H1
Char Bansi (Ba) 59 G6
Char Bhadrasan (Ba) 59 F4
Char Gazi (Ba) 73 H1
Char Haim (Ba) 59 G5
Char Jagabandhu (Ba)
    59 H6
Char Lalmohan (Ba) 73 G2
Char Manpura (Ba) 73 H2
Char Matua (Ba) 59 H6
Charadva 49 E6
Charakunda 87 E3
Charalia Hat (Ba) 74 B1
Charama 68 D6
Charamaddi (Ba) 73 G1
Charambadi 95 E3
Charan 84 C2
Charang 19 E3
Charangaon 76 D1
Charanwas 33 E2
Charap (C) 26 C4
Charasa 14 C1
Charaut 39 E3
Charduar 42 D2
Charegaon 68 A2
Chareimna 28 D5
Chargram (Ba) 60 C1
Charhanta 54 C3
Charikot (N) 39 E1
Charkaria 55 G2
Charkha 63 F4
Charkhai (Ba) 60 B1
Charkhardi 63 E3
Charkhari 35 H6
Charkhi Dadri 22 A4
Charmadi 90 D6
Charmal 70 B4
Charme (C) 26 D4
Charnali (P) 16 A2
Charpokhri 38 B6
Charthana 78 A2
Charthari 37 G2
Charthawal 22 C2
Charwa 66 B2
Charwan 32 B5
Chas (Wbg) 57 F4
Chas (Mah) 76 C4
Chassad 61 G1
Chat (M) 75 F3
Chat Bamori 52 D3
Chatalpar (Ba) 59 H3
Chataparti 91 G2
Chatar 62 D2
Chatari 78 D2
Chatarpur 53 H1
Chatgaon 80 A1
Chatmohar (Ba) 58 D3
Chatoli 52 D3
Chaton 43 F6

Chatori 78 B4
Chatra (N) 39 H2
Chatra (Bih) 56 C3
Chatra (Wbg)58 A3
Chatrappatti 95 H6
Chatrapur 82 C3
Chatru 13 G4
Chatta (P) 16 D1
Chattak (Ba) 60 A1
Chattanahalli 95 E2
Chattargarh 20 B4
Chatukhera Sondia 52 B4
Chatung 28 D3
Chatwai 67 G2
Chau 32 D1
Chaube 57 E3
Chaubia 35 G2
Chaubisho (N) 24 C1
Chaudda (Ba) 59 H5
Chaudepalle 92 D5
Chaudni 18 C5
Chaudri Ka Nagal 21 H6
Chaugacha (Ba) 58 D5
Chaugain 38 B6
Chauk (M) 75 H5
Chauk (Utt) 37 H2
Chauk (Mah) 76 B4
Chauka 53 H2
Chaukhandi (P) 47 E1
Chaukhutia 23 G1
Chauki (*) 13 F1
Chauki (Mad) 65 H1
Chauki Maniar 18 A3
Chaukpu (M) 45 E2
Chaukrauda 34 D3
Chauku S1 H6
Chaul 76 A5
Chaulpani 67 F1
Chaung-U (M) 75 G3
Chaunggyank (M) 61 F6
Chaungma (M) 75 H2
Chaungmuktsa (M) 75 E4
Chaungne (M) 74 D6
Chaungwa (M) 61 G6
Chaungyung (M) 75 E4
Chaungyyin (M) 61 G5
Chaungzongyi (M) 75 H3
Chauntra (P) 12 A4
Chauntra (P) 12 B5
Chaupal 18 C4
Chauparan 56 D2
Chaura 101 F3
Chauradadar 68 D1
Chauri (Utt) 37 F2
Chauri (Goa) 90 A1
Chauri Khas 17 H1
Chausa 38 A6
Chausala 77 G4
Chausana 22 C2
Chautam 39 G6
Chauth Ka Barwara 33 H4
Chautha (N) 25 E2
Chavad 63 F3
Chavakkad 94 D6
Chavara 98 B3
Chawand 50 C3
Chawmaw (M) 45 G4
Chawinda (P) 17 E1
Chawngdam (M) 45 G3
Chawngte 60 C6
Chayul (C) 26 D5
Chaz (P) 12 A3
Chebrolu 88 A4
Chechat 51 H2
Chechi 51 F1
Cheingsanu (M) 75 E4
Chejerla 93 E2

Chekawn 60 D5
Chelakara 95 E5
Chelur (Kar) 91 H5
Chelur (Kar) 92 B4
Chelvai 80 A5
Chelyama 57 G4
Chemeti 82 C1
Chemma 81 G3
Chemre 14 D3
Chen 43 H3
Chendebi (B) 41 F1
Chenekotapale 92 A3
Chengalpattu 93 F6
Chengam 96 C2
Chengar Char (Ba) 73 H2
Chengele 28 C4
Chenggalgiri 41 F5
Chengka (C) 45 H4
Chenkatbari 67 E2
Chennimalai 95 H4
Chenuru 93 F3
Chepai (C) 29 H5
Chepang (N) 24 D5
Chepwe 28 A4
Cheraiya 57 E2
Cheran 41 G5
Cherial 79 G6
Cherla 80 C6
Cherlopalle (And) 87 G6
Cherlopalle (And) 91 H2
Cherrapunji 42 A6
Cherukuru 88 A5
Cheruppulasseri 95 E5
Cheruthuruthi 95 E5
Cheruvalli 98 B2
Cheshorr 43 H4
Chetamale 101 F1
Chetiagaon 43 G1
Chetipalaiyam 95 F5
Chetput 96 D1
Chevella 86 D2
Chewara 57 E1
Cheyyur 97 E1
Chhaba 17 F3
Chhabra 52 B2
Chhachhrauli 18 C6
Chhachpur 18 D4
Chhadvel 64 D4
Chhaen 50 D6
Chhaensa 22 C5
Chhajli 21 H1
Chhain 31 G2
Chhaktala 64 D2
Chhalala 63 G1
Chham 19 E5
Chhamb 13 E6
Chhanautiya (N) 38 B1
Chhanbari (Ba) 59 H1
Chhanga Manga (P) 16 D4
Chhani Bari 21 F3
Chhanta 54 C6
Chhanua (Ba) 74 B3
Chhanz 13 E3
Chhapar (Raj) 21 E6
Chhapar (Utt) 22 D2
Chhapera 52 A4
Chhapoli 21 G6
Chhapra (Raj) 32 D1
Chhapra (Bih) 38 D4
Chhaprauli 22 C3
Chhapre (N) 24 C4
Chharah 22 B4
Chharchh 34 C6
Chharra 23 E6
Chhata 22 C6
Chhatapur 39 G4
Chhatardighi (Ba) 58 D2
Chhatarpada 71 F5

Chhati 68 D5
Chhatiain (Ba) 60 A3
Chhatna 57 G5
Chhatrapur 56 B3
Chhattain (Ba) 59 H3
Chhattargam 13 F3
Chhattargul 13 G4
Chhaundan 17 H6
Chhaygaon 42 A4
Chhegaon Makhan 65 H3
Chheligada 82 B3
Chhibramau 35 G2
Chhibro (N) 25 E1
Chhihdipada 70 C4
Chhika 18 C1
Chhila 31 H2
Chhimluang 60 D2
Chhindwara 67 F2
Chhinod 34 B6
Chhipa Barod 52 A2
Chhipaner 66 C1
Chhipawar 66 B2
Chhitar ka Par 31 G5
Chhitauni 38 A2
Chhorang 18 C2
Chhota Baisdia (Ba) 73 G2
Chhota Chhindwara 53 H6
Chhota Donger 80 D3
Chhota Gajara (Ba) 59 H3
Chhoti Sadri 51 E3
Chhuikhadan 68 C4
Chhukha Dzong (B) 41 E2
Chhura 69 E5
Chhuri Hills 55 G6
Chi-Kyaw (M) 75 F6
Chiahpui 61 E3
Chichawatni (P) 16 A5
Chichgarh 68 A5
Chichola 68 B5
Chicholi (Mad) 66 D2
Chicholi (Mad) 67 F4
Chichondi 77 F4
Chichpalli 79 G1
Chichra 71 G1
Chidam (C) 29 G6
Chidambaram 97 E4
Chigateri 91 F1
Chiglai (M) 45 G5
Chihtzelo (C) 45 H3
Chihuapa (C) 45 F6
Chik Banavar 92 A5
Chikal Bhir 77 H4
Chikalda 66 C4
Chikali Kalan 67 F2
Chikalthan (Mah) 77 F1
Chikalthan (Mah) 77 G2
Chikamamdi 87 F2
Chikandi (Ba) 59 F5
Chikar Khas 12 C3
Chikara 51 E2
Chikballapur 92 B5
Chikhli (Raj) 50 D5
Chikhli (Guj) 64 D4
Chikhli (Mah) 66 A6
Chikhli (Mah) 84 D4
Chikitigarh 82 C3
Chikjajur 91 F3
Chikkerur 90 D2
Chikli (Guj) 64 B5
Chikli (Mah) 79 E2
Chiklitan 14 B2
Chikmagalur 91 E5
Chiknayakanahalli 91 G5
Chikodi 84 D4
Chikodi Road 85 E4
Chikong (C) 29 E4
Chikupalle 80 B5
Chilakalurupet 88 A4

Chilakanahatti 91 F1
Chilakhana 41 E4
Chilam 13 F1
Chilamanuru 93 F3
Chilamatturu 92 A4
Chilamullah (P) 47 G2
Chilangdong (C) 29 H6
Chilguda 81 G2
Chilhia 37 G1
Chiling 14 C3
Chilkana 22 C1
Chilkha (N) 24 D3
Chillanwala (P) 12 C6
Chillargi 78 D6
Chillur 91 E3
Chilmari (Ba) 41 E6
Chilong Kungma (C) 15 G5
Chilpa 55 E5
Chilpi 68 C2
Chilupar 37 H4
Chilwani 34 D5
Chilwaria 36 D1
Chimakurti 87 H5
Chimalgi 85 G4
Chimata 87 H6
Chimur 67 G6
Chinari 12 D3
Chinbyit (M) 75 H2
Chinchani 76 A2
Chinchar Gompa (C) 27 E4
Chinchli 85 E3
Chinchner 84 C1
Chincholi (Mah) 77 E5
Chincholi (Kar) 86 C1
Chinchwad 76 C5
Chinda (C) 26 D1
Chindaung (M) 75 G5
Chindru (C) 28 B2
Chineni 13 G5
Chingai 43 G6
Chinghkranghka (M) 45 F5
Chingkou (C) 45 G6
Chingmei 43 H4
Chingyaung (M) 61 G4
Chingyaung (M) 61 H5
Chinhat 36 C2
Chinia 55 H3
Chiniot (P) 16 B3
Chinji (P) 12 A6
Chinkurali 95 E1
Chinna Annaluru 93 F1
Chinna Dharapuram 95 H5
Chinna Ganjam 88 A5
Chinna Salem 96 C3
Chinna Taki 78 C5
Chinnakraka 93 F1
Chinnamandem 92 C4
Chinnamanur 98 D1
Chinoni 34 C4
Chinpurtar (N) 39 E1
Chintaguda 79 G3
Chintakani 80 A5
Chintakunta 86 B6
Chintaladevi 93 F1
Chintalapudi 88 C2
Chintalcheru 87 E1
Chintalnar 80 C5
Chintamani 92 B5
Chintanian 40 C6
Chintapale 81 F6
Chintapalli (Mad) 80 B4
Chintapalli (And) 87 F3
Chinturu 80 D6
Chinur 79 H4
Chiol 64 B6
Chiplun 84 B1
Chipoketami 43 G5

Chipurupalle 81 H5
Chira 24 A2
Chiraghpalli 86 C1
Chirai 32 A3
Chiraidongri 68 A1
Chiraikund 55 F4
Chirak 17 F5
Chirakkal 94 B3
Chirala 88 A5
Chiramana 93 F2
Chirang (B) 41 F2
Chirapatla 66 C2
Chirawa 21 G5
Chirgaon 35 F6
Chiriakot 37 G5
Chirikipadasyasan 82 C2
Chiriya Tapu 100 B6
Chirki 57 E3
Chirod 49 E5
Chiroli Hills 68 B6
Chisapani (N) 39 F2
Chisot 14 A5
Chispani Garhi (N) 38 D1
Chispur 77 G5
Chistian Mandi (P) 20 B1
Chit Frozepur 38 A5
Chital 63 F3
Chitalancheri 95 E6
Chitalwana 49 G1
Chitapur 86 B2
Chitar 32 D4
Chitkal 19 E3
Chitmanikarbaripara (Ba)
  60 B5
Chito 14 A5
Chitoli 34 D5
Chitoor 93 E5
Chitopipalgaon 77 G2
Chitosi (Ba) 59 H5
Chitpalgarh 37 E5
Chitradurga 91 F3
Chitrakot 81 E3
Chitrakut 36 C6, 54 C1
Chitraon 54 D4
Chittagong (Ba) 74 B1
Chittamur 97 E1
Chittanahalli 91 H5
Chittaranjan 57 G4
Chittial 86 D2
Chittivalasa 81 H6
Chittorgarh 51 E1
Chittur 95 F5
Chituh (C) 45 H4
Chitvel 93 E3
Chityal (And) 79 H5
Chityal (And) 87 F2
Chizami 43 G5
Cho Dzong (C) 28 C1
Chobari (Guj) 48 D5
Chobari (Guj) 63 F2
Chochvihire 77 E3
Chodavaram 81 G6, 88 D1
Chodia 20 D4
Chodo 43 F1
Choga (P) 12 A1
Chogallia 23 H3
Chogat 94 D3
Choglamsar 14 D3
Choha Khalsa (P) 12 C5
Choharwa (N) 39 F3
Chohtan 31 F6
Choi (P) 12 A4
Chok 63 G4
Chokan 55 E5
Chokkarlaputtu 81 G4
Chokorgye (C) 26 D2
Chokpot 41 G6
Chokri 63 F1

Cholapur 37 G6
Cholavandam 99 E1
Cholavaram 93 G5
Cholmpuram 98 D3
Choma 51 H4
Chomo Dzong (C) 27 G2
Chomu 33 G2
Chonggye Dzong (C) 26 A3
Chonghymsen 43 G3
Chongmoche (C) 26 A3
Chonkham 28 C6
Chonp 33 H2
Chonta (Ba) 59 H3
Chontson (C) 29 G6
Chopan 55 G2
Chopda 65 G4
Chopra 40 B4
Choranda 64 B2
Chorhat 54 D2
Chorimal 50 B4
Chorivad 50 B4
Chorkai (Ba) 40 D6
Chorkata 57 G3
Chorwad 62 D5
Chorwan 13 F2
Chot (P) 16 B1
Chota Udaipur 64 D2
Chotal (P) 49 E1
Chotala 21 E1
Chotila 63 F1
Chowpani (P) 48 C2
Chuadanga (Ba) 58 D4
Chuang Tong 15 E6
Chuchakwas 22 A4
Chuchekanda (N) 24 C4
Chuda 63 G1
Chuganwan 17 E3
Chuhar Jamali (P) 47 G2
Chuhar Kana (P) 16 D3
Chuharpur 18 D6
Chui 32 D2
Chukmtapalli 80 A2
Chuknagar (Ba) 58 D6
Chumar 15 F6
Chumatang 15 E5
Chumbi 77 G5
Chumdo (C) 28 B1
Chumdo Khyang (C) 26 B4
Chunampettai 97 E2
Chunapughat (Ba) 60 A3
Chunar 55 G1
Chunari 41 G4
Chunawdh 20 C1
Chunchankate 95 E1
Chundi 87 H6
Chunga (P) 14 B1
Chungi (P) 16 D3
Chungkar (B) 42 A2
Chungtia 43 G4
Chungtsa (C) 29 H3
Chunian (P) 16 D4
Chuniba 26 C6
Chupalong (C) 29 H1
Chuprial (P) 12 A1
Chura 63 E3
Churachandpur 61 E3
Churala 79 H1
Churani 23 F1
Churchu 56 D4
Churelia 52 B3
Churelkhera 34 D5
Churgang (C) 15 H6
Churi Ajtgarh 21 F6
Churi Jodhan 21 F6
Churki (Utt) 55 G2
Churki (Mad) 55 G4
Churu 21 F5
Churulia 57 H4

Churup 19 F2
Chusa (C) 29 F4
Chushul 15 F4
Chutak 14 D5
Chutia 42 D3
Clifton (P) 47 E2
Clutterbuckganj 23 G5
Cnuchak (P) 16 C4
Codal 90 B1
Coimbatore 95 F5
Colachel 98 C5
Colgong 39 H6
Colonelganj 36 D2
Comilla (Ba) 59 H5
Contai 72 A3
Cooch Behar 41 E4
Coondapoor 90 B4
Coonoor 95 F4
Copalsar 20 C3
Coromandel 93 G5
Cossimbazar 58 B3
Covelong 93 F6
Cox's Bazar (Ba) 74 B4
Crowpara (Ba) 74 C2
Cuddalore 97 E3
Cuddapah 92 D2
Cumbum 87 G5
Cuncolim 84 C6
Curchorem 84 C6
Cuttack 71 E6

Dabagram 58 B4
Daban (N) 25 F5
Dabar Wahan (P) 30 A1
Dabha 79 H2
Dabhaura 54 C1
Dabhoda 50 A5
Dabhoi 64 C2
Dabhol 84 A1
Dabi (N) 25 G1
Dabihan 38 D4
Dabka (Mad) 34 D5
Dabka (Guj) 64 B2
Dablana 33 G5
Dabli 20 D2
Daboh 35 F5
Dabra (Mad) 35 E5
Dabra (Mad) 69 G3
Dabugam 81 F3
Dabwali 21 E1
Dachepalle 87 H3
Dachung (C) 26 A5
Dachung Yogma 15 F4
Dachuru 93 E2
Dadahu 18 C5
Dadai (P) 12 D1
Dadenggiri 41 F5
Dadhia 33 F3
Dadhiali 63 F4
Dadi 84 D4
Dado Siba 17 H2
Dadon 23 E4
Dadori 34 D5
Dadpar (Ba) 59 G6
Dadrewa 21 F4
Dadri 22 C4
Dadu 21 F1
Dadwara 32 C3
Dag 51 H4
Daga 55 F3
Daganbhuiya (Ba) 59 H6
Dager 13 E5
Daggar (P) 12 A2
Dagmara 39 G4
Dagru 17 F5
Dagshai 18 B5
Dagyeling (C) 26 B3

Dahanu 76 A1
Daharabandar 63 F5
Daharanwala (P) 20 A2
Dahida 63 F4
Dahigaon 66 A5
Dahigaon 77 F2
Dahihanda 66 B5
Dahijuri 71 G1
Dahina 22 A5
Dahinsara 49 E6
Dahivad 65 F4
Dahivadi 84 D1
Dahivel 64 D5
Dahmi 33 G3
Dahmot 17 H5
Daiali Dhani 20 B5
Daidarda 49 G2
Daijar 32 B4
Daikra 32 B3
Dailekh (N) 24 D4
Dainhat 58 B4
Daisara 48 B6
Dakahin Simulea (Ba)
  59 F3
Dakhakot (N) 25 F5
Dakhan 31 H5
Dakhinpara (Ba) 74 C5
Dakoank 101 G6
Dakor 50 B6
Dakupi (Ba) 73 E1
Dala 17 F5
Dalabda 51 F4
Dalash 18 C3
Dalbung 27 H4
Daletma (M) 74 D3
Dalgaon 42 C3
Dalgoma 41 G4
Dalhousie 17 H1
Dalimb 78 A6
Dalkhania 63 E4
Dalkola 40 A5
Dalmau 36 C4
Dalpatpur 53 E3
Dalphu (N) 25 F2
Dalsingh Sarai 39 E5
Daltonganj 56 B3
Dalu 41 F6
Daluabari (Ba) 58 C2
Dalunag 13 H2
Dalwa 20 D5
Dama 49 H3
Damadara 31 E3
Damadua 82 B2
Damak (N) 40 A3
Damakhera 69 E3
Damalchoruvu 93 E5
Daman 64 A4
Damargidda 86 C3
Dambal 85 G4
Dambuk 28 B5
Dambukso 43 E4
Damchara 60 C3
Damdwali (N) 25 E5
Dami 13 F6
Damji (B) 41 E2
Damjipura 63 F3
Dammapeta 88 C2
Damnagar 63 F3
Damni 33 G3
Damni (Mad) 68 D1
Damoh (Mad) 53 G4
Damoh (Mad) 68 B3
Damotse (B) 42 A1
Damra 14 D5
Damrala 63 E3
Damroh 28 A4
Damze (C) 27 F3
Dana (N) 25 H4

Danapur 38 C5
Danauda 21 H2
Danayanicheruvu 92 C3
Danda (Raj) 20 B4
Danda (Raj) 20 D3
Dandakharka (N) 39 G2
Dandaut (P) 17 F1
Dandeldhura (N) 24 B2
Dandeli 84 D6
Dandhera 21 E3
Dandi 64 A4
Dandiganahalli 91 F6
Dandinshirehallu 91 G1
Dandma 21 H4
Dandot (P) 12 B6
Dangarh 68 C5
Dangashilbhata 81 G3
Dangchura 19 F6
Dangiawas 32 B4
Dangri 31 F3
Dangusurada 82 A2
Daniawan 38 D6
Dankaur 22 C5
Dankhar Gompa 19 E2
Danlat 85 F2
Danli 28 B4
Danna 13 E3
Danpur 51 E5
Danta (Raj) 33 F1
Danta (Guj) 50 A3
Dantan 71 H2
Dantewara 80 D4
Dantivada 49 H3
Dantrai 50 A2
Dantur 71 F4
Danwara 51 G6
Danwro 32 B3
Daowala (P) 16 B3
Daphu (B) 40 D2
Dapivli 76 A3
Dapoli 76 B6, 84 A1
Daporijo 27 G5
Dappal 13 E1
Dapur 76 D2
Daraganj 40 C4
Daran Ghati 18 D3
Daranagar (Utt) 23 E3
Daranagar (Utt) 36 D5
Darangibra 43 E6
Darapur (P) 12 C6
Darauli 38 A4
Darba (Har) 21 F2
Darba (Mad) 81 E4
Darbe 57 F3
Darbhanga 39 E4
Darbi 21 F2
Darcha 14 C6
Daregaunra (N) 25 F4
Darekasa 68 B4
Darelo (P) 48 B1
Dargawan 53 G2
Darhal Gangan 12 D5
Darhi 68 D3
Darhial 23 F3
Darhuk 15 E3
Dariapur (Bih) 38 C5
Dariapur (Wbg) 58 B2
Dariawad 51 E3
Dariba 50 D1
Darigawan 56 A1
Darima 55 H6
Daring 27 H6
Daringbadi 82 B1
Darjanwala (P) 16 A2
Darjeeling 40 B2
Darjin 70 C2
Darkha 57 E1
Darkhai (M) 61 E4

Darkoti 18 C4
Darlawn 60 D3
Darli 13 F1
Darma (N) 25 E2
Darman (P) 17 F1
Darman 55 H2
Daro (P) 47 G2
Daroh Khas 18 A2
Darpur 18 C6
Darranga 42 A3
Darsana (Ba) 58 C4
Darsano Chano (P) 47 F1
Darsi 87 H5
Daru Kharika 56 D3
Darugiri 41 G5
Darugmul 13 E2
Darur 85 E3
Darwani (Ba) 40 C5
Darwha 66 D6
Daryabad 36 D2
Daryapur 66 C5
Das 13 F1
Dasada 49 G5
Dasai 51 F6
Dasala 78 A3
Dasamantapur 81 G3
Dasamapatti 96 A2
Dasave 76 C5
Dasghara 58 B6
Dashapalla 70 C6
Dashing Gompa (C) 28 B1
Dasingabadi 82 B2
Daska (P) 17 E1
Daskalgram 58 B4
Daslana 49 H5
Dasmina (Ba) 73 G2
Dasna 22 C4
Daspur (Wbg) 72 A1
Daspur (Ori) 81 G1
Dasua 17 G2
Dasuria (Ba) 58 D3
Dataganj 23 G6
Datha 63 G4
Dathwekyauk Atet (M) 61 G4
Datia 35 E5
Datigaon 51 F6
Datma 41 F3
Dato (P) 48 A2
Datrpur Rakri 17 G2
Dattapulia 58 C5
Dattapur 67 E5
Dattuhar 20 A5
Datwas 33 H3
Daudkandi (Ba) 59 G5
Daudnagar (Bih) 38 D5
Daudnagar (Bih) 56 B1
Daudpur 38 B5
Dauki 42 B6
Daula 22 C3
Daulat (P) 30 B3
Daulat Nagar (P) 12 D6
Daulatabad (Mah) 77 F1
Daulatabad (And) 86 C2
Daulatabad (Tam) 96 A1
Daulathkau (Ba) 73 G1
Daulatpur (Ba) 59 E3
Daulatpur (Ba) 59 E6
Daulatpur (Pun) 17 H2
Daulatpur (Raj) 33 E1
Daulatpur (Wbg) 40 B6
Daulatpur (Mad) 52 B6
Daulatpura 20 C1
Daulia (Ba) 73 G1
Daultala (P) 12 B5
Daund 77 E5
Daura (N) 25 F2
Daurala 22 D3

Dausa 34 A2
Daut (P) 12 B1
Davangere 91 F2
Davri 84 C2
Daw 30 D4
Dawa 32 D3
Dawaniwara 68 A3
Dawarwari 77 G2
Dawasar 20 C4
Dawath 38 B6
Dayul Gompa (C) 29 G3
De (C) 26 D1
Deatra 20 A6
Deb (N) 24 B1
Debari 50 C2
Debhata (Ba) 72 D1
Debiapur 35 G3
Debichaur (N) 38 B1
Debidwar (Ba) 59 H4
Debiganj (Ba) 40 C4
Debikat (N) 25 F6
Debipur 58 C3
Debipura 35 F3
Debra 72 A1
Dechen Dzong (C) 26 A2
Dechu 31 H3
Dedadra 49 G6
Dedan 63 F5
Dedarda 63 G4
Dedasri 31 H1
Dedha 31 E3
Dediapada 64 C3
Dedusar (P) 31 E6
Deeg 34 C1
Degam 82 C2
Deganga 58 C6
Degaon 67 E5
Dehar 18 B3
Dehare 77 E3
Dehej 64 A3
Dehemai 50 B5
Dehgam 50 A5
Dehgaon 53 E5
Dehithan 77 F4
Dehlan 18 A3
Dehlen 17 H5
Dehni 78 D1
Dehori 53 F5
Dehra Dun 19 E6
Dehri (Mad) 52 D3
Dehri (Bih) 56 B1
Dehri (Mad) 65 F2
Deinnyin (M) 61 G5
Dekan 51 F2
Delang 83 E1
Delath 18 C4
Delduar (Ba) 59 F3
Delhi Cantonment 22 B4
Delpatpur 53 G3
Delvad 64 D6
Delwada 63 E5
Delwara 64 A5
Dem (C) 28 A1
Demagiri 60 C6
Demchok 15 G6
Demmi 79 E5
Demra 53 E6
Dena Nanak 17 F2
Dengashi Met 76 B2
Dening 28 C5
Denkanikota 95 H1
Denog 32 A2
Deo 56 B2
Deoban (Utt) 18 D5
Deoban (Har) 22 A2
Deoband 22 D2
Deobhog 81 F2

Deocha 58 A3
Deodha Bhadaur 39 E3
Deodongra 76 B1
Deogad 64 B4
Deogan 71 E5
Deogaon (Raj) 33 G4
Deogaon (Utt) 37 G5
Deogaon (Mad) 54 A4
Deogaon (Mad) 69 E6
Deogaon (Ori) 69 H6
Deogaon (Ori) 71 E4
Deogarh (Raj) 32 D6
Deogarh (Utt) 53 E2
Deogarh (Mad) 54 D4
Deogarh (Ori) 70 C3
Deoghar 57 G2
Deohati 64 D1
Deokali 24 A5
Deokar 68 C3
Deolali 76 C1
Deolali Pravra 77 E2
Deolapar 67 G3
Deolari 66 A3
Deoli (P) 12 C1
Deoli (Raj) 32 C4
Deoli (Raj) 33 G5
Deoli (Mah) 67 E5
Deoli (Ori) 71 G2
Deolia (Raj) 33 F5
Deolia (Guj) 49 E6
Deolia (Raj) 51 E3
Deona Joliani (P) 12 D6
Deopara (Ba) 59 F2
Deopura 33 G6
Deora (Raj) 31 E4
Deora (Mad) 55 F3
Deora (Guj) 62 C3
Deoranian 23 G4
Deorha 18 D4
Deori (Him) 18 C4
Deori (Raj) 34 C6
Deori (Mad) 53 F5
Deori (Mah) 68 B5
Deoria (Utt) 23 H5
Deoria (Bih) 38 C4
Deosari 41 G3
Deosil 55 E4
Deotal 19 G4
Deottana 78 B3
Depal 72 A3
Depalpur 51 G6
Deparkhera 52 D3
Deppeguda 82 A3
Depura 32 A5
Deqen (C) 29 H4
Dera (P) 16 A2
Dera Gopipur 18 A2
Derapur 35 H4
Derasar 20 C6
Derdi 63 E3
Derdi Janbai 63 F3
Derebara 42 D6
Dergaon 43 F3
Deri 35 H5
Dero 31 H3
Derol 50 A4
Deroli 50 B6
Derwa 36 D5
Desabpur (Ba) 58 D6
Desalpur 49 E4
Deshgaon 65 H3
Deshiatoli 40 A4
Deshkit 14 C2
Deshnoke 20 B6
Desilsar 20 B6
Desli 66 C3
Desur 96 D1
Desuri 32 C6

Deswal 32 D2
Detroj 49 H5
Detwara 50 C2
Deulgaon Mahi 77 H1
Deulgaon Raja 77 H1
Deura 76 D6, 84 C1
Devadurga 86 B4
Devakaparam 96 C1
Devakottai 99 G1
Devala 95 E4
Devanakonda 86 C6
Devanhalli 92 B5
Devanur 91 F5
Devaprayag 19 F6
Devapur (And) 79 E2
Devapur (Kar) 86 A4
Devarapalle 88 D2
Devarkadra 86 D3
Devarkonda 87 F3
Devarkulam 98 B3
Devarshola 95 E3
Devarsugur 86 C4
Devgad Baria 50 D6
Devgaon 77 F1
Devgarh (Mah) 76 B6
Devgarh (Mah) 84 B4
Devi Dhura 23 H2
Devigol 13 H5
Devikolam 98 C1
Devikolhi 14 A5
Devikop 90 C1
Devikot 31 F3
Devimane 90 B2
Devipatnam 88 D2
Devipattinam 99 G2
Devla 84 B2
Devlia 49 G6
Devpur 76 D2
Devruk 84 B2
Dewa (Raj) 31 E2
Dewa (Utt) 36 C2
Dewair 32 D6
Dewal 50 C4
Dewal Thai 24 A2
Dewalmari 80 A3
Dewan 64 D6
Dewangiri (B) 42 A2
Dewar Nat 41 E4
Dewara 79 G2
Dewaria 52 B6
Dewas 51 H6
Dewdand 55 F6
Deyai 79 H2
Deyalapura 91 G6
Deyi 33 H5
Dhab 57 E2
Dhaba 20 C3
Dhabai 55 F2
Dhaban (Raj) 20 D2
Dhaban (Raj) 21 E1
Dhabrot 13 E4
Dhagwan 35 H5
Dhaia 20 B5
Dhain 67 E1
Dhaisar 31 F2
Dhaita 64 D4
Dhaje (B) 41 F2
Dhak (P) 16 A1
Dhaka (Ba) 59 G4
Dhaka 38 D3
Dhakadakshin (Ba) 60 B1
Dhakauli 52 D2
Dhakauni 36 B2
Dhakela (N) 24 D5
Dhakki 13 E1
Dhakuakhana 43 G2
Dhalakria 43 G3
Dhalan 13 E5

Dhalbumagarh 71 G1
Dhalghata (Ba) 74 B3
Dhali (N) 25 F4
Dhali 95 G6
Dhalkebar (N) 39 E2
Dhama 70 A4
Dhamak 66 D6
Dhamangaon (Mah) 65 H5
Dhamangaon (Mah) 67 E5
Dhamangaon Khurd 66 A2
Dhamaur 37 E4
Dhamaura (N) 39 E3
Dhambola 50 C4
Dhamda 68 C4
Dhamdaha 39 H5
Dhamdhama 42 A3
Dhamhara Ghat 39 F5
Dhammod 65 G2
Dhamnagar 71 F5
Dhamnand 84 B1
Dhamni (Mad) 55 H4
Dhamni (Bih) 57 H2
Dhamni (Mah) 66 C6
Dhamni (Mah) 78 C2
Dhamnia (Raj) 33 F6
Dhamnia (Mad) 51 F2
Dhamotar 51 F3
Dhampur 23 F3
Dhamrai (Ba) 59 F4
Dhamtan 21 H2
Dhamtari 68 D5
Dhamtaur (P) 12 B3
Dhamthal (P) 17 F1
Dhana 53 F4
Dhanaj 66 D6
Dhanan 12 D4
Dhanana 30 D3
Dhanapur 37 H6
Dhanaria 32 D3
Dhanaula 17 G6
Dhanaulti 19 E6
Dhanaura 23 E3
Dhanauri 21 H1
Dhanbad 57 F4
Dhanbari (Ba) 59 F2
Dhand 33 H2
Dhandalpur 63 F2
Dhandamunda 69 G5
Dhandharphal 76 D2
Dhandhuka 63 G1
Dhandni 21 E6
Dhanepur 37 E2
Dhanera 49 H2
Dhanesa 36 D3
Dhangan 56 C2
Dhangaon 65 H2
Dhangarhi (N) 24 B4
Dhangari 23 G2
Dhangrol (P) 12 C5
Dhani (Raj) 21 E4
Dhani (Utt) 37 G2
Dhaniakhali 58 B6
Dhanin 32 D6
Dhank 62 C3
Dhankakri 53 H6
Dhanki 78 D2
Dhankoli 33 E1
Dhankot 22 B4
Dhankuta (N) 39 H2
Dhano 21 F4
Dhanoa 17 G2
Dhanora (Mah) 64 D4
Dhanora (Mah) 65 G4
Dhanora (Mad) 67 F1
Dhanora (Mah) 68 A6,
   80 A1
Dhanora (Mah) 77 G1
Dhanora (Mad) 80 D1

Dhanpur (Guj) 64 D1
Dhanpur (Mad) 81 E3
Dhansia 21 E4
Dhansimukh 43 E3
Dhansoi 38 A6
Dhansura 50 B5
Dhantola 40 B4
Dhanuka (N) 39 E3
Dhanushkodi 99 H3
Dhanwada 86 C3
Dhanwahi 54 A6
Dhanwar (Bih) 57 E2
Dhanwar (Mad) 68 B2
Dhanyacharanbari 60 B4
Dhaod 33 F1
Dhaoli 65 G4
Dhap (N) 24 B1
Dhapai (P) 16 B6
Dhaparao (C) 19 G4
Dhappa 13 G1
Dhar (Pun) 17 H1
Dhar (Him)18 D3
Dhar (Mad) 65 F1
Dhar (Mah) 65 H6
Dhara 18 C2
Dharakot 82 B2
Dharambandha 69 F5
Dharamgarh 81 G2
Dharampur 64 B6
Dharampura 54 B1
Dharampuri 65 F2
Dharamsala 18 A1
Dharamtul 42 C4
Dharan (N) 39 H3
Dharangaon 65 F5
Dharapuram 95 G5
Dharar 13 E4
Dharchula 24 B1
Dharhara 39 F6
Dhari 63 E4
Dhariala (P) 12 B6
Dharindharo (P) 48 D1
Dhariwal 17 G2
Dharmabad 78 D4
Dharmagar (Ba) 60 A3
Dharmaj 64 A1
Dharmajigudem 88 C3
Dharmal 17 H2
Dharmanagar 60 B2
Dharmapur 100 B4
Dharmapura 91 G3
Dharmapuri 96 A2
Dharmarpuri 79 F4
Dharmastala 90 D6
Dharmavaram 92 B2
Dharmjaygarh 69 G1
Dharmkot 17 G4
Dharmpur (P) 16 C3
Dharmpur 18 C4
Dharmpuri 77 E6
Dharmsal (P) 30 C6
Dharmsala (J&K) 13 E5
Dharmsala (Ori) 71 F5
Dharnaoda 52 C2
Dharni 66 B3
Dharoli 64 B3
Dharsana 64 A5
Dharsinwa 68 D4
Dharson 21 H5
Dharsul 21 G2
Dharuadihi 70 B2
Dharuhera 22 B5
Dharur (Mah) 77 H4
Dharur (And) 86 D2
Dharwad 85 E6
Dharwas 14 A5
Dhasa 63 F3
Dhasai 76 C3

Dhasania 31 H3
Dhata 36 C6
Dhatrat 22 A2
Dhatrial 13 E6
Dhauj 22 C5
Dhaukora (Ba) 59 F4
Dhaulana 22 D4
Dhaunkal (P) 16 D1
Dhaura 53 E2
Dhaurahra 24 C6
Dhaurpur 81 F2
Dhavalgi 85 H4
Dhawalpur 69 E6
Dhawalpuri 77 E3
Dhayda 65 H6
Dhechuapalong (Ba) 74 B4
Dheklajuli 42 C3
Dhekna 66 C2
Dhemaji 43 G1
Dhenkanal 71 E5
Dhenkikot 71 E3
Dheri 13 E4
Dhertalai 66 B4
Dhiawa 33 E1
Dhib Santeka (P) 20 B1
Dhikala 23 F2
Dhikola 33 F6
Dhilwan 17 F3
Dhima 49 F2
Dhindi (N) 24 B2
Dhing 42 C3
Dhinoj 49 H4
Dhipri 34 A5
Dhirasram (Ba) 59 G3
Dhirera 20 C5
Dhiruwas 21 F4
Dhita (N) 25 E3
Dhoa 18 C6
Dhobe 80 C3
Dhobgawan 39 E5
Dhodha (P) 17 E2
Dhodhar 51 F4
Dhodramou 66 C2
Dhoha 34 D4
Dhol 50 C1
Dhola 63 G3
Dhola Ka Gaon 32 B6
Dholan (P) 17 E4
Dholapani 51 E3
Dholera 63 H2
Dholerao 32 C5
Dholesar 31 G3
Dholia (Raj) 31 F2
Dholia (Guj) 50 B3
Dholipal 21 E2
Dholka 49 H6
Dholpur (Raj) 34 D3
Dholpur (Ori) 70 B5
Dholunda 69 H3
Dholvira 48 D4
Dhondhatarai 69 G2
Dhondrai 77 G3
Dhone 86 D6
Dhor Jalgaon 77 F3
Dhoraji 62 D3
Dhorian (P) 12 D6
Dhorighat 37 H4
Dhoriniana 31 F6
Dhorkingaon 77 F2
Dhoro (P) 30 A6
Dhoro Naro (P) 30 B6
Dhorpatan (N) 25 G4
Dhorpur 55 H5
Dhosha 72 C2
Dhotre 77 E2
Dhowa 57 G3
Dhrangadhra 49 F6
Dhrema (P) 16 A2

Dhrmapasha (Ba) 59 H1
Dhrol 62 D1
Dhuanuali 82 D1
Dhudial (P) 12 B5
Dhudial (P) 12 C2
Dhuin (Ba) 60 A6
Dhulasar (Ba) 73 F3
Dhuli (N) 24 C1
Dhulia 65 E5
Dhulian 58 B2
Dhuliana (P) 16 D5
Dhulikhel (N) 38 D1
Dhulkot 65 G3
Dhull 12 D3
Dhuma 53 H6
Dhumri 35 F1
Dhumvad 85 E6
Dhunaghat 23 H2
Dhunat (Ba) 59 E2
Dhundras (N) 24 C3
Dhundsi 90 D1
Dhung (N) 24 B2
Dhupagari 40 D3
Dhupdhara 41 H5
Dhuraia 57 G1
Dhuri (Pun) 17 H6
Dhuri (Mad) 52 D2
Dhuriapar 37 H4
Dhurjanna (N) 24 C4
Dhurki 55 H3
Dhurnal (P) 12 A5
Dhurung (Ba) 74 B3
Dhurwai 35 F6
Dhznasar 21 E3
Dialpura Bhaika 17 F5
Diamond Harbour 72 B2
Dibai 23 E5
Dibni (N) 38 A1
Dibrugarh 43 H1
Dichpalli 79 E4
Didarganj 37 G5
Didauli 23 F4
Didihat 24 A1
Didu 31 G2
Didwana 33 E1
Digah 31 E1
Digaman (N) 24 C3
Digambarpur 72 B2
Digaon 86 B2
Digapahandi 82 C3
Digau 51 F3
Digaura 53 F1
Digboi 44 B1
Digdaul 13 F5
Diggi 33 G4
Digha 71 H3, 72 A3
Dighal 22 B4
Dighalbank 40 A4
Dighaltarang 28 A6
Digharchi 85 E1
Dighi (Bih) 57 F1
Dighi (Mah) 76 A5
Dighinala (Ba) 60 B5
Dighol 77 H4
Dighori 67 H5, 68 A5
Dighwara 38 C5
Digi 82 B1
Digligiri 41 E6
Diglur 78 D5
Dignagar (Wbg) 58 A5
Dignagar (Wbg) 58 C5
Digod 33 H6
Digpait (Ba) 59 E2
Digras (Mah) 78 B2
Digras (Mah) 78 C4
Digras (Mah) 78 D1
Digri (P) 48 A1
Digsar 49 F6

Digtoli 34 C6
Digwal 86 C1
Dihai (M) 61 E6
Dihajan 43 H2
Dihra 56 B1
Dijkot (P) 16 B4
Dijmur 27 H6
Diju 43 F1
Dijungania 42 C1
Dikam 43 H1
Dikling (C) 26 D4
Dikomukh 43 G2
Diktel (N) 39 G2
Dikthan 65 G1
Dilhori 13 E5
Dilkawn 61 E5
Dillikot (N) 24 D3
Dilwara 50 B3
Dilyat (P) 30 B5
Dimapur 43 F5
Dimarkhera 54 B5
Dimbam 95 F3
Dimla (Ba) 40 D4
Dimlo (M) 61 E5
Dina (P) 12 C5
Dinajpur (Ba) 40 C5
Dinanagar (Pun) 17 G2
Dinanagar (Pun) 21 E1
Dinara 38 A6
Dindigul 95 H6, 96 A6
Dindori (Mad) 54 C6
Dindori (Mad) 76 C1
Dindrur 77 H4
Dinga (P) 12 C6
Dingla (N) 39 G2
Dingla (N) 39 H1
Dingna (C) 26 B2
Dinhata 41 E4
Dinjan 44 A1
Dip 52 C5
Dipadih 55 H5
Dipalpur (P) 16 C5
Dipas 21 H6
Diphu 43 E5
Dipling 43 H2
Diplo (P) 48 C2
Dipnagar 38 D6
Diptsang (B) 42 B2
Dirai (Ba) 59 H2
Dirang Dzong 42 C1
Dirba 21 H1
Dirji 42 D2
Deesa 49 H3
Disangmukh 43 G2
Dispur 42 B5
Ditdako 101 G5
Dithori 68 A1
Diu 63 E5
Diuri 24 A3
Diwan Bazar (Ba) 60 B5
Diwanbari (Ba) 60 B5
Diwanganj (Ba) 41 E6
Diwanganj 52 C5
Diwanji 32 B5
Diyodar 49 G3
Do-Im (M) 75 F4
Doani (Ba) 73 F2
Doari 55 E3
Doarian 12 D1
Dob Dabyan 13 F4
Dobata (N) 24 B3
Dobathua 22 D3
Dobbspet 91 H5
Doberan (P) 12 C4
Dobhi 56 C2
Dobrajpur 57 H4
Doburji (P) 17 E5

Dod Belvangala 92 A5
Doda (P) 17 F2
Doda (J&K) 13 G5
Doda (Pun) 17 E6
Doda Gompa (C) 29 G2
Dodaguni 91 G5
Dodballapur 92 A5
Dodda Magge 91 F6
Dodderi 91 G3
Doddumatta 81 E5
Dodi 52 A6
Dodih (P) 16 B2
Dodvad 85 E5
Doga (P) 12 D6
Doga 21 H1
Doggada 23 F1
Dogoli 80 C4
Dohad 50 D6
Dohar (Ba) 59 F4
Dohazari (Ba) 74 B2
Doiangmukh 42 D5
Doimara 42 C2
Doisanagar 56 C5
Doiwala 19 E6
Dolalghat (N) 39 E1
Dolar 66 B4
Dolaria 66 C1
Dolasa 63 E5
Dolasne 76 D3
Doli 32 A4
Dolkharab 76 C2
Dolluang (M) 61 F5
Dolungmukh 43 G1
Dolwan 64 B5
Domaila 23 G1
Domar (Ba) 40 C4
Domariaganj 37 F2
Dombivli 76 B3
Dombri 77 G4
Domchanch 57 E2
Domel (*) 12 C2
Domel (J&K) 13 F6
Domela (P) 12 C1
Domeli (P) 12 C5
Domganj 38 C5
Domka (B) 41 H2
Domkipali 69 G5
Domli 19 E1
Domohani 40 C3
Domukonda 79 E5
Dona Paula 84 C6
Donakonda 87 G5
Donbaik (M) 74 C6
Dondaicha 65 E4
Dong (C) 29 H4
Dong 29 E5
Dongaon 78 B1
Dongar (Guj) 63 G5
Dongar (Mad) 80 D2
Dongargaon (Mah) 68 B4
Dongargaon (Mad) 68 B5
Dongargarh 68 B4
Dongba (C) 25 H1
Dongkar (C) 26 B5
Dongti Pass (C) 29 H2
Donkar (B) 41 H1
Donli 28 C5
Donmatia 42 A5
Donsar (C) 19 H3
Doraha 17 H5
Doranala 87 F5
Dorje Gompa (C) 28 C1
Dorka 54 C4
Dornakal 88 A1
Doronagaon (B) 41 E3
Doru 13 F4
Dorwa 65 H2
Dosapadu 88 C3

Dostpur 37 F4
Dotanang (B) 41 E1
Dotihal 85 H5
Dotria 51 F6
Dou (P) 14 A1
Dowlaiswaram 88 D2
Drafa 62 C2
Draklund 18 A1
Draksharama 89 E3
Dramthal 13 F5
Drang 13 E3
Dranga 13 G5
Drass 13 G2
Dri (C) 28 D4
Drogulika 14 B3
Drowa Gompa (C) 29 F4
Drubil 13 G5
Druk (C) 28 A2
Drummondganj 55 E1
Dsoba (C) 29 F3
Duarmara 44 B1
Dubacherla 88 C3
Dubak 79 F5
Dubari 37 H4
Dubaulia 37 F3
Dubbi 34 A2
Dubere 76 C2
Dubi 34 A4
Dublat 72 B3
Dubra 57 G4
Dubri 41 E4
Duda 49 G1
Dudaberi 31 E5
Dudada 79 F6
Dudda 91 F5
Duddukuru 88 A5
Dudgaon 79 E4
Dudhai 48 C5
Dudhala 63 E4
Dudhalia 50 B5
Dudhani 85 H2
Dudhara 37 G2
Dudhgaon 78 B3
Dudhi 55 G3
Dudhia 50 D6
Dudhnai 41 G5
Dudhnial 12 D2
Dudhsagar 84 C6
Dudi 13 E2
Dudiras 80 D4
Dudkha 49 G4
Dudna 21 F5
Dudu (J&K) 13 G6
Dudu (Raj) 32 D1
Dudu (Raj) 33 F3
Dudwa 24 B4
Duff Dunbhar 18 C1
Dugari 33 H5
Dugasra 52 D4
Duggipar 68 A4
Duggirala 88 B4
Duguvametta 87 F6
Duhubi (N) 39 H3
Dui Yambi 27 E6
Duimial (P) 12 B6
Dujana 22 A4
Dukye Dzong (B) 40 D1
Dulahazara (Ba) 74 B3
Dulai (Ba) 59 E3
Dulai (Raj) 32 C3
Dulanwala (P) 12 D6
Dulhi 24 C5
Duliajan 44 A1
Dulla (P) 12 A5
Dullanan (P) 16 A5
Dullu (N) 24 D3
Dulumbari 60 B5
Dulur 12 C2

Dum Duma 44 B1
Duman (P) 12 B6
Dumanata 80 C2
Dumari 14 A6
Dumaria (Bih) 56 B2
Dumaria (Bih) 71 F1
Dumarpara 55 H6
Dumas 64 A5
Dumbaguda 81 G3
Dumbalo (P) 48 A1
Dumbur 60 B5
Dumgul 13 H1
Dumja (N) 39 E1
Dumka 57 H3
Dumkhal 64 C3
Dumkhar 14 B2
Dummagudem 80 C6
Dumnichanki 42 B4
Dumra (Raj) 21 G6
Dumra (Bih) 38 D3
Dumra (Guj) 48 A6
Dumrahar 55 G4
Dumraon 38 A6
Dumri (Utt) 37 H3
Dumri (Bih) 56 B5
Dumri (Bih) 57 E3
Dumsa 44 B1
Dumte (B) 40 D2
Dumuhan (N) 40 A1
Duna Dzong (B) 41 E2
Dunara 32 A5
Dunawa 67 E3
Dunda 19 E5
Dundlod 21 F6
Dundwaraganj 23 F6
Dunera 17 H1
Dunga Bunga (P) 20 B2
Dungaon 76 B6
Dungarpur (Raj) 50 C4
Dungarpur (Guj) 63 G4
Dungarwatal 49 G1
Dungi 81 H3
Dungla 51 E2
Dungra 50 D5
Dungrana 21 F3
Dungri 50 D6
Dungripali 69 H5
Duni 33 G5
Dunkar (C) 19 H3
Dupadu 87 G5
Dupara 51 H5
Dupchanchia (Ba) 58 D1
Dupugong (C) 29 H3
Duraguda 81 E4
Duraha 52 C5
Durail (Ba) 59 F1
Duraundha 38 B4
Durbaldhan 22 A4
Durg 68 C4
Durgachak 72 B2
Durgada 91 H5
Durgadahalli 92 A5
Durgaon (N) 25 F3
Durgapur (Ba) 58 D2
Durgapur (Ba) 59 G1
Durgapur (Wbg) 57 H5
Durgapur (Wbg) 40 B6
Durgarajupatnam 93 G3
Durgauti 37 H6
Durgi 87 G4
Durgu Kondal 68 C6
Durjana 21 F3
Durkaranja 81 H1
Dusana 65 E4
Duthwa 49 F1
Duttaluru 93 E1
Dutung 15 E6
Duva 49 G2

Duvapera 82 B5
Duvvuru 92 D1
Dwara Bazar (Ba) 60 A1
Dwarahat 23 G1
Dwaranhalli 86 B3
Dwarapudi 89 E2
Dwarband 60 D2
Dwarikhal 23 F1
Dwarka 62 A2
Dwarkaganj 37 E4
Dzachung (C) 29 E4
Dze (C) 26 D3
Dzem (C) 27 F1
Dzeng (C) 27 G2
Dzinchi (C) 26 C2
Dzokang Dzong (C) 29 F1
Dzong (B) 26 A6
Dzong (B) 42 A1
Dzong 42 C1
Dzonga Dzong (B) 40 C2
Dzongutraphuk (C) 29 E3
Dzron (C) 29 H3

Edakkad 94 C3
Edappal 94 D5
Edavanna 94 D4
Edlabad 65 H5
Edugurallapalle 80 C6
Edupadu 80 D6
Eghra 56 B3
Ehadaur 17 G6
Ekangar Sarai 38 D6
Eklingji 50 C2
Ekma 38 B5
Ekoya 101 H5
Eksambe 84 D3
Elamanchili 89 G1
Elavasanur 96 C3
Elavirampannai 99 E3
Elayavor 94 C2
Eleswaram 89 E2
Elgur 80 A2
Elivala 95 E2
Elladakere 91 G4
Ellanuru 92 B2
Ellasiri 93 G4
Ellaturu 87 H3
Elliotganj (Ba) 59 G4
Ellora 77 F1
Elmagonda 80 C5
Elumalai 99 E1
Eluru 88 C3
Elwinpet 82 A4
Emaluru 80 C6
Emani 88 B4
Embal 99 G1
Embragon 28 B4
Eminabad (P) 17 E2
Emmiganur 86 A6
Emmiganuru 86 C5
Endaka (C) 27 E3
Enfok 101 G5
English Bazar 58 A1
Enneli 79 F6
Ennore 93 G5
Eppodumvernran 99 E3
Eraballi 91 G3
Erachh 35 G5
Erad 15 E3
Erakampatti 95 G5
Eral 99 E4
Erannoli 94 C3
Erattupeta 98 C2
Erdangkramsa 43 E4
Erimayur 95 E6
Erinpura 32 B6

Eriyodi 96 A6
Erki 56 D6
Ernakulam 98 B1
Erode 95 H4
Erpedu 93 F4
Erragondapalem 87 G4
Erragundlakota 93 E3
Erraguntla 92 C2
Erravaripalem 93 E4
Ersama 71 F6
Erumaipatti 96 A4
Eruru 86 A6
Eruvadi 98 D5
Etah 35 F1
Etawah (Raj) 34 A6
Etawah (Utt) 35 F3
Etikoppaka 89 F1
Etmadpur 35 E2
Ettaiyapuram 99 E3
Ettapur 96 B3
Ettumanur 98 B2
Eturnagaram 80 A5
Ezas 14 C3

Fagu 18 C4
Faisalabad (P) 16 B3
Faizabad 37 E3
Faizpur 65 H4
Fakhrupur 36 D1
Fakiraghona (Ba) 74 B3
Falakata 40 D3
Falam (M) 61 E6
Falka 39 H5
Fanchanpur 56 C1
Fandpur 57 H4
Fanepura (P) 16 B3
Faqira Bazar (M) 74 C4
Faradi 48 B6
Farah 34 D1
Farakka 58 A2
Faralpura (P) 16 B4
Faranshat 13 G2
Farashganj (Ba) 59 G6
Fardapur 65 G6
Fariabad 13 H5
Faridabad 22 C5
Faridganj (Ba) 59 G5
Faridkot 17 F5
Faridnagar 22 D4
Faridpur (Ba) 59 E3
Faridpur (Ba) 59 E4
Faridpur (Har) 22 B2
Faridpur (Utt) 23 H5
Farkawn 61 E5
Farmanah 22 B3
Farooqnagar 86 D2
Farozeshah 17 F5
Farukhabad 35 H1
Farrukhnagar (Har) 22 B5
Farrukhnagar (Utt) 22 C4
Farshabad 87 E4
Faruka (P) 16 A2
Fatehabad (Pun) 17 F3
Fatehabad (Har) 21 G2
Fatehabad (Raj) 22 B6
Fatehabad (Utt) 35 E2
Fatehabad Chandrawati-
  ganj 51 G6
Fatehgadh 49 E4
Fatehganj Sharki 23 G5
Fatehganj West 23 G4
Fatehgarh (Pun) 17 G6
Fatehgarh (Pun) 18 A5
Fatehgarh (Raj) 33 F4
Fatehgarh (Utt) 35 H1
Fatehgarh (Raj) 52 B2
Fatehgarh Churian 17 F2

Fatehjang (P) 12 A4
Fatehnagar 50 D1
Fatehpur (N) 39 G3
Fatehpur (P) 16 C4
Fatehpur (Him) 17 H2
Fatehpur (Raj) 21 F6
Fatehpur (Utt) 22 D1
Fatehpur (Utt) 22 D6
Fatehpur (Utt) 36 B5
Fatehpur (Utt) 36 C2
Fatehpur (Mad) 53 G3
Fatehpur (Bih) 56 D2
Fatehpur (Wbg) 58 A3
Fatehpur (Mah) 65 H6
Fatehpur (Wbg) 72 B2
Fatehpur Sikri 34 D2
Fatehpura 50 D5
Fathkhelda 78 A1
Fatikebhari (Ba) 60 B6
Fatikrai 60 B3
Fattuwal 17 F4
Fatuhiwala 21 E1
Fatwa 38 D6
Fazilka 16 D6
Fazilpur (Ba) 60 A6
Fenchuganj (Ba) 60 B2
Feni (Ba) 60 A6
Ferokh 94 D4
Ferozepur (P) 16 C6
Finjeshwar 69 E5
Firdaus (P) 16 A6
Firozabad (Utt) 35 E2
Firozabad (Kar) 86 A2
Firozpur 17 E5
Firozpur Cantonment 17 E4
Firozpur Jhirka 22 B6
Fitna (P) 16 B6
Folowai 13 E1
Forbesganj 39 H4
Fort Abbas (P) 20 B3
Fort White (M) 61 F5
Furkating 43 F3

Gabargaon (Ba) 59 E1
Gabat 50 B5
Gabindasti (Ba) 59 H2
Gabur 86 B4
Gachhipura 33 E2
Gad Boriad 64 C2
Gadag 85 G6
Gadarwara 53 F6
Gaddige 95 E2
Gadechi 62 A2
Gadekallu 91 H1, 92 A1
Gadhada (Guj) 48 D4
Gadhada (Guj) 63 F2
Gadhagra 63 F4
Gadhali 63 G3
Gadhia 63 F4
Gadhinglaj 84 D4
Gadhka (Guj) 62 B2
Gadhka (Guj) 63 E2
Gadhula 63 G3
Gadidemadugu 86 D5
Gadiganuru 86 A6
Gadigarevula 87 E5
Gadra (P) 31 E5
Gadra Road 31 E5
Gadro Charan (P) 49 E2
Gadulabadi 82 B1
Gadwal 86 C4
Gagargarh 37 G3
Gagaw Nok (M) 44 C3
Gaggan (P) 12 A4
Gaggo (P) 16 A6
Gagron 51 H2
Gagu Mahal (P) 16 A4
Gagurni 52 A3

Gahira (Ba) 74 B2
Gahmar 38 A6
Gaibanda (Ba) 41 E6
Gaigath 24 C6
Gaighat (N) 39 G3
Gaighata 58 C6
Gaighatti 39 E4
Gaik 15 E4
Gaikhuri Hills 67 H4
Gaila (Ba) 59 F6
Gaimbar (P) 16 C5
Gaindakanda (N) 24 D4
Gaindoli 33 H6
Gaini 23 G5
Gainsari 37 F1
Gainta 34 A5
Gairagaon (N) 25 F5
Gaisabad 53 H3
Gajapajinagaram 81 H5
Gajar Gola (P) 16 C2
Gajawari (P) 48 B3
Gajendragarh 85 G5
Gajipura 49 H1
Gajner (Guj) 20 B6
Gajner (Utt) 36 A4
Gajol 40 B6
Gajraula 23 E4
Gajsinghpur 20 B2
Gajwer 79 F6
Galag 86 A4
Galatgi 84 D3
Galau (P) 48 B3
Galayang (M) 45 E4
Galchipa (Ba) 73 F2
Galgali 85 F4
Galhar 13 H5
Galiakot 50 D5
Galimpur (Ba) 59 H5
Galivedu 92 C3
Galkot (N) 25 H5
Galleri 82 B1
Galli Jagir (P) 12 A5
Galsi 58 A5
Galund 50 D1
Galvada 65 F4
Gama Sagar 72 B3
Gamar Khurd 79 E2
Gambat Brok (P) 14 A1
Gamharia 57 F6
Gampalagudem 88 A2
Gampbellpore (P) 12 A4
Ganagajal 70 B2
Ganagapur 86 A2
Ganapavaram 88 C3
Ganaur 22 B3
Ganavaram 88 B3
Ganda Kas (P) 12 A4
Gandabahali 81 F1
Gandamara (Ba) 74 B2
Gandap 49 G1
Gandarvakottai 96 C6
Gandasi 91 F5
Gande 57 F3
Ganderbal 13 F3
Gandeva 64 B5
Gandevi 64 B5
Gandhari 79 E5
Gandheli 21 E3
Gandhidham 48 D6
Gandhinagar 50 A6
Gandpa Gompa 15 F5
Ganeshganj 34 A6
Ganga 21 E1
Gangadevipalle 87 G5
Gangadhara 79 F5
Gangaikandapuram 96 D4
Gangajalghati 57 G5
Gangakher 78 B4

Gangakondacholapuram
  96 C4
Gangalur 80 C4
Ganganagar (Raj) 20 D1
Ganganagar (Ass) 60 D2
Gangapur (Raj) 33 E6
Gangapur (Raj) 34 B3
Gangapur (Mah) 77 F2
Gangapur (Ori) 82 C2
Gangapur Siswan 38 B5
Gangarajumadugula 81 F6
Gangaram 80 A6
Gangareddigudem 88 C2
Gangasagar (Ba) 59 H4
Gangavalli 96 B3
Gangavathi 86 A6
Gangaw (M) 75 G2
Gangdhar 51 G4
Ganghasara 49 F1
Gangi (Utt) 19 F5
Gangi (Raj) 20 A4
Gangiasar 21 F5
Gangidem (C) 28 A2
Gangli 65 F2
Gangni (Ba) 58 C4
Gangoh 22 C1
Gangoli 90 C4
Gangotri 19 F4
Gangra 15 E4
Gangrampur 40 C6
Gangrar 51 E1
Gangri 23 E6
Gangtha 17 H2
Gangti 57 G1
Gangtok 40 C1
Ganguvada 82 B4
Gania 70 C6
Ganiari 69 E2
Ganika 13 G5
Ganj 54 B2
Ganj Dinara 35 E6
Ganj Muradabad 36 A2
Ganjam 82 D3
Ganjigunti 92 B5
Ganjivaripalle 87 F4
Ganjoti 78 A6
Ganod 62 D3
Ganor 33 G4
Ganrapota 58 C5
Ganutia 58 A4
Gaoran 13 G4
Gaorisar 21 E5
Gar Dzong (C) 19 H2
Gara (Raj) 34 B2
Gara (Mad) 52 C2
Gara (And) 82 B5
Garabdesar 20 D5
Garag 85 E5
Garah 32 B6
Garahi (P) 47 H2
Garai (P) 12 A1
Garampani 43 F3
Garampant 42 C6
Garautha 35 G6
Garbandh 82 B4
Garbi Haubaullah Khan (P)
  12 C2
Garbor 32 C6
Garbyang 24 B1
Gardi 38 B1
Gareahgarh 20 D1
Garenga 81 E3
Gareya (Ba) 40 C4
Garhbeta 57 H6
Garh (P) 16 B5
Garh (J&K) 13 E6
Garh (Mad) 54 D2

Garh Anapur 49 H2
Garh Krishnaprasad 82 D2
Garha 53 H5
Garhakota 53 G4
Garhani 38 B6
Garhchiroli 80 A1
Garhdiwala 17 G3
Garhi (*) 12 C3
Garhi (Utt) 22 C2
Garhi (Raj) 34 B2
Garhi (Mad) 34 C4
Garhi (Raj) 50 D4
Garhi (Mad) 53 E5
Garhi (Mad) 68 B2
Garhi Harsaru 22 B5
Garhmukteswar 23 E4
Garho (P) 47 F3
Garhshankar 18 A4
Gariaband 69 E6
Gariyadhar 63 F4
Garjania (Ba) 74 B4
Garjia 23 G2
Garkha 38 C5
Garladine 92 A1
Garladinne 86 D6
Garlamarla 33 E6
Garli 18 A2
Garmali 63 F4
Garnawad 51 H2
Garnia 32 C4
Garnimitta 92 D4
Garobadha 41 F5
Garot 51 G3
Garpos 70 B2
Garrauli 53 G1
Garrda 33 G6
Garsia 30 C2
Garsisar 20 D5
Garu 56 B4
Garubhasa 41 F3
Garwa (Utt) 24 D6, 36 D1
Garwa (Bih) 56 A3
Gasheng 27 H4
Gasigaon 27 G6
Gasipur 71 F6
Gatasilli 69 E6
Gategaon 78 A5
Gathaura 53 H1
Gaudgaon 77 H6
Gaudikota 92 C2
Gaumukh 19 G4
Gaur 58 B1
Gaura Umarai 36 C4
Gauribidanur 92 A4
Gauriganj 36 D4
Gauripur 41 F4
Gauritiar 36 A6
Gaumadi (Ba) 59 F6
Gaviridevipeta 88 C1
Gavridad 63 E1
Gavunipalli 92 B5
Gawahati 42 B4
Gawal (M) 29 F6
Gawan 57 E2
Gawana 19 F5
Gawnaha 38 B2
Gaya 56 C2
Gaziphema 43 G6
Gazulapalle 87 E6
Gedi (Guj) 49 E4
Gedi (Guj) 63 G1
Gejeragaon 43 G2
Geleki 43 H3
Genapara 41 F6
Gerba (C) 26 A2
Gersar 20 C5
Gersopa 90 C3
Geta (N) 24 B4

Getta Dzong (B) 41 E2
Gettavadi 95 F3
Gette 27 H4
Gevrai 77 G3
Ghafargaon (Ba) 59 G2
Ghafurwah (P) 20 A1
Ghaggar 21 H1
Ghaghra 56 B5
Ghagra (Ba) 59 G1
Ghagra 55 E6
Ghairatganj 53 E5
Ghakhar (P) 16 D1
Ghalvad 76 A1
Ghamarwin 18 B3
Ghambi 84 C1
Ghambiraopet 79 F5
Ghan Sawangi 77 H2
Ghana 64 C5
Ghanauli 18 B4
Ghanaur 18 B6
Ghandwala 17 F2
Ghanerao 32 C6
Ghania (P) 16 C1
Ghanpur 79 G6
Ghanshampur 39 F4
Ghanshyampur 49 F6
Ghansor 67 H1
Ghantapara 69 H6
Ghanteswar 71 G5
Ghantiali (Raj) 31 F1
Ghantiali (Raj) 32 B1
Ghantila 49 E6
Ghantwar 63 E5
Gharaunda 22 B2
Ghargaon 76 D3
Gharghoda 69 H2
Ghari Ghat 37 F2
Gharibwal (P) 12 B6
Gharo (P) 47 F2
Gharyala 17 E4
Ghasera 22 B5
Ghaswani 34 C5
Ghat (Utt) 19 G6
Ghat (Raj) 34 B3
Ghat Bilod 65 G1
Ghat Borul 78 B6
Ghatal 58 A6
Ghatampur 36 A4
Ghatang 66 C4
Ghatanji 79 E1
Ghatera 53 H4
Ghatgaon 71 E4
Ghatgarh 76 C2
Ghatghar 76 C3
Ghatiaoli 51 E1
Ghatigaon 34 D4
Ghatkar 84 C4
Ghatkesar 87 F1
Ghatnagar (Ba) 58 C1
Ghatnandra 65 G6
Ghatol 51 E4
Ghatoli 51 H1
Ghatsila 71 F1
Ghattu 92 C4
Ghatwa 33 F1
Ghatwari 33 H2
Ghaura 53 G2
Ghausganj 36 A2
Ghazi 12 C3
Ghaziabad 22 C4
Ghazipur (Utt) 36 B5
Ghazipur (Utt) 37 H5
Ghazipur (Bih) 38 B5
Ghens 69 H4
Gheora 22 B4
Gherdi 85 F2
Gheura 32 A3
Ghiar 22 B1

Ghidni 71 G1
Ghila (P) 12 A5
Ghior (Ba) 59 F4
Ghiri 18 B3
Ghiror 35 F2
Ghitrari 18 A1
Ghod 76 C4
Ghodadar 50 C3
Ghodasivadi 76 D2
Ghodra 18 C4
Ghoga 39 H6
Ghogaon 65 G3
Ghogardiha 39 F4
Ghogari 78 D3
Ghogha 63 H3
Gholau 50 C6
Ghona 32 A5
Ghora Gali (P) 12 C3
Ghorabari (P) 47 F3
Ghoraghat (Ba) 40 D6
Ghorasahan 38 C3
Ghorasar 50 A6
Ghorawal 55 G2
Ghori 12 C2
Ghoriajor 70 A2
Ghosar 70 B5
Ghosi (Utt) 37 H4
Ghosi (Bih) 38 C6, 56 D1
Ghosia 37 F6
Ghosla 51 H5
Ghot 80 A2
Ghota 49 E6
Ghotan 77 F3
Ghotaru 30 C2
Ghoti 76 C2
Ghughi 68 B1
Ghugus 79 G1
Ghui 55 G4
Ghulam Wadera (P) 46 D1
Ghumka 68 C4
Ghunada 49 E6
Ghund 18 C4
Ghungchiai 24 A5
Ghunghuti 54 C5
Ghungrilla (P) 12 B5
Ghunkarah (B) 42 A1
Ghura 53 H2
Ghurain 18 A6
Ghurani 17 H5
Ghurghushti (P) 12 A3
Ghurkur 18 A2
Ghuma (N) 39 H3
Ghut 86 C4
Ghutku 69 E2
Ghutra 55 F5
Giabong 19 E2
Giala (B) 41 F1
Giamda Dzong (C) 26 D1
Gianpura (P) 16 A6
Giarlam Aliwals 20 A4
Gidam 80 D4
Gidar (P) 12 B1
Giddalur 87 F6
Giddarbana 17 E6
Gidpur (P) 16 D5
Gigasaran 63 E4
Gigrial (P) 13 E6
Gijgarh 34 B2
Gilduru 88 C4
Gingee 96 D2
Gingla 50 D3
Ginigera 85 H6
Ginjia 43 E3
Ginnurgarh 52 C6
Girab 31 E5
Girandi 20 A6
Girar 53 F3
Girart 67 G6

Girasar 20 A6
Girdawara 80 B2
Girdhariwala (P) 20 B1
Girdharpura 51 G1
Girgaon 24 A1
Giriak 56 D1
Giridih 57 F3
Girisola 82 C3
Girri 32 D4
Girwan 36 B6
Gittidas 12 D1
Gnimthenla (B) 41 E2
Goalpara 41 G4
Goalpokhar 40 B4
Goaltor 57 H6
Goalundo (Ba) 59 E4
Goanra 50 D1
Gobak (C) 15 H5
Gobardanga 58 C6
Gobardhan 34 C1
Gobardhan Vilas 50 C2
Gobardhana 38 B1
Gobindaganj (Ba) 60 A1
Gobindapur (Ba) 60 A3
Gobindapur 58 B5
Gobindganj (Ba) 58 D1
Gobindgar 18 A5
Gobindpur (Pun) 17 H3
Gobindpur (Bih) 57 E2
Gobindpur (Bih) 57 G4
Gobindpur (Ori) 70 B2
Gobra Nawapara 69 E5
Gobur 86 A2
Godagari (Ba) 58 B2
Godapiasal 71 H1
Godarpura 65 H2
Godawari (N) 38 D1
Godda 57 H1
Godh 24 C6
Godhegaon 77 E3
Godhra (Guj) 50 C6
Godhra (Guj) 63 E5
Godia Creek 47 H5
Godipara 82 D1
Godra 48 B6
Godri 68 B3
Godusara (M) 74 C5
Goela 33 F4
Gof 67 E2
Gogan (N) 24 B3
Gogaon 68 A6
Gogarpur 52 A3
Goghat 58 A6
Gogonda 80 D5
Gogri Jamalpur 39 G6
Gogulapelle 87 G6
Gogunda 50 C2
Gogwa 70 C4
Goh 56 C1
Gohad 35 E4
Gohan 35 G4
Gohana 22 B3
Gohand 35 H5
Goharganj 52 D6
Gohpur 43 E2
Gohra (P) 12 B4
Goi 12 D4
Goibarigaon 42 A3
Goichran 19 E4
Goilkera 70 D1
Gojra (P) 16 A4
Gojra (P) 16 B3
Gojra (P) 16 C1
Gokak 85 E4
Gokal 34 D1
Gokalpura 49 G4
Gokand (P) 12 A2
Gokarn 90 B2

Gokarna (Ba) 59 H3
Gokarna 58 B3
Gokavaram 88 D2
Gokhatar 49 F4
Gol 31 H6
Gola 57 E4
Gola Bazar 37 H4
Gola Gokarnanath 24 B5
Golaghat 43 F3
Golakganj 41 E4
Golantra 82 C3
Golapalle 80 C6
Golconda 87 E2
Golegaon 66 B6
Golepangri 77 G2
Goler 18 A2
Golewala 17 E5
Golgeri 85 H3
Golhalli 92 A5
Golikatte 90 C4
Golitattu 90 D6
Golla 91 H2
Gollagudem 88 B1
Gollapalle 88 C3
Gollapalli 79 F5
Golmuri 57 F6
Golpur (P) 12 B6
Golri 20 B6
Goluwali 20 D2
Goma Hanu 14 B2
Gomdandi (Ba) 74 B1
Gomoh 57 F4
Gompa 14 C1
Gompo Ne (C) 27 H1
Gomta 14 A5
Gona 53 E2
Gonapallo 93 E3
Gonda (Utt) 22 D6
Gonda (Utt) 37 E2
Gondal (P) 13 E6
Gondal 63 E2
Gonde 76 D2
Gondher 33 F5
Gondi 35 H5
Gondia 71 E5
Gondiwal (P) 16 D1
Gondiya 68 A4
Gondla 18 B1
Gondoch 32 B5
Gondpalli 80 C5
Gonebidu 91 E5
Gonegandla 86 C5
Gongba (C) 29 F1
Gongchuandgaon (B) 41 G2
Gongrali (N) 25 F4
Gongshan (C) 29 H6
Gonkor (M) 75 G4
Gonour 54 A2
Gonphu (B) 41 G2
Gooty 92 A1
Gop 83 E1
Gopala Singavaram 86 D5
Gopalganj (Ba) 59 E6
Gopalganj (Ba) 60 B1
Gopalganj (Bih) 38 B3
Gopalganj (Mad) 67 G2
Gopalpur (Ba) 58 D1
Gopalpur (Ba) 59 F2
Gopalpur (N) 39 E2
Gopalpur (Bih) 39 H6
Gopalpur (Ori) 70 A2
Gopalpur (Wbg) 72 A3
Gopalpur-on-Sea 82 C3
Gopalpura 21 G6
Gopalpuram 88 D2
Gopalsar 32 A3
Gopamau 36 A1

Gopavaram 88 B3
Gopiballabhpur 71 G2
Gopichettipalaiyam 95 G4
Gopiganj 37 E6
Gopikandar 57 H2
Gopikat 61 E1
Gopinattam 95 H2
Gora (C) 29 H2
Gora 34 D6
Gorabond 81 H1
Goraj 64 C2
Gorakhpur (Har) 21 G2
Gorakhpur (Utt) 37 H3
Goramari 42 C4
Gorana 50 C2
Gorantla 92 B3
Goras 34 B6
Gorau 32 D1
Goraul 38 D5
Gordal (P) 16 A2
Gordhanpura 52 A2
Goreakothi 38 C4
Goregaon (Mah) 68 A4
Goregaon (Mah) 76 B6
Goregaon (Mah) 78 B1
Gorera 32 C1
Gorgat 62 B2
Gorhar (P) 48 D2
Gorhe 76 B2
Goria 49 G6
Gorkhe (N) 40 B2
Gorkhpur 54 D6
Gormi 35 F3
Gorthan 76 C1
Gorubathan 40 C2
Gorur 91 F6
Gosainganj (Utt) 36 C3
Gosainganj (Utt) 37 F3
Gosairhat (Ba) 59 F6
Gosalpur 54 A5
Gosava 72 C2
Gossaigaon 41 E4
Gosti 14 A5
Gosunda 51 E1
Gotan 32 C3
Gotarka 49 F4
Gote 85 F3
Goth Bacho (P) 47 F1
Goth Bagauah (P) 47 G3
Goth Baloch Khan (P) 47 F1
Goth Ghulam (P) 47 E1
Goth Kapat (P) 47 F1
Goth Khamisani (P) 47 F1
Goth Musa (P) 47 F3
Goth Yar Muhammad (P) 46 D1
Gothiana 33 F4
Gothini 38 A4
Gothna 84 B2
Gothva 50 A4
Goti 80 C3
Gotia 81 E3
Gotitoria 53 F6
Gotlagartu 87 G6
Gotsa (C) 40 D1
Gotsong (C) 29 E2
Gour 58 B1
Gouripur (Ba) 59 G2
Gourjhamar 53 F4
Gourpali 70 B3
Govada 76 A1
Govindapalle 81 F5
Govindgarh (Raj) 34 B1
Govindgarh (Mad) 54 C3
Govindghat 19 H5
Govindpur 70 D3
Govindwal 17 F4

Govundlapalem 93 G2
Goyain (Ba) 60 B1
Goyerkata 40 C3
Gozer 13 E1
Grama 91 F6
Gramag 18 B2
Gramphu 18 C1
Grantala (Ba) 60 B2
Grantunag 13 H2
Gua 70 D2
Guani (N) 24 C3
Guanuwala (P) 12 B6
Guatala (Ba) 59 G1
Gubbi 91 H5
Gubra 53 H5
Gudali 50 C1
Gudalur 95 G4
Gudari 82 A3
Gudekota 91 G1
Gudem 81 F6
Gudgaon 66 D3
Gudgeri 90 D1
Gudha (Raj) 21 G6
Gudha (Raj) 33 G6
Gudha (Raj) 34 B3
Gudibanda 92 A4
Gudikallu 86 C5
Gudivada 88 C4
Gudiyattam 92 D6
Gudluru 93 F1
Gudraipattu 96 D2
Gudur (Kar) 85 G5
Gudur (And) 87 H1
Gudur (And) 93 F3
Guduru 86 D5
Guduvancheri 93 G6
Gugauli 25 E6
Gugera (P) 16 C4
Gugi 86 A3
Guhagar 84 A1
Guhisar 35 E4
Guhla 22 A1
Gujar Khan (P) 12 C5
Gujararu 13 G5
Gujhandi 56 D2
Gujo (P) 47 F2
Gujranwala (P) 16 D2
Gujrat (P) 12 A2
Gujrat (P) 12 D6
Gujri (P) 30 A4
Gujri 65 G2
Gujrotar (P) 30 A4
Gul 13 F5
Gulab Ali (P) 20 B2
Gulabgarh 13 H5
Gulaothi 22 D4
Gularia 24 C5
Gulbarga 86 B2
Guledagud 85 G4
Gulganj 53 G2
Guliana (P) 12 B5
Gulmarg 13 E3
Gulmatungo 14 A3
Gulmikot (N) 25 H5
Gultari 13 G1
Gulu 70 D1
Guluba 82 D2
Gum (N) 25 E2
Gum Ga (M) 44 B3
Guma 18 B2
Gumagarh 70 B6
Guman 50 C3
Gumba 14 B6
Gumia 57 E4
Gumla 56 B6
Gumlai 70 B3
Gumma (Mad) 81 E5
Gumma (Ori) 82 B4

Gummidipundi 93 G5
Gumri 80 A1
Gumsar 69 H6
Gumshen (M) 45 F3
Gumthala Gadhu 22 A1
Gumtharla 22 C1
Guna 52 C2
Gunabati (Ba) 59 H5
Gunaga 52 C5
Gunamanipara 60 B4
Gunasvel 64 B5
Gund (J&K) 13 F2
Gund (J&K) 13 F4
Gunda 62 C2
Gundal (Kar) 85 F3
Gundal (And) 87 G1
Gundardehi 68 C5
Gundevadi 85 E3
Gundiali 63 G1
Gundipet 87 E1
Gundlabrahmeswaram
  87 F5
Gundlakonda 86 C6
Gundlupet 95 F3
Gundmal 86 C3
Gundrampalli 87 F2
Gundribadi 70 C6
Gundugolanu 88 C3
Gundusar 20 D6
Gunerbari (Ba) 59 E1
Gunga 31 F4
Gungvad 85 E3
Gunhana (N) 24 D5
Gunjavan 90 C1
Gunji 84 D6
Gunjong 42 D6
Gunna (P) 17 E1
Gunnaur 23 E5
Gunra 62 C2
Gunta 22 A6
Guntakal 86 C6, 92 A1
Guntur 88 A4
Gunupur (Ori) 81 G2
Gunupur (Ori) 82 A3
Gunwara 54 B3
Gupta Kashi 19 G5
Guptapur 82 D2
Gura 31 G6
Gurach 50 C2
Gurampod 87 F3
Guraora 22 A5
Gurbakhshganj 36 C4
Gurda 69 G2
Gurdaspur 17 F2
Gurgaon (Har) 22 B5
Gurgaon (Mah) 78 C3
Gurgunta 86 A4
Gurh 54 D2
Gurha 32 C2
Gurha Andla 32 B5
Guri Hatnur 79 E2
Guriani 22 B5
Gurjakhana (N) 25 G4
Gurla 51 G2
Gurlapur 85 E4
Gurmatkal 86 C3
Gurna (P) 16 B2
Gurnaoda 34 A5
Gurpur 90 C6
Gurramkonda 92 D4
Gursahaiganj 35 H2
Gursarai 35 G5
Gurtedu 81 E6
Gurua 56 C2
Guruharsahai 17 E5
Gurur 13 E2
Gurusar 17 E6
Gurusula 70 C4

Guruvajipeta 87 G6
Guruvayoor 94 D5
Guruzala 87 H3
Gushria Chuk 43 E3
Guskhara 58 A5
Guthan 21 G4
Guthli 50 B6
Gutni 36 D5
Gutta 80 A2
Guttal 91 E2
Gutturu 92 B3
Guvindapur 82 B3
Guvvalacheruvu 92 D3
Guwarghat 53 H5
Gwabin (M) 75 G5
Gwala 21 G6
Gwaldam 23 H1
Gwalior (Mad) 35 E4
Gwalior (Mad) 51 F1
Gwara 68 C1
Gwazon (M) 74 C6
Gwegyo (M) 75 H5
Gya 14 D4
Gyakateng (C) 27 H2
Gyala (C) 27 H2
Gyalshing 40 B1
Gyanpur 37 F6
Gyao (C) 26 B5
Gyara (C) 27 F3
Gyatsa Dzong (C) 26 D3
Gyetsa (B) 41 G1
Gyisum (C) 26 C5
Gyokkon (M) 75 H6
Gyraspur 53 E4

Ha Dzong (B) 40 D1
Hab Nadi Chowki (P) 47 E1
Habaipur 42 D5
Habib 12 D1
Habibpur 58 B1
Habiganj (Ba) 60 A3
Habra 58 C6
Habri 22 B2
Habur 30 D2
Hachcholli 86 B5
Hachi 27 F6
Hadadi 91 E3
Hadagli 85 G3
Hadali (P) 16 A1
Hadapsar 76 D5
Hadda (Raj) 20 B6
Hadda (Raj) 31 E1
Hadgaon 78 D2
Hadgaon Buzurg 78 A3
Hadobhangi 82 A4
Hadol 50 A4
Hadrukh 35 G4
Hadsar 18 B1
Hafizabad (P) 16 C2
Haflong 42 D6
Hagalvadi 91 G5
Hagari 91 H1
Hagaribomanahalli 91 F1
Hagnis 14 A2
Haia Ghat 39 E4
Haicin (M) 61 E3
Haidarganj 37 E3
Haidargarh 36 C3
Haidarnagar 56 A2
Haide (C) 26 A4
Hailakandi 60 C2
Haileymandi 22 B5
Hajan 13 E2
Hajganj (Ba) 59 G5
Haji Darya Khan (P) 46 D1
Hajipur (Raj) 22 A6, 34 A1
Hajipur (Bih) 38 D5
Hajira (*) 12 D4

Hajira (Guj) 64 A4
Hajjipur 17 G2
Hajminia (N) 38 D3
Hajo 42 A4
Hajua 41 H3
Hakha (C) 29 F3
Hako 14 A5
Halagli 85 F4
Halalpur (P) 16 B2
Halanjur 80 B1
Halbarga 78 C6
Haldaur 23 E3
Haldi 84 D3
Haldia 72 B2
Haldibari 40 C4
Haldikhora 40 A4
Haldipur 90 B3
Haldwani 23 G3
Halebid 91 F5
Halena 34 C2
Halenda 63 E2
Halgar 78 B6
Halge 90 B1
Halgeri 91 E2
Halgur 95 G1
Halhali 60 B3
Hali 78 B5
Halia 55 F2
Haliapur 36 D3
Halimai 83 E2
Halimpur 38 D4
Halisahar 58 C6
Haliwara 80 A2
Haliyal 85 E6
Halkarni 84 D4
Halki 85 F4
Halla (P) 16 C4
Halli Mysore 91 F6
Hallowal (P) 17 E2
Halog 18 C4
Halol 64 C1
Halsangi 85 G2
Halsi (Bih) 57 E1
Halsi (Kar) 84 D6
Halsur 78 B6
Haltugaon 41 F3
Haluaghat (Ba) 41 F6
Haludpukhur 71 E1
Halvad 49 E6
Halvi 86 B5
Halwara 17 G5
Hamira 31 E2
Hamirpur (Him) 18 A3
Hamirpur (Utt) 36 A5
Hamoka (P) 16 A2
Hampatnam 85 H6
Hampapura 95 E2
Hampasagaram 91 F1
Hampet 13 G3
Hampi 86 A6
Hanagal 91 G2
Hanbal 91 E6
Handapa 70 C5
Handauk-Ale (M) 75 G6
Handia (Utt) 37 E6
Handia (Mad) 66 B1
Handwara 13 E2
Hanegaon 78 C5
Hang Habai 42 D5
Hangal 90 D2
Hangrum 43 E6
Hankar 14 C4
Hanker 80 B1
Hanle 15 F6
Hanmant Vadiya 84 D2
Hanmsagar 85 H5
Hannur 85 H1
Hanotia 33 E5

Hansat 64 A3
Hansbini 43 E3
Hanship 61 E3
Hansi (Him) 18 D1
Hansi (Har) 21 H3
Hanskhali 58 C5
Hanslawala (P) 12 C6
Hanspura 56 B1
Hanti 39 F5
Hanudaki 91 H5
Hanuman Chatti 19 G5
Hanumangarh 21 E2
Hanummana 55 E2
Hanur 95 G2
Hanzal 13 G4
Haochong 61 E1
Hapagaon 42 C3
Hapur 22 D4
Haracha (B) 41 F2
Haragauri (Ba) 60 B2
Haraiya 37 F3
Haranhalli 91 F5
Haranpur (P) 12 B6
Harappa (P) 16 A5
Harappa Road (P) 16 B5
Harasnath 33 F1
Harau 21 G1
Harawah 54 B5
Harbang (Ba) 74 B3
Harbhanga 70 B5
Harchandpur 36 C4
Harchowal 17 G3
Harda 66 C2
Hardesar 21 E4
Hardi 38 D4
Hardia Chauki (N) 38 D1
Hardo Warpal (P) 16 D1
Hardoi 36 A1
Hardot 53 E4
Hardote 53 E5
Hardua 54 C1
Harduaganj 23 E6
Hargam 24 B6
Hari 18 B3
Hari Rampur 37 H3
Hari Singhpura 20 C3
Haria (N) 39 G3
Haria (P) 12 C6
Hariadhana 32 C4
Hariala 12 C3
Hariana 62 D1
Hariara (Pun) 17 H3
Hariara (Raj) 32 C4
Hariarpara 58 B3
Hariarpur 57 G2
Harichandanpur 71 E4
Haridaspur 71 E5
Haridwar 23 E1
Harigarh 52 A2
Harihar 91 E2
Hariharganj 56 B2
Hariharpur (Ba) 40 B4
Hariharpur (Bih) 55 H2
Hariharpur (Mad) 55 H4
Hariharpur (Kar) 90 D5
Hariharpur Garhi (N) 38 D2
Harij 49 G4
Harijaipara 60 C5
Harike 17 F4
Harina Buzar (Ba) 60 C6
Harinakunda (Ba) 58 D4
Haringhata 58 C6
Haripad 98 B3
Haripur (P) 12 B3
Haripur 82 C4
Harirampur (Ba) 59 E4
Harisal 66 B4
Harishchandrapur 40 A6

Harivanam 86 B5
Hariyali 49 G1
Hariyasar 21 E4
Harji 32 A6
Harkhapur 24 C5
Harlakhi (N) 39 E3
Harlalpur 18 B6
Harmal 19 H6
Harmara 33 F3
Harnahalli 90 D3
Harnai 76 B6, 84 A1
Harnaoda 52 B2
Harnatanr 38 A1
Harnaut 38 D6
Harni (Ba) 73 H1
Harohalli (Kar) 92 A6,
  95 H1
Harohalli (Kar) 95 F2
Harohoka 54 D4
Haroli 18 A3
Harpalpur (Utt) 35 G6
Harpalpur (Utt) 35 H2
Harpanahalli 91 E2
Harpoke (P) 16 D2
Harpur (N) 38 D2
Harrai 67 G1
Harratola 54 D6
Harsani 31 E5
Harsauli 22 B6
Harsawa 21 F6
Harse Shekh (P) 16 B2
Harsidhi 38 C3
Harsil 19 F4
Harsol 50 B5
Harsor 33 E3
Harsud 66 B2
Harsul 76 C1
Harta (N) 38 C1
Harua 72 C1
Harunabad (P) 20 B2
Harur 96 B2
Harvale 84 C6
Harwa 31 G4
Hasan Abdal (P) 12 A3
Hasanabad 79 G6
Hasanganj 36 B3
Hasanpur (Har) 22 C6
Hasanpur (Utt) 23 E4
Hasanpur (Bih) 39 F5
Hasaparti 79 G6
Hasaud 69 G3
Hasimara 40 D3
Haslia 20 D7
Hasnabad (Wbg) 72 C1
Hasnabad (Mah) 77 G1
Hasnai (Ba) 59 F2
Hassan 91 F6
Hastinapur 23 E3
Haswa 36 C5
Hat Banjari 68 B5
Hat Gamaria 71 E2
Hat Piplia 52 A6
Hata (Utt) 37 H3, 38 A3
Hata (Bih) 55 H1
Hataia (Ba) 59 F3
Hatgarh 64 C6
Hathazari (Ba) 74 B1
Hathgaon 36 C5
Hathiana 51 E1
Hathibari 70 C1
Hathni Kurd 18 C6
Hathras 35 E1
Hathusar 20 C3
Hathwa 38 B4
Hatian 12 C3
Hatibandha (Ba) 40 D4
Hatibar 71 E5
Hatid 85 E2

Hatigarh 71 H2
Hatikhuli 43 E3
Hatkalanda 84 D3
Hatkhambe 84 B2
Hatkhuri 54 A3
Hatkoli 80 D3
Hatli 17 G1
Hatnura 86 D1
Hatod 51 G6
Hatranga (N) 24 B2
Hatron 66 B5
Hatta (Mad) 53 H3
Hatta (Mah) 78 B3
Hattigam 81 E1
Hattigudur 86 A3
Hattili 82 A4
Hattin 22 C5
Hattur 85 G1
Hatur Khas 17 G5
Haulawng 60 D6
Haungpa (M) 44 C6
Hausdiha 57 H2
Havannur 91 E1
Havasbhavi 90 D2
Haveli 76 C4
Haveli Lakkha (P) 16 C6
Havelian (P) 12 B3
Haveri 90 D2
Hawal 13 H4
Hawalbagh 23 H2
Hayuliang 28 C5
Hazaribagh 56 D3
Hazrat Jandaha 38 D5
Hazro (P) 12 A3
Hazurpur (P) 16 B1
Hebatpur 63 H2
Hebbetti 86 B5
Hebbur 91 H5
Hebby 91 E4
Hebertpur 18 D6
Hebli 85 F6
Hebri 90 C5
Hebsur 85 F6
Hediyal 95 E2
Heggadadevankote 95 E2
Heinsum (M) 44 B5
Heirnkut (M) 43 H6
Heiwati (C) 29 H6
Helan (P) 12 C4
Helan (P) 16 C1
Helem 43 E2
Helwak 84 B2
Hemaliu (M) 61 H1
Hemis 14 D3
Hemkund 19 H5
Hempur 24 B6, 36 B1
Hemtabad 40 B5
Henglep 61 E2
Hengtam 61 E3
Henhoaha 101 H6
Henima 43 E6
Hentoin 101 G4
Her 78 B5
Herberthad 100 A5
Herga 90 C5
Herhanj 56 C4
Heria Hatmaran Chak
   72 A2
Hesadi 56 D6
Hesrur 85 G6
Hetanpur 58 C3
Hiangzang (M) 61 F4
Higona 52 C3
Hijla (Ba) 59 G6
Hijraon 21 G2
Hilawng (M) 75 F4
Hilaya (P) 47 G1
Hili (Ba) 40 D6

Hilli 40 D6
Hilsa 38 D6
Himaigaon 43 E4
Himatnagar 50 B4
Hinam 101 F4
Hinamandalam 82 A4
Hindaun 34 B3
Hindiganal 92 B5
Hindol 70 D5
Hindoli 33 G5
Hindoria 53 G4
Hindu Malkot 16 D6
Hindubari (Ba) 60 A5
Hindupur 92 A4
Hingalganj 72 D1
Hinganghat 67 F6
Hingir 70 A3
Hingoli 78 C2
Hingpur 13 G4
Hiniskut 14 B2
Hinjilikatu 82 C2
Hipparga 85 H1
Hippargi 85 H3
Hira (P) 16 A6
Hira 86 A4
Hirad 50 B3
Hiranagal 17 G1
Hirangaon 52 B6
Hiranpur 58 A2
Hirapur (Mad) 53 G3
Hirapur (Tri) 60 A5
Hirasar 21 E6
Hirawari 67 E3
Hire Kotankal 86 B5
Hirehadagalli 91 E1
Hirekerur 90 D2
Hirisave 91 G6
Hiriyur 91 G4
Hirmi 69 E3
Hirnagaon 86 B1
Hirodih 57 E2
Hisamki 20 B3
Hisar 21 G3
Hisilpur (P) 20 A2
Hisua 56 D1
Hitaura (N) 38 C1
Hiwarkhed 66 B4
Hiwarkheri 67 G2
Hkaingzi (M) 75 F5
Hkalak Ga (M) 44 C3
Hkamho (M) 45 E2
Hkamkawn (M) 45 G4
Hkindawng (M) 45 G3
Hkinlun (M) 45 G2
Hkonthonzin (M) 61 G5
Hkyenhpa (M) 29 E6
Hlaikhan 61 E5
Hlup (M) 75 E5
Hmawngzaw 61 E4
Hmindingyin (M) 75 F5
Hmuntha 60 D5
Hnahlan 61 E4
Hodal 22 C6
Hodka Jho 48 B4
Hodu 31 G6
Hoinar 80 D3
Hojai 42 D4
Holalagondi 86 B6
Holalkere 91 F3
Holalu 91 E2
Holalur 91 E3
Holavanhalli 92 A4
Hole Narsipur 91 F6
Holehonnur 91 E3
Homlich Thach 19 E3
Homna (Ba) 59 G4
Honavar 90 B3
Hong 43 F1

Honganur 95 G1
Honnakere 91 G6
Honnali 91 E3
Honnavalli 91 F5
Honotgi 85 G3
Honupatta 14 B3
Honuru 91 H1
Honwada 86 D3
Hooghly-Chinsura 58 B6
Horlonga 81 H1, 82 A1
Horomoto 70 D2
Horti (Mah) 78 A6
Horti (Kar) 85 G2
Hosakote 91 H3
Hosanagara 90 D4
Hosangadi 90 C4
Hosdrug 94 B2
Hosdurga 91 F4
Hosehalli 91 G2
Hoshalli 92 A5
Hoshangabad 52 D6
Hoshiarpur 17 H3
Hoskote 92 B6
Hospet 85 H6, 86 A6
Hosur (Kar) 90 D2
Hosur (Tam) 92 B6
Hosuru 92 A4
Hota (P) 16 B6
Howli 41 H3
Howrah 72 B1
Hpala (M) 45 H3
Hpansing (M) 61 H2
Hpare (M) 45 G5
Hpizaw (M) 45 G2
Hponnyoliek (M) 74 C5
Hpontha (M) 75 E6
Hpunchan (M) 45 F3
Hpungan (M) 45 F5
Hpungnye (M) 44 C4
Hpusu Nok (M) 44 C3
Hriangkhan (M) 61 E6
Hriphaw (M) 45 G5
Hriphi (M) 75 E1
Hruizam (M) 60 C6
Htangsan (M) 44 A4
Htangtum (M) 75 E3
Htawgaw (M) 45 G5
Hti Seru (C) 29 G5
Hting Bu Ga (M) 45 F2
Htouwaing (M) 75 G1
Hualtu 60 D4
Hubli 85 F6
Hudugru 92 A4
Hudiara (P) 17 E3
Hudukhata 41 H3
Huikai (C) 45 G6
Hujian (M) 16 B1
Hujra (P) 16 C5
Hujra Shah Meqeen (P)
   16 D5
Hukeri 84 D4
Hukeri Road 85 E4
Hukitola 71 G6
Hulasganj 56 C1
Hulekal 90 C2
Hulgur 90 D1
Hulihaidar 85 H5
Hulijanli 85 F2
Hulikunte 91 G3
Huliyar 91 G4
Huliyurdurga 91 H6
Hulki 53 H6
Hulkur 91 F5
Hullahalli 95 E2
Hulloli 85 F2
Humachadakatte 90 D4
Humbarna 84 B2
Humcha 90 D4

Humgarh 57 H6
Hunasagi 86 A4
Hunawng (M) 61 H1
Hundar 14 C2
Hundarki 86 B2
Hundru 57 E5
Hung (M) 75 E4
Hungdu (M) 75 E5
Hungund 85 H4
Hunsur 95 E2
Hunterganj 56 C2
Hura (Wbg) 57 G5
Hura (Kar) 85 G2
Huralihalu 91 G2
Hurra 33 E5
Hurshi 58 B3
Husain 35 E1
Husainganj (Har) 22 A4
Husainganj (Utt) 36 C5
Husainpur (Ba) 59 G2
Husainpur 22 C3
Husnabad 86 C3
Hussainabad 56 A2
Hussaingunj 38 B4
Hutti 86 A4
Huturgi 85 G2
Huvin Hipparga 85 H3
Hawinahadagalli 91 E1
Huzurabad 79 G5
Huzurnagar 87 H3
Huzurpur 36 D1
Hwehka (M) 44 C6
Hwekum (M) 44 A4
Hyderabad 87 E1

Ibniyi 28 B4
Ibrahimpatan (And) 79 F4
Ibrahimpatan (And) 87 E2
Ichagarh 57 E6
Ichak 56 D3
Ichalkaranji 84 D3
Ichchapuram 82 C3
Ichhapur 65 H4
Ichhawar 52 B6
Ichora 79 E3
Idaiseval 99 E3
Idaiyakottai 95 H6
Idaiyappatti 96 A6
Idappadi 95 H3
Idar 50 B4
Idgaon (Ba) 74 B3
Idgarh (Ba) 74 B3
Idgundi 90 C1
Idilin 28 C4
Idukki 98 C2
Igatpuri 76 C2
Iglas 22 D6
Ignoitijala 101 E1
Ij 86 C4
Ijeri 86 A3
Ijhora 77 G5
Ikauna 37 E1
Ikhale 13 G4
Ikhlas (P) 12 A5
Ikhlaspur (P) 17 F1
Iklod 34 C4
Ilam (N) 40 A2
Ilam Bazar 58 A4
Ilangakkurichchi 96 B6
Ilav 64 A4
Ilayankudi 99 G2
Iliuru Kotapeta 87 E6
Ilkal 85 H5
Illatur 98 D3
Ilol 50 A4
Iluhar (Ba) 59 F6
Iluppur 96 B6
Ilupu 28 B4

Imamganj 56 B2
Imla Khas 37 H4
Imlota 22 A4
Imphal 61 F1
Inaka 101 G4
Inarwa (N) 39 H3
Inathganj (Ba) 60 A2
Indagaon 81 F1
Indapur (Mah) 76 B5
Indapur (Mah) 77 F6
Indargarh (Raj) 34 A5
Indargarh (Mad) 35 F5
Indaror 31 E4
Indas 58 A5
Indaw (M) 61 H4
Indawar 32 D3
Indergarh 35 H2
Indi 85 G2
Indin (M) 61 F6
Indipur 71 F6
Indiu (M) 74 C6
Indora 17 G2
Indore 51 H6, 65 H1
Indpur 57 G5
Indrana 31 H5
Indri 22 B1
Indukurpeta 93 G2
Indur 96 A2
Ingohta 36 A3
Ingyi (M) 61 H6
Inhauna 36 D3
Inkillu 88 A5
Inshan 13 G4
Int 77 G4
Inwara 20 D6
Ipuru 87 H4
Iradtnagar 35 E2
Iraiyur 96 C3
Irakam 93 G4
Irikkur 94 C2
Irinjalakuda 95 E6
Iritti 94 C2
Isagarh 52 D1
Isanagar (Mad) 53 G1
Isanagar (Utt) 24 C6
Isanattam 96 A5
Isarda 33 H4
Isauli 37 E4
Isganiep 14 A2
Ishkiali 12 D4
Ishurdi (Ba) 58 D3
Ishwaria 63 E2
Iskagundam 87 F5
Islahpur 79 E3
Islamabad (P) 12 B4
Islamkot (P) 48 D2
Islamnagar (Utt) 22 C1
Islamnagar (Utt) 23 F5
Islampur (Ba) 59 E1
Islampur (Wbg) 40 B4
Islampur (Bih) 56 D1
Islampur (Wbg) 58 C3
Islampur (Raj) 21 G5
Islur 90 C2
Ismailabad 18 B6
Isvej 63 G4
Iswal 50 C5
Iswarganj (Ba) 59 G2
Iswaripur (Ba) 72 D2
Iswerpur 71 G4
Itahar 40 B6
Itahari (N) 39 H3
Itakhola (Ba) 60 A3
Itamati 82 D1
Itanagar 43 E2
Itaria 63 F2
Itarsi 66 D1
Itaunja 36 B2

Itchu 14 A3
Iteshu (C) 29 H3
Itiathok 37 E1
Itiki 91 F1
Itkhori 56 D3
Itkur 77 H5
Itna (Ba) 59 H2
Itwa 37 F1
Itwari 67 G4
Izatnagar 23 G5

Jaba (P) 12 A6
Jabalpur 53 H5, 54 A5
Jabarhera 22 D1
Jabera 53 H4
Jabori (P) 12 C2
Jabra 56 C3
Jadakal 90 C4
Jadan 32 C5
Jadcherla 86 D3
Jaddangi 89 E1
Jade 90 D2
Jadewari (P) 47 F3
Jadhala 78 B4
Jadho 77 E6, 84 D1
Jafarabad (Guj) 63 F5
Jafarabad (Mah) 77 H1
Jafarganj (Ba) 59 H4
Jaflang (Ba) 42 B6
Jagadalapur 81 H2
Jagadevipalaiyam 96 A1
Jagadhri 18 C6
Jagal (P) 12 B3
Jagalur 91 G2
Jagamapur 35 G4
Jaganna Thaprasad 82 C1
Jagannath 83 E2
Jagannath Hat (Ba) 74 B1
Jagannathpur (Ba) 60 A2
Jagannathpur (Ori) 70 C5
Jagannathpur (Bih) 71 E2
Jaganndharju Chattram
  82 A5
Jagaon 66 B1
Jagargonda 80 D5
Jagasar 20 A5
Jagat 23 G6
Jagatballabhpur 58 B6
Jagatpur (Utt) 36 C4
Jagatpur (Ori) 71 E6
Jagatsingpur 71 F6
Jagatsukh 18 C2
Jagayyapeta 88 A3
Jagdala 41 H3
Jagdalpur (Ori) 69 G4
Jagdalpur (Mad) 81 E3
Jagdevwala 20 C5
Jagdishpur 69 G4
Jagdispur (Utt) 36 D4
Jagdispur (Bih) 38 B6
Jaggampeta 89 E2
Jagi Road 42 C4
Jagmabba 21 E2
Jagnair 34 D3
Jagoti 51 G5
Jagpura 51 E4
Jagraon 17 G5
Jagtial 79 F4
Jagudan 49 H5
Jahan Khan (P) 16 B5
Jahanabad (Ba) 74 A1
Jahanabad (P) 16 A2
Jahanabad (Utt) 23 H4
Jahangir (P) 16 B4
Jahangira (P) 12 A3
Jahangirabad 23 E5
Jahangirganj 37 G4

Jahangirpur 22 C5
Jahazpur 33 G5
Jahman (P) 17 E4
Jahri 78 B3
Jaigarh 84 B2
Jaijaipur 69 G3
Jaijon 17 H4
Jaikhedan 64 D5
Jaiko Lahri 17 G2
Jaimalsar 20 B5
Jain (N) 24 B4
Jainagar 57 E3
Jainath 79 F2
Jainpur 37 G4
Jaintgarh 71 E2
Jainti 41 E3
Jaintiapur (Ba) 42 B6
Jaipur (Raj) 33 H2
Jaipur (Ass) 44 A2
Jaipur (Wbg) 57 F5
Jaipurhat (Ba) 58 D1
Jairambati 58 A6
Jais 36 D4
Jaisalmer 31 E2
Jaisindhar 30 D5
Jaisinghnagar (Mad) 53 F4
Jaisinghnagar (Mad) 54 C4
Jait 34 D1
Jaitapur 84 B3
Jaitaran 32 D4
Jaitsar 21 E6
Jaitgiri 81 E3
Jaithari 53 F5
Jaithra 35 G1
Jaitipur (Utt) 23 H6
Jaitipur (Bih) 38 C6
Jaito (Pun) 17 F6
Jaito (Har) 22 B3
Jaitpur (Raj) 20 D4
Jaitpur (Mad) 53 G5
Jaitpura 33 G2
Jajal 19 E6
Jajarkot (N) 25 E4
Jajau 34 D2
Jajpur 71 F5
Jajpur Road 71 E5
Jajur 91 H3
Jakar 82 C3
Jakh 32 D1
Jakhal 21 G1
Jakhalabandha 42 D3
Jakhan 32 B2
Jakhar (P) 16 A5
Jakhar 13 E6
Jakharawali 20 D2
Jakhau 47 H5
Jakhauli 22 A2
Jakhaura 53 E1
Jakhim 56 B1
Jakhlaun 53 E2
Jakhoda 34 C5
Jakonia 34 B6
Jakrem 42 A6
Jalakandapuram 95 H3
Jalalabad (Pun) 17 E5
Jalalabad (Utt) 22 C2
Jalalabad (Utt) 23 H6
Jalalabad (Utt) 35 H2
Jalalgarh 39 H5
Jalali 23 E6
Jalalkhera 67 E4
Jalalpur (P) 16 B2
Jalalpur (Utt) 35 H5
Jalalpur (Utt) 37 F4
Jalalpur (Ass) 60 C1
Jalalpur (Guj) 64 A5
Jalalpur Dhai 36 C5
Jalam 66 A5

Jalandhar (Pun) 17 G4
Jalandhar (Mad) 53 E4
Jalandhar Cantonment
  17 G4
Jalangi 58 C3
Jalapur (P) 12 C6
Jalapur (P) 13 E6
Jalara 50 D3
Jalaun 35 G4
Jalbai (P) 12 A3
Jaldega (Mad) 55 G6
Jaldega (Bih) 70 C1
Jaldhaka (Ba) 40 D4
Jaldi (Ba) 74 B2
Jale 39 E4
Jalesar 35 E1
Jaleshwar 71 H3
Jaleswar (N) 39 E3
Jalgaon (Mah) 65 E6
Jalgaon (Mah) 65 G5
Jalgaon (Mah) 66 A5
Jalgaon (Mah) 77 F4
Jalgaon (Mah) 84 A1
Jalia 62 D1
Jaliapara (Ba) 74 C5
Jalihalli 86 A4
Jalikbari 42 A4
Jalimura 42 B4
Jalkot 78 C5
Jallan (P) 16 D2
Jallivari Pullalacheruvu
  87 F6
Jallo (P) 17 E3
Jalmana 22 B2
Jalna 77 G2
Jalndra 82 C4
Jalod 65 F4
Jalor 32 A6
Jalotra 50 A3
Jalpaiguri 40 C3
Jalwali 20 B5
Jalwara 52 B1
Jam 67 H4
Jam Sahib (P) 30 A4
Jamal 21 F3
Jamali (P) 48 A2
Jamalpur (Ba) 59 E1
Jamalpur (P) 20 A2
Jamalpur (Har) 21 H3
Jamalpur (Bih) 39 F6
Jamalpur (Wbg) 58 B5
Jamania 24 A4
Jamanpur 49 G4
Jamaro Head (P) 30 A4
Jamb (Mah) 67 F6
Jamb (And) 79 E3
Jambahal 70 B1
Jambani 71 G1
Jambar (P) 16 C4
Jambhor 78 A1
Jambhulpada 76 B4
Jambo 32 A2
Jamboti 84 D5
Jambu (C) 19 F2
Jambu 71 G6
Jambughoda 64 C1
Jambur (Guj) 63 E5
Jambur (Kar) 94 D1
Jambura 62 D1
Jamda (Mah) 65 F6
Jamda (Bih) 70 D2
Jamdaha 52 D2
Jamesabad (P) 30 B6
Jamgaon (Mah) 77 E3
Jamgaon (Mah) 85 G1
Jamhuri 50 B3

Jami 81 H6
Jamikunta 79 G5
Jamiri 42 C2
Jamjodhpur 62 C3
Jamka 63 E4
Jamkandorna 62 D3
Jamke Chatta (P) 16 D1
Jamkhandi 85 F4
Jamkhed (Mah) 77 G2
Jamkhed (Mah) 77 G4
Jamki (P) 17 E1
Jamli (Mad) 51 F6
Jamli (Mad) 65 F3
Jammalamdugu 92 C1
Jammu 13 F6
Jamnagar 62 C1
Jamner (Mad) 52 C3
Jamner (Mah) 65 G5
Jamod 66 A4
Jamra 70 A3
Jampara 70 C5
Jamshedpur 57 F6
Jamsher (P) 16 D5
Jamtali 37 E5
Jamtara 57 G3
Jamua 57 F3
Jamuguri (Ass) 42 D3
Jamuguri (Ass) 43 F4
Jamui 57 F1
Jamuna 40 D6
Jamunamukh 42 C4
Jamunia 52 B6
Jamunkira 70 B3
Jamuria 57 H4
Jamurki (Ba) 59 F3
Jamwa Ramgarh 33 H2
Jamwala 63 E5
Janakal 91 F3
Janakpur (N) 39 E3
Janakpur 54 D4
Janan 48 D4
Jandanwala (P) 16 B3
Jandiala (Pun) 17 F3
Jandiala (Pun) 17 G4
Jandiala Sherkhan (P)
  16 C2
Jandraka (P) 16 C4
Jandwala 20 D1
Janephal 66 A6
Jang 42 B1
Jangalwar 13 H5
Jangamakote 92 B5
Jangaon (And) 79 G4
Jangaon (And) 87 G1
Jangel 55 G2
Janghira 71 E4
Jangi (Him) 19 E3
Jangi (Guj) 48 D5
Jangid 79 H5
Jangipur 58 B2
Janglot 17 G1
Jangra 70 C3
Jani 22 D3
Janiwala (P) 16 A4
Janjgir 69 F2
Janjira (Ba) 59 G5
Jankia 82 D1
Jansath 22 D3
Jantra Khani (N) 39 F1
Janur 78 B2
Janvi 49 F2
Janwada 78 C6
Jaola (Raj) 33 E3
Jaola (Mah) 78 A5
Jaola (Mah) 78 B8
Jaola (Mah) 78 C2
Jaoli (Mah) 76 C6
Jaoli (Mah) 78 A6
Jaoli (Mah) 84 C1

Jaora 51 F4
Japla 52 B2
Jara 48 A4
Jarada 82 B3
Jaraikela 70 D2
Jarandh 69 F6
Jaranwala (P) 16 C3
Jarau 82 B2
Jardundha 55 E6
Jared (P) 12 C1
Jareru 34 D4
Jarha 54 B5
Jari (*)12 D5
Jari (Him) 18 C2
Jaria Jhanjail (Ba) 59 G1
Jaridhih 57 E4
Jarmundi 57 F3
Jarod (Mad) 52 D4
Jarod (Guj) 64 B1
Jarpara 70 C5
Jarvar 76 C2
Jarwa (Him) 18 C5
Jarwa (Utt) 25 F6
Jarwa (Utt) 37 F1
Jarwal 36 D2
Jarwe 69 G2
Jasana 21 F3
Jasdan 63 F2
Jashipur 71 E2
Jashpurnagar 56 B6
Jasidih 57 G2
Jasma 50 D1
Jasmergarh 17 F1
Jaso 54 B2
Jasol 31 H5
Jaspur (Utt) 23 F3
Jaspur (Mad) 69 G3
Jaspura 36 A5
Jasrana 35 F2
Jasrapura 21 G6
Jasrasar 20 C6
Jassar (P) 17 F2
Jasuntsar 20 C4
Jaswantnagar 35 F2
Jaswantpura 50 A2
Jaswari 66 A3
Jat 51 F1
Jatar Daul 72 C2
Jatara 53 G1
Jatawada 49 E4
Jath 85 F2
Jathwara 36 D5
Jati (Mughalbhin) (P) 47 H3
Jatkul (P) 12 B1
Jatli (P) 12 B5
Jatni 71 E6
Jaton ki Dhani 49 E1
Jatramanipara 60 C5
Jatrapur (Ba) 59 E6
Jatusana 22 B5
Jatwar 18 B6
Jatwara 34 A2
Jauli 22 D2
Jaulka 66 C4
Jaunpur 37 F5
Jaura (P) 12 C6
Jauta 13 H5
Javagallu 91 F5
Javanagondanahalli 91 G4
Jawad 51 F2
Jawaja 32 D5
Jawal 78 D1
Jawala Mukhi 18 A2
Jawalgeri 86 B5
Jawali (Him) 17 H2
Jawali (Raj) 32 C6
Jawar (Mad) 52 A6
Jawar (Mad) 66 A3

Jawassa 35 F3
Jawhar 76 B1
Jayal 32 D2
Jayantipur 82 B3
Jayapatna 81 G2
Joydevpur (Ba) 59 G3
Jayganj (Ba) 40 C5
Jaynagar (Ba) 73 G1
Jaynagar (Bih) 39 F3
Jaynagar (Wbg) 72 C2
Jaypur (Bih) 57 G2
Jaypur (Wbg) 57 H6
Jaysingpur 84 D3
Jehanabad (Bih) 38 C6
Jehanabad (Bih) 56 A1
Jehanian (P) 16 C2
Jehpoyo (P) 48 C2
Jejuri 76 D5
Jeketa 18 D4
Jelam 19 H5
Jemir Ghat (N) 25 H5
Jenapur 71 F5
Jengpata 43 E4
Jepa (C) 29 E1
Jerain 42 C6
Jerruck (P) 47 G1
Jeruwakhera 53 E3
Jesawa 31 G6
Jesawara 50 D6
Jessami 43 G5
Jessore (Ba) 58 D5
Jesurana 31 E2
Jetalsar 62 D3
Jethana 33 E4
Jetpur (Guj) 49 E6
Jetpur (Guj) 63 E3
Jeur (Mah) 77 E3
Jeur (Mah) 77 F5
Jevargi 86 A2
Jewar 22 C5
Jeypur 81 F4
Jhab 49 G1
Jhabran (P) 16 D2
Jhabua 51 E6
Jhabugam 64 C2
Jhadabhumi 82 C1
Jhadupudi 82 C3
Jhagadiya 64 B3
Jhagar 52 C2
Jhailar 66 D3
Jhajha 57 F2
Jhajham 49 F4
Jhajhar 22 C5
Jhajjar 22 B4
Jhajju 20 B6
Jhajra 18 D6
Jhak 33 G3
Jhaknawad 51 E6
Jhalai 33 H4
Jhalakati (Ba) 73 F1
Jhalambi 64 C4
Jhalar (P) 12 A4
Jhalarpatan 51 H2
Jhalawar 51 H2
Jhalida 57 E5
Jhalki 85 G2
Jhalod 50 D6
Jhalra 33 H5
Jhalu 23 E2
Jhamra (P) 12 A3
Jhanda (P) 12 A3
Jhando Marri (P) 30 A5
Jhandoke 21 G2
Jhanfli 31 E4
Jhang (P) 12 A4
Jhang (P) 16 A4
Jhangurbara 40 A6
Jhanjahrpur 39 F4

Jhanjhmer 63 H4
Jhanjwa 50 B3
Jhansi 35 F6
Jhanwar 32 A4
Jhanzi 43 G2
Jhapa (N) 40 A3
Jhara Sangaru 78 D6
Jharapapra 80 B1
Jharda 51 G4
Jhargram 71 G1
Jharia 57 F4
Jharkatta 80 B1
Jharli 22 A4
Jharol 50 C2
Jharsuguda 70 A3
Jharwasa 33 E4
Jhatingri 18 B2
Jhawani (N) 38 B1
Jhawarian (P) 16 A1
Jhedasar 21 E3
Jhelum (P) 12 C5
Jhenaidah (Ba) 58 D4
Jhenida (Ba) 59 E4
Jherda 49 H3
Jhikabasti (N) 24 C3
Jhikra 72 A1
Jhilimili 57 G6
Jhilla 53 E4
Jhilmili (Mad) 55 G5
Jhilmili (Mad) 67 G2
Jhimpir (P) 47 G1
Jhingergacha (Ba) 58 D5
Jhinjhak 35 H3
Jhinjhana 22 C2
Jhinjhuvada 49 F5
Jhinkali 31 E4
Jhinkpani 71 E1
Jhiraua 33 G4
Jhirna 23 F2
Jhodge 65 E6
Jhok Hamand (P) 16 C4
Jhol (P) 30 A5
Jhonpra 33 H4
Jhulaghat 24 A2
Jhumra Chak (P) 16 B3
Jhumritilaiya 56 D3
Jhungi 18 C3
Jhuniar 21 F1
Jhunjhunu 21 G5
Jhunpa 21 G4
Jhura 48 C5
Jhuran 48 C5
Jhusi 37 E6
Jiawan 55 F3
Jibti 24 B1
Jidkal 87 F1
Jido 27 H3
Jigal 23 H2
Jigna 35 E5
Jigni (Mad) 35 E3
Jigni (Utt) 35 G5
Jigthan 77 F2
Jihtzu (C) 29 H5
Jikhipali 69 H4
Jikyop (C) 26 A4
Jilluba 82 C7
Jilugumilli 88 C2
Jimkhar (B) 26 A6
Jinang 82 B4
Jind 22 A3
Jindrah 13 F6
Jinduka (C) 29 H4
Jinghanu 13 F6
Jining 27 H5
Jinjhiniali 31 E4
Jinthanggaon 42 D4
Jinti 77 F5

Jintur 78 B2
Jio (C) 29 G2
Jior (C) 29 G3
Jiphum 74 C1
Jirampal 80 D5
Jiran 51 F3
Jiri (N) 39 F1
Jirigam 28 C6
Jirighat 60 D1
Jispa Camp 14 C6
Jitpur 23 G3
Jiwan (C) 29 H6
Jiwan Shah (P) 16 B6
Jiwana 33 E5
Jobat 65 E1
Jodasar (Raj) 20 A5
Jodasar (Raj) 20 D5
Jodhatti 85 E4
Jodhka 21 F2
Jodhpur 32 B4
Jodiya 62 D1
Jodiya Bandar 48 D6
Jodmoha 67 E6
Jogapatti 38 B3
Jogbani 39 H4
Jogbura (N) 24 B3
Joghara 39 E3
Jogi Tila (P) 12 C6
Jogighopa 41 G4
Jogindar Nagar 18 B2
Jogiwala 21 G3
Joianwala (P) 16 D2
Jojomura 70 B4
Jokche (C) 19 G2
Joki Hat 40 A4
Jolarpet 96 B1
Jonai Bazar 28 A6
Jongohetpara 41 F6
Jonha 57 E5
Jonnagiri 86 C6
Jora 34 D4
Joranda 71 E5
Jorera 22 C6
Jorhat 43 F3
Jori 56 C3
Joriapani (N) 24 B3
Jorigam 81 F2
Jormu 70 C6
Jorpakuri 40 C3
Joshiana (Utt) 19 F6
Joshiana (Utt) 23 F1
Joshimath 19 G5
Joteswar Hat 40 D3
Jouljibi (N) 24 B2
Jowai 42 B6
Jowar (P) 12 A2
Jowla 77 F5
Joya 23 E4
Joyag (Ba) 59 H6
Jrongnel (C) 29 G5
Juan 22 B3
Jub (N) 24 C3
Jubarajpur 81 G3
Jubbal 18 D4
Judpur 53 H3
Juhu 76 A3
Jujkhola (Ba) 60 B6
Jukal 78 C5
Jukehi 54 B3
Julana 22 A3
Julwania 65 F3
Jumabari (Ba) 59 E1
Jumla (N) 25 E2
Juna Raj 64 C3
Junagadh 62 D3
Junagarh 81 G2
Junbesi (N) 39 F1
Jundla 22 B2

Junga 18 C4
Jungkar (C) 27 E3
Jungo Jalbani (P) 47 G3
Jungshahi (P) 47 G2
Junia 33 F4
Junnar 76 C3
Junoni 85 E2
Jupatarai 68 A6
Juri (Ba) 60 B2
Juribela (N) 38 D2
Juryar (P) 48 B2
Jusri 33 F2
Jwalpur 23 E1

Kabadak (Ba) 72 D2
Kabaing (M) 75 H2
Kabirganj 24 A4
Kabirpur 71 F5
Kabrai 36 A6
Kabulgram (P) 12 A2
Kabuli 49 F1
Kabulshah 16 D6
Kabzauk (M) 74 D5
Kachai (N) 24 B4
Kachaura (Utt) 23 F6
Kachaura (Utt) 35 F3
Kachautla 52 A4
Kachchhiahana 67 F3
Kachchirayapalaiyam
  96 B3
Kachelo (P) 30 C1
Kachhapind 13 F6
Kachhauna 36 B2
Kachhwa 37 F6
Kachnar 52 D2
Kachnara 51 F4
Kachola 33 F6
Kachua (Ba) 59 H5
Kachua (Ba) 73 F1
Kada 77 F4
Kadaba (Kar) 91 E6
Kadaba (Kar) 91 H5
Kadach 62 C4
Kadaiyam 98 D4
Kadaiyanallur 98 D3
Kadakkal 98 C4
Kadakkavur 98 B4
Kadaladi 96 C1
Kadambur 99 E3
Kadamtala 100 B4
Kadana 50 C5
Kadanwari (P) 30 B2
Kadapara 70 B5
Kadarbana (N) 38 D3
Kadattur 96 A2
Kadaura 35 H5
Kadavakuduru 88 A5
Kadegaon 84 D2
Kadera 33 H5
Kadhan (P) 48 A2
Kadi 49 H5
Kadichur 86 C3
Kadipur 37 F4
Kadirabad 77 H2
Kadiri 92 C3
Kadiyampatti 96 A3
Kadligarh 70 B5
Kadma 21 H5
Kadra 90 B1
Kadrangyang (M) 45 E4
Kadu (M) 61 G4
Kadum 28 C6
Kadur 91 F4
Kadus 76 C4
Kadval 64 C1
Kadwa 40 A5
Kadwaha 52 D1

Kafara 24 C5
Kagada 82 C1
Kagal 84 D3
Kagaraul 34 D2
Kagaznagar 79 H3
Kagdari 63 E1
Kaglipur 92 A6
Kahani 67 H1
Kahao 29 E5
Kahim 76 A4
Kahnaur 22 A4
Kahnuwan 17 G2
Kahuta (P) 12 C4
Kahuta 12 D3
Kahwabakra 69 E6
Kaihoa 101 G4
Kaij 77 H4
Kaikarem 88 C3
Kailali (N) 24 B4
Kailana 18 D5
Kailaras 34 C4
Kailashabar 60 B3
Kailia 35 G5
Kaimganj 35 G1
Kaimori 53 H5
Kaing (M) 75 H4
Kainur 23 G1
Kainwaha 34 D6
Kaiphundai 61 E2
Kaipuram 82 B4
Kairana 22 C2
Kairon 17 F4
Kairot 33 F5
Kairu 21 H4
Kaisarganj 36 D2
Kaisi 74 D2
Kaitha 51 H5
Kaithal 22 A1
Kajalia (Ba) 59 F6
Kajgaon 65 F6
Kajlagarh 72 A2
Kajra 21 G5
Kakachawa 37 G1
Kakana 101 F2
Kakanpur 50 C6
Kakarbai 35 G5
Kakarbhitta (N) 40 B3
Kakarwao 53 F2
Kakatpur 83 F1
Kakching 61 F2
Kakching Khunou 61 F2
Kakdwip 72 B3
Kakelao 32 B4
Kakhandri 85 F3
Kakinada 89 E2
Kakkabe 94 C2
Kakkirigumma 81 G4
Kakmari 85 F3
Kako 38 C6
Kakor 33 H4
Kakora 23 G6
Kakori 36 B3
Kakraban 60 A5
Kakrala (Raj) 20 B4
Kakrala (Utt) 23 G6
Kakreji 49 E6
Kaksa 57 H5
Kakset 15 F4
Kakshar 13 H2
Kaku 32 C1
Kakul (P) 12 C3
Kakwan 35 H3
Kala (P) 12 C5
Kala 17 G4
Kala Afghanan 17 F2
Kala Amb 18 C5
Kala Dera 33 G2

Kala Pipal 52 B5
Kala-Ywa (M) 74 C6
Kaladan (M) 74 D4
Kaladan 74 D1
Kaladgi 85 F4
Kaladhungi 23 G3
Kalagarh 23 F2
Kalagechhia 72 A2
Kalaia (Ba) 73 G1
Kalaigaon 42 B3
Kalain 60 C1
Kalaiya (N) 38 C2
Kalakada 92 D4
Kalakankar 36 C5
Kalakot (P) 12 A1
Kalaksar 18 D1
Kalaktang 42 B2
Kalale 95 E2
Kalalia 32 D5
Kalam 67 E6
Kalamadi 85 F3
Kalamangalam 95 H1
Kalamati 56 D5
Kalamb 76 D4
Kalambela 91 H4
Kalamnuri 78 C2
Kalamrida (Ba) 59 F5
Kalan (Pun) 17 G5
Kalan (And) 87 E2
Kalana 62 D3
Kalanaur (Pun) 17 F2
Kalanaur (Har) 22 A4
Kalandri 50 A1
Kalangini 96 A4
Kalanpur (Raj) 32 A4
Kalanpur (Utt) 36 A3
Kalanwali 21 F1
Kalapahar 43 F6
Kalapathar Patna 70 D6
Kalapatti 95 F4
Kalapettai 97 E2
Kalapur (Ba) 74 B2
Kalaraoa (Ba) 58 D6
Kalarmarchara (Ba) 74 B3
Kalarua (M) 74 B4
Kalas 77 E6
Kalasa (And) 87 G3
Kalasa (And) 90 D5
Kalasapadu 92 D1
Kalaud 21 G4
Kalava 87 E5
Kalavad 62 D2
Kalavi 93 E6
Kalayat 22 A2
Kalchaundi 85 E1
Kalchini 41 E3
Kalda 54 B3
Kaldabi 13 E5
Kale (Mah) 84 C2
Kale (Mah) 84 C3
Kaledhon 85 E1
Kalegaon 77 H4
Kalemyo (M) 61 F5
Kaletwa (M) 74 D3
Kalewa (M) 61 G5
Kalgaon 77 F2
Kalghatgi 85 E6
Kalgi 86 B1
Kalgupur 78 B6
Kalhel 14 A6
Kali (P) 17 E2
Kali 78 D1
Kalia Shan (P) 20 B1
Kaliachak 58 B1
Kaliakain (Ba) 59 F3
Kaliakpur 71 F1

Kalian Awan (P) 12 B4
Kaliana (P) 16 B6
Kaliana (Har) 21 H4
Kaliana (Guj) 62 D2
Kaliani 43 F3
Kalianwala (P) 16 C2
Kaliaseri 94 C2
Kalichandbari (Ba) 60 B5
Kalidaha (Ba) 40 D5
Kaliganj (Ba) 58 D5
Kaliganj (Ba) 72 D1
Kaliganj 58 B4
Kaligiri 93 F2
Kalikapur (Ba) 59 H6
Kalikavu 95 E4
Kalikiri 92 D4
Kalikot (N) 24 D3
Kalimala 81 E6
Kalimpong 40 C2
Kalinagar 24 A4
Kalindha 36 A1
Kalingapatam 82 B5
Kalingia 82 B1
Kalingupatti 99 F2
Kalinjara 50 D5
Kalipith 52 B3
Kalipur (Ba) 74 B2
Kalit 13 E6
Kaliyaganj 40 B5
Kalka 18 B5
Kalkadambur 95 G3
Kalkini (Ba) 59 F5
Kalkote 13 E5
Kallakkurichchi 96 B3
Kallakudi 96 C5
Kallakuru 88 C3
Kallam 77 H5
Kallangudi 91 F5
Kallar (P) 12 A6
Kallar (P) 12 C4
Kallar (J&K) 13 F1
Kallar (Ker) 94 B1
Kallar (Ker) 98 C1
Kallidaikurichi 98 D4
Kalligud 99 E2
Kallimandayam 95 H6
Kallupatti 99 E2
Kallur (Kar) 86 B4
Kallur (And) 88 B2
Kalma 86 B4
Kalmanda 52 A1
Kalmargu 79 F3
Kalmeshwar 67 F4
Kalmora 65 E1
Kalna 58 B5
Kalnai 55 H6
Kalnsar 20 B5
Kalohi (P) 48 B2
Kalol (Guj) 49 H5
Kalol (Guj) 64 C1
Kaloli 84 C1
Kalom 27 G6
Kalot 21 G5
Kalowal (P) 16 B2
Kalpa 19 E3
Kalpetta 94 D3
Kalpi 35 H4
Kalra (P) 16 A1
Kalri (P) 16 A3
Kalri 32 C2
Kalsapura 91 E5
Kalsi 18 D5
Kalu (P) 47 G1
Kalu 20 D5
Kalu Khan (P) 12 A3
Kalugumalai 99 E3
Kaluma Kanda (Ba) 59 G1
Kaluvaye 93 E2

Kalvan 64 D6
Kalwa 76 B6
Kalwakurti 87 E3
Kalwari 37 F3
Kalyan 76 B3
Kalyandrug 91 H2
Kalyani 78 B6
Kalyanpur (Bih) 38 C3
Kalyanpur (Tri) 60 A4
Kalyanpur (Kar) 90 C5
Kalyansingapuram 81 G2
Kalyarkoil 99 G1
Kama 50 C1
Kamaing (M) 44 D6
Kamakhyanagar 70 D5
Kamalapuram 92 C2
Kamalganj (Ba) 60 B3
Kamalganj 35 H2
Kamalia (P) 16 A5
Kamalnagar 78 C5
Kamalpur (Bih) 39 H4
Kamalpur (Ass) 42 A4
Kamalpur (Tri) 60 B3
Kamalpur (Guj) 63 G1
Kaman 22 C6
Kamanayakapaiyam 95 G5
Kamanjani (Ba) 41 E6
Kamankol 85 E4
Kamanpur 79 H4
Kamar 12 D4
Kamareddi 79 E5
Kamarhati 58 B6
Kamarji 55 E4
Kamarkhal (Ba) 60 A1
Kamarpur 43 E2
Kamasin 36 C6
Kamavarapukota 88 C2
Kambadur 91 H3
Kambalapalle 87 E5
Kamban 98 C2
Kambeng 27 G5
Kambhampadu 88 B2
Kambi 77 G3
Kambohanwala (P) 16 B5
Kamchang (C) 27 E3
Kamdara 56 C6
Kamdhia 63 E3
Kameli 80 D4
Kameng 42 D2
Kameri 84 D2
Kameria 32 D1
Kamgana (B) 41 E2
Kamhtawngdam (M) 45 H2
Kaminpur (P) 16 B3
Kamir (P) 16 B6
Kamjaw Ga (M) 45 F3
Kamku 44 D1
Kamlagarh 18 B2
Kamlapur (Utt) 36 C1
Kamlapur (Kar) 86 B1
Kamlial (P) 12 A5
Kamoke (P) 16 D2
Kamola 23 G3
Kampang 61 G2
Kampara 69 H2
Kampel 65 H1
Kampil 23 G6
Kampli 86 A6
Kamptee 67 G4
Kampur 42 C4
Kampura 35 G4
Kamarakhanda (Ba) 59 E2
Kamrana 20 B3
Kamrej 64 B4
Kamri 13 F1
Kamrkupur 58 A6
Kamsandra 92 C6

Kamsin (N) 24 B1
Kamta 84 B4
Kamtaul 39 E4
Kamtha 68 A3
Kamudi 99 F3
Kamvadi 77 F5
Kan (M) 75 F1
Kana 85 H5
Kanaganapalle 92 A2
Kanagton (M) 61 H5
Kanairghat (Ba) 60 B1
Kanakamajalu 94 C1
Kanakanur 80 A5
Kanakapura 95 G1
Kanakaramchattram 93 F5
Kanakatte 91 F4
Kanalla 101 H6
Kanang (M) 74 D3
Kanangla 84 D4
Kanar 51 H4
Kanas (Mah) 65 E1
Kanas (Ori) 83 E1
Kanasan 31 F4
Kanasar 31 H1
Kanaudi 54 C4
Kanauj 51 E2
Kanayannur 98 B1
Kanbya (M) 75 G6
Kanbya Ashe (M) 75 H6
Kanchannagar (Ba) 60 B6
Kanchannagar (Ba) 74 B2
Kanchanpur (N) 39 G3
Kanchanpur 60 B3
Kanchikacherla 88 A3
Kanching 43 H3
Kanchipuram 93 F6
Kanchrapara 58 C6
Kanda (Utt) 18 D5
Kanda (Utt) 23 F2
Kandaghat 18 B4
Kandahar 78 C4
Kandahu (M) 30 B1
Kandar 18 B3
Kandar 80 B2
Kandarkhi 23 F4
Kandauli 38 A4
Kandbara 70 D4
Kandfari (P) 30 A5
Kandgal 85 H5
Kandh 64 B3
Kandhla (P) 30 B1
Kandhla 22 C3
Kandhrapur 37 G4
Kandi (Him) 18 C3
Kandi (Utt) 23 E1
Kandi (Wbg) 58 B3
Kandi (And) 86 D1
Kandiala 31 E2
Kandigaon (Ba) 59 H2
Kandikere 91 G5
Kandili 96 B1
Kandkurti 78 D4
Kandla 48 D6
Kando (N) 24 C2
Kandorna 62 C3
Kandra (P) 30 A1
Kandra (Mad) 56 A5
Kandra (Bih) 57 E6
Kandran Garhi (N) 38 C1
Kandri 80 B1
Kandukur 87 H6
Kandur 93 F6
Kanduru 92 D4
Kandwal (P) 12 A6
Kane Chak Nagrota 13 E6
Kanegiri 90 C1
Kanekallu 91 H1
Kanepalli 79 H3

Kanera 51 F2
Kanesan 33 F5
Kanethi 18 C4
Kangan 13 F3
Kanganpur (P) 16 D5
Kangaon 67 F6
Kangayam 95 H5
Kangchen (C) 26 A1
Kangfang (M) 45 H4
Kanghmun 60 C4
Kangkung (M) 45 H3
Kanglatongbi 61 F1
Kangpar (B) 42 A2
Kangra 18 A2
Kangti 78 D5
Kangundi 92 C6
Kangyi (M) 61 F5
Kangyu (C) 28 A2
Kanha (Mad) 68 B2
Kanha (Mah) 78 D2
Kanhargaon 78 C1
Kanhla (M) 75 H4
Kanhor 20 D3
Kanhur 77 E3
Kanhwara 54 B4
Kani (M) 75 H1
Kanigiri 87 G6
Kanij 50 A6
Kanika 70 A3
Kanina 22 A5
Kanini 13 H5
Kaniwara 67 H2
Kaniyambadi 93 E6
Kanjale (Mah) 76 C6
Kanjale (Mah) 84 B1
Kanjalgi 85 E4
Kanjang 43 F6
Kanjangaon Ganpati 76 D4
Kanjanwali (P) 16 A5
Kanjar Kot (P) 48 B3
Kanjarda 51 F2
Kanjed 80 A3
Kanjia 53 E3
Kanjirapalli 98 B2
Kanjwani (P) 16 B4
Kankani 32 B4
Kankanwadi 85 F4
Kankapal 81 E4
Kankauli 84 C4
Kanker 68 D6
Kanker Khera 22 D3
Kankhal 23 E1
Kanki 40 A4
Kankipudu 88 B4
Kankiu (M) 45 F1
Kankroli 50 C1
Kanna (P) 17 E3
Kannad 65 F6
Kannandahalli 96 A1
Kannapuram 88 C2
Kannauj 35 H2
Kannod 66 B1
Kannoli 85 H3
Kannur 94 C3
Kanod 31 F2
Kanodar 49 H3
Kanol 19 H6
Kanor 50 D2
Kanota 33 H2
Kanpati 42 C3
Kanpetlat (M) 75 F4
Kanpur (J&K) 17 G1
Kanpur (Utt) 36 B3
Kanpur (Ori) 70 D6
Kanpura 33 F4
Kansar (Raj) 21 E3
Kansar (Ori) 70 B4
Kanseth (Ba) 58 B2

Kansi (M) 44 C5
Kansivni 66 C6
Kantabanji 69 G6
Kantai 38 D4
Kantamurnad 94 D2
Kantan (M) 44 C3
Kantanagar (Ba) 40 C5
Kanteli 68 D2
Kanth 23 F3
Kantha 36 B3
Kantharia 63 G1
Kanthet (M) 75 G2
Kanthkoti 48 D5
Kanti 22 A5
Kantilo 70 D6
Kanun 51 F6
Kanuparti 88 A5
Kanur (Mah) 78 C4
Kanur (Kar) 85 G2
Kanutse 14 B2
Kanwas 51 H1
Kanwat 33 G1
Kanyakumari 98 D6
Kanzalwano 13 E2
Kaohni 55 F3
Kaonlesar 32 C1
Kap (Mah) 79 E1
Kap (Kar) 90 C5
Kapadna 65 E5
Kapadvanj 50 B6
Kapal 84 D4
Kapanga 101 G4
Kaparkot (N) 25 E5
Kapasan 51 E1
Kapasia (Ba) 59 G3
Kapasia 50 A2
Kaphra 23 H2
Kapi Dzong (B) 41 E1
Kapileswarapundi 88 B4
Kapilmum (Ba) 58 D6
Kapkot 23 H1
Kapra (M) 45 E4
Kapren 33 H6
Kaptai (Ba) 74 C1
Kaptei (M) 61 E5
Kaptipada 71 F3
Kapu (C) 28 A2
Kapur 86 B3
Kapuria 32 B2
Kapurisar 20 D4
Kapurthala 17 F3
Kar Bhoaga 86 A1
Kara 36 C5
Karachi (P) 47 E1
Karad 84 C2
Karadge 84 D3
Karadi 91 G5
Karadkhel 78 C5
Karadoho 76 A1
Karagur 96 A2
Karahal 34 C6
Karaia 35 E5
Karaiahai 52 B2
Karaikal 97 E5
Karaikela 56 D6
Karaikkudi 99 G1
Karajgi (Mah) 85 F2
Karajgi (Mah) 85 G1
Karajgi (Kar) 90 D1
Karak (C) 19 F1
Karakat 38 B6
Karakhera 35 E6
Karakthal 49 G6
Karali 64 C2
Karambad 78 C6
Karambakudi 96 C6

Karampa 77 G6
Karampur 34 B4
Karanchedu 88 A5
Karandighi 40 A5
Karangania 42 D1
Karangulam 98 D5
Karanja (Mah) 66 C6
Karanja (Mah) 67 E4
Karanja (Mah) 76 A4
Karanji (Mah) 77 F3
Karanji (Mah) 79 F1
Karanjia (Mad) 54 D6
Karanjia (Mad) 68 B1
Karanjia (Ori) 71 E3
Karanphan 84 C3
Karanpur (P) 20 A1
Karanpur 37 F2
Karantela 82 C3
Karanwas 52 B4
Karapa 89 E3
Karapgaon 53 F6
Karar 55 H2
Karari 36 D6
Karauli 34 B3
Karavadi 88 A6
Karban 49 G2
Karbigwan 36 B4
Karbos 13 G1
Karbudurun 13 G4
Karchana 37 E6
Karde 76 D4
Karedu 88 A6
Karegaon 77 F2
Kareli 53 G6
Karempudi 87 H4
Karera (Raj) 32 D6
Karera (Mad) 35 E6
Kargani 85 E2
Karghar 56 A1
Kargil 14 A2
Karhaia Khoh 52 C4
Karhal 35 F2
Karhati 77 E5
Kari 77 H5
Kariala (P) 12 B6
Kariala (P) 12 C6
Kariana 63 F3
Karianwala (P) 13 E6
Karimangalam 96 A2
Karimganj (Ba) 59 H2
Karimganj 60 C1
Karimnagar 79 G5
Karimpur 58 C4
Karimuddinpur 38 A5
Karivalamvandalur 98 D3
Karivemula 86 C5
Kariyapatti 99 E2
Karjan 64 B2
Karjat (Mah) 76 B4
Karjat (Mah) 77 F5
Karjat (Mah) 77 G2
Karka (J&K) 12 D1
Karka (Mad) 80 D4
Karkal 90 D5
Karkalmatti 85 F4
Karkamb 77 F6
Karkasur (P) 48 C2
Karkheli 78 D4
Karki 54 D4
Karko 27 H4
Karkoma 69 G2
Karla 76 B4
Karlaghati 82 A2
Karlapet 81 G2
Karlup 13 F6
Karmad 77 G2
Karmala 77 F5
Karmatani 57 F3

Karmawas 32 A5
Karna (P) 30 B6
Karnal 22 B2
Karnana (P) 12 D6
Karnaota 32 D1
Karnaprayag 19 G6
Karnapur 41 E4
Karnesar 20 A6
Karnisar 20 B5
Karon 57 G3
Karonda 53 E3
Karong 43 F6
Karoni 32 A4
Karora (P) 12 B1
Karora 22 D5
Karpo (C) 26 D4
Karra 56 C5
Karrapur 53 F4
Karru 20 D3
Karsado 34 B2
Karsgaon 66 D4
Karsi 55 H5
Karsog 18 C3
Karta (C) 26 C5
Kartal 54 B1
Kartala 69 G2
Kartapur 17 G3
Kartse 13 H2
Karu 14 D3
Karuar (P) 20 A3
Karuj 33 E6
Karumattapatti 95 F4
Karumbakkam 93 F6
Karunda 51 E2
Karungapalli 98 B3
Karunguli 97 E1
Karur (P) 12 C4
Karur (Kar) 90 C3
Karur (And) 92 A1
Karur (Tam) 96 A5
Karuru 86 B6
Karuvambram 94 D4
Karva 84 D2
Karvetnagar 93 E5
Karwa 54 D5
Karwapa 80 A1
Karwar (Raj) 33 H5
Karwar (Mad) 51 H6
Karwar (Kar) 90 B2
Karwara 49 H1
Karwi 36 C6
Kas 84 C1
Kasa 76 B2
Kasal 84 B4
Kasamba 18 B2
Kasar 51 H1
Kasar Sirsi 78 B6
Kasara 76 C2
Kasaragod 94 B1
Kasarda 84 C4
Kasare 64 D5
Kasari 51 G4
Kasau (M) 45 F6
Kasauli 18 B5
Kasba (Bih) 39 H5
Kasba (Kar) 85 H4
Kasba Kamarda 71 H3
Kasba Narayangarh 71 H2
Kasba Pataspur 72 A2
Kasbo (P) 49 E3
Kasdol 69 F3
Kasegaon 84 C2
Kasel 17 E3
Kasganj 23 F6
Kasha (Ba) 59 H4
Kashedi 76 C6
Kashinagar (Ba) 59 H5
Kashipur (Utt) 23 F3

Kashipur (Wbg) 57 G5
Kashipur (Ori) 81 G3
Kashti 77 E5
Kasia 38 A3
Kasiabad (Ba) 72 D1
Kasimabad 37 H5
Kasinathpur (Ba) 59 E3
Kasipet 79 G4
Kasmara 35 G2
Kasni 22 B4
Kasodа 65 G5
Kasol 18 C2
Kasom Khullon 61 G2
Kaspur 81 E1
Kasran (P) 12 A4
Kaswad 65 G2
Kassoke (P) 16 C2
Kassowal (P) 16 A5
Kasti 32 B3
Kasukanga 81 E1
Kasumkasa 68 C6
Kasur (P) 17 E4
Kat 18 B3
Kat Ram Chand (P) 20 A1
Katahul 65 E4
Katak Chincholi 78 C6
Kataklik 15 E1
Katalberi 67 G2
Katamgia 82 B2
Katangi (Mad) 53 H5
Katangi (Mad) 67 H3
Katangjhiri 68 A3
Katangur 87 G2
Katapuram 80 B5
Katarkhatav 84 D1
Katarki 85 H6
Katarukonda 86 C6
Katea 38 B3
Katepalli 79 H3
Katgora 69 F1
Katha Saghral (P) 16 A1
Kathal 50 B6
Kathala (P) 12 D6
Kathalia (Ba) 73 F1
Kathalia 60 A5
Kathana 22 A2
Kathgodam 23 H3
Kathi 64 D3
Kathia 52 C2
Kathiatali 42 D4
Kathiwara 64 D1
Kathlaur 17 G1
Kathmandu (N) 38 D1
Kathor 64 B4
Kathore (P) 30 A2
Kathori 31 E2
Kathoti 33 E2
Kathu 33 E2
Kathu Nangal 17 F3
Kathua 17 G1
Kathuli (Ba) 58 C4
Kathumar 34 B1
Kati 77 H6
Katiadi (Ba) 59 G3
Katigara 60 C1
Katihar 39 H6
Katikund 57 H3
Katkamsari 56 D3
Katkol 85 E5
Katkuiyan 25 E6
Katkut 65 H1
Katlichara 60 C2
Kato (C) 26 B3
Katoda 51 F1
Katol (Him) 19 E4
Katol (Mah) 67 F4
Katomato (N) 24 B3
Katosan 49 H5

Katpadi 93 E6
Katphal 77 E5
Katra (J&K) 13 F5
Katra (Utt) 23 H5
Katra (Utt) 37 E1
Katra (Bih) 39 E4
Katra (Mad) 54 D1
Katrabani 57 G3
Katrain 18 B2
Katral 85 G2
Katrangia 70 A6
Katras 57 F4
Kattampatti 95 G5
Katti (N) 24 D4
Kattipuram 94 D5
Kattumavadi 99 H1
Kattuputhur 96 A5
Kattur 90 C1
Katunje (N) 24 B4
Katur 78 C4
Katuria 57 G2
Katutra (C) 27 E5
Katwa 58 B4
Katwara 51 E6
Kauakol 57 E1
Kauhi 68 D5
Kaukachal 98 B2
Kaukky (M) 61 H5
Kaukuntla 86 D3
Kaul 22 B1
Kaulas 78 D5
Kauli 18 A6
Kaunghein (M) 44 A5
Kauria 54 B4
Kauriram 37 H3
Kausani 23 H1
Kautalam 86 B5
Kauthe 76 D4
Kav 90 D6
Kavalandi 95 F2
Kavali 93 G1
Kavallur 85 G6
Kavarapetai 93 G5
Kavathe Mahankal 85 E2
Kaveripakkam 93 E6
Kaveripattinam 96 A1
Kavital 86 A4
Kaviti 82 C3
Kavlapur 84 D2
Kavutaram 88 C4
Kawa 33 H2
Kawai (P) 12 C2
Kawai 52 B2
Kawant 64 D2
Kawara (P) 12 A1
Kawardha 68 C2
Kawi 64 A2
Kawitang (M) 61 H1
Kawlkulli 60 D4
Kawnglanghpu (M) 45 G2
Kawngtim (M) 44 C2
Kawta 78 C4
Kawton (M) 75 G5
Kawya (M) 61 H1
Kaya (P) 12 B3
Kayalpattinam 99 F4
Kayankulam 98 B3
Kayar 79 F2
Kayattar 99 E4
Kayundapadi 95 G4
Kaza 19 E1
Kazipet 79 G6
Kazir Char (Ba) 59 G6
Kazir Hat (Ba) 60 A6
Kaziranga 43 E3
Kazu (M) 45 E6
Kbarhara 20 C3
Ke Sakan (M) 75 G2

Kebang 27 H5
Kedarnath 19 G5
Kedarpur 54 A6
Kedavur 94 D4
Kedgaon 76 D5
Kedua 69 G4
Kegaon 81 G1
Keitumkawn 60 D5
Kekri 33 F5
Kekrima 43 G5
Kel 13 E1
Kelambakkam 93 G6
Kelan Devi 34 B4
Kelangkania 42 D2
Kelapara (Ba) 73 F2
Kelasar 20 B4
Kelgawan 53 F1
Kelghar 76 C6
Kelhari 55 E5
Kelnor 31 E6
Kelod 67 F4
Kelwa 32 C6
Kelwara (Mad) 34 B6,
    52 B1
Kelwara (Raj) 50 C1
Kelwara (Utt) 53 E2
Kelzar 79 H1
Kem 77 F6
Kembhavi 86 A3
Kemmanugundi 91 E4
Kemri 23 G4
Kenchaman Hoskota 91 E6
Kenda (Wbg) 57 F5
Kenda (Mad) 69 E1
Kendai 55 F6
Kendgali 85 H3
Kendghata 57 H3
Kendrapara 71 F6
Kendua (Ba) 59 H2
Kendujhargarh 71 E3
Kendumundi 71 E3
Kengeri 92 A6
Kengklan (B) 41 H2
Keolari 67 H2
Keonchi 68 D1
Keora 50 C2
Keoripur 37 F4
Ker 21 G6
Kera 48 C6
Keran 12 D2
Kerap 33 E2
Kerar 54 D6
Kerawa 101 G4
Kerbana 53 G3
Keredari 56 D4
Keri (C) 29 G4
Kerimeri 79 G3
Kermigaon 28 B6
Kerpani 53 G5
Kertasar 20 C6
Keru 31 F2
Kerur 85 F5
Kerwada 64 A3
Kesaibahal 70 B2
Kesaram 78 D6
Kesardesar 20 C6
Kesariya 38 C4
Keshannagar 71 F6
Keshiyari 71 H2
Keshli 53 F5
Keshod 62 D4
Keshorai Patan 33 H6
Keshpur 71 H1, 72 A1
Keshwan 13 G5
Kesinga 81 G1
Keskal 80 D1
Kesla 66 D1
Kesrawandih 38 D5

Kesturu 91 H6
Kesur 51 G6
Keswana 32 A6
Ketar 55 H2
Kethong (C) 27 F3
Kethun 51 H1
Keti Bandar (P) 47 F3
Ketu Barabas 31 H3
Ketugram 58 B4
Kevdi 64 C4
Keylong 14 B6
Khabha 31 E3
Khachhar (P) 48 A1
Khachrod 51 F5
Khada 38 A2
Khadaro (P) 48 A1
Khadi Thach 19 F3
Khadma 69 E5
Khadrala 18 D4
Khadreha (N) 24 B4
Khadro (P) 30 A4
Khaga 36 C5
Khagaria 39 F6
Khagasari 62 C3
Khagaul 38 C5
Khagrachhari (Ba) 60 B5
Khagrachhari (Ba) 60 C6
Khai (P) 30 B5
Khaiala 30 D2
Khair 22 D6
Khair Muhammad Jat (P)
    47 H2
Khaira (Bih) 38 C5
Khaira (Mad) 54 D5
Khaira (Bih) 57 F1
Khaira (Mah) 68 C3
Khaira (Ori) 71 F4
Khaira Gali (P) 12 B3
Khaira Tela 38 A2
Khairabad (P) 12 A3
Khairabad (Utt) 36 B1
Khairabad (Raj) 51 H2
Khairagarh 34 D2
Khairi 13 F6
Khairipur (P) 30 A1
Khairla 32 B5
Khairlanji 67 H3
Khairwara 50 C3
Khaitong 28 D5
Khaiyan 21 F2
Khajipeta 92 D2
Khajiripada 82 B3
Khajuha 36 B4
Khajuraho 53 H2, 54 A2
Khajurdihi 70 C3
Khajurgaon 36 C4
Khajurhat 37 E3
Khajuri (Utt) 38 A5
Khajuri (Bih) 57 E2
Khajuri (Wbg) 72 B3
Khajuri (Kar) 86 A1
Khajuria 50 B2
Khajwana 32 C2
Khakarti 33 F2
Khaki (P) 12 B2
Khaki Hat 71 G5
Khakurdi 65 E5
Khal 20 C3
Khalabat (P) 12 B3
Khalapur (P) 16 C3
Khalapur 76 B4
Khalari 69 F4
Khalem 13 G5
Khalghat 65 G2
Khaliajuri (Ba) 59 H2
Khaliakani 81 G1
Khalilabad 37 G3
Khallar 66 C5

Khallikot 82 D2
Khalra 17 E3
Khalsar 14 C2
Khalsi 14 B2
Khalwe 66 B3
Khalyabari 60 C3
Kham 50 B2
Khamanon 18 A5
Khamar (Mad) 69 G2
Khamar (Ori) 70 D4
Khamaria (Mad) 54 C5
Khamaria (Mad) 68 C3
Khamaria Pul 23 H4
Khamarpani 67 F3
Khamaswari 77 H5
Khambale 65 F4
Khambha 63 F4
Khambhaliya 62 B2
Khambhodar 62 B3
Khamera 51 E4
Khamgaon 66 A5
Khamharia 69 F5
Khamla 66 C3
Khammam 88 A2
Khampar 38 A4
Khamtalai 67 H4
Khana 58 A5
Khanabal 13 F4
Khanag 18 C3
Khanakot (N) 24 C2
Khanakul 58 A6
Khanal 17 G1
Khanapur (Mah) 78 C2
Khanapur (Mah) 78 C4
Khanapur (And) 79 F3
Khanapur (Kar) 84 D5
Khanapur (Mah) 85 E2
Khanapur (Kar) 86 B3
Khandaghosh 58 A5
Khandagiri 71 E6
Khandala (Mah) 76 B4
Khandala (Mah) 76 D6
Khandala (Mah) 77 E1
Khandala (Mah) 78 C1
Khandar 23 H6
Khandarpara (Ba) 59 F5
Khandauh 35 E2
Khandbari (N) 39 H1
Khandela (Raj) 33 G1
Khandela (Raj) 34 B6
Khandera 62 D2
Khandhar 34 B4
Khandpara 70 D6
Khandsara 68 D3
Khandu 51 E5
Khandwa 66 A3
Khangah Dogran (P) 16 C2
Khangra 25 E6
Khangta 32 C3
Khani 67 H1
Khaniadhana 53 E1
Khanjar 14 B5
Khanjeri (P) 12 C4
Khanjpur (N) 39 F3
Khankar 34 D6
Khanna (Pun) 18 A5
Khanna (Utt) 36 A6
Khanpur (P) 12 B3
Khanpur (Utt) 23 E4
Khanpur (Raj) 52 A2
Khansahibpuram 98 D2
Khanspur (P) 12 C3
Khanta 40 B5
Khantapara 71 G4
Khanua 34 C2
Khanuan 35 G4
Khapa (Mad) 67 E1
Khapa (Mad) 67 G1

Khapa (Mah) 67 G4
Khapari 66 C1
Khar 19 E2
Khar Kot (P) 12 B3
Khar Talegaon 66 D5
Khara (Pun) 17 E5
Khara (Raj) 31 H2
Kharagarh 68 C4
Kharagdiha 57 F2
Kharagpur (Bih) 57 F1
Kharagpur (Wbg) 71 H2
Kharai (Utt) 52 D1
Kharai (Mad) 54 D5
Kharai Kotbar 71 H2
Kharak 22 A4
Kharakvasla 76 C5
Kharal 13 H2
Kharang (N) 39 H2
Kharangna 67 E5
Kharar (Pun) 18 B5
Kharar (Utt) 55 G3
Kharar (Wbg) 58 A6
Kharari 35 F6
Kharba (Wbg)40 B6
Kharba (Utt) 62 C2
Kharba (Wbg) 71 E4
Kharbara (P) 12 A3
Kharbu 13 H2
Kharchi 32 C5
Kharchia 49 E6
Kharda (Mah) 67 E6
Kharda (Mah) 77 G4
Kharder (P) 12 A6
Khardi (Raj) 52 C5
Khardi (Mah) 76 B2
Khardi (Mah) 85 F1
Khardung 14 C2
Kharela 35 H6
Kharepatan 84 B3
Khareri 62 D2
Khargon 65 G3
Khargram 58 A3
Khargurpur 37 E1
Khari (Raj) 32 B3
Khari (Mad) 52 B6
Khari Robar 48 D6
Kharia (Raj) 32 A1
Kharia (Guj) 62 D4
Kharian (P) 12 D6
Khariar 69 G6
Khariar Road 69 F5
Kharibari 40 B3
Khario (P) 48 D2
Kharipur (P) 48 B1
Kharipur 33 G6
Kharka 78 C5
Kharkari 33 E3
Kharkhauda (Utt) 22 D4
Kharkhauda (Har) 22 B4
Kharmang (P) 14 A1
Kharmauza 41 G4
Kharola 78 B5
Kharora 69 E4
Kharpada 76 B4
Kharra 31 H4
Kharsawan 57 E6
Kharsia 69 G2
Kharsod 51 G5
Kharsumdi 85 E2
Khartaksho 13 H1
Kharu 14 C2
Kharuk (P) 48 B2
Kharunda 51 G2
Kharupatia 42 B3
Kharwa 33 E4
Kharwandi 77 G3
Kharyal 21 E2
Khas Marala (P) 13 E6

Khaser Hat (Ba) 73 H1
Khashdhar 18 D4
Khasnar 66 A4
Khat 67 H4
Khata (C) 28 B1
Khatai 55 F2
Khatali 65 E2
Khatan (P) 20 B2
Khatao 84 D1
Khataul 54 B4
Khatauli 22 D3
Khataura 52 D1
Khategaon 66 B1
Khatima 23 H3
Khating 19 F5
Khatoli 33 H5, 34 A5
Khatora 67 G6
Khatra 57 G6
Khatu 33 G1
Khaur Oil Field (P) 12 A5
Khavda 48 C4
Khawad 49 H5
Khawasa 67 G3
Khawbung 61 E5
Khawhai 60 D5
Khawthlir 60 D4
Khayrasole 57 H4
Khebuching 61 E1
Khed (Mah) 76 C4
Khed (Mah) 76 C5
Khed (Mah) 77 E5
Khed (Mah) 84 B1
Khed Brahma 50 B3
Kheda 50 A6
Khedapada 50 D5
Khede 65 E5
Khedoi 48 C6
Kheduli 32 D3
Khedwa 50 B3
Khejra 21 E4
Khejuri 71 F3
Khejurpara 70 B6
Khekra 22 C4
Khela 24 B1
Khelma 43 E5
Khemat 49 H2
Kheng (M) 75 E4
Khengyoi 61 F3
Kheni Karan 17 E4
Khenkhar (M) 74 D2
Khentar 12 D4
Khera (Raj) 20 C5
Khera (Raj) 32 D5
Khera (Raj) 32 D6
Khera (Raj) 50 D3
Khera Jagispur 35 H2
Kherala 49 G3
Kherali 63 F1
Kheralu 50 A4
Kherapa 32 B3
Kherapara 41 F6
Kherda 66 C6
Kherewa 26 D6
Khergam 64 B5
Kheri (Utt) 24 C6
Kheri (Mah) 52 B6
Kheri (Mad) 66 D3
Kherli 67 E3
Kherna 71 E2
Kheroda 50 D2
Khertri 21 H6
Khetlal (Ba) 58 D1
Khetolai 31 G2
Khetri 42 B4
Khetwaro Tar (P) 30 C1
Khewari (P) 30 A3

Khewra (P) 12 B6
Khichan 31 H2
Khichchiwala (P) 20 B3
Khichohi (P) 12 A6
Khidirpur (Ba) 59 G5
Khidora 34 D3
Khieunaten (C) 29 G5
Khijadia 63 E3
Khijariya 62 D2
Khilchipur 52 A3
Khinda 70 A3
Khindasar 32 A1
Khinia 33 G6
Khinlasa 53 E3
Khinsar 31 G4
Khinwara 32 C6
Khinwasai 32 C2
Khinyan 31 E2
Khipri (P) 30 B6
Khipro (P) 30 B5
Khiraitangri 71 E3
Khirasra 63 E2
Khiri 55 E1
Khirpai 58 A6
Khiwa (P) 16 A3
Khizr Sarai 56 D1
Khizrabad (Pun) 18 B5
Khizrabad (Har) 18 C6
Khnapi (M) 75 F1
Khod 32 B6
Khoda 49 G3
Khodade 84 B2
Khodala 76 B2
Khodri 69 E1
Khodu 49 F6
Khohar (P) 12 C6
Khohir 55 G4
Khoirabari (Ass) 42 A3
Khoirabari (Ass) 42 B2
Khojachora 48 B6
Khojarnath (C) 24 D1
Khokara 52 B5
Khokarmoho 77 G4
Khokhar (P) 30 A6
Khokhri 63 E3
Khoksa (Ba) 58 D4
Khol 22 A5
Kholapur 66 C5
Khombhadi 48 B5
Khondar 37 E6, 55 E1
Khonsa 44 B2
Khopa 55 G5
Khopoli 76 B4
Khorana 63 E1
Khorbani 13 E5
Khorewah (P) 47 H2
Khori (P) 12 C6
Khormul 55 F5
Khotal 77 H3
Khotang (N) 39 G2
Khotaria 63 E2
Khothian 33 E5
Khowai 60 A3
Khowang 43 H2
Khreuh 13 F3
Khreum (M) 75 E4
Khuaiyum (M) 61 E4
Khuapual (M) 61 E5
Khuarsi 18 A1
Khudaganj (Utt) 23 H5
Khudaganj (Utt) 35 H2
Khudiala 32 A3
Khudian (P) 17 E4
Khugaung (M) 45 G4
Khuhi Khengi (P) 30 B1
Khuhian 21 E1
Khuiratta 12 D5

Khuisah (M) 75 E4
Khujianwali (P) 16 D1
Khujner 52 A4
Khuldabad 77 F1
Khuldo 15 F6
Khulna (Ba) 59 E6
Khulri 53 F6
Khumbad (P) 12 C4
Khumbi 61 F2
Khundala 31 G6
Khundaur 37 E4
Khundian 18 A2
Khuntaora 63 G4
Khunti 56 D5
Khuntpani 71 E1
Khur 33 F1
Khura (P) 16 A1
Khurai 53 E3
Khurampura 65 F2
Khurasa 37 E2
Khurda 71 E6
Khurel 65 H1
Khurhom 13 E2
Khuri (Raj) 21 E6
Khuri (Raj) 32 D2
Khuria (Utt) 37 H1
Khuria (Mad) 68 D1
Khurja 22 D5
Khurpa (N) 25 E4
Khurrianwala (P) 16 B3
Khushah (P) 16 A1
Khushpur (P) 16 B4
Khutar 24 A5
Khutauna 39 F3
Khutgaon 70 C1
Khuzami 43 G5
Khwajakhela (P) 12 A1
Khyatsa (C) 26 C3
Khyekhye (C) 26 C3
Kiagi 15 E4
Kiamari (P) 47 E2
Kiar 18 C4
Kiari 15 E4
Kibar 19 E1
Kibbanshalli 91 G5
Kichanapalle 80 B6
Kichha 23 G3
Kidianagru 49 E5
Kigan (P) 12 C1
Kihunian 54 C1
Kikdeshwar 51 F2
Kikkeri 91 G6
Kila 52 B3
Kilakkarai 99 G3
Kilakkottara 95 F6
Kilar 14 A5
Kilarni 78 A6
Kilchen 93 F6
Kilchu 14 B3
Kileshwar 62 C3
Kilimannur 98 C4
Kiliyanur 97 E2
Kilkar Kungma (C) 15 H5
Killar 13 H6
Killarbagh 60 C3
Kiloi 22 B3
Kilor 13 H6
Kilski (P) 16 D1
Kimi 14 C1
Kimin 43 F1
Kimos 101 F2
Kin (M) 61 H6
Kinana 22 A3
Kinbin (M) 61 H6
Kinchamanda 81 G5
Kindas (M) 61 G4
Kingaon 78 B4
Kingaon Jatu 78 A1

Kingaon Raja 77 H1
Kinhalu 85 H6
Kinhi 86 B1
Kinhton (M) 75 E5
Kinlivli 76 B3
Kinmungyon (M) 75 G5
Kinol 31 E3
Kinwat 79 E2
Kipsi (C) 27 E3
Kirakat 37 G5
Kirandul 80 D5
Kiranur (Tam) 96 B6
Kiranur (Tam) 96 D3
Kiraoli 34 D2
Kiratpur (N) 24 C4
Kiratpur (Pun) 18 B4
Kiratpur (Utt) 23 E2
Kirba 70 A4
Kirhan 21 G2
Kiria Mai 23 F5
Kirjhrapur 37 H4
Kirkee 76 C5
Kirko (P) 17 E2
Kirloskarvadi 84 D2
Kirmara 21 G2
Kirmahar 58 A4
Kimapur 68 B3
Kirpalian (P) 12 B2
Kirvatti 90 C1
Kishanganj (Bih) 39 G5
Kishanganj (Bih) 40 A4
Kishanganj (Raj) 52 B1
Kishangarh (Raj) 22 B6
Kishangarh (Raj) 33 G2
Kishangarh (Raj) 33 F3
Kishangarh (Mad) 53 H2
Kishanpur (Utt) 9 E5
Kishanpur (Utt) 36 C5
Kishanpur (Bih) 39 F4
Kishanpur Baral 22 C3
Kishanpura 17 F5
Kishni 35 G2
Kishonrganj (Ba) 40 D5
Kishorganj (Ba) 59 G2
Kishtwar 13 G5
Kisinda 70 B4
Kisko 56 B5
Kistaram (Mad) 80 C6
Kistaram (And) 88 A1
Kisumpet 87 E2
Kitagha 43 F4
Kitari 67 H5
Kithar 13 H6
Kithor 22 D4
Kittur 85 E5
Kivarli 50 B2
Klangklang (M) 61 E6
Klangpi (M) 61 E6
Klau (M) 61 E6
Kliehriat 42 C6
Klorzan (M) 61 F6
Knanki (P) 16 D1
Knari 20 B6
Knedaseri 21 E3
Knot 21 H2
Koath 38 B6
Kobo 28 A6
Kobur 78 D3
Koch 56 C1
Kochadhamin 40 A4
Kochas 38 A6
Kochi 98 A1
Kochugaon 41 F3
Kod 90 D2
Kodad 87 H2
Kodae 48 B6
Kodaganur 91 F3
Kodaikanal 95 G6

Kodala 82 C2
Kodanad 95 F3
Kodapakha 80 B1
Kodarma 57 E2
Kodavaluru 93 G2
Koddekal 85 H4
Kodh 49 F6
Kodigenhalli 92 A4
Kodihalli 95 H1
Kodikonda 92 B4
Kodikulam 98 D2
Kodinar 63 E5
Kodinga 81 F3
Kodingauk (M) 74 C6
Kodikkarai 97 E6
Kodiyeri 94 C3
Kodli 86 B1
Kodlipet 91 E6
Kodmial 79 F5
Kodoli 84 D3
Kodram 49 H4
Kodsanar 80 D3
Kodumud 95 H4
Kodumuru 86 D5
Kodungallur 95 E6
Kodunigud 80 D1
Koduru (And) 81 G6
Koduru (And) 88 C4
Koduru (And) 93 E4
Koduru (And) 93 G2
Kodwa 68 D3
Koelibeda 80 C1
Koelwar 38 C5
Koaria 50 D1
Kohala (P) 12 C3
Kohalli 85 F3
Kohi 31 G5
Kohima 43 F5
Kohina 21 E4
Kohir 86 C1
Kohnia 35 G6
Koikonda 86 D3
Koilkuntla 87 E6
Koimekeah 101 G4
Koira 70 D2
Kojala 17 G3
Kojarjaola 78 A3
Kokamag 13 G4
Kokavada 81 E4
Kokesra 84 B3
Kokilamukh 43 F3
Kokkanti 92 C3
Kokrajhar 41 F3
Kokri 17 G5
Koksalung (N) 39 G3
Koksara 81 G2
Kolabira 70 B3
Kolad 76 B5
Koladit 65 H3
Kolaghat 72 A1
Kolai (P) 12 B1
Kolakaluru 88 B4
Kolambi 67 E6
Kolar (Him) 18 C6
Kolar (Kar) 92 C5
Kolar Gold Fields 92 C6
Kolaras 34 D4
Kolari 34 D3
Kolarue 101 G4
Kolattupuzha 98 C4
Kolayat 20 B6
Kolebira 56 C6
Kolgaon (Mah) 76 D2
Kolgaon (Mah) 77 E4
Kolhapur (Mah) 84 C3
Kolhapur (And) 87 E4
Kolhar (Mah) 77 E2
Kolhar (Mah) 85 G4

Kolimigundla 92 C1
Kolithar 63 E2
Kolki 62 D3
Kollam (Quilon) 98 B4
Kollangud 95 F5
Kollattur 94 D5
Kollegal 95 G2
Kollur 90 C4
Kolluru 88 B4
Kolosib 60 D3
Kolshi 76 B6
Kolu 31 H2
Kolukheri 52 B3
Kolur 80 C1
Kolvan 76 C5
Kolwihir 66 D4
Komarola 87 F6
Konakanametla 87 G5
Komatlapeta 81 H3
Komattiyar 96 C1
Kombong 27 H5
Komha 69 F6
Kommi 93 F1
Komordungi 71 E2
Kon 55 H2
Konada 82 A6
Konapeta 92 D3
Konark 83 F1
Konch 35 G5
Kond (Mah) 78 A5
Kond (Mah) 84 B1
Kondagaon 80 D2
Kondakamberu 81 E6
Kondakarla 89 G1
Kondalwadi 78 D4
Kondanar 80 D3
Kondapalle 88 B3
Kondapi 87 H6
Kondapur 87 E1
Kondapuram 92 C2
Kondhali 67 F4
Kondotti 94 D4
Kondrapole 87 H3
Kongad 95 E5
Kongadak 95 G3
Konglu (M) 45 F1
Kongnoli 84 D3
Kongnyu 43 H3
Kongtal 61 F3
Kongto (C) 26 C3
Kongtsuka (C) 29 H2
Koni 98 C3
Konka 67 G2
Konnur (Kar) 85 E4
Konnur (Kar) 85 H3
Konrra 56 B6
Konta 80 D6
Kontha (M) 61 G5
Kopaganj 37 H4
Kopal 85 H6
Kopargaon 77 E1
Koparia 39 G5
Koparti 65 E4
Kopela 80 A4
Kopol 87 G3
Koppa (Kar) 90 D4
Koppa (Kar) 91 H6
Kora (Utt) 36 B4
Kora (Bih) 39 H5
Kora (Mah) 67 G6
Koradgaon 77 F3
Koragbal Gurias 13 F2
Korai 71 F5
Korajgi 85 H2
Korandh 78 C3
Korangal 86 C2

Koraput 81 G4
Korat 78 D2
Koratagere 91 H5
Koratgi 86 A5
Koratla 79 F4
Korba 69 F1
Korbo 27 H3
Korda 49 F4
Koregaon 84 D1
Korhalli 85 H2
Kori 47 H4
Koriras 80 D4
Koriyamangalam 96 B2
Korkop 85 E4
Korla 86 B2
Koma 32 A4
Korondi 81 E2
Koropani (N) 25 G5
Korosavada 82 B4
Koroth 94 D3
Korti 77 F5
Korukollu 88 C4
Korukonda (Ori) 81 E5
Korukonda (And) 88 D2
Korwai 53 E3
Korwar 85 H3
Korwatanr 57 E2
Kosa 47 H5, 48 A5
Kosamba 64 A4
Kosana 32 C4
Kosapuram 92 C4
Kosar 18 C1
Kosdani 78 D1
Kosdol 69 H2
Kosgi (And) 86 B5
Kosgi (And) 86 C2
Koshalpur (Ba) 40 C5
Kosi 22 C6
Kosithal 32 D6
Kosli 22 A5
Kosri 78 B3
Kot (J&K) 13 E6
Kot (Har) 22 C6
Kot (Raj) 32 C6
Kot Bainka 13 E4
Kot Banhtu 21 F1
Kot Bhai 17 E6
Kot Diji (P) 30 A2
Kot Fateh 17 F6
Kot Faten Khan (P) 12 A4
Kot Fatuhi 17 H4
Kot Fazldad Khan (P) 16 B5
Kot Ghazi (P) 16 B2
Kot Hakim Khan (P) 16 B1
Kot Imamgarh (P) 30 B3
Kot Kapura 17 F5
Kot Khai 18 C4
Kot Lsa Khan 17 F4
Kot Mir Md Khan (P) 30 A1
Kot Mumin (P) 16 B2
Kot Najbulian (P) 12 B3
Kot Nikka (P) 16 B2
Kot Pindi Das (P) 16 D3
Kot Putli 21 H6
Kot Qasim 22 B6
Kot Radha Kishan (P)
    16 D4
Kot Sarang (P) 12 A5
Kot Sarthara 34 D4
Kot Sultan (P) 16 A3
Kota (Raj) 33 G6
Kota (Utt) 55 G2
Kota (Mad) 69 E2
Kota (And) 93 G3
Kota Bagh 23 G2
Kota Uratla 89 F1
Kotabommali 82 B5
Kotada (Guj) 49 G3

Kotada (Mad) 52 C4
Kotada (Guj) 63 G4
Kotadi 48 B6
Kotagad 82 A2
Kotagaon 76 D4
Kotagiri 95 F4
Kotakkal 94 D5
Kotakunda 86 C3
Kotalgi 85 F2
Kotalpur 58 A6
Kotamangalam (Tam)
    95 F4
Kotamangalam (Ker) 98 B1
Kotananduru 89 E1
Kotapad 81 F3
Kotapadu 81 G6
Kotapalli 79 G5
Kotapeta 89 E3
Kotar 54 C2
Kotarlia 69 H3
Kotatattu 90 C4
Kotayam 94 C3
Kotchandpur (Ba) 58 D5
Kotda Nayani 63 E1
Kotda Sangani 63 E2
Kotdwara 23 F1
Kotepalli 86 D2
Koterki 86 B3
Koteshwar 47 H4
Kotgal 68 B6
Kotgir 78 D5
Koth 63 H1
Kotha Guru 17 F6
Kothakota 86 D4
Kothala 78 A3
Kothar 76 B1
Kothara 48 A6
Kothari 79 H2
Kothi (Mad) 54 B2
Kothi (Mad) 55 E5
Kothi (Bih) 56 B3
Kothi (Mah) 80 B2
Kothli (Utt) 37 F2
Kotil 12 D4
Kotipalle 89 E3
Kotla (P) 12 B4
Kotla (P) 12 D6
Kotla (Him) 17 H1
Kotla (Har) 22 B4
Kotli (P) 12 C4
Kotli Daim (P) 16 C1
Kotli Loharan (P) 13 E6
Kotli Surat Malli 17 F2
Kotma 55 E5
Kotra (Raj) 32 D4
Kotra (Utt) 35 G5
Kotra (Raj) 50 B3
Kotra (Raj) 50 C2
Kotra (Mad) 53 G6
Kotra (Mad) 69 H3
Kotra Pitha 63 F2
Kotri (Raj) 31 E3
Kotri (Raj) 33 F5
Kotri (Raj) 33 F6
Kotri (Raj) 34 A5
Kotri (Mad) 52 B4
Kotri (Mad) 52 B6
Kotri Allahrakhio (P) 47 G3
Kotsamlai 70 A5
Kottagudem (And) 80 B6
Kottagudem (And) 88 B1
Kottagudi 98 D1
Kottaippattanam 99 H1
Kottaiyur 99 G1
Kottakota (And) 81 G6
Kottakota (And) 92 C4
Kottampatti 96 A6
Kottapatnam 93 G3

Kottapeta 92 D3
Kottappatti 96 B2
Kottarakara 98 B3
Kottatti 95 F1
Kottavalasa 81 H6
Kottayam 98 B2
Kottuchery 97 E5
Kottur 91 F2
Kotturu (Mad) 80 B4
Kotturu (And) 82 A4
Kottuvally 98 B1
Kotul 76 C3
Kotwa 54 D1
Kouni 55 E6
Kovalam 98 C5
Kovattur 97 E1
Kovillor 98 C5
Kovilpatti 99 E3
Kovilur 96 A5
Kovur 93 G2
Kovvur 88 D2
Kovvur Plain 88 C2
Kowar 57 F3
Kowdalli 95 G2
Kowtta Buzurg 78 C6
Koyul 15 G6
Koyyalgudem 88 D2
Koyyuru 89 E1
Kozhikode 94 D4
Krar 13 E3
Krawandiya 56 A1
Kriebnapatnam 93 G3
Krishna 86 C4
Krishnadevipeta 89 F1
Krishnaganj 58 C5
Krishnagar 58 C5
Krishnagiri (And) 86 C6
Krishnagiri (Tam) 96 A1
Krishnai 41 G4
Krishnapur 58 B2
Krishnarajanagara 95 E1
Krishnarajpet 95 E1
Krishnarajpur 92 B6
Krishnarayapuram 96 A5
Krishnur 78 C4
Krosuru 87 H3
Kru (M) 74 D4
Kseh Kyntharg 42 C5
Ksehkma Bazar 42 B5
Ku Tung Kal (C) 45 G6
Kuakhera 51 G2
Kuakonda 80 D4
Kuamara 71 G3
Kuanar 70 D3
Kuarpur 54 D4
Kuba 63 E4
Kuchai 57 E6
Kuchai Kot 38 B3
Kuchaman 33 E2
Kuchaur 33 F1
Kuchchri 30 D2
Kuchera 32 D2
Kuchesar 22 D4
Kuchi 85 E2
Kuchinda 70 B3
Kuchipudi 88 B4
Kuchrod 51 F4
Kud 13 G5
Kuda (Guj) 49 F5
Kuda (Mah) 76 B5
Kudal 84 B5
Kudalia 49 F2
Kudan 76 B2
Kudarkot 35 G3
Kudatin 86 A6
Kudavasai 96 D5
Kudaw (M) 75 H1

Kudchi 85 E3
Kuderu 92 A2
Kudibali 70 A6
Kudligi 91 F1
Kudor 13 E2
Kudpura 53 G5
Kudra 56 A1
Kudsu 32 B1
Kudumulagumma 81 E5
Kuduru 91 H6
Kueke Bahawal (P) 16 C5
Kugti 18 B1
Kuhi 67 G5
Kuhuri 82 D1
Kuiri 43 G6
Kujang 71 F6
Kukadgaon 77 G5
Kukana 77 F3
Kukanar 81 E4
Kukarmunda 64 D3
Kukiehara 60 C2
Kukma 48 C5
Kuknur 85 G6
Kuknurpalli 79 F6
Kukra 24 B5
Kukri Ser 18 C2
Kukshi 65 F2
Kuku (M) 43 H6
Kulaisila 71 F1
Kulanchavadi 96 D3
Kulang 14 C6, 18 C1
Kularun 17 H6
Kulasekarapatinam 99 E5
Kulasgaram 98 D5
Kultali 72 C2
Kulattur (Tam) 96 B5
Kulattur (Tam) 99 F3
Kulaura (Ba) 60 B2
Kuldharan 77 F5
Kulgam 13 F4
Kulgeri 85 F5
Kulhar 53 E3
Kuliana 71 F2
Kuliar Char (Ba) 59 G3
Kuligam 13 E2
Kulittalai 96 A5
Kulkulapalli 87 E2
Kulluwal (P) 13 E6
Kulpahar 35 H6
Kulpi 72 B2
Kulrian 21 G1
Kulti 57 G4
Kulu 18 C2
Kum 17 H5
Kumai 40 C2
Kumaltar (N) 25 G5
Kumana 20 C4
Kumar Bazidpur 38 D5
Kumaralingam 95 G6
Kumardhubi 57 G4
Kumargam 98 B2
Kumarganj 40 C6
Kumarghat 60 B3
Kumargram 41 E3
Kumarkhad 39 G4
Kumarkhali (Ba) 58 D4
Kumarmunda 70 C2
Kumbakonam 96 D5
Kumbalgod 92 A6
Kumbasar 20 C4
Kumbhagin 93 E2
Kumbhalgarh 32 C6
Kumbhari 85 G1
Kumbhariputtu 81 H3
Kumbharvada 90 B1
Kumbhikota 81 H3
Kumbher (N) 24 D5
Kumbhir 60 D1

Kumbhraj 52 B2
Kumbla 94 B1
Kumdok 15 E4
Kumerhin 55 E5
Kumguri 41 H3
Kumha 68 C1
Kumhari 53 H4
Kumharsain 18 C4
Kumher 34 C1
Kumira (Ba) 74 A1
Kumngwei (M) 61 F4
Kumrikhata 42 A3
Kumsi 90 D3
Kumta (Mah) 84 D1
Kumta (Kar) 90 B2
Kunaipur (Ba) 59 E4
Kunamanur 86 C3
Kunamkulam 94 D5
Kunar 13 G2
Kunaraui (P) 20 B2
Kunathunadu 95 F6
Kunavaram 88 C1
Kund 13 F5
Kund Bara 14 A6
Kunda (Utt) 36 D5
Kunda (Ass) 41 G3
Kunda (Mad) 67 G2
Kunda (Mad) 68 G2
Kundadam 95 G5
Kundagram (Ba) 58 D2
Kundahit 57 H3
Kundai 81 E1
Kundali 53 G6
Kundam 54 B5
Kundanganj 36 C4
Kundanpur 51 E6
Kundara 98 B3
Kundaria 23 G6
Kundgol 85 G5
Kundlu 18 B4
Kundolu 13 H6
Kundora 81 F4
Kundukur 92 B4
Kundur 91 F6
Kundurgaon 80 D3
Kundurpi 91 H3
Kungjara 69 H1
Kungpiho (C) 45 H5
Kuniamuttur 95 F5
Kunigal 91 H6
Kunja Dinga (P) 20 A2
Kunjer 52 A1
Kunjpura 22 B2
Kunkavay 63 E3
Kunkheri 66 C3
Kunkuri (Mad) 55 H6
Kunkuri (Mad) 56 A6
Kunlaung (M) 75 E4
Kunnamangalam 94 D4
Kunnandarkoil 96 C6
Kunnathur 98 B3
Kunnattur 96 B1
Kunnatur 95 G4
Kunore 13 H2
Kunria (Guj) 48 C4
Kunria (Guj) 48 D5
Kuntrila (P) 12 B5
Kunwar 36 C5
Kunwar Kotri 52 B4
Kunze (M) 75 G2
Kupaluvur 96 C5
Kupat 66 D6
Kuppagadde 90 D2
Kuppagallu 86 B5
Kuppam 92 C6
Kuppam (And) 92 D5
Kupwara 13 E2
Kurabalakota 92 C4

Kurabar 50 D2
Kurai (P) 16 A5
Kuraitha 40 A6
Kural 64 A2
Kurali 18 A5
Kuram 66 C5
Kuran Sarai 38 B6
Kurandvad 84 D3
Kuraon 55 E1
Kurara 36 A5
Kurasia 55 F5
Kurauli 35 F1
Kurawar 52 B5
Kurchhola 19 F6
Kurchi (Raj) 32 B2
Kurchi (Raj) 94 D2
Kurdeg 70 A1
Kurdi 86 B4
Kurduvadi 77 F6
Kurebhar 37 E4
Kurgaon 34 B3
Kurgiakh 14 C5
Kurha 67 E5
Kurhani 38 D4
Kurhegaon 76 C2
Kuri 31 E3
Kuria (P) 12 A2
Kurichchi 95 H3
Kurichi 95 F5
Kurichodu 87 H5
Kurigram (Ba) 41 E5
Kurinjippadi 96 D3
Kurkhera 68 A6
Kurki 32 D4
Kurkumb 77 E5
Kurkundi (Kar) 86 B3
Kurkundi (Kar) 86 B4
Kurla 76 A3
Kurlasi 51 G3
Kurnool 86 D5
Kurra Jarawan 35 G2
Kursakatta 39 H4
Kurse Korhi 80 B1
Kursela 39 H6
Kurseong 40 B2
Kursha Gompa 14 B4
Kursi 36 C2
Kurson 39 F4
Kurtamagarh 82 A1
Kurtha 56 C1
Kurtkoti 85 F6
Kuru 56 C4
Kurud 68 D5
Kurugodu 86 A6
Kurukkuchalai 99 F4
Kurukshetra 22 B1
Kurul 85 G1
Kurumbalur 96 B4
Kurupam 81 H4
Kuruskela 56 B6
Kurwal 37 E4
Kusera 55 F2
Kuseri (N) 24 B2
Kushalgarh 51 E5
Kushalnagar 94 D1
Kushinagar 38 A3
Kushmahar 54 D3
Kushmanchi 87 H2
Kushmandi 40 B6
Kushol 14 B4
Kushtagi 85 H5
Kushtia (Ba) 58 D4
Kusi 84 C1
Kuslamb 77 G5
Kusma (N) 25 H5
Kusmi 56 A5
Kusnur 78 C5
Kusumbe 65 E5

Kusumi 70 B3
Kut (Ba) 59 H4
Kuta 17 G1
Kutal 13 G5
Kutana 22 C3
Kutharpekot (N) 25 G5
Kuthaund 35 G4
Kuthaunda 35 G4
Kuthiala Shaikhan (P)
 16 C1
Kuthpathri 13 F2
Kutipi 70 D1
Kutiyana 62 C3
Kutku 56 A4
Kutnaur 19 E5
Kutragada 81 H2
Kutravada 88 D1
Kutri 70 C6
Kutru 80 C3
Kuttalam (Tam) 96 D4
Kuttalam (Tam) 98 D4
Kuttanailur 96 D5
Kuttattukulam 98 B1
Kuttiyadi 94 C3
Kutumba 56 B2
Kuvadra 63 E2
Kuwa 49 F6
Kuwala (P) 49 E3
Kuwar 49 G5
Kuyung (C) 45 G6
Kuzhitturai 98 D5
Kwar 13 H5
Kwate Tu Kwage 101.E1
Kwazon (M) 74 C5
Kwitu (M) 45 F6
Kyabin (M) 61 G6
Kyadet (M) 75 H3
Kyanggyigou (M) 61 H5
Kyatsandra 91 H5
Kyaukmasin (M) 75 G3
Kyauko (M) 75 G5
Kyauksit (M) 75 F4
Kyauktaw (M) 74 D5
Kyaukye (M) 75 H5
Kyaupyok (M) 61 G6
Kyaw (M) 75 G2
Kyenpalawn (M) 45 E1
Kyimpuk (C) 19 G3
Kyin (M) 75 G3
Kyindwe (M) 75 F5
Kymdong (C) 27 E3
Kyonon 14 C5

La-Awn Ga (M) 45 F2
Labaid 69 G1
Laban (M) 44 D5
Laban 34 A6
Labpur 58 A4
Labrang 19 E3
Labu (N) 25 E4
Lachh 13 E2
Lachharas 64 C3
Lachharsar 21 E5
Lachhmangarh (Raj) 21 F6
Lachhmangarh (Raj) 34 B1
Lachhmipur 23 F5
Lachmipos 70 B2
Lachung 40 C1
Lachyan 85 G2
Lad Bharol 18 B2
Ladana 20 C3
Ladania 39 F3
Ladhaura 53 F1
Ladhuka (P) 16 D5
Ladhurka 57 G5
Ladhuwala 17 E5

Ladi 70 A5
Ladiun (P) 47 G3
Ladkhed 66 D6
Ladnum 21 E6
Lado (C) 27 E3
Ladpura (Raj) 33 H6
Ladpura (Raj) 51 H1
Ladsawangi 77 G1
Laduna 51 G4
Laeja 48 B6
Lagairong 61 E2
Lagam 42 C1
Lagcha 24 C6
Lagung (C) 28 A1
Lagwi (M) 45 G5
Lahai 98 C2
Lahail 21 H1
Lahan (N) 39 F3
Lahar 35 F4
Laharpur 24 C6
Lahawa (M) 74 C3
Lahchuraghat 35 G6
Lahe (M) 44 A4
Laheria Sarai 39 E4
Lahir 80 C3
Lahli 22 A4
Lahor (P) 12 A3
Lahore (P) 17 E3
Lahori 77 H4
Lahorighat 42 C4
Lahri 13 H6
Laiho (C) 45 H6
Laikera 70 B3
Laiksar 23 E1
Lailaw (M) 75 E6
Lailenpi (M) 74 D2
Lailente (M) 74 D3
Laimakuri 27 H6
Laimura 70 B3
Lainkalangpara (Ba) 74 C3
Laisawrai 60 C5
Laisong 43 E6
Laitak (M) 75 F1
Laitlyngkot 42 B6
Lajakawng (M) 45 F2
Lajoshi (C) 29 H3
Laju 44 B2
Lajun Chamik (C) 19 H1
Lajwana 22 A3
Lak (P) 16 A1
Lakadiya 48 D5
Lakadong 42 C6
Lakarpata (N) 24 D4
Lakavalli 91 E4
Lakawas 50 D2
Lakema 43 F5
Lakh 77 E2
Lakha 31 E4
Lakhai (Ba) 59 H3
Lakhaipur 56 D2
Lakhamara 69 G5
Lakhandur 67 H5
Lakhanpuri 68 D6
Lakhanwada 66 A6
Lakhanwal (P) 13 E6
Lakhasar 20 D2
Lakhaura 38 C3
Lakhawala (P) 20 A2
Lakhbahat 81 H2
Lakheri 34 A5
Lakhimpur 24 B6
Lakhipur (Ass) 41 G4
Lakhipur (Ass) 60 D2
Lakhisarai 39 F6
Lakhkhan (P) 16 A4
Lakhmana 31 F3
Lakhna 35 G3

Lakhnadon 67 H1
Lakhnauti 22 C2
Lakhni (Guj) 49 G3
Lakhni (Mah) 67 H5
Lakhona 33 E6
Lakhpat 48 A4
Lakhpuri 66 C5
Lakhren (M) 44 D6
Lakhtar 49 E6
Lakin (M) 45 G3
Lakiredipalle 92 D3
Lakkamapayakkanpatti
 95 G5
Lakkavarapukera 81 G6
Laksham (Ba) 59 H5
Lakshettipet 79 G4
Lakshimpur (Ba) 59 G6
Lakshimpur (And) 81 F5
Lakshimpur (Kar) 90 C4
Lakshmanath 71 H3
Lakshmanpur 55 G6
Lakshmeshwar 85 F6
Lakshimcharipara (Ba)
 60 B6
Lakshmikantapur 72 B2
Lakshmipur 100 B2
Laksmisagar 57 G6
Lakundi 85 G6
Lakyen Ga (M) 44 C3
Lal Dhang 23 E1
Lala 60 C2
Lala Musa (P) 12 D6
Lalamdesar 20 B6
Lalauli 36 B5
Lalbagh 65 H4
Lalbiti (N) 39 E2
Lalbunra 68 A3
Lalganj (Utt) 36 C4
Lalganj (Utt) 36 D5
Lalganj (Utt) 37 G5
Lalganj (Bih) 38 D5
Lalganj (Utt) 55 F1
Lalgarh (Raj) 20 D1
Lalgarh (Wbg) 71 H1
Lalgola 58 B2
Lalgopalganj 36 D5
Lalgudi 96 C5
Lalian (P) 16 B2
Laligam 96 A2
Lalitpur (N) 38 D1
Lalitpur 53 E2
Lalkua 23 G3
Lallen 60 C4
Lalmanir Hat (Ba) 41 E5
Lalna (Ba) 73 F2
Laloi 62 D2
Lalpani 61 E1
Lalpur (Ba) 58 C3
Lalpur (J&K) 13 E2
Lalpur (Raj) 20 B2
Lalpur (Mad) 54 D5
Lalpur (Guj) 62 C2
Lalsong 60 D1
Lalsot 34 A3
Lalu (P) 30 B3
Lalu 14 A2
Lam Tso 15 E6
Lama (Ba) 74 C3
Lama Disa 42 D6
Lamache 19 F3
Lamaj 76 C6, 84 B1
Lamakhera 52 B2
Lamayuru 14 B2
Lamba (Raj) 33 F4
Lamba (Guj) 62 B3
Lambagraon 18 A2
Lambhua 37 E4
Lambi 21 E1

Lambia 32 D4
Lamdo (C) 27 G2
Lammasingi 81 F6
Lamobagar Gola (N) 39 H1
Lamri (N) 25 F2
Lamta 68 A2
Lamti (B) 41 G1
Lamunja (C) 45 H3
Lanchiati (C) 45 H3
Landour 19 E6
Lang Loharani (P) 47 E1
Lang Thanga 19 E2
Langadu Bazar (Ba) 60 C6
Langar Makhdum (P) 16 B2
Langarpeth 85 E2
Langau Ga (M) 44 D4
Langdiangngai 41 G6
Langera 13 H6
Langhnaj 49 H5
Langi 71 E6
Langja 19 E1
Langjon 28 C5
Langkang (C) 27 F3
Langkapara Hat 40 D3
Langmo (C) 26 A1
Langokhkaw (M) 45 G4
Langtao (M) 45 E2
Langyang (M) 45 G5
Lanja 84 B3
Lanji 68 B4
Lanjigarh 81 H2
Lanjora 80 D2
Lanka (Utt) 19 F4
Lanka (Ass) 42 D5
Lankui 52 C6
Lanlegwa (M) 61 H3
Lansdowne 23 F1
Lanting 42 D6
Lanywa (M) 75 H5
Lao (B) 26 A6
Lao (C) 29 G2
Laogang Bazar 60 A5
Laohala 66 A6
Laotiki (M) 45 G5
Lapa 43 H2
Lapati 101 F2
Lapchaura 52 C1
Lapri 54 D4
Lapundra 31 H4
Lapung 56 C5
Lapyep Ga (M) 44 B4
Lar 38 A4
Lara 19 E2
Laresune 70 A4
Larji 18 C3
Laroka 12 D5
Laruri 43 H5
Las 50 A1
Lasalgaon 76 D1
Lasaria (Raj) 33 E6
Lasaria (Raj) 50 D3
Lashari (P) 30 B4
Lashkarhat 40 C6
Laskein 42 C6
Laski 101 F4
Lasrawan 51 E2
Lasundra 50 B6
Lasur (Mah) 65 F4
Lasur (Mah) 77 F1
Lasurne 77 E6
Lathau 28 B6
Lathi (Ass) 60 C2
Lathi (Guj) 63 F3
Lathipada 82 C2
Lathor 69 G6
Latif (P) 30 B3
Latipur 62 D1

Latoti 32 C4
Latrang (C) 29 G4
Latsa (C) 45 H1
Latu (Ba) 60 C1
Latur 78 A5
Lauhkaung (M) 45 G5
Lauho (M) 45 H5
Laukaha 39 F3
Laukahi 39 F3
Laungonal 17 G6
Laungshe (M) 75 G4
Lauri 54 A1
Lauriya Mandangarh 38 B2
Lavanuru 92 C2
Lawa 33 G4
Lawahi 54 D4
Lawamjula (N) 25 F5
Lawan 31 H3
Lawana 36 D5
Lawang (C) 29 G6
Lawha 78 C4
Lawngkyaw (M) 45 G5
Lawngngaw (M) 44 A4
Lawngtlai 74 D1
Lawrencepur (P) 12 A3
Lawtha (M) 61 H4
Laxar Chumik (C) 19 G3
Layawng Ga (M) 45 E5
Layshi (M) 43 H6
Laza (M) 45 F3
Le (C) 26 B6
Lebon (M) 75 F5
Ledaing (M) 75 G4
Ledama (M) 75 G3
Ledo 44 B1
Legaing (M) 75 H6
Legara 69 H6
Leh 14 D2
Lehragaga 21 H1
Lehtrar (P) 12 C4
Leike 43 E6
Leite 60 D6
Lekhaw (M) 44 A5
Lekhparajuli (N) 24 D5
Lekong Yok 15 G6
Lelava 49 G2
Lele (N) 38 D1
Leleka (P) 16 B6
Lemru 69 G1
Lendara 80 D1
Lengauk (M) 75 H2
Lengrabhita 41 F4
Lengteng 42 D3
Lenikot (M) 61 F4
Lepa (C) 29 E4
Lepakshi 92 A4
Lepanglat 28 D6
Leslieganj 56 B3
Leta (N) 25 H4
Leteri 52 C3
Letha (M) 75 F3
Lethang (C) 26 A5
Letpanbya (M) 74 D6
Letse (M) 75 G4
Letwedet (M) 74 C5
Letyetma (M) 75 H3
Lewri (N) 39 E3
Lhagyari (C) 26 C3
Lhakhangra (C) 29 G5
Lhapso (C) 26 C3
Lhatsa Gompa 27 G4
Lhung (C) 29 H2
Lhuntse Dzong (C) 26 C5
Lhuntsi Dzong (B) 41 H1
Liamaia (M) 74 D2
Libanggaon (N) 25 F5
Libasi 64 A1
Lichu 18 C1

Lieta (C) 15 H5
Lifripara 70 A2
Lihinwan 13 G4
Likehe 14 D4
Likhapani 44 B1
Likhi 65 G2
Likhmisar 20 D6
Lilam (J&K) 13 E1
Lilam (Utt) 24 A1
Lilauni (P) 12 A1
Liliani (P) 16 B2
Liligumma 81 H3
Liliya Mota 63 F3
Lilla (P) 12 A6
Lilong 61 F2
Lilung (C) 26 D3
Limba Ganesh 77 G4
Limbda 63 F3
Limbdi 63 G1
Limdi 50 D6
Limkhera 50 D6
Linga 67 F2
Lingadahalli 91 E4
Lingadaw (M) 75 H3
Lingal 87 E4
Lingala (And) 80 A6
Lingala (And) 92 C2
Lingampalli 87 E1
Lingampet 79 E5
Lingapur 79 G4
Lingasanpalli 87 E3
Lingdev 76 D3
Lingi 78 B2
Lingkha (C) 29 E2
Lingsugur 86 A4
Linhpa (M) 44 B5
Linshot 14 B3
Lisa (C) 45 H1
Litakot (N) 25 E3
Litham 19 E3
Litipara 69 F6
Loakara 70 A1
Loang 13 G6
Lobang 42 C6
Lobeng 82 A1
Loch 42 A3
Lochipur 69 H5
Lodai 48 C5
Lodhika 63 E2
Lodhikheda 67 F3
Lodhma 56 D5
Lodrani 49 E4
Lohaganj (Ba) 59 G5
Lohagara (Ba) 59 E5
Lohaghat 24 A2
Lohani 21 H4
Lohara (Mah) 65 G5
Lohara (Mah) 67 E6
Lohara (Mad) 68 D3
Lohara (Mah) 78 A6
Lohardaga 56 B5
Loharghat 42 A5
Lohari (Har) 21 H3
Lohari (Mad) 55 E6
Loharia (Raj) 50 D4
Loharia (Raj) 51 G1
Loharkhet 23 H1
Loharsi 69 F3
Loharu 21 H5
Lohat Baddy 17 G5
Lohatipur 28 C5
Lohawat 32 A2
Lohba 23 G1
Loheswar 79 E4
Lohgaon 78 D4
Lohgarh 18 B5
Lohsna 21 F5
Loipaw (M) 44 C6

Loisingha 69 H5
Lokapur 85 F4
Lokar 18 D5
Lokhartalai 66 C1
Lokhuni 43 G3
Lokia 50 D5
Lokikere 91 F3
Lokkanahalli 95 G2
Lokondo (N) 24 C2
Loma (C) 29 E3
Lonand 76 D6
Lonar 78 A1
Lonavla 76 B4
Lonbehela 78 D1
Londa (Ba) 73 G2
Londa (Aru) 42 D1
Londa (Kar) 84 D6
Longdam (C) 29 G5
Longhar 76 A4
Longhrawh (M) 61 E5
Longkamgaon 43 E4
Longkin (M) 44 C5
Longku 42 D5
Longpi 61 E2
Longsa 43 G4
Longting 44 A2
Longyi (M) 75 F5
Longyul (C) 28 A1
Loni (Utt) 22 C4
Loni (Mah) 66 D5
Loni (Mah) 77 E2
Loni (Mah) 77 F4
Loni (Mah) 77 F5
Loni Bapkar 77 E5
Loni Kalbhor 76 D5
Lonsapur 63 F5
Lopoke 17 E3
Lora (P) 12 B3
Lori 19 E2
Lorma 69 H5
Lormi 68 D2
Loroto (C) 26 C5
Lorrikki (P) 17 E1
Losal 33 F1
Losar 18 D1
Lotan 37 G2
Lothal 63 H1
Lotia 67 F1
Lotpuri 63 F5
Lotsun 14 A2
Lotugadda 81 F6
Louri (B) 42 B2
Lowada 72 A1
Lowalang 56 C3
Lowan 33 H3
Lu 44 A2
Lubanwala (P) 17 E3
Lucknow 36 C3
Luddan (P) 20 A1
Ludesar 21 F2
Ludewala (P) 16 A2
Ludhiana 17 H4
Lugam 79 H2
Lugasi 53 H1
Luhara 64 A3
Luharu 34 C2
Luk (C) 19 G3
Luk Saung (C) 29 G5
Lukhamui 61 E1
Lukla (N) 39 G1
Lukou (C) 45 H5
Lukung 15 E3
Lukwasa 52 C1
Lukwei (C) 45 H4
Lukyi (M) 45 F6
Lulliani (P) 17 E4
Lumbini (N) 37 G1
Lumding 43 E5

Lumoko (C) 45 H5
Lumsal (N) 24 B2
Lumtui 60 D4
Lumu 14 A2
Luna 31 G3 (Raj)
Luna 48 B4 (Guj)
Lunang (C) 27 H1
Lunar 30 D3
Lunavada 50 C5
Lunda 51 E3
Lundarwan 12 D2
Lundra 55 H5
Lung Chen (B) 41 F1
Lungchwanchiang (C) 45 G6
Lungdar 61 E5
Lungding (M) 61 E6
Lungding (Ass) 42 D5
Lungding (Ass) 43 E5
Lungiya 63 E4
Lungkar (C) 15 H5
Lunglei 60 D6
Lungler (M) 61 E6
Lunglung Nang (C) 29 H4
Lungmo (C) 27 G1
Lungngo (M) 75 E2
Lungpho 60 D5
Lungrang (M) 75 E2
Lungring (M) 75 F2
Lungsawi (M) 75 E2
Lungsen 60 C6
Lungtar (M) 75 F2
Lungthung (N) 40 A1
Lungthung 60 A5
Lungtian (Ba) 60 C4
Lunh (N) 25 F3
Lunhyar (P) 48 C2
Lunia (P) 48 D2
Lunishera (N) 25 E3
Lunkaransar 20 C4
Lunkha (P) 14 A1
Lunsar 63 F1
Luntsum (N) 25 G4
Lurigaon (N) 25 G2
Lushui (C) 45 H4
Lutu 21 F5
Luwari (P) 48 A2
Lwedup (M) 75 F4
Lyngkhoi 42 A6

Mabdeitikra 55 F6
Macchiwara 18 A5
Mach (P) 16 D3
Machai (P) 12 A2
Machalpur 52 A3
Macharla 86 C4
Machchand 35 G4
Macheri 34 B2
Macherla 87 G4
Machgaon 83 F1
Machhi Singh (P) 16 B6
Machhlishahr 37 F5
Machhoi 13 G2
Machhrehta 36 B1
Machilpar 34 C3
Maching 43 F6
Machkhoa 43 G1
Machkund 81 F5
Madakasira 91 H4
Madalmoi 77 G3
Madanapalle 92 C4
Madanganj 33 E3
Madankeri 90 B2
Madanpur (Utt) 35 G2
Madanpur (Bih) 39 H4
Madanpur (Utt) 53 F3
Madanpur (Bih) 56 B2

Madanpur (Wbg) 58 C6
Madanpur (Mad) 69 G1
Madaora 53 F3
Madapalli 96 B1
Madari Hat 40 D3
Madaripur (Ba) 59 F5
Madattukkulam 95 G6
Madaula 22 D5
Madawara 33 H6, 34 A6
Madded 80 B4
Maddikera 86 C6
Maddimadugu 92 D3
Maddipadu 87 H5
Maddoke (P) 17 F2
Madduluru 87 H6
Maddupur 55 G1
Maddur (And) 86 C3
Maddur (Ker) 95 F1
Madeswaramalai 95 H2
Madh (Ba) 59 H3
Madh 76 C3
Madha 77 G6
Madharianwala (P) 16 C2
Madhavaram 86 C5
Madhavpur 62 C4
Madhepur 39 F4
Madheri 67 F6
Madhi 62 A2
Madhipura 39 G5
Madhira 88 A3
Madho Shinghana 21 E2
Madho Tanda 24 A4
Madhoganj 36 A2
Madhogarh 35 G4
Madhopur 17 G1
Madhorajpura 33 G3
Madhu (M) 75 E4
Madhuban (Utt) 37 H4
Madhuban (Bih) 38 D4
Madhuban (Mad) 69 G4
Madhubani (Bih) 38 A2
Madhubani (Bih) 39 E4
Madhugiri 91 H4
Madhupur (Ba) 59 F2
Madhupur (Ba) 59 H4
Madhupur (Bih) 57 G3
Madhupur (Tri) 60 A4
Madhupur Garh 71 E5
Madhura 39 H4
Madhwas 50 C5
Madhyamaheshwar 19 G5
Madia (Ba) 59 E2
Madiali 20 C4
Madikeri 94 C1
Madina 22 A3
Madinaguda 87 E1
Madipenta 87 F5
Madivedu 92 C4
Madka 49 F3
Madlauda 21 H2
Madli 32 A4
Madlia 32 D3
Madnakal 86 C4
Madnapur 23 H6
Madnur 78 D5
Madpura 32 C2
Madras 93 G5-6
Madri 50 C3
Madua (Ba) 59 H3
Madugula 81 G6
Madukkar 96 D6
Madukkarai 95 F5
Madurai 99 F1
Madurantakam 97 E1
Maduvanhalli 95 G2
Madwapur 39 E3
Madwas 55 E3
Maeshpur 40 A5

Magadi 91 H6
Magarwara 36 A3
Magaturu 87 F5
Magawng (M) 45 G5
Mageda 81 E2
Maggowal (P) 16 D1
Maghar 37 G3
Maglona 21 F6
Magna Hat 72 B2
Magnama (Ba) 74 B3
Magnur 86 C4
Magori (Utt) 34 C1
Magori (Guj) 50 C5
Magra (Ba) 59 E3
Magra 58 B6
Magroni 34 D5
Maguchi (C) 45 H1
Magura (Ba) 59 E5
Magwana 48 B5
Magyichaung (M) 74 C6
Magyigon (M) 75 G6
Magyiywa (M) 75 G5
Mahabaleshwar 76 C6
Mahabalipuram 97 F1
Mahaban 34 D1
Mahad 76 C6
Mahadanapuram 96 B5
Mahadebpur (Ba) 58 C1
Mahadeopalli 69 H3
Mahadeopur 80 A4
Mahadu (M) 75 E5
Mahadwani 54 B6
Mahagama 57 H1
Mahagaon (Mah) 78 D1
Mahagaon (Mah) 78 D2
Mahagaon (Mah) 84 D4
Mahagaon (Kar) 86 A1
Mahagarh 51 F2
Mahajan 20 D4
Mahakalguri 41 E3
Mahal 92 D4
Mahalabari (Ba) 60 B6
Mahalchhari (Ba) 60 B6
Mahalgaon 67 G5
Mahalingpur 85 E4
Mahalpur 17 H3
Maham 22 A3
Mahan 66 C6
Mahandraganj 41 E6
Mahandri (P) 12 C1
Mahanga 71 F6
Mahansar 21 F5
Mahar 84 C2
Maharajagadai 96 A1
Maharjaganj 36 C4
Maharjanagar 36 C1
Maharaj Gund 12 C2
Maharajganj 38 B4
Maharajpur (Bih) 40 A6
Maharajpur (Mad) 53 G5
Maharajpur (Mad) 68 C3
Maharan (P) 20 B1
Maharganj 37 G4
Maharj 17 F6
Maharjpur (Utt) 36 B4
Maharjpur (Mad) 53 H1
Mahasamund 69 E5
Mahatpur 17 G4
Mahbubabad 87 H1
Mahbubnagar 86 D3
Mahe (J&K) 15 F5
Mahe (Ker) 94 C3
Maheji 65 G5
Mahendragarh (Har) 21 H5
Mahendragarh (Mad) 55 E5
Mahendranagar (N) 39 G3
Mahesa 56 D3
Mahesana 49 H4

Maheshmunda 57 F3
Maheshpur 58 A2
Maheshwar 65 G2
Maheshwaram 87 E2
Maheskhali 74 B4
Mahespur (Ba) 58 D5
Mahewa 54 A3
Mahfuzbhendaru 82 B5
Mahgalpur 35 H3
Mahgawan 35 F3
Mahi Nag 13 E4
Mahidharpur 70 C5
Mahiganj (Ba) 40 D5
Mahim 76 A2
Mahisama 87 E2
Mahisar (Ba) 59 G5
Mahishadal 72 A2
Mahisi 39 F5
Mahlan 33 G3
Mahmadpur 50 A3
Mahmudabad 36 C1
Mahmudpur (P) 16 C2
Mahnar Bazar 38 D5
Mahoba 35 H6
Mahodra 52 B1
Maholi (Utt) 24 B6
Maholi (Utt) 34 D1
Maholpada 70 D3
Mahrajganj 37 H2
Mahrauli 22 C4
Mahroni 53 F2
Mahrua 37 F4
Mahrwala 21 E2
Mahsa (M) 45 E6
Mahshol 12 D4
Mahson 37 G3
Mahsrang 84 C4
Mahta 17 F3
Mahua 38 A3
Mahuadanr 56 A5
Mahud 85 F1
Mahudha 50 B6
Mahul 37 F4
Mahuli 37 G3
Mahur (Ass) 42 D6
Mahur (Mah) 65 H6
Mahur (Mah) 78 D2
Mahura 12 D3
Mahuria 51 H4
Mahuva (Guj) 63 G5
Mahuva (Guj) 64 B5
Mahuver 64 A5
Mahuwa 38 D5
Mahwah 34 B2
Maibong 42 D6
Maidan Kili (P) 12 B2
Maidukuru 92 D2
Maigabo (B) 41 F2
Maihar 54 B3
Maihma Sawai 17 E6
Maijdi (Ba) 59 H6
Maika Hans (P) 16 B6
Maikalganj 24 B6
Maikot (N) 25 G4
Mailakanda (Ba) 59 G1
Mailani 24 A5
Mailavaram 88 B3
Mailepalli 87 F3
Maili (M) 45 H5
Maili 12 D3
Mailpir 57 E6
Maina 52 A5
Mainaguri 40 C3
Mainamati (Ba) 59 H5
Mainatanr 38 C2
Maindargi 85 H1
Maingkwan (M) 44 D4
Maingkwan 43 H3

Maingnyaung (M) 61 D3
Maingpok (M) 44 C6
Maini (P) 12 A3
Mainoraipara 60 B3
Mainpuri 35 F2
Maipadu 93 G2
Maipur 64 D5
Maira (P) 12 C5
Mairang 42 A5
Mairh 33 H1
Mairwa 38 B4
Maisandra 91 G6
Maitbhanga (Ba) 74 A1
Maiunli 28 C5
Maiyan 12 D3
Majal 48 B5
Majali 90 A1
Majbat 42 C3
Majgaon 55 E4
Majhaul 39 E6
Majhauli 38 A4
Majhgawan (Mad) 54 A5
Majhgawan (Mad) 54 B1
Majhiaon 56 A3
Majholi 53 H5
Majholi (Mad) 54 D3
Majhwalia 38 C3
Maji Mandri 80 B3
Majitha 17 F3
Majna 53 G2
Majorganj 38 D3
Majpuri 77 H2
Majra (Him) 18 C6
Majra (Utt) 19 E6
Majri 79 G1
Majuli 43 F2
Makanpur 35 H2
Makardhokra 67 G5
Makariagaon 42 C4
Makaw (M) 44 D3
Makdala 49 G3
Maker 38 C5
Makhdumnagar 37 F3
Makhdumpur 56 C1
Makhera 51 F2
Makhjan 84 B2
Makhor 32 A1
Makhtal 86 C4
Makhu 17 F4
Makhya 81 F3
Makkapeta 88 A2
Makkuva 81 H4
Makrai 66 C2
Makrana 33 E2
Makrandpur 39 E4
Makri 81 E2
Makrohar 55 F4
Makron 51 H5
Maksi 51 H5
Maksudangarh 52 C3
Makum 44 A1
Makwanpur Garhi (N) 38 D1
Makware 43 H5
Mal (Utt) 36 B2
Mal (Wbg) 40 C2
Mal Mari Makan (P) 47 F1
Mala (Raj) 33 F3
Mala (Ker) 95 E6
Malab 22 B6
Malacca 101 F2
Malachua 54 C5
Malahar 53 H1
Malai 19 F6
Malaiyur 96 D1
Malakanagiri 81 E5
Malakavemula 92 B3
Malakhera 34 B1

Malakheti (N) 24 B4
Malal (P) 12 A4
Malalavadi 95 E1
Malampalli 79 H6
Malampuzha 95 E5
Malan 13 G5
Malana 18 C2
Malangpa 42 D6
Malangwa (N) 38 D2
Malappuram 94 D4
Malapur 90 B3
Malara 33 G5
Malari 19 H5
Malasisar 21 F3
Malaudh 17 H5
Malaut 17 E6
Malavalli 95 F1
Malavi 91 F1
Malavucad 98 A1
Malawan 35 F1
Malawar 52 B4
Malayadivaram 96 A5
Malchalma 86 C1
Malda 58 B1
Malebennur 91 E3
Malegaon (Mah) 65 E6
Malegaon (Mah) 77 H5
Malegaon (Mah) 78 B4
Malegaon (Mah) 78 C3
Malegaon Jahagir 66 B6
Malehra 53 G2
Malepur 57 F1
Malerkolta 17 H5
Malewara 68 B6
Malgaon (Mah) 65 E3
Malgaon (Mah) 85 E3
Malgund 84 A2
Malhar (Raj) 31 H2
Malhar (Mad) 69 F3
Malhargarh (Mad) 51 F3
Malhargarh (Guj) 53 E3
Malharia 39 H4
Malhera 22 C3
Malhiwri 78 D1
Malhura 78 G2
Mali Kot 13 F4
Malia (Mad) 51 F3
Malia (Guj) 62 D4
Malial 79 F4
Malian (P) 16 B1
Maliara 57 H5
Malihabad 36 B2
Malikpeth 77 G6
Malipara 40 C4
Malipur 37 F4
Maliya 49 E6
Malkana 21 F1
Malkapur (Mah) 65 H5
Malkapur (Mah) 66 A5
Malkapur (And) 78 D6
Malkapur (Mah) 84 C2
Malkapur (And) 87 E2
Malkhaid 86 B2
Malkhed 66 D5
Malkhurda 69 G3
Malkot 78 C3
Malla 86 A3
Mallah (P) 17 F2
Mallan 17 E6
Mallanpur 24 C6
Mallanwan 36 A2
Mallapuram 79 F4
Mallasamudram 96 A4
Mallepalli 80 C5
Malliau (P) 16 D3
Mallipatna 91 F3
Mallur 96 A3
Maloni 34 D3

Malotha 18 B2
Malpe 90 C5
Malpur (Guj) 50 B5
Malpur (Mah) 65 E4
Malpura (Raj) 33 G4
Malpura (Raj) 34 D2
Malsiras 77 F6
Malthan 76 D4
Malther 18 B3
Maluani 21 E2
Malud 82 D2
Maluk Singh (P) 48 B1
Malunje 77 E2
Malur (Kar) 90 D4
Malur (Kar) 92 B6
Malusar 21 E5
Malwan (Utt) 36 B4
Malwan (Mah) 84 B4
Malwara 49 H2
Mamarkera 20 D1
Mamana 33 F3
Mamandur 93 F6
Mamda 79 E3
Mamdapur 85 F3
Mamdipalli 79 G3
Mamdot 17 E5
Mamit 60 C4
Mamu Kanjan (P) 16 A5
Man (M) 75 G4
Man (J&K) 15 F3
Man (Mah) 66 C5
Man Ming (M) 45 F6
Man Namsai (M) 45 E1
Mana 19 G5
Manadar 32 B6
Manadipet 96 D2
Manak (P) 16 D4
Manakhur 34 C4
Manaklao 32 B3
Manakpur 18 B5
Manali 18 C1
Manalurpettai 96 C2
Manamadurai 99 F2
Manamelkudi 99 H1
Manamodu 96 D4
Manana 22 B3
Manantavadi 94 D3
Manannur 87 E4
Mananwala (P) 16 C3
Manapadu 99 E5
Manaparai 96 A6
Manapuram 96 A2
Manasa 51 F2
Manasar 21 E6
Manatu 56 B3
Manauri 36 D6
Manavadar 62 D3
Manawar 65 F2
Manbazar 57 G5
Manchar 76 C4
Mancharpur 70 D1
Manchikeri 90 C1
Manchippa 79 E5
Manchirayal 79 H4
Manda (Ba) 58 C1
Manda (Raj) 31 E2
Manda (Raj) 32 C5
Manda (Utt) 55 E1
Manda (Ori) 71 F2
Mandagadde 90 D4
Mandai 31 E4
Mandakla 50 D2
Mandal (Raj) 33 E6
Mandal (Guj) 49 G5
Mandala 64 B2
Mandalamanikam 99 F2
Mandalgarh 33 F6

Mandangad 76 B6
Mandaora 34 A1
Mandaori 34 A3
Mandapalli 79 F3
Mandapam 99 G3
Mandapeta 89 E3
Mandapur 77 E2
Mandapur Rampur 81 H1
Mandar 56 D5
Mandari 49 H2
Mandasa 82 B4
Mandavalli 88 C4
Mandavgan 77 E4
Mandawa (Raj) 21 F5
Mandawa (Raj) 33 H4
Mandawar (Raj) 22 A6
Mandawar (Utt) 23 E2
Mandawar (Raj) 52 A2
Mandeli 32 C1
Mandem 80 B4
Mandera 51 G1
Mandgaon 67 F6
Mandhal 67 G5
Mandhan 22 A5
Mandhar 68 D4
Mandi (J&K) 13 E4
Mandi (Him) 18 B3
Mandi Bahauddin (P) 12 C6
Mandi Burewala (P) 16 A6
Mandikal 92 A4
Mandipalle 81 G4
Mandisadiganj (P) 16 C6
Mandkaula 22 C5
Mandki 77 E6
Mandla 68 B1
Mandleshwar 65 G2
Mandlioli 21 G4
Mandodra 62 C4
Mandoli 50 A1
Mandore 32 B4
Mandori (P) 12 A4
Mandpur (N) 24 D5
Mandra (P) 12 B5
Mandrael 34 C4
Mandrela 21 G5
Mandrup 85 G1
Mandsaur 51 F3
Mandu (Bih) 56 B4
Mandu (Bih) 56 D4
Mandu (Mad) 65 G1
Mandva 64 B6
Mandve 76 A4
Mandved 65 E6
Mandvi (Guj) 48 B6
Mandvi (Guj) 49 G4
Mandvi (Guj) 64 B4
Mandvi (Mah) 76 A2
Mandwala 32 A6
Mandwara 65 F2
Mandwe 76 D3
Mandya 95 F1
Mane 27 H6
Manebhanjyang (N) 39 F2
Manechan 15 E6
Manegaod 66 A5
Manegaon (Mad) 67 H2
Manegaon (Mah) 77 G6
Manekwara 63 E4
Maner 38 C5
Manerajuri 85 E2
Maneri (Utt) 19 E5
Maneri (Mad) 54 A6
Maneri (Mad) 54 B6
Maneri (Mah) 84 C5
Mang (P) 12 C4
Manga (P) 16 D4
Mangalagiri 88 A4
Mangalam (Tam) 96 D3

Mangalam (Tam) 99 G2
Mangalapuram 98 C4
Mangaldai 42 B3
Mangalgi 86 B1
Mangali 21 G3
Mangalkot 58 A4
Mangalore 90 C6
Mangalwada 91 H3
Mangalwar Hat (Ba) 74 B1
Mangalwedha 85 F1
Mangan 40 C1
Mangaon (Mah) 76 B5
Mangaon (Mah) 84 C5
Mangapet 80 B5
Mangarh 18 C5
Mangarwar 51 E2
Mangat (P) 16 C1
Mangat 13 F4
Mangawah 54 D2
Mangchibuk (M) 45 G3
Mangial 78 C4
Manginipudi 88 C4
Mangkheng (M) 61 F6
Mangkyi (M) 45 G4
Mangla (P) 12 C5
Manglaor 18 C3
Manglaur (P) 12 A1
Manglaur 22 D1
Manglia 51 H6
Mangliawas 33 E4
Manglur 85 H6
Manglutan 100 B6
Mangnang (C) 19 H3
Mangoke (P) 16 D2
Mangoli 85 G3
Mangom 13 F2
Mangoor 80 C6
Mangowal (P) 16 A1
Mangri (N) 25 F2
Mangrol (Raj) 34 A6
Mangrol (Mad) 34 C4
Mangrol (Guj) 62 C4
Mangrol (Guj) 64 B4
Mangrul (Mah) 67 E5
Mangrul (Mah) 76 B3
Mangrul (Mah) 77 H6
Mangrul Chaval 66 D6
Mangrul Pir 66 C6
Mangrup 33 E6
Mangwal (P) 12 A5
Mangwal 17 H2
Manhairu 22 A4
Manhargudi 96 D4
Mani (Him) 19 E2
Mani (Kar) 90 D6
Mani Dabwali 21 E1
Mania 34 D3
Maniar 38 A5
Maniari Aliganj 37 E4
Maniarwa 39 F3
Manigachi 39 F4
Manihala (P) 17 E3
Manihari 40 A6
Manik Chak 58 A1
Manika 56 B4
Manikapur (N) 24 D5
Manikaran 18 C2
Manikchhari (Ba) 60 B6
Manikdaundi 77 F3
Manikganj (Ba) 59 F4
Manikiala (P) 12 B4
Manikpara 71 H1
Manikpur (Mad) 54 B5
Manikpur (Utt) 54 C1
Manimangalam 93 F6
Manipal 90 C5
Maniramkanda (N) 24 D4
Maniwali 20 D1

Maniyachchi 99 E4
Manja (C) 19 F2
Manjakot (P) 12 B2
Manjalampeta 93 E4
Manjampati 95 G6
Manjapara 70 B2
Manjar Sumba 77 G4
Manjarabad 91 E6
Manjeri 94 D4
Manjeshwara 90 C6
Manjhagarh 38 B4
Manjhanpur 36 D6
Manjhaoli 22 C5
Manjhari 71 E1
Manjhi 38 B5
Manjhiara 57 H3
Manjhra (Utt) 24 A4
Manjhra (Utt) 24 C5
Manjlegaon 77 H3
Manjpur 49 G4
Manjram 78 C4
Manjur 76 D1
Mankachar 41 E6
Mankali (N) 24 C3
Mankasar 20 A5
Mankeshwar 77 G5
Manki 90 B3
Mankot (N) 24 B1
Mankrin (M) 45 E6
Mankuwa 48 B5
Manlajur (C) 15 H5
Manmad 77 E1
Manmao 44 B2
Manna 20 D1
Mannachchanellur 96 B5
Mannargudi 96 D5
Mannarkad 95 E5
Mannemkonda 81 E6
Mannu (M) 45 E1
Mano 13 H5
Manohar Thana 52 B3
Manohardi (Ba) 59 G3
Manoharpur 33 H1
Manoli 85 E5
Manomonda 70 A5
Manor 76 A2
Manora (P) 47 E2
Manora 78 C1
Manori 76 A3
Manpui 60 C3
Manpur (Har) 22 C6
Manpur (Raj) 50 B3
Manpur (Mad) 54 C4
Manpur (Mad) 55 H5
Manpur (Bih) 56 C1
Manpur (Mad) 65 G1
Manpur (Mad) 68 B6
Manpur Khurd 69 F6
Manpura 55 H4
Mansa (Pun) 21 G1
Mansa (Guj) 50 A5
Mansar 67 G4
Mansehra (P) 12 B2
Mansein (M) 44 B6
Mansinghpur (Ba) 40 D6
Mansum (M) 44 C5
Mansuram (P) 20 A3
Mansurwali (P) 16 D1
Mantala (Ba) 59 H1
Manteswar 58 B5
Mantha 78 A2
Manthani 79 H4
Mantralayam 86 B5
Mantur 85 F4
Mantzo (C) 29 H6
Manu (P) 20 A4
Manu 60 B3
Manu Bazar 60 A6

Manubrolu 93 F3
Manumukh (Ba) 60 B2
Manung (N) 25 G5
Manur (Mah) 77 G3
Manur (Tam) 99 E4
Manushmuria 71 G1
Manvel 63 E4
Manvi 86 B4
Manwat 78 A3
Manwe (M) 44 C6
Manyapadu 86 D5
Manywet (M) 44 D6
Manzgom 13 F4
Mao Songsang 43 G6
Maochao (C) 45 H4
Mapating (C) 29 H4
Mapusa 84 C5
Mara (M) 45 F5
Mara (C) 29 H3
Mara (Aru) 27 F5
Mara (Mad) 55 F4
Marad 62 D3
Maradam 81 H5
Maradugu 87 F4
Marahalli 95 G2
Marahchi 23 F6
Marahra 23 E6
Marakkanam 97 E2
Marakpur 22 B6
Maralvadi 95 G1
Maram 43 G6
Marang Ponga 70 D2
Marangadh 49 H3
Marangaon 43 E2
Marangkong 43 H3
Maranhali 91 F6
Maraulianwala (P) 16 B2
Maraur 18 C2
Margao 84 C6
Margherita 44 B2
Margram 58 A3
Marhaura 38 C5
Marho Bula Khan (P) 47 G3
Mari (P) 16 A2
Mariad 53 H3
Mariahan 55 F1
Mariahu 37 F5
Mariani 43 G3
Maricha 39 F4
Marihal 85 E5
Marikal 86 C3
Maripeda 87 H2
Marka 36 C5
Markacho 57 E3
Markakasa 68 B5
Markan (P) 30 B3
Markandi (Mah) 79 H1
Markandi (Ori) 82 C3
Markapur 87 G5
Markha 14 C3
Markham Dzong (C) 29 H2
Markik 79 F6
Markuli (Ba) 60 A2
Marla 31 H3
Marmat 62 C3
Maroa 42 A4

Marod 68 D5
Maroda 80 B1
Marol (P) 14 A1
Marosile 69 F5
Marot (P) 20 A3
Marot 33 F2
Marpalli 86 D1
Marrayagudem 80 C6
Marri 50 A1
Marrigudem 80 B6
Marsalang 14 C3
Marshaghai 71 F6
Martand 13 F4
Martung (P) 12 A2
Martur 86 B2
Maru 101 G4
Maru Gahtawng (M) 45 F4
Marua 33 F3
Marudur 96 B5
Marungapuri 96 B6
Maruru 92 A2
Marutadu 96 D1
Maruteru 88 D3
Maruthi 13 G6
Maruturu 87 F5
Maruwa Ghat (N) 38 B1
Marvad 65 F4
Marve 76 A3
Marwadi 78 C1
Marwas 52 C3
Masabdisa 43 E5
Masaigah 18 B6
Masaipet 79 F6
Masakhali (Ba) 59 G3
Masalang (Ba) 60 B5
Masanjor 57 H3
Masarkal 86 B4
Masauli 36 D2
Masaurhi 38 C6
Maschhari (Ba) 60 B6
Maseiu (M) 61 G5
Mashal 85 H2
Mashkubha (Ba) 74 C1
Mashubra 18 C4
Masinagudi 95 F3
Masira 54 C4
Masisar 21 F5
Masitan 21 E1
Maski 86 A5
Masod 87 E3
Masrakh 38 C4
Massa 77 H5
Massa Jogi 77 H4
Masterpara (Ba) 60 B5
Masti 92 B6
Masturi 69 F2
Masuda 33 E4
Masulipatam 88 C4
Masumzup (M) 45 E2
Masur 84 D1
Masura 84 B4
Mat 22 D6
Matabhanga 40 D4
Matala 78 B6
Matalkunta 78 D6
Matanhei 22 A4
Matanomadh 48 A5
Matar 64 A1
Matarbari (Ba) 74 B3
Mataundh 36 A6
Matayan 13 G2
Matbar Hat (Ba) 60 A6
Matbarar Char (Ba) 59 F5
Matbari (Ba) 73 F2
Mated 87 H1
Matera Bazar 24 D6
Mateswar (Ba) 59 F3
Mathak 49 E6

Mathania 32 B3
Matheran 76 B4
Matho 14 C3
Mathrala (P) 12 A5
Mathu Barog 13 G1
Mathura (Utt) 34 D1
Mathura (Utt) 37 E1
Mathurapur (Bih) 40 B5
Mathurapur (Ass) 43 H2
Mathurapur (Wbg) 72 C2
Mathwada 79 H6
Mathwar 64 D2
Matiali 40 C2
Matiari 58 C5
Matibhanga (Ba) 59 E6
Matili 20 D1
Matin 55 F6
Matiyal (*) 13 G1
Matiyal (J&K) 17 F1
Matkuli 67 E1
Matla 68 B3
Matlab Bazar (Ba) 59 G5
Matli (P) 47 H1
Matmari 86 C4
Mato 71 G5
Matola 78 A6
Mator (P) 13 G1
Matra 63 F2
Matsalwang (C) 29 G6
Matsel 14 A4
Mattampalli 87 H3
Matteke (P) 16 C2
Mattigatta 91 G5
Mattigiri 95 H1
Mattihalli 91 F2
Mattili 81 F5
Mattod 91 G4
Matwa 62 D2
Matwad 64 A5
Mau (Raj) 33 G1
Mau (Raj) 34 A6
Mau (Mad) 35 F4
Mau (Utt) 36 D6
Mau (Mad) 52 C4
Mau (Mad) 54 D3
Mau (Bih) 56 C1
Mau (Mad)68 A2
Mau Aimma 37 E5
Mau Ranipur 35 G6
Maudaha 36 A5
Maudanga 42 D4
Mauganj 55 E2
Mauhar 36 B4
Maujpur 34 B1
Maukkadaw (M) 61 G6
Maulavi Bazar (Ba) 60 B2
Maulipader 81 E4
Maunath Bhanjan 37 H5
Maunda 67 G4
Maung Te (M) 44 A5
Maungdaung (M) 75 H1
Maunggyihtaung (M) 74 C5
Maungkan (M) 61 H1
Maur 17 F6
Maurawan 36 C4
Mauvum (M) 61 E4
Mavalli 90 B3
Mavelikara 98 B3
Mavingundi 90 C3
Mavli 50 D2
Mawai 68 C1
Mawal 50 A2
Mawana 22 D3
Mawaynram 42 A6
Mawden 42 A5
Mawdoh 42 A5
Mawhati 42 B5
Mawke (M) 61 H5

Mawkyrwat 42 A6
Mawlai 42 B5
Mawlaik (M) 61 G4
Mawle (M) 75 F2
Mawlyngkneng 42 B5
Mawmarin 41 H6
Mawphlang 42 A6
Mawrongor 42 A6
Mawskei 42 A5
Mawtongyi (M) 61 H4
Maya Chikhi 37 F3
Mayabandar 100 B3
Mayakonda 91 F3
Mayang Imphal 61 F2
Mayapur (Mad) 52 B5
Mayapur (Wbg) 58 C5
Mayamagar 49 F6
Mayem 84 C6
Mayin (M) 75 G2
Mayna 72 A2
Mayni 84 D1
Mayuram 96 D4
Mayureswar 58 A3
Mc Leodganj (P) 16 C6
Mebsi 38 C4
Mebu 28 A5
Mechcheri 95 H3
Medak 79 E6
Medakul (Ba) 59 F6
Medana 81 F2
Medapadu 89 E2
Medarmetla 87 H5
Medchal 87 E1
Medha (Mah) 76 C6'
Medha (Mah) 84 C1
Medha (Mah) 84 C2
Medikurti 92 D4
Medkanhal 86 A5
Medsi 66 B6
Medu Kongkar Dzong (C)
  26 B1
Meenachi 98 B2
Meerut 22 D3
Mega 27 G4
Megalwa 31 H6
Megarvalli 90 B4
Meghatari 56 D2
Meghpur 63 E1
Meghraj 50 C5
Mehandiganj (Ba) 59 G6
Mehda 35 F4
Mehdawal 37 G2
Meherpur (Ba) 58 C4
Mehervara 49 H4
Mehidpur 51 G5
Mehkar 78 A1
Mehmadabad 50 A6
Mehnagar 37 G5
Mehrawan 37 F5
Mehro Pilo (P) 12 A5
Mehunbare 65 E6
Meilangtlang (M) 74 C2
Meipanjra 67 F4
Meiring 61 G2
Meja (Raj) 33 E6
Meja (Utt) 55 E1
Mekha 28 B5
Mekhuganj 40 C4
Mel Mattur 96 C4
Melabon (M) 61 H1
Melandaha (Ba) 59 E1
Melapalayam 99 E4
Melattur 95 E4
Melchhamunda 69 H5
Melghat 66 B4
Meliyaputtu 82 B4
Mellapur 85 G5
Melliyakarai 96 B3

Melmandai 99 F3
Melpadi 93 E6
Melpatti 92 D6
Melkote 95 F1
Melun (M) 75 E6
Melung (N) 39 E1
Melur 99 F1
Meluri 43 H5
Melvisharam 93 E6
Memari 58 B5
Mendarda 62 D4
Mendhar 12 D4
Mendipur (Ba) 59 H2
Mendradem (C) 28 A2
Mendwas 33 G4
Mengka (C) 45 F6
Mengni 63 E2
Mengta (C) 45 H6
Menki 67 H6
Menkong (C) 29 G4
Mennanyam 94 C3
Menshaw (M) 75 E6
Mentada 81 H5
Meppadi 94 D3
Mepumna 28 D5
Merak 15 F4
Meral 56 A3
Meramsar 20 C6
Merandahalli 96 A1
Merasar 20 B5
Meri (C) 28 A2
Mero 50 A1
Merpalli 80 A3
Merta 32 D3
Meshing 27 G5
Mesuria 63 E1
Meswan 62 D4
Metala 65 H6
Methan 49 G6
Methraipara 60 B4
Meting (P) 47 G1
Metpalli 79 F4
Mettupalayam 95 F4
Mettur 95 H3
Metwan 13 G4
Metwara 52 A6
Mevasa 63 F2
Mewali 64 B1
Mewasa 62 D3
Mezali (M) 75 G6
Mhaisgaon 77 G6
Mhaismal 77 F1
Mhasdi 65 E5
Mhasla 76 B6
Mhasvad 85 E1
Mhow 65 G1
Miajlar 30 D4
Mian Channun (P) 16 A6
Mian Hussain (P) 47 H3
Mian Pirdad Faqir (P) 47 G3
Miana (P) 12 A2
Miana 52 C1
Miana Gondal (P) 16 B1
Miani (P) 12 B6
Miani (Pun) 17 G3
Miani (Utt) 19 E5
Mianpur 53 E1
Mianwal (P) 16 C1
Mianwali 20 C1
Miao 44 C1
Miaon 23 G6
Miar Hat (Ba) 59 H6
Midda 17 E6
Midh Ranjah (P) 16 B2
Midigeri 91 H4
Midnapore 71 H1
Midutura 87 E5
Miganj 23 G4

Miging 27 H4
Migto (C) 28 D2
Mihijam 57 G4
Mihona 35 F4
Mijakpur 34 B1
Mikaw (M) 45 H2
Mikirbheta 42 C4
Mikirgaon 42 D4
Milak 23 G4
Milkipur 37 E3
Milupara 69 H2
Mimbil (M) 61 F4
Mimisal 99 H1
Minapur 38 D4
Minbu (M) 75 H6
Minbya (M) 75 E6
Minchinabad (P) 16 C6
Mindaingbin (M) 75 H2
Mingachhi (Ba) 59 E2
Mingala (M) 74 C5
Mingaora (P) 12 A1
Mingin (M) 61 G6
Mingtanwala (P) 16 C3
Minigaon (N) 25 F3
Minimarg 13 F1
Minjur 93 G5
Minkiani 18 A1
Minsin (M) 44 A6
Mintha (M) 61 G2
Minthami (M) 61 G4
Minutang 28 D5
Minyin (M) 75 G5
Minywa (M) 75 F2
Minzong 28 D6
Mipi 28 B3
Mirabat (P) 12 B1
Miragwas 52 B3
Mirahu (P) 30 B2
Miraj 84 D3
Mirajgaon 77 F4
Miraliwala (P) 16 D2
Miran 21 F6
Mirando Gompa (C) 27 F2
Mirapur 39 E4
Miraspur 22 D3
Mirau 21 G4
Mirchaduri 55 G3
Mirgani 38 B4
Mirgarh (P) 20 A3
Miri 77 F3
Mirialguda 87 G3
Mirian 90 B2
Mirik 40 B2
Mirle 95 E1
Mirmau 36 D3
Mirowal (P) 17 E2
Mirpur (Ba) 59 F4
Mirpur (P) 12 C5
Mirpur (*) 12 D2
Mirpur (*) 12 D5
Mirpur Batoro (P) 47 G2
Mirpur Khas (P) 30 A6
Mirpur Sakro (P) 47 F2
Mirsarai (Ba) 60 A6
Mirthal 17 G2
Mirwah (P) 30 A6
Miryan 86 C1
Mirza Murad 37 F6
Mirzaganj (Ba) 73 F1
Mirzapur (Ba) 59 F3
Mirzapur (Utt) 23 G6
Mirzapur (Utt)) 37 F6
Mirzapur (Bih) 56 B2
Mirzapur (Wbg) 58 B3
Mirzo Laghari (P) 47 G2
Misa 42 D3
Misamari 42 C3
Misha 101 G4

Mishrikot 85 E6
Misni 62 B3
Misrikh 36 B1
Missa Keswal (P) 12 C5
Mitamain (Ba) 59 H2
Mitasar 21 E5
Mitauli 24 B6
Mitha Bel 37 H3
Mitha Lak (P) 16 B2
Mitha Tar (P) 48 D1
Mithapur (Guj) 49 G5
Mithapur (Guj) 62 A1
Mithi (P) 48 A3
Mithi (P) 48 A2
Mithria 20 A6
Mitrahu (P) 30 B4
Mittemari 92 B4
Miuda (M) 75 F4
Miyagam 64 B2
Miyanganj 36 B3
Mkai-Imnu (M) 75 E4
Moana 22 A2
Mobarakpur (Ba) 58 D6
Modasa 50 B5
Modhera 49 G4
Modhwara 62 B3
Modinagar 22 C4
Moga 17 F5
Mogalturu 88 D4
Mogaung (M) 44 D6
Mogaung (M) 75 H1
Mogiyabari 60 B4
Mogli 78 D3
Moglipenta 93 E4
Mogra (Raj) 32 B4
Mogra (Mah) 67 G4
Moha 77 H5
Mohakalpara 71 G6
Mohala 68 B6
Mohan (Utt) 18 D6
Mohan (Utt) 36 B3
Mohana (Har) 22 B3
Mohana (Raj) 33 G3
Mohana (Mad) 34 D5
Mohana (Ori) 82 B2
Mohanganj (Ba) 59 H1
Mohanganj 36 D4
Mohangarh 53 F1
Mohania (Utt) 37 H6
Mohania (Bih) 55 H1
Mohankot 51 E6
Mohanlalganj 36 C3
Mohanpur (Ba) 58 C2
Mohanpur (Ba) 59 G5
Mohanpur (N) 39 G3
Mohanpur (Guj) 50 B5
Mohanpur (Wbg) 71 H3
Mohanur 96 A4
Mohardh 55 F4
Mohari 67 H4
Mohasa 52 D3
Mohattanagar (P) 30 A4
Mohdra (Mad) 53 H3
Mohdra (Mad) 54 A3
Mohean 101 G4
Mohena 22 C5
Mohendro ro Par (P) 30 D6
Mohera 69 E5
Mohgaon (Mad) 54 B6
Mohgaon (Mad) 68 A3
Mohgaon (Mad) 68 B2
Mohjuddinnagar 39 E5
Mohkher 67 F3
Mohoda 67 E6
Mohol 77 G6
Mohona 51 G2
Mohpa 67 F4
Mohpadar 81 E4

Mohri 13 E1
Mohurli 79 G1
Moi 52 A1
Moinabad 86 B1
Moirang 61 F2
Moka 86 B6
Mokal (P) 17 E5
Mokal (Raj) 31 E2
Mokal (Guj) 62 C3
Mokala 32 D3
Mokalsar (Raj) 20 D3
Mokalsar (Raj) 32 A5
Mokameh 39 E6
Mokampur 20 D4
Mokhada 76 B1
Mokheri 31 H2
Mokhpal 80 D4
Mokokchung 43 G4
Mokso (M) 44 C6
Moktha (M) 61 G6
Moku (C) 29 G2
Molagavalli 86 B6
Molakalmuru 91 G2
Molaman 20 C5
Molen 84 D6
Mollahat (Ba) 59 E6
Molnom 61 E3
Molong 61 E1
Molvailup 61 G2
Mombi New 61 F3
Momer 50 B3
Mon 43 H3
Mona Remout Depot (P) 16 B1
Monachara 60 C2
Monakhali (Ba) 74 B4
Moncombu 98 B2
Mond 84 B4
Mondari 14 C2
Mondemkhallu 82 A4
Mone Leh 14 C5
Mongar Dzong (B) 41 H2
Monghyr 39 F6
Mongku (C) 27 H3
Mongla (Ba) 73 E2
Mongotong (C) 29 G1
Monka (B) 41 H1
Montgomerywala (P) 16 A4
Monu 13 E4
Moohiwala (P) 16 A4
Moorang 19 E3
Mop 78 B1
Mopadu 93 E1
Mopung 27 H5
Mor (Raj) 33 G4
Mor (Bih) 39 E6
Morab 85 F5
Morabgi 85 F2
Moradabad 23 F4
Moragang 60 C2
Morageri 91 F1
Moraim 49 G1
Morala 85 E2
Moram 78 A6
Moranam 93 E6
Morang 18 D1
Morangpalli 86 D1
Moranhat 43 H2
Morappur 96 B2
Morar (P) 16 C3
Morar 35 E4
Moratgi 85 H2
Morath 78 D2
Morena 35 E3
Morgaon 76 D5
Morgram 58 B3
Mori (Raj) 33 E2
Mori (Mad) 51 G2

Morla 33 F4
Mormugao 84 C6
Mornai 41 G4
Morni 18 C5
Moro 50 B2
Morpa 49 G3
Morpur 62 C3
Morrelganj (Ba) 73 E1
Morsi 66 D4
Mortad 79 E4
Mortakka 65 H2
Morvi 49 E6
Morwai 56 B5
Morwan 51 F2
Mosh 14 A5
Moshrot 42 C5
Motagaon 50 D4
Motai 32 A2
Motanga 70 D5
Moteh 87 H2
Moter 81 G2
Moth 35 F5
Mothala 48 A5
Motibennur 91 E2
Motigarh 20 B5
Motihari 38 C3
Motinala 68 B2
Motipur 24 C5
Motkur 87 G1
Mottugudiam 80 D5
Mottur 96 B1
Motu 80 D6
Mouana 49 E4
Mount Abu 50 A2
Movan 62 B2
Moviya 63 E3
Mowa 88 C4
Mozo (M) 75 G1
Mrambon 28 B5
Mrawehaung (M) 74 D5
Mualbem (M) 61 F5
Mualbu Kawnpui 74 D2
Mualpi (M) 61 F4
Mualvum 60 C3
Mubarakpur 37 G4
Mudabidri 90 C6
Mudan Turzio 98 C4
Mudana 78 D2
Mudavadi 92 C5
Mudbal 86 A3
Muddanuru 92 C2
Muddur 79 G6
Mudebihal 85 H4
Mudel Town (P) 17 E3
Mudenur 85 H5
Mudetha 49 G3
Mudga 85 H4
Mudhol (And) 78 D4
Mudhol (Kar) 85 F4
Mudia 47 H4, 48 A4
Mudigere 91 E5
Mudigubba 92 B3
Mudil 15 E5
Mudkavi 85 F4
Mudkhed 78 C3
Mudki 17 F5
Mudong (M) 45 E1
Mudra 52 D2
Mudukulatur 99 F3
Mudumala 86 C4
Mudumalai 95 E3
Mudumpadu 92 D4
Mugad 85 E6
Mughal Maidan 13 G4
Mughal Sarai 37 G6
Mughalgidda 86 D2
Mughalpur 23 F3

Muglih 15 E3
Mugu (N) 25 F1
Muguru 95 F2
Muhamdi 24 A6
Muhammad Bazar 58 A3
Muhammad Bin Qasim (P) 47 E2
Muhammadabad (Utt) 35 G2
Muhammadabad (Utt) 37 H4
Muhammadabad (Utt) 38 A5
Muhammadabad (And) 86 C3
Muhammadganj 56 A2
Muhammadgarh 53 E4
Muhammadpur (Ba) 59 E5
Muhammadpur (P) 16 B6
Muhammadpur (Utt) 24 A6
Muhammadpur (Mad) 65 G3
Muhar 30 D2
Muharwari (P) 20 B1
Muhri 13 E2
Muirpur 55 G3
Mujahad (P) 12 A5
Mujigaon (N) 24 C2
Mujika 42 D2
Mujjagad 82 B1
Mujkot (N) 25 E4
Mukabeli 80 B3
Mukalmua 42 A4
Mukam Dalfur (P) 48 B2
Mukandpur 17 H4
Mukandwara 51 H1
Mukapara 80 C4
Mukhab 31 F4
Mukhacharidwar 60 B5
Mukhed 77 E1
Mukher 78 C4
Mukhim 19 E5
Mukiana (P) 16 A3
Mukki 27 G5
Muklawa 20 C2
Mukpalli 80 A2
Mukrian 17 G2
Muksar (N) 39 F3
Muktagacha (Ba) 59 F2
Muktagiri 66 D4
Mukteswar 23 H2
Mukti 65 F5
Muktsar 17 E5
Mukundgarh 21 F6
Mukutban 79 F2
Mul 79 H1
Mul Dwarka 63 E5
Mulad (Ba) 59 G6
Muladhuli (Ba) 58 D3
Mulaikaraippatti 99 E4
Mulana 18 C6
Mulanur 95 H5
Mulawa (P) 12 B5
Mulawa 78 C2
Mulbagal 92 C5
Mulbekh 14 A2
Mulgund 85 F6
Mulhalli 95 G1
Muli 63 F1
Mulila 62 D2
Mulki 90 C6
Mulla Katyar (P) 47 H1
Mullianpur 60 C6
Mulshi 76 B5
Multai 67 E3
Mulug 79 H6, 79 A6
Mulvad 85 G3
Mumbra 76 B3

Mumidivaram 89 E3
Mummasar 21 E5
Munabao 30 D5
Munak 22 B2
Munda (J&K) 13 F4
Munda (Raj) 21 E2
Mundahal Kalan 22 A3
Mundakayam 98 C2
Mundargi 85 G6
Mundarwa 35 H2
Mundgaon 66 B5
Mundgod 90 C1
Mundha Pande 23 F4
Mundher 70 A4
Mundhevadi 85 G1
Mundhri 67 H4
Mundi 66 A2
Mundlana 22 B3
Mundlapadu 87 F6
Mundra 48 C6
Mundra Bandar 48 C6
Mundsar 20 C6
Mundwa 32 D2
Mundwara 50 A1
Mung (P) 12 C6
Munga (N) 39 H2
Mungala 87 H2
Mungamuru 93 G1
Mungaoli 83 G2
Mungaram (C) 26 A3
Mungeli 68 D2
Mungi 77 G3
Mungod 87 F2
Mungra Badshahpur 37 E5
Mungsaria 20 D6
Mungwani (Mad) 53 G6
Mungwani (Mad) 67 G2
Mungwe (M) 44 A6
Munirabad 85 H6
Munjasar 32 A2
Munjola 81 E3
Munjpur 63 F1
Munnar 98 C1
Munnawar 13 E6
Munradaippu 99 E4
Munshi Bazar (Ba) 60 B2
Munshiganj (Ba) 59 G4
Munshir Hat (Ba) 59 G1
Munsyari 24 B1
Munund 69 G2
Mupa 42 D6
Mupaw Ga (M) 44 D5
Mupawaram 87 G3
Muphlang 42 B6
Muqam 13 E2
Mura 70 A3
Murad Kari (P) 30 B3
Muradnagar (Ba) 59 G4
Muradnagar 22 C4
Muragacha 58 B4
Murajhar 42 D4
Muralnuam (M) 61 E5
Muramgaon 68 B6
Muraral 58 A2
Murat (P) 12 B4
Murbad 76 B3
Murdol 70 A5
Murerea 37 H3
Murgod 85 E5
Murgud 84 D3
Murhar 30 C3
Murheri 34 D6
Murhipar 68 B4
Murhu 56 D6
Murid (P) 12 A6
Muridke (P) 17 E2
Muridwala (P) 16 A5

Murinda 18 A5
Murkal 95 E2
Murkunda 56 C6
Murlen 61 E4
Murliganj 39 G5
Murree (P) 12 C3
Murshidabad 58 B3
Murtajapur 66 C5
Murud (Mah) 76 A5
Murud (Mah) 77 H5, 78 AH
Murud 78 A5
Muruda 71 G3
Murugamale 92 B5
Murum 76 D6
Murwara 54 B4
Mus 101 F2
Musafirkhana (P) 47 H3
Musafirkhana 36 D4
Musaiyur 96 D2
Musalimadugu 87 E5
Musalvadi 77 E3
Musani Hingorja (P) 47 H2
Musapet 86 D3
Musepur 22 C6
Mushabani 71 F1
Musikot (N) 25 H5
Musiri 96 B5
Musk 13 G2
Muskira 35 H5
Musrumgond 80 B2
Mussoorie 19 E6
Mustabada 88 B3
Mustafabad (P) 16 C4
Mustafabad (Har) 18 C6
Mustafabad (Utt) 36 C5
Mutampet 79 H2
Mutaram 79 H5
Mutgi 85 G3
Muthli 31 H5
Mutssukota 92 B1
Muttapuram 80 B6
Muttattur 96 D2
Muttukula 87 G4
Muttukuru (And) 92 D5
Muttukuru (And) 93 G3
Muttpet 96 D6
Muttur 95 H5
Mutukula 87 G4
Mutukulivayal 98 D5
Mutylapadu 92 D1
Muvalrevu 82 B4
Muvatagupudur 95 F5
Muvatupuzha 98 B1
Muyyabompeta 79 H3
Muzaffarabad (*) 12 C2
Muzaffarabad (Utt) 18 C6
Muzaffarnagar 22 C2
Muzaffarpur 38 D4
Mwei Shi (M) 75 E4
Myaing (M) 75 H3
Myang (C) 19 F3
Myanimukh (Ba) 60 C6
Myari 62 C4
Myaukchun (M) 61 G5
Myaungbwe (M) 75 E6
Myene (M) 61 H2
Myinza (M) 75 G2
Myitche (M) 75 H4
Myitkyinya (M) 45 E6
Mylliem 42 B6
Mymensingh (Ba) 59 F2
Mynser 42 C5
Myohaung (M) 75 E6
Myothit (M) 61 G2
Mysore 95 F2

Nab Chote (B) 41 G1
Nabadwip 58 B5

Nabagram 100 B3
Nabha 18 A6
Nabiganj (Ba) 60 A2
Nabinagar (Ba) 59 H4
Nabinagar 56 A2
Nabisar (P) 48 C1
Nabisar Road (P) 48 B1
Nabu Ghat (N) 39 E1
Nabung (M) 75 F2
Nachani 24 A1
Nachankhadak 64 B6
Nachar 18 D3
Nachinda 72 A3
Nachna 31 G1
Nachuga 101 E1
Nadapuram 94 C3
Nadaul 38 C6
Nadaun 18 A3
Nadawan 54 B4
Nadbai 34 C2
Nadiad 50 A6
Nadigaon 35 F4
Nadol 32 C6
Nadria 54 D3
Naduvattam 95 E4
Naenwa 33 H5
Naerung 14 B3
Nagabal 13 E4
Nagad 65 F6
Nagai (Mad) 69 F1
Nagaj (Mah) 85 E2
Nagal 22 D1, 23 E2
Nagaladime 86 C5
Nagalamdike 92 A3
Nagalapuram 86 D5
Nagalpuram 99 F3
Nagalvadi 65 G3
Nagalwadi 67 G3
Nagansur 85 H1
Nagaon (Nawgong) 42 C4
Nagaon 76 A4
Nagapattinam 97 E5
Nagapur 78 A4
Nagar (Raj) 33 F3
Nagar (Raj) 33 H5
Nagar (Raj) 34 B1
Nagar (Mad) 55 F5
Nagar (Kar) 90 D4
Nagar Devla 65 F6
Nagar Kamul 87 E3
Nagar Khas 31 G6
Nagar Mewa 31 H5
Nagar Parkar (P) 49 E3
Nagar Untari 55 H3
Nagaram 80 B5
Nagarbari (Ba) 59 E2
Nagarbari (Ba) 59 E4
Nagarbera 41 H4
Nagargaon 43 F2
Nagarhole 94 D2
Nagari 93 F5
Nagarkunda (Ba) 59 E5
Nagarmangala 91 G6
Nagarnar 81 E3
Nagarpur (Ba) 59 E3
Nagarsul 77 E1
Nagasamudram 92 B3
Nagasari 63 F5
Nagaur 32 C2
Nagavetlu 93 F6
Nagda (Mad) 51 G5
Nagda (Mad) 51 G6
Nagdirgram 60 D2
Nagelao 33 E4
Nagercoil 98 D5
Nageshwari (Ba) 41 E5

Nagevadi 84 D2
Naggar 18 C2
Nagina 23 E2
Naginimara 43 H3
Nagjhari 77 F4
Nagjua 56 C5
Nagnur 79 F6
Nagod 54 B2
Nagoki 21 F2
Nagor (C) 25 H2
Nagore 97 E5
Nagothana 76 B5
Nagpur (Har) 21 G2
Nagpur (Mah) 67 G4
Nagpur (Mad) 79 F6
Nagra (Utt) 38 A5
Nagra (Bih) 38 C5
Nagra (Guj) 64 A1
Nagrai (P) 12 A2
Nagraibari 60 A4
Nagrajsar 20 A6
Nagrakara 40 D2
Nagram 36 C3
Nagri (Bih) 56 D5
Nagri (Mah) 67 F6
Nagri (Mad) 69 E6
Nagrota 17 H2
Nagrota Khas 18 A2
Nagslapuram 93 F5
Nagthan 85 G3
Nahala 21 G2
Nahan 18 C5
Nahapa 64 B1
Nahar 22 A5
Nahargarh (Mad) 51 F3
Nahargarh (Raj) 52 B1
Nahata (Ba) 59 E5
Nahianwala 17 F6
Nahil 24 A5
Nahisar (P) 48 D3
Nahna 18 B5
Nahoria 55 E2
Nai Sarai 52 D2
Naidhal 13 E2
Naihati 58 C6
Naika 50 A6
Naikaneri 92 C6
Naikul 70 C4
Nainakot (P) 17 F2
Naini 37 E6
Naini Tal 23 G2
Nainpur 68 A1
Naitola (B) 41 H2
Naiwala (P) 16 B5
Najafgarh 22 B4
Najahat (P) 17 E5
Najibabad 23 E2
Nakachari 43 G3
Nakapalle 89 F1
Nakasipara 58 B4
Nakawas 13 F4
Nakhola 42 C4
Nakhtarana 48 B5
Nako 19 F2
Nakodar 17 G4
Nakrasar 21 E5
Nakrekal 87 G2
Nakrtiaganj 38 B2
Naksalbari 40 B3
Nakur 22 C1
Nala (Bih) 57 G3
Nala (Guj) 64 D3
Nalagarh 18 B4
Nalaghat 82 B2
Nalahallu 91 H4
Nalanda 56 D1
Nalapara 41 H5
Nalatvad 85 H4

Nalbari 42 A3
Nalcha 65 G1
Nalchiti (Ba) 73 F1
Naldera 18 C4
Naldhara 64 B5
Naldurg 78 A6
Nalegaon 78 B5
Nalgonda 87 G2
Nalgora 72 C2
Nalhati 58 A3
Nalhiapur 37 F3
Nalikodur 87 H1
Nalitabari (Ba) 59 F1
Naliya 48 A5
Nalkhera 51 H4
Nallajerla 88 D2
Nallapalem 93 F2
Nallur (Kar) 91 E3
Nallur (Tam) 95 H4
Nalwar 86 B2
Namai (N) 25 F6
Namakal 96 A4
Namanagar 82 B4
Namano 50 D1
Nambiyur 95 G4
Namboi 61 F2
Namchi 40 B2
Namdang 43 G2
Namgia 19 F2
Namgiripettai 96 A4
Namik 24 A1
Namjara (M) 45 G2
Namkalan (M) 45 F6
Namkhana 72 B3
Namkom 56 D5
Namla (C) 25 H1
Namli 51 F5
Namlit (M) 44 B6
Namoli 18 B4
Nampak (M) 45 E1
Nampali 87 F3
Nampamun (M) 61 G4
Nampaung (M) 45 E6
Namphu Gompa (C) 27 G1
Nampur 65 E5
Namrup 44 A2
Namsai 44 B1
Namthang 40 C2
Namting (M) 44 C5
Namyu (M) 45 E5
Nana 50 B1
Nanaj 77 F5
Nanasi 64 C6
Nanauta 22 C2
Nanbon (M) 61 D3
Nancherla 86 D3
Nand 67 G6
Nandagaon 22 C6
Nandail (Ba) 59 G2
Nandalai (Ba) 58 C2
Nandalgaon 77 H3
Nandalur 93 E3
Nandanapur 39 H4
Nandaprayag 19 G6
Nandasan 49 H5
Nandauti 34 B3
Nandavaram (And) 86 C5
Nandavaram (And) 93 E2
Nanded 78 C3
Nander 51 H5
Nandewaro (P) 30 B1
Nandgad 84 D5
Nandgaon (Mah) 65 E6
Nandgaon (Mah) 66 D5
Nandgaon (Mah) 76 A5
Nandgaon (Mah) 76 C2
Nandgaon Kaji 66 D5
Nandghat 69 E3

Nandi Hills 92 B5
Nandia 31 G6
Nandigam 82 B4
Nandigama 88 A3
Nandigram 72 A2
Nandikhila (Ba) 59 G2
Nandikotkur 87 E5
Nandipadu (And) 92 B1
Nandipadu (And) 93 E2
Nandipalli 86 B3
Nandivargam 87 E6
Nandnee 85 G1
Nandod 64 C3
Nandol 50 A5
Nandora 68 B4
Nandori 67 F6
Nandpur (N) 38 A1
Nandra (Mad) 65 G2
Nandra (Mah) 65 G4
Nandul (81 G1
Nandur (Mah) 77 G3
Nandur (Mah) 77 H4
Nandur Shingoti 76 D2
Nandura 66 A5
Nandurbar 64 D4
Nandvadgi 85 H4
Nandwai 51 F1
Nandyal 87 E6
Nang Xian (C) 27 E3
Nangal 18 B3
Nangal 18 B4
Nangal Dunne Singh (P) 17 E2
Nangaleswar 71 H3
Nangarecha 48 B6
Nangavalli 95 H3
Nangavaram 96 B5
Nangli 92 C5
Nangloi Jat 22 B4
Nangor 48 C5
Nangraon (N) 24 B2
Nangtraw 42 B5
Nanguneri 99 E5
Nanichang 15 E4
Nanjangud 95 F2
Nankana Sahib (P) 16 C3
Nankatti 68 C4
Nankhari 18 C4
Nanlotang (C) 29 H5
Nanmad 65 E6
Nannial 79 H3
Nannilam 96 D5
Nanpara 24 D6
Nanpur (Bih) 39 E4
Nanpur (Mad)65 E2
Nanta 33 G6
Nanur 58 A4
Nanyaseik (M) 44 D5
Nanzalein (M) 61 G5
Naogai 55 G4
Naogaon (Ba) 58 C1
Naohata (Ba) 58 C2
Naojan 43 F4
Naoli 86 A5
Naorangdesar 20 C5
Naoshera 13 H6
Napaz 13 G4
Nar 64 A1
Nar Bozdar (P) 30 A2
Nar Kot 13 E5
Nara (P) 12 B3
Nara Datla (P) 16 A4
Nara Nag 13 F2
Narahia 39 F4
Narahipeta 93 E6
Naraina 33 F3
Naraini 36 B6, 54 B1
Narainpur (Utt) 38 A5

Narainpur (Mah)80 D2
Narakal 98 A1
Naral (Ba) 59 E5
Naran (P) 12 C1
Narang (P) 17 E2
Naranji (P) 12 A2
Naranjigundlapalle 91 H2
Naranpur 56 A6
Naransigapuram 79 G6
Narapala 92 B2
Narasannapeta 82 B5
Narasapura 92 B5
Narasar 87 H4
Narasigarayanpet 93 E5
Narasimharajapura 91 E4
Narasimharaopalem 88 B2
Narasingapuram 93 E4
Narasinghpur 70 D6
Narasinhpur (Ba) 59 G5
Narauli 23 F4
Naravarikuppam 93 G5
Narayanapar 82 B4
Narayanavanam 93 F5
Narayanganj (Ba) 59 F4
Narayanganj 54 A6
Narayangaon 76 C3
Narayangarh 51 F3
Narayanker 78 D6
Narayanpet 86 C3
Narayanpur (Raj) 34 A1
Narayanpur (Bih) 57 F3
Narayanpur (Wbg) 58 A3
Narayanpur (Tri) 59 H4
Narayanpur (Guj) 64 C4
Narayanpur (And) 87 F2
Narayapatnam 81 G4
Narayargadh (N) 38 B1
Narayngarh 18 B5
Narcheng (N) 25 H4
Nardana 65 F4
Nardiganj 56 D1
Nare 17 F4
Naregal 85 G6
Narela 22 B4
Narendranagar 19 E6
Narendrapur 82 C3
Narera 21 H6
Nargaon (N) 24 B3
Nargaon 65 H5
Nargol 64 A6
Nargora 69 F2
Nargund 85 F5
Narharpur 68 D6
Narhat 56 D2
Narhatta (Ba) 58 D1
Nari (P) 16 A1
Naria (Ba) 59 G5
Nariana 13 E6
Narikal 14 B2
Naring (M) 75 E2
Narkanda 18 C4
Narkatapalli 87 G2
Narkatia 38 C3
Narkhed 77 G6
Narkher 67 F4
Narki 35 E2
Narlapur 80 A5
Narmada 68 A1
Narnaul 21 H5
Narnaund 21 H3
Narnuru 86 D5
Naroli 64 B6
Narona 86 A1
Narora 50 A6
Narot 17 G1
Narowal (P) 17 E2
Narpatganj 39 G4
Narsampet 79 H6

Narsana 49 H1
Narsapur (And) 79 E3
Narsapur (And) 79 E6
Narsapur (And) 88 D4
Narsar 32 C3
Narsi 78 B2
Narsimharpur 53 G6
Narsingdi (Ba) 59 G4
Narsinghargh (Mad) 52 C4
Narsinghgarh (Mad) 53 G3
Narsingi 79 E6
Narsingpur 77 F6
Narsipatnam 89 F1
Narsipur 22 B4
Narsro 20 D4
Narsu 13 F5
Narundi (Ba) 59 F1
Narvauli 53 F4
Narwa 32 B4
Narwai 34 D5
Narwal 36 B4
Narwana 21 H2
Narwar (Raj) 33 E3
Narwar (Mad) 34 D5
Narwar (Mad) 52 D5
Nasik 76 C1
Nasik Road 76 C1
Nasirabad (Ba) 59 H4
Nasirabad (Raj) 33 E4
Nasirabad (Utt) 36 D4
Nasirabad (Mah) 65 G5
Nasirnagar (Ba) 59 H3
Nasirpur (P) 30 A6
Nasrapur 76 C5
Nasriganj 56 B1
Nasrullahganj 52 C6
Naswadi 64 C2
Natabari Hat 41 E4
Natadaha (Ba) 58 C4
Natau 50 D4
Natchaung (M) 61 F6
Nateputa 77 E6
Nateran 52 D4
Nathana 17 F6
Nathdwara 50 C1
Natherpetna (Ba) 59 H5
Nathiagali (P) 12 C3
Nathkaw (M) 44 C2
Nathnagar 39 G6
Nathuwala (P) 16 A6
Natkyigon (M) 61 F5
Natore (Ba) 58 D2
Nattam 96 A6
Nattarasankottai 99 F1
Natu La (C) 40 C1
Natusar 32 B1
Naubatpur 38 C6
Naugachhia 39 H6
Naugam 12 D2
Naugarh (Utt) 37 G1
Naugarh (Utt) 55 H2
Nauhatta (Bih) 39 F5
Nauhatta (Bih) 56 A2
Nauknyo (M) 44 B3
Naukot (P) 48 B2
Naultha 22 B3
Naunggauk (M) 61 H4
Naungmana (M) 61 H2
Naupada 82 B4
Naupadapenth 82 B3
Naupara 55 F5
Naura 55 G5
Nauranga (N) 24 B4
Naushahra (P) 16 C4
Naushahra Panwah 17 F3
Naushehra 20 A4
Naushera Virkhan (P)
    16 D2

Nautanwa 37 H1
Navalgund 85 F6
Navalyal 85 E3
Navapur 64 C4
Navdi 84 B2
Navibandar 62 C4
Navira 82 A3
Navsari 64 B5
Navuru 90 D6
Nawa 56 B3
Nawa Unt ka Palia (P)
    49 E2
Nawab Basoda 53 E4
Nawabandar 63 E5
Nawabanj 37 E2
Nawabganj (Ba) 40 D6
Nawabganj (Ba) 58 B2
Nawabganj (Ba) 59 F4
Nawabganj (Utt) 23 H4
Nawabganj (Utt) 35 G1
Nawabganj (Utt) 36 C2
Nawabganj (Mad) 51 F5
Nawabganj Aliabad 24 D6
Nawabpet (And) 86 D3
Nawabpet (And) 87 G1
Nawada (Utt) 36 A2
Nawada (Bih) 56 D1
Nawada (Wbg) 58 B4
Nawadih 57 E4
Nawagai (P) 12 A2
Nawagam 64 C2
Nawagaon 69 F4
Nawai 33 H4
Nawakot (N) 24 B3
Nawakot (N) 25 H6
Nawalgarh 21 G6
Nawan (P) 12 C4
Nawanagar (Utt) 38 A4
Nawanagar (Bih) 38 B6
Nawangar 55 F3
Nawanshahr (P) 12 C3
Nawansharh 17 H4
Nawanshahr 13 E6
Nawapara (Ba) 59 E6
Nawapara 69 F5
Nawargaon 67 G6
Nawaushahr 13 E6
Nawe Kili (P) 12 A2
Nawegaon (Mah) 68 A5
Nawegaon (Mah) 80 A1
Nawngpu Awng (M) 61 H1
Nawngsankyin (M) 61 H2
Nawt (M) 75 F3
Naya Chor (P) 30 C6
Nayagaon (Mad) 51 F2
Nayagaon (Mad) 53 G6
Nayagarh (Ori) 70 C6
Nayagarh (Ori) 82 C1
Nayagram 71 H2
Nayaikal 78 D6
Nayakanahatti 91 G2
Nayamasti (Ba) 74 A1
Naydongri 65 E6
Nayegaon 78 D4
Nayu (C) 27 G3
Nayudupeta 93 F4
Nazarabad 52 C4
Nazareth 99 E4
Nazir Hat (Ba) 74 B1
Nazira 43 H2
Nazirpur (Ba) 59 F6
Nbawn Ga (M) 44 D4
Ndup Tumsa (M) 44 D3
Ndurenchu (C) 29 H2
Neamati 43 G3
Nearan 33 E4
Neazipur 38 B5
Neddiguda 70 B6

Nedong Dzong (C) 26 B3
Nedumangad 98 C4
Nedungadu 97 E5
Neibbawi 60 D4
Neihdawn 61 E5
Nekarikallu 87 H4
Nekmard (Ba) 40 B5
Nekonda 79 H6
Nelamangala 92 A6
Nelang 19 F4
Nellayi 95 E6
Nelligere 91 G6
Nellikkuppam 96 D3
Nellimarla 81 H5
Nellipaka 80 C6
Nellore 93 G2
Nellurupalem 93 F2
Nemawar 66 B1
Nemmara 95 E6
Neogha 78 C2
Neora 69 E3
Neora Nadi 40 C3
Neoria Husainpur 23 H4
Nepa (N) 25 E4
Nepa Nagar 66 A3
Nepalganj (N) 24 D5
Nepaltar (N) 39 F3
Nepar (C) 27 F3
Nepasar 20 C6
Nepka (N) 25 E1
Nepoklu 94 C2
Ner (Mah) 65 E5
Ner (Mah) 66 D6
Ner Pinglaj 66 D4
Nera Gonsar (C) 28 D1
Neral 76 B4
Neravailu 93 E4
Neravy 97 E5
Nerbole 15 F6
Neredikonda 79 E3
Nereducherla 86 D6
Nerhema 43 F3
Neri 65 G5
Nermand 18 C3
Nerua 18 D5
Nerur 84 B5
Nesari 84 D4
Neta (N) 24 D4
Netarhat 56 B5
Nethersole Dam 76 C4
Neto (N) 24 D2
Netra 48 A5
Netrakona (Ba) 59 G1
Nettapakkam 96 D3
Neur 68 D1
Nevasa 77 F2
Nevra 84 B2
New Delhi 22 C4
New Township 57 H4
Newari 52 A6
Neyveli 96 D3
Neyyatinkara 98 C5
Ngahan (M) 74 C4
Ngaiphaipi (M) 75 E2
Ngajathku (M) 45 E3
Ngakura (M) 74 C4
Ngalang Ga (M) 44 D3
Ngalangkang (B) 42 A1
Ngalung Ga (M) 44 C2
Ngandaung (M) 74 D5
Nganinme (M) 75 H5
Nganiyinthaung (M) 74 D4
Ngapo (C) 27 E1
Ngarap (C) 26 C3
Ngasha (M) 74 D3
Ngathayauk (M) 75 H5
Ngotewngrowa (M) 74 C4
Ngunla (C) 28 A2

Ngunsaing (M) 75 F5
Ngur 61 E4
Nhkyengbum (M) 45 E3
Nhpi Ga (M) 45 F2
Nhtem (M) 44 C4
Ni Kondapa 87 H2
Niagzu (C) 15 F3
Niali 83 F1
Niamatpur (Ba) 58 C1
Nianyu 44 A3
Niausa 44 A2
Nibase (M) 75 F6
Nibel Singhwala 17 G5
Nibua Raiganj 38 A2
Nichinal 13 F7
Nichlaul 37 H1
Nichole (Ba) 58 B2
Nichuguard 43 E5
Nidadavole 88 D3
Nidagundi 85 G5
Nidamangalam 96 D5
Nidgundi 85 G4
Nidni 86 B1
Nidubrolu 88 B4
Nidugal 91 H3
Nidumolu 88 C4
Nigan 58 B5
Nighasan 24 B5
Nighaw 78 D3
Nighoj 76 D4
Nigohau 36 C3
Nigohi 23 H5
Nigri 55 E3
Nihal Khera 16 D6
Nihalamba 65 E3
Nihang (P) 16 A2
Nihtaur 23 E2
Nijgarh (N) 38 C2
Nijhar 64 D4
Nij Narajol 72 A1
Nikara 62 D2
Niktak 27 F6
Nikuran 22 A2
Nilakkottai 99 E1
Nilambazar 60 C2
Nilambur 95 E4
Nilambur Road 95 E4
Nilanga 78 B6
Nileshwar 94 B2
Nilgaon 36 C2
Nilgiri 71 G4
Nilguda 88 B2
Nilji 81 F1
Nilkant 32 A5
Nilkund 90 C2
Nilokheri 22 B1
Nilphamari (Ba) 40 C5
Nilvala 63 F3
Nim Ka Khera 33 G6
Nim Ka Thana 21 H6
Nimach 51 F2
Nimaj 32 D4
Niman 21 G2
Nimapara 83 E1
Nimba 78 A3
Nimbagalu 91 H1
Nimbahera 51 E2
Nimbal (Kar) 85 G2
Nimbal (Kar) 85 H1
Nimbarga 86 A1
Nimbavda 85 E1
Nimbgaon Jali 77 E2
Nimbgaon Ketki 77 F6
Nimbi Jodban 33 E1
Nimbod 51 F4
Nimbola 66 A4
Nimdih 57 F6
Nimera 33 G1

Nimgaon 65 E6
Nimgong (B) 41 H2
Nimkhar 36 B1
Nimkhera 65 F1
Nimbli Uda 32 C5
Nimmakhandipeth 82 B3
Nimmu 14 C3
Nimnan 55 G3
Nimon 76 D2
Nimpani 66 D2
Nimri 32 D2
Nindo Shahr (P) 48 A2
Ningbau Ga (M) 44 B4
Ningbyen (M) 44 C3
Ningdibuta (M) 44 D3
Ninging 27 H3
Ninglum (M) 45 E6
Ningrawng (M) 44 C4
Ningru 28 B6
Ninguani 55 E5
Nioku 27 G6
Nior Nis 15 E4
Nipal 32 C6
Nipani 84 D4
Nipani Dongri 67 H3
Nipania 69 E3
Niphad 76 D1
Nira 76 D6
Nirakarpur 83 E1
Niraun 31 F3
Nirbana 20 C2
Nirgunda 86 B2
Nirmal 79 E3
Nirmali 39 F4
Niruna 48 B5
Nirvada 65 G4
Nisalgaon (N) 25 G2
Nisampur 76 B5
Nisang 22 B2
Nisapui 60 D3
Nisarpur 65 E2
Nischintapur (Ba) 58 C1
Nithor 34 B2
Nithrana 21 F3
Niti 19 H5
Nitrur 77 H4
Nitte 90 D5
Nittur 91 H5
Nitur 78 B3
Nituria 57 G4
Nivali 65 F3
Nivari 35 F6
Niwari 22 C4
Niwas 54 B6
Nizamabad (Utt) 37 G4
Nizamabad (And) 79 E4
Nizamabad (And) 87 E3
Nizamghat 28 B5
Nizampatam 88 B5
Nizampet 78 D6
Nizampur 65 E4
Nizapur 20 C2
Noagaon 71 E4
Noakhali (Ba) 59 H6
Noamundi 70 D2
Noawan 37 H6
Noghanvadar 63 G3
Nogmung (M) 45 F1
Noh 15 H4
Nohar 21 F3
Nohjhil 22 D6
Nohta 53 H4
Nohtun Jo Goth (P) 48 B1
Noju 43 E2
Nokh 31 H1
Nokha (Rasj) 32 C1
Nokha (Bih) 56 A1
Nokhar (P) 16 D2

Nokhra (Raj) 20 A6
Nokhra (Raj) 31 G6
Noklal 43 H4
Nola (C) 27 F1
Nonanpanji 53 H2
Nonavinkere 91 G5
Nondopuru 81 G5
Nongkhlaw 42 A5
Nonglang (M) 61 F5
Nongpoh 42 B5
Nongstoin 41 H6
Nongthymmai 42 B6
Noonkha (Ba) 41 E5
Norang 26 D6, 42 D1
Noria 17 F1
Norla 81 H1
North Dum Dum 72 C1
North Gawahati 42 B4
North Lakhimpur 43 F2
North Salmara 41 G4
Nosra 32 A6
Nossam 92 C1
Nowganwa 22 B6
Nowgong (Ass) 42 C3
Nowgong (Mad) 53 G1
Nowrangapur 81 F3
Noya (C) 29 F3
Nring 44 C1
Nsopzup (M) 45 E5
Nu Laluk 43 F2
Nua 21 F5
Nuagam 82 A1
Nuagan 70 C6
Nuagaon 71 F6
Nuakot 70 D3
Nugihalli 91 G6
Nugur 80 C3
Nuh 22 B5
Num (N) 39 H1
Numaligarh 43 F3
Numari (C) 26 C1
Nungba 61 E2
Nunhat 57 G2
Nur Sarai 38 D6
Nur Shah (P) 16 B5
Nur Shah (P) 20 A1
Nurabad 35 E4
Nurewala (P) 16 A2
Nurganj 52 C6
Nuriala 30 D4
Nurkot (P) 17 F1
Nurla 14 B2
Nurmahal 17 G4
Nurpur (P) 16 A1
Nurpur (P) 16 B5
Nurpur (Him) 17 H1
Nurpur (Pun) 18 A4
Nurpur (Utt) 23 E3
Nurpur Shahan (P) 12 B4
Nursar (P) 20 B1
Nuruddin 17 F3
Nutalapadu 88 A5
Nutan Bazar 60 B5
Nutimagudu 92 A2
Nuzvid 88 B3
Nyahalode 65 F5
Nyamati 91 E3
Nyamoshung (C) 26 A3
Nyangan (M) 75 H6
Nyanglu (C) 27 F2
Nyasia 44 A3
Nyauaggan (M) 75 H1
Nyaung-U (M) 75 H4
Nyaungbin (M) 61 G5
Nyaungbinywa (M) 75 H6
Nyaunghla (M) 75 H6
Nye (C) 26 D2
Nyellung (C) 26 B5

Nyengo (C) 26 A2
Nyereng 27 H3
Nyerong (C) 26 D5
Nyeying 27 G4
Nylo (C) 28 A1
Nyoma Rap 15 E5
Nyorak 27 H5
Nyukmadong 42 C1
Nyung-Imnu (M) 75 E4
Nyuri 26 C6

Obaidullaganj 52 D6
Obalapuram 91 H1
Obo (M) 61 G4
Obolam 93 E2
Obra 56 B1
Od 64 B1
Odania 31 G2
Odepur 70 A6
Odhan 21 F2
Odiyatur 96 D2
Odugattur 92 D6
Odur 13 E3
Oel Thakwa 24 B6
Oghi (P) 12 B2
Oila Jawand Singh (P)
   16 C5
Oinamlong 61 E2
Ojhar 76 D1
Ojna (N) 24 B3
Oka (C) 26 C2
Okara (P) 16 C5
Okha 62 A1
Okhaldhunga (N) 39 F1
Okhimath 19 G6
Okrara (P) 30 D6
Olakkur 96 D1
Old Disa 49 H3
Old Goa 84 C6
Oligaon (N) 24 D2
Ollur 95 E6
Olpad 64 A4
Olthingthang (P) 14 A1
Oluru 93 F4
Omalur 96 A3
Omati (C) 45 H3
Omawe (M) 75 E3
Onda 57 H5
Onder 52 D3
Ondo (C) 29 G4
Ong (M) 75 F4
Ongole 88 A6
Ongur 97 E2
Onkar 65 H2
Onkareshwar 65 H2
Onpa (C) 27 E1
Ontimita 93 E3
Ooru 49 G5
Oppicherla 87 G4
Oragadam 97 E1
Oragaon 82 C1
Orai 35 G5
Orampadu 93 E3
Oran 36 B6
Orang (C) 27 F3
Orang 42 C3
Orattanadu 96 C5
Orchha 35 F6
Ordeltong 80 D5
Ormanjhi 56 D5
Osian 32 B3
Osmanabad 77 H5
Osmanagar 77 E5
Othian (P) 17 E1
Ottappalam 95 E5
Ottappidaram 99 E4
Otur 76 D3
Outbal (P) 12 A4

Ovari Paravamatam 99 E5
Owen (P) 12 C4
Owk 86 D6
Oyautapah 101 G4
Ozhukarai 97 E2

Pa-Aing (M) 75 G6
Pabai 52 D4
Pabargarh 34 C4
Pabel 76 D4
Pabhoi 43 E2
Pabna (Ba) 58 D3
Pabram 61 E1
Pabuhar (P) 48 B2
Paburiya 82 B1
Pacha (P) 12 A2
Pachagarh (Ba) 40 C4
Pachar (Raj) 20 D4
Pachar (Raj) 33 G2
Pachavada 63 G3
Pachchal 96 C2
Pachchalur 95 G6
Pachegaon 67 E5
Pacheri 21 H5
Pachgachhiya (N) 38 D2
Pachh Elasin (Ba) 59 E3
Pachhapur 85 E4
Pachhegam 63 G3
Pachhewar 33 G3
Pachmarhi 67 E1
Pachnai 42 C3
Pachor 52 B4
Pachora 65 G6
Pachpadra 31 H5
Pachpahar 51 H2
Pachperwa 37 F1
Pachud 77 G2
Padalam 97 E1
Padali (M) 74 D6
Padalur 96 C4
Padampur (Raj) 20 C2
Padampur (Ori) 69 G5
Padampura 51 F1
Padana 82 B6
Padank (M) 75 G5
Padarri 32 B6
Paddhari 62 D1
Pade (M) 45 G3
Paderu 81 G6
Padghe 76 B3
Padhana 17 E3
Padhri (P) 12 C6
Padigaon 69 H3
Padival 50 A1
Padkal 87 E2
Padma 56 D3
Padmanabnapuram 98 C5
Padmi (N) 25 G4
Padmur 80 C4
Padoli 77 H5
Padra 64 B2
Padrauna 38 A2
Padriya (N) 38 C1
Padru 31 H6
Padsali 84 C3
Padshabane (P) 12 B5
Padu 33 E3
Padua (Ba) 74 B2
Padum 14 B4
Paduna 50 D3
Padwa 81 G5
Paga (M) 61 H6
Pagan (M) 75 H4
Pagara (Raj) 33 G5
Pagara (Mad) 54 A3
Pagara (Mad) 67 E1
Pagaria 51 H3
Pagdhal 66 C1

Paghachang (Ba) 59 H4
Pagidyala 87 E5
Pagla (Ba) 60 A1
Paglapir (Ba) 40 D5
Pagowal (P) 17 E1
Pah 63 G4
Pahad 21 G4
Pahalagam 13 G3
Paharapur 38 B3
Pahari (Raj) 22 C6
Pahari (Raj) 35 E3
Pahari (Utt) 36 C6
Pahari (Mad) 55 E2
Paharikhera 54 B1
Pahartali (Ba) 74 B1
Pahasu 23 E5
Pahaurka 21 F2
Pahla (Mad) 34 B6
Pahla (Mad) 67 H5
Pahlagaon 100 B3
Pahritol (N) 38 D2
Pahur 65 G5
Pai 22 A2
Paidim (M) 61 F4
Paikaulia 37 F2
Paikbara 23 F4
Paikgacha (Ba) 72 D1
Paikhai 60 D4
Pail (P) 12 A6
Pail 17 H5
Pailani 36 B5
Pain Kufar 18 C5
Paina 38 A4
Painavu 98 C1
Pairuj 70 A6
Paithan 77 G2
Paiti (P) 12 A1
Pajo (B) 41 E1
Paka (C) 27 H1
Pakala 93 E5
Pakari (N) 39 H3
Pakari 82 A1
Pakaur 58 A2
Pakhriguri 41 G4
Pakhyong 40 C2
Pakka Sarnoka 20 D2
Pakka Sidhar (P) 16 B6
Pakkam (Tam) 96 C2
Pakkam (Tam) 97 E1
Pakni 85 G1
Pakokku (M) 75 H4
Pakpattan (P) 16 C6
Pakri (N) 37 G1
Pakribarawan 57 E1
Pakridayal 38 C3
Paksoi (Ba) 58 D3
Pakuria (Ba) 58 D2
Pakuria 58 A3
Pal (Guj) 63 E2
Pal (Mah) 65 H4
Pal (Mah) 84 C1
Pal Lahara 70 D4
Pala (Kar) 90 D2
Pala (Ker) 98 B2
Palahal 12 D5
Palai (Raj) 33 H3
Palai (Raj) 33 H5
Palaiyam 96 A5
Palakkad 95 F5
Palakkodu 96 A2
Palakollu 88 D3
Palalankwe 101 E1
Palali 63 G1
Palam (Del) 22 C4
Palam (Mah) 78 B4
Palamedu 99 E1
Palampur 18 B2
Palana 20 B6

Palandaw (M) 75 H6
Palandri (P) 12 C4
Palandur 68 A5
Palang (Ba) 59 F5
Palanghat 60 D2
Palangphabari 60 A5
Palani 95 G6
Palanpur 50 A3
Palari (Mad) 67 H2
Palari (Mad) 69 E4
Palas (P) 12 B1
Palasa 82 B4
Palasamudram 92 A4
Palasbari 42 A4
Palasdev 77 E5
Palashbari (Ba) 40 D6
Palasi 39 H4
Palasla 32 B2
Palasner 65 F3
Palasni (Raj) 32 C4
Palasni (Guj) 64 C2
Palaspal 71 E4
Palasponga 70 D3
Palasrihir 64 C5
Palavanettam 99 E2
Palavna 76 B6
Palayangadi 94 B2
Palayankottai 99 E4
Paldhar 18 D1
Paldhi 65 G5
Pale (M) 75 H2
Palehra 68 B2
Palera 53 G1
Paletwa (M) 74 D4
Palghar 76 A2
Palhana 36 D6
Pali (Raj) 32 C5
Pali (Raj) 34 A5
Pali (Utt) 53 E2
Pali (Mad) 54 C5
Pali (Mad) 69 F1
Pali (Mah) 76 B5
Pali (Mah) 77 G4
Pali (Mah) 84 B2
Palia 24 B5
Palianawa 49 E5
Paliganj 38 C6
Palitana 63 G3
Paliyad 63 G2
Paliyur 96 A5
Paljori 57 G3
Palkonda 82 A4
Palkot 56 B6
Palla 12 C2
Palladam 95 G5
Pallamo 93 F4
Pallapatla 88 B5
Pallapatti 95 H5
Pallavapuram 93 G6
Pallavaram 93 G6
Pallevada 88 C3
Palli 80 B3
Pallikonda 92 D6
Pallipatti 96 B2
Pallu 20 D3
Palma 55 G5
Palmala 80 A4
Palmaner 92 D5
Paloha 53 F6
Paloje 76 B3
Paloncha 88 B1
Palpa (N) 25 H6
Palpur 34 C5
Palra 36 B5
Palri (Raj) 32 C3
Palri (Raj) 33 E3
Palri (Raj) 50 B1
Palsada 69 G5

Palsana (Raj) 33 G1
Palsana (Guj) 64 B5
Palsi 85 E2
Palsud 65 F3
Palturu 91 H1
Palugurallapalle 92 D1
Palukallu 86 C5
Palur 93 F6
Palus 84 D2
Paluvayi 87 F3
Paluzawa (M) 61 G5
Palwal 22 C5
Pamarru 88 B4
Pambadi 98 B2
Pamban 99 H3
Pambha 22 B1
Pambriew 41 H6
Pamen (C) 29 H3
Pamgarh 69 F3
Pamidi 92 A1
Pampore 13 F3
Pamuduru 92 B3
Pamuru 93 E1
Panadra 48 A4
Panagar 54 A5
Panaikklam 99 G3
Panaipakkam 93 E5
Panaji 84 C6
Panakkudi 98 D5
Panamaram 94 D3
Panamik 14 C1
Panar 64 A5
Panari 42 B3
Panasar 32 B2
Panaspada 82 D2
Panbari (N) 25 H6
Panbihar 51 G5
Panchabhat 82 C1
Panchal 57 H5
Panchanandapur 58 A1
Panchapalli 95 H1, 96 A1
Panchasar (Guj) 49 E6
Panchasar (Guj) 49 G5
Panchat 17 H4
Panchbibi (Ba) 40 C6
Panchgani 76 C6
Panchgaon 67 G5
Panchla (Raj) 30 D5
Panchla (Wbg) 72 B1
Panchmura 57 H6
Panchori 32 B2
Panchun 32 B1
Panda (C) 26 D3
Pandadah 68 B4
Pandalkudi 99 F2
Pandare 77 E6
Pandaria 68 D2
Pandaul 39 E4
Pandayapura 95 F1
Pande 77 F5
Pandhana 65 H3
Pandharkawada 79 F1
Pandharpur 85 F1
Pandharwara 79 F2
Pandhurli 76 C2
Pandhurna 67 E3
Pandiam 88 A1
Pandoh 18 B3
Pandola 34 B6
Pandrapat 55 H6
Pandri Shivgarh 55 G1
Pandridand 55 F6
Pandripada 82 C2
Pandu 42 A4
Pandua (Bih) 58 B1
Pandua (Wbg) 58 B5
Pandukeshwar 19 H5
Pandusar 21 E4

Paneli 62 D3
Panem 87 E6
Panemangluru 90 D6
Paneri 42 B3
Panetha 64 B3
Pangaon (Mah) 77 G6
Pangaon (Mah) 78 B4
Pangate 36 B6
Pangdro (C) 28 B2
Panghari Bazar (Ba) 60 B5
Pangi 19 E3
Pangin 28 A5
Panglang (M) 45 E5
Pangnamdim (M) 29 F6
Pangra 78 C2
Pangri (P) 48 B2
Pangri (Mah) 76 D2
Pangri (Mah) 77 H5
Pangsa (Ba) 59 E4
Pangshing (C) 28 A2
Pangthang (B) 42 A2
Pangzawl 60 D5
Panhala 84 C3
Panhori 34 C1
Pani Mines 64 C1
Panian (P) 12 B3
Panigata (N) 40 A3
Panihari 21 F2
Panihati 58 B6
Panikunda 41 H6
Panipat 22 B2
Panjappatti 96 A5
Panjar (P) 12 C4
Panje 94 C1
Panjeke 17 E5
Panjeri 12 D5
Panjigiran 12 C2
Panjipara 40 B4
Panjnadi (P) 12 B1
Panjrehe 55 F3
Panjwara 57 H1
Panka (B) 41 H2
Pankhabari 40 B3
Panki 56 B3
Panna 54 A2
Panniar 35 E4
Panniwala 20 D1
Panol 17 G1
Panpa (M) 45 E6
Panposh 70 C2
Panruti 96 D3
Pansemal 65 E3
Pansera Bahbaipur (P)
    16 A3
Pansina 63 G1
Panskura 72 A1
Pantalam 98 B3
Pantapara 40 A3
Panth Piplia 51 F3
Panth Piploda 51 G4
Pantha (M) 61 G3
Pantha (M) 61 G4
Pantheri 31 H6
Pantnagar 23 G3
Pantra 62 B2
Panuria 57 G4
Panvas 84 B3
Panvel 76 B4
Panvi 63 G2
Panwad 64 D2
Panwar 33 G5
Panwari 35 H6
Panzgam 12 D3
Panzul 13 E2
Paoni 13 E5
Paonta Sahib 18 C6
Papaldo 13 H1
Papanasam (Tam) 96 C5

Papanasam (Tam) 98 D4
Papannapet 79 E6
Paparda 34 A3
Paphund 54 C3
Papinayankanahalli 86 A6
Papiniseri 94 B2
Papireddippatti 96 A3
Pappadahandi 81 F3
Pappambadi 95 H3
Pappampatti 95 G6
Pappinivatti 94 D6
Paprenda 36 B5
Par 27 F6
Para (N) 25 F3
Para (Raj) 33 F5
Para (Wbg) 57 F4
Para (Mah) 77 G4
Para (Mah) 85 F2
Paradarami 92 D6
Paradip 71 G6
Paraiya 56 C1
Paral 50 B6
Parali 76 B2
Paralkote 80 B2
Paramakudi 99 F2
Paramanandal 96 B2
Paramankurichi 99 E5
Paramati 96 A4
Parambikulam 95 F6
Parambul 90 C6
Parantij 50 A5
Parao (P) 12 A1
Paraoli 50 C2
Parappanangadi 94 C4
Parapur 81 E3
Pararia 54 A5
Parbatpur 80 C1
Parasamba 82 B4
Parasgad 85 F5
Parasgaon 80 D2
Parashuram (Ba) 60 A5
Parasi (N) 37 H1
Parasi (Mad) 54 C4
Parasi (Bih) 57 E6
Parasia 67 F2
Parasnath 57 F3
Paraspur 36 D2
Parasunanpur 91 G3
Parasuram Kund 28 B4
Paraswani 69 F4
Paraswar 55 H5
Paraswara 68 A2
Paratwada 66 C4
Paravur 98 B4
Parbal 13 G5
Parbat 82 B3
Parbatipur (Ba) 40 D5
Parbatsar 33 E2
Parbhani 78 B3
Parbung 60 D3
Parchuri 84 B1
Pardi 64 B6
Pardi Takmor 78 C1
Parenda 77 G5
Pareng 27 H5
Parerkola 58 A2
Pargaon (Mah) 77 E5
Pargaon (Mah) 77 F4
Pargi 86 D2
Parhari 53 E4
Parial (P) 12 B5
Pariar 36 B3
Parichha 35 F6
Parichhatgarh 22 D3
Parigi 92 A4
Parihara (Raj) 21 E6
Parihara (Bih) 39 F6
Pariharpur 39 E3

Parinche 76 D5
Pariwat 31 E2
Parjang 70 D5
Parkal 79 H5
Parkaryan 13 H3
Parkutsa 13 H3
Parlakimidi 82 B4
Parlia 52 A4
Parmanand 17 G2
Parmandal 13 F6
Parnasala 80 C6
Parner 77 E4
Paro Dzong (B) 41 E1
Parodi 63 G3
Parola (Utt) 19 E5
Parola (Mah) 65 F5
Paroli 33 F6
Paron (Mad) 52 B1
Paron (Utt) 53 F1
Paror 18 A2
Parpatia 55 H6
Parsa 55 G6
Parsabad 57 E3
Parsad 50 C3
Parsapalle 92 B2
Parsar 35 E4
Parsendi 36 C1
Parseoni 67 G4
Parshadepur 36 D4
Parsipada 76 B1
Parsol 52 D1
Parsola 51 E4
Parsoli 51 F1
Parsora 71 E2
Partabgarh 33 H2
Partabpur 80 C1
Partapgarh 51 E3
Partappur 71 G3
Partapur (N) 24 C4
Partapur 50 D4
Partibanur 99 F2
Partol (N) 24 D2
Partur 77 H2
Paruchuru 88 A5
Parumanchala 87 E5
Paruraj 38 C4
Parvatabad 86 A2
Parvatipuram 81 H4
Parwa 20 B5
Paryang (C) 25 G1
Pasan 55 E6
Pasandhara (N) 25 F4
Pasewada 80 B3
Pashkyum 14 A2
Pashwari 13 F1
Pasighat 28 A5
Pasok (M) 75 G4
Pasrur (P) 17 E1
Paston 13 F3
Pasupugallu 87 H5
Pata Polavaram 89 G1
Patachhari (Ba) 60 B6
Patadottacheruvu 86 C6
Patagunta 93 E5
Patahi 38 D3
Pataiya 95 F3
Patakata 41 F5
Patamda 57 F6
Patamdesar 20 D5
Patamunda 70 D3
Patamundai 71 F6
Patan (N) 24 B2
Patan (*) 13 E5
Patan (Raj) 33 E5
Patan (Guj) 49 G4
Patan (Mad) 52 B4
Patan (Mad) 53 H5

Patan (Bih) 56 B3
Patan (Mah) 68 D5
Patan (Mah) 84 C2
Patancheru 87 E1
Patani 21 H1
Patansaongi 67 G4
Patapalya 92 B4
Patapur 82 C2
Patarbar 57 E4
Patas 77 E5
Patauda 22 B5
Pataudi (Har) 21 H4
Pataudi (Har) 22 B5
Patchur 96 B1
Patdarha 69 F6
Patdi 49 G5
Patera 53 H3
Patewa 69 F4
Patgaon 41 F3
Patgram (Ba) 40 D4
Patha 53 F2
Pathakhuri 60 C3
Pathako 34 B5
Pathalgaon 69 H1
Pathalia (N) 38 C2
Pathalipam 43 G1
Pathanamthitta 98 C3
Pathankot 17 G1
Pathapkandi 60 C2
Pathardewa 38 A3
Pathardi 77 F3
Pathargama 57 H1
Patharghata (Ba) 73 F2
Patharia (Mad) 53 G4
Patharia (Mad) 69 E2
Pathariya (Ba) 60 A1
Patharkhnang 41 H5
Patharkot (N) 39 E2
Patharughat 42 B3
Pathavada 49 H2
Pathena 34 B2
Pathna 58 A1
Pathoda 21 F5
Pathpur 71 E6
Pathrala 21 F1
Pathraora 54 D3
Pathri (Mah) 78 A3
Pathri (Mah) 79 H1
Pathro 12 D2
Pathrot 66 C4
Pathrud 77 G5
Pati 65 E3
Patia (Ba) 74 B2
Patiala 18 A6
Patiali 23 G6
Patian 12 C2
Patithia 37 E5
Patiraj 40 B6
Patiram 40 C6
Patkura 71 F6
Patlahara (N) 38 B1
Patna (Utt) 24 D6
Patna (Bih) 38 D5
Patna (Ori) 71 E3
Patna (Kar) 92 C6
Patnagarh 69 G5
Patnam 92 B3
Patnitola (Ba) 58 C1
Patnitop 13 G5
Pato (N) 39 G3
Patoda (Raj) 21 F6
Patoda (Mah) 77 G4
Patodi 31 H4
Patoli 34 B2
Patonda 65 F4
Patpara 55 E4
Patrapur 82 C3
Patrasaer 57 H5

Patratu 56 D4
Patri 81 E2
Patroputtu 81 F4
Patrur 78 A3
Patsanda 57 F1
Patsikuri 81 G1
Patsio 14 C6
Patsul 66 B5
Patta 18 B4
Pattadakal 85 G5
Pattambi 95 E5
Pattan (J&K) 13 E3
Pattan (Mad) 67 E3
Pattanapuram 98 C3
Patti (Pun) 17 F4
Patti (Utt) 35 H2
Patti (Utt) 37 E5
Patti (And) 79 H5
Pattikonda 86 C6
Pattoki (P) 16 C4
Pattukkottai 96 D6
Patua 101 H5
Patuakhali (Ba) 73 F2
Patuli 58 B4
Patun 70 D1
Patur 66 B6
Paturda 66 B5
Paturu 82 D2
Patwa 32 C4
Patwai 23 F4
Paud 76 C5
Pauk (M) 75 G4
Pauktaw (M) 74 D6
Paumyaung (M) 75 E5
Paunar (Mah) 67 F5
Paunar (Mad) 67 G1
Paungbyin (M) 61 H3
Paunggwe (M) 75 H3
Pauni 67 H5
Pauri 19 F6
Pausesavli 84 D1
Pavagada 91 H3, 92 A3
Pavagadh 64 C1
Pawahku (M) 45 H4
Pawai (Mad) 54 A3
Pawai (Bih) 56 B2
Pawakhali 40 A4
Pawayan 24 A5
Payagpur 36 D1
Payalakunte 92 D1
Payang 28 C5
Payaw (M) 44 A4
Payoli 94 C3
Payu (C) 28 B1
Payyanur 94 B2
Pebindaik (M) 75 H3
Pechampalli 87 F2
Pechi 52 B3
Pechipara 98 D5
Pedana 88 C4
Pedapalli 87 E4
Pedda Alavalapadu 87 H6
Pedda Aravidu 87 G5
Pedda Arikatla 87 G6
Pedda Irlapadu 87 G6
Pedda Munugal 88 A2
Pedda Nayakkanpalaiyam
   96 B3
Pedda Sana 82 B4
Peddaballe 92 C3
Peddachama 87 F5
Peddachappalle 92 D2
Peddacheruvu 87 G3
Peddakurapadu 88 A3
Peddamal 86 C2
Peddamanapuram 81 H5
Peddapalli 79 G4
Peddapariya 93 F3

Peddapasupula 92 C1
Peddapavani 93 F1
Peddapudi 89 E2
Peddapur 78 D6
Peddapuram 89 E2
Peddatippasamudram
   92 C4
Peddavalasa 81 F6
Pedgaon 77 E5
Peduru 92 D6
Pehowa 22 A1
Peint 64 C6
Pejorling (C) 26 D4
Pemaden (C) 27 H1
Pemakochung (C) 27 H1
Pemayangtse 40 B1
Pen 76 B4
Penagalaru 93 E3
Pendo (C) 26 C5
Pendra (Mad) 55 E6
Pendra (Mah) 64 D3
Pendra Road 55 E6
Pendur 84 B4
Pendurti 81 H6
Pengkhua 41 F3
Penkua 101 G5
Pennadam 96 D4
Pennagaram 95 H2
Pennattur 96 C2
Pennur 78 C4
Penta 80 D6
Pentakota 89 F2
Penuganchiprolu 88 A3
Penugonda 88 D3
Penukonda 92 A3
Penumuru 93 E5
Penur 77 G6
Peontra 18 D5
Peralam 96 D5
Peralassery 94 C2
Perambalur 96 B4
Peranamallur 96 D1
Peravurani 96 C6
Perayur 99 E2
Perdala 94 B1
Perdur 90 C5
Peringom 94 C2
Peritalmana 95 E5
Periya 94 D3
Periyakulam 98 D1
Periyanayakampalaiyam
   95 F4
Periyapalaiyam 93 F5
Pernampet 92 D6
Pernem 84 C5
Perumbalai 95 H2
Perumbavur 98 B1
Perumkulam 98 C4
Perunali 99 F3
Perungalur 96 C6
Peruru 92 A2
Pesavar 65 G6
Pesiduvaripalle 92 D2
Pet Sirur 86 B2
Peth (Mah) 76 D4
Peth (Mah) 84 C2
Peth Wadaj 78 C4
Petlad 64 A1
Petlawad 51 F6
Petro (P) 30 C3
Phacharia 63 F5
Phachishekha (C) 26 A1
Phacona 23 E3
Phaggu 21 F1
Phagi 33 G3
Phagne 65 E5
Phagwara 17 G4
Phaiapong 100 B2

Phaileng 60 C4
Phaiphengmun 61 E3
Phaisat (M) 61 E3
Phaiyeng 61 F1
Phala 62 D1
Phalabang (N) 25 E5
Phalasia 50 C3
Phalauda 22 D3
Phalghat 65 G2
Phalla (P) 16 C1
Phalsund 31 G4
Phalta 72 B2
Phaltan 77 E6
Phampini 81 F4
Phancha 18 D3
Phanda 52 C5
Phangchogaon 43 E3
Phanjila 14 B3
Phansidewa 40 C3
Phaphund 35 G3
Pharal 22 A1
Pharenda 37 H2
Phariaro (P) 30 A2
Phariha 35 F1
Pharkia 39 H5
Pharona 13 H2
Pharping (N) 38 D1
Pharrod 32 D2
Phatepur 65 E3
Phatnikka (P) 16 B3
Phe 14 B4
Phek 43 G5
Phellong 61 E1
Phembu (N) 40 A1
Phenaing (M) 75 E3
Pherod 32 C2
Phesar 56 B1
Phidim (N) 40 A2
Phijorgaon (N) 25 G2
Phillora (P) 17 F1
Phinch 32 A4
Phirangipuram 88 A4
Phiringia 70 A6
Phisugaon 41 F3
Phlangmawphra 41 H6
Phobrang 15 E3
Pholodi (Raj) 31 H2
Pholodi (Raj) 32 D3
Phonda 84 C4
Phopagaon (N) 25 G2
Phopnar 66 A4
Photaksar 14 B3
Phuchu (C) 27 G2
Phuglana 17 G3
Phugru (N) 25 E4
Phuitani 43 F6
Phuktal Gompa 14 C5
Phuladiyon Dherwali (P)
   30 B5
Phulambri 77 G1
Phulang (C) 27 E2
Phularwan (P) 16 B1
Phulaut 39 G6
Phulbani 70 B6
Phulbari (Ba) 40 D6
Phulbari (Wbg) 41 E5
Phulbari (Meg) 41 F5
Phulbaria (Ba) 59 F2
Phulbaroda 52 B2
Phulbihar 24 B5
Phulera 33 G3
Phuljhuri (Ba) 73 F2
Phullen 60 D4
Phulo 21 F1
Phulpur (Ba) 59 F1
Phulpur (Utt) 37 E6
Phulpur (Utt) 37 F6

Phulpur (Utt) 37 G4
Phulra (P) 12 B2
Phulra (P) 20 A3
Phulsangvi 98 D2
Phulsar (Raj) 20 B4
Phulsar (Guj) 63 H4
Phulsari 69 G1
Phultala (Ba) 59 E6
Phultola (Ba) 40 B4
Phulwari 38 D6
Phungnangtar (N) 40 A3
Phungotah 17 G1
Phungyar 61 G1
Phuntsholing 40 D2
Phuparang (C) 28 A1
Phupher 52 D4
Phursungi 76 D5
Phusibuang 60 D4
Phyang 14 C3
Pi 33 E3
Piarewaro Tar (P) 30 C2
Pichavaram 97 E4
Pichhor 35 E5
Pichor 35 E6
Pichwa 63 E5
Pidikalo 55 H6
Pidmu 14 B4
Piduguralla 87 H3
Pieksao (B) 41 H2
Pihani (Utt) 24 A6
Pihani (Utt) 36 A1
Pihuj 64 A1
Piklon 52 D2
Pilani 21 G5
Pilar 84 C6
Pileru 92 D4
Pili Bangan 20 D2
Pilibhit 23 H4
Pilkhua 22 C4
Pillutla 87 H3
Piloro (P) 48 B2
Pilu (P) 49 E2
Pilwa (Raj) 33 E3
Pilwa (Utt) 35 F1
Pimi (B) 41 H1
Pimpalgaon (Mah) 65 G6
Pimpalgaon (Mah) 76 D4
Pimpalgaon (Mah) 78 B4
Pimpalgaon Baswant
   76 D1
Pimpalgaon Raja 66 A5
Pimpalner (Mah) 77 F6
Pimpalner (Mah) 77 H3
Pimpalwandi 76 D3
Pimparkher 77 H3
Pimpla 77 G3
Pimplner 64 D5
Pimpri (Guj) 64 C5
Pimpri (Mah) 78 A1
Pimpri (Mah) 78 C2
Pimpri (Mah) 85 E1
Pinahat 35 E2
Pind Dadan Khan (P) 12 A6
Pind Sultani (P) 12 A4
Pinda (M) 75 G5
Pindi Bhattian (P) 16 B2
Pindi Cheb (P) 12 A5
Pindi Rawan (P) 16 B1
Pindi Saidpur (P) 12 C6
Pindi Shaikh Musa (P)
   16 B4
Pindipole 87 H2
Pindkapar 67 G3
Pindra 68 A1
Pindwara 50 B2
Pingli (Mah) 78 B3
Pingli (Mah) 84 D1
Pingma Ga (M) 45 F2

Pingna (Ba) 59 E2
Pinjar 66 C6
Pinjaur 18 B5
Pinkapar 68 C5
Pinlawng (M) 45 F4
Pinswar 19 F5
Pinwa (M) 75 H6
Pipalda 34 A4
Pipalgaon (Mah) 77 H2
Pipalgaon (Mah) 79 E2
Pipaljhopa 65 G3
Pipalkhera (Mad) 52 C4
Pipalkhera (Mad) 65 G1
Pipalkot (N) 24 C2
Pipalkoti 19 G6
Pipalrawan 52 A5
Pipalsana 23 F3
Pipalwa 63 F4
Pipalwara 34 A4
Pipar 32 C4
Piparia (Mad) 54 B6
Piparia (Mad) 55 F6
Pipariya (Bih) 38 C3
Pipariya (Mad) 53 E6
Piparkhed 65 G5
Piparwani 67 H3
Piphena 21 F2
Piplawandi 81 E3
Pipli (Har) 21 F1
Pipli (Raj) 50 D1
Pipli (Ori) 83 E1
Piplia 65 H2
Piplod (Raj) 33 F6
Piplod (Mad) 66 A3
Piploda (Mad) 51 F4
Piploda (Mad) 51 G5
Piplu 51 G6
Piplun 58 B5
Pipo (C) 28 A2
Pippara 88 D3
Pipra (Utt) 37 G3
Pipra (Bih) 38 C3
Pipra (Bih) 39 G4
Pipraha (N) 24 C4
Piprai 52 D2
Pipraich 37 H3
Piprala 49 F4
Pipri (P) 47 F2
Pipri (Utt) 55 G3
Pipri (Mad) 65 F3
Pipri (Mah) 77 G2
Piprod 54 A4
Piproda 52 C1
Pir Ali Mardan (P) 47 H1
Pir Ghani (P) 16 C6
Pir Jo Ghot (P) 30 B5
Pir Jo Goth (P) 30 A1
Pir Kampria 21 E2
Pir Kot (P) 16 C2
Pir Mangho (P) 47 E1
Pira Fatehal (P) 12 A6
Pirakata 71 H1
Pirangut 76 C5
Pirawa 51 H3
Pirganj (Ba) 40 B5
Pirganj (Ba) 40 D6
Pirhapal 80 C1
Piria 55 F6
Piriyapatna 94 D1
Pirmed 98 C2
Pirmeli 80 B3
Piro 38 B6
Pirojpur (Ba) 73 F1
Pirona 35 G5
Pirpainti 39 H6
Pirthala 22 C5
Pirthipur 35 F6
Pisangan 33 E4

Pisawa 22 D5
Pithal 82 C2
Pithapuram 89 E2
Pithi 77 G4
Pithora 69 F4
Pithoragarh 24 A2
Pithoro (P) 30 B6
Pitij 56 C3
Pitlam 78 D5
Piun (P) 14 B1
Piuthan (N) 25 G5
Plassey 58 B4
Plonliang 28 C5
Pnulan 20 B3
Po-Rhi-Byin (M) 74 D6
Poahat 101 G4
Pochannapet 79 F6
Podalakur 93 F3
Podile 87 G5
Podla 80 D5
Podur 86 C4
Poduru 88 D3
Podzo Sumdo (C) 27 E4
Pogullapalle 88 B1
Pohegaon 77 E2
Pohri 34 C6
Pokaran 31 G2
Pokharia 57 G4
Pokhra 23 F1
Pokhri 19 G6
Pokuru 87 H6
Poladpur 76 C6
Polaia Kalan 52 A5
Polang 18 B2
Polasara 82 C2
Polatala 92 D3
Polavaram 88 D2
Poling (C) 19 G4
Pollachi 95 F5
Polur 96 C1
Pomalvadi 77 F5
Pomuma 79 H2
Ponad 76 A4
Ponda 84 C6
Pondang (C) 29 H6
Pondi 69 E1
Pondicherry 97 E2
Pondlo 32 C3
Ponduru (And) 82 A5
Ponduru (And) 87 H6
Pongchau 44 B2
Pongode 87 H3
Pongunagu 14 D5
Ponmudi 98 C4
Ponna (M) 75 F3
Ponnagyun (M) 74 D6
Ponnai 93 E5
Ponnamaravati 96 B6
Ponnampet 94 D2
Ponnani 94 D5
Ponneri 93 G5
Ponnuru 88 A4
Ponpadi 93 F5
Ponyo (M) 44 A4
Poompuhar 97 E4
Poonamallee 93 F6
Poonawadu 90 B1
Poradaha (Ba) 58 D4
Poraiyar 97 E4
Porata 81 G5
Porbandar 62 B3
Poreya 57 H2
Porka 21 E3
Porla 84 C3
Porsa 35 E3
Port Blair 100 B5
Port Meadows 100 B5

Porto Novo (Parangi-
  ppettai) 97 E3
Porumamilla 92 D1
Poshuk (C) 28 B1
Posina 50 B2
Posora 70 B6
Potangi 81 G5
Potha 13 E4
Pothia (Bih) 39 H6
Pothia (Bih) 40 B4
Pothungoli 80 C2
Potin 43 F1
Potka 71 F1
Potkapalli 79 H5
Potlan 50 D1
Potrang (C) 26 B3
Potrang (C) 27 E4
Pottasingi 82 A3
Poundul 78 D2
Pouri 54 C4
Pragpura 33 H1
Prahnu (P) 14 B1
Prakasha 65 E4
Prakkilanka 88 D2
Pranhera 33 F5
Prarapnagar 72 C1
Praserganj 72 B3
Pratabnagar 19 F6
Pratabpur 55 H5
Pratapgarh (Utt) 37 E5
Pratapgarh (Mah) 76 C6
Pratapnagar (Ba) 72 D1
Pratapur 82 C2
Prattipadu (And) 88 A4
Prattipadu (And) 89 E2
Pravara Sangam 77 F2
Pravasuni 70 B3
Priphema 43 F5
Priya 82 B5
Proddatur 92 C2
Psiar 42 C5
Pubail (Ba) 59 G4
Puchung (C) 28 A3
Pudamari 82 B2
Puddukkottai 99 E4
Pudimadaka 89 G1
Pudu Chatram 95 H6
Pudukad 95 E6
Pudukkottai 96 B6
Pudumadurai 100 B3
Pudunagaram 95 E5
Puduppadi 93 E6
Puduppattai 98 D2
Pudur (Tam) 95 F4
Pudur (Tam) 99 F3
Puduvayal 93 G5
Pugal 20 A4
Puh 19 F3
Puichari (Ba) 74 B2
Puipani 82 B3
Puiwa (M) 75 F5
Pujarikaker 80 C5
Pukhrayan 35 H4
Pul Bajuan (P) 13 E6
Pulain (Ba) 60 B2
Pulambadi 96 B4
Pulanto (N) 24 D2
Pulasar 21 E5
Pulbazar 40 B2
Pulga 18 C2
Pulgaon 67 E5
Pulicat 93 G5
Pulivendla 92 C2
Puliyangudi 98 D3
Pulkusma 57 G6
Pullalacheruvu 87 G4
Pullambadi 96 B5
Pullampet 93 E3

Pulomi 43 F5
Pulsa 67 E4
Pulunj 85 F1
Puluvappatti 95 F5
Pulwama 13 F3
Pulyara 98 C3
Pumkahtawng (M) 45 F6
Pumsin (M) 44 C5
Punadra 50 B6
Punahana 22 C6
Punalur 98 C3
Punas (Raj) 32 D2
Punas (Raj) 49 H1
Punasa 66 A2
Punawas 31 H6
Punch 12 D4
Puncha 57 G5
Punchh 35 G5
Pundri 22 B2
Pundro (C) 26 C4
Pune 76 C5
Pungan (M) 44 D6
Punganuru 92 C5
Pungka (M) 45 F4
Punguk 15 F6
Punho Chandia (P) 48 A2
Punjaipugalur 96 A4
Punjaipuliampatti 95 G4
Punjalkatte 90 D6
Punjapura 66 A1
Punji 66 D2
Punjur 95 G3
Punlumbum (M) 45 F4
Punpun 38 C6
Punrasar 20 C5
Punsa (P) 14 A2
Puntamba 77 E2
Punwat 79 G1
Pupri 39 E3
Pur (Utt) 22 D2
Pur (Raj) 33 E6
Pura 34 B5
Purandarpur 37 H2
Purandhar 76 D5
Purangarh 84 B3
Purani 23 E2
Puranigudam 42 D4
Puranpur 24 A4
Puras 66 B5
Purasa 49 F1
Purbasthali 58 B5
Purbba Dhala (Ba) 59 G1
Puri 83 E2
Purigal 95 F2
Purkahur 80 B3
Purkhas 22 B3
Purli 78 A4
Purna 78 B3
Purnakot 70 C5
Purnia 39 H5
Purnoor 80 B2
Purorr 43 H4
Pursura 58 A6
Purti Ghat (N) 25 H5
Purtsang 28 D3
Purulia 57 F5
Purulia Muffasil 57 F5
Purunagarh 70 C5
Purunakatak 70 B5
Purusand 71 F4
Purushottampur 82 C2
Purwa 36 B3
Pusa 39 E5
Pusad 78 C2
Pushal 13 G4
Pushkar 33 E3
Pushpagiri 96 C1

Putalapattu 93 E5
Putao (M) 45 E1
Puthia (Ba) 58 C3
Putluru 92 B2
Puttanattam 96 A6
Puttaparthi 92 B3
Puttha (M) 61 G3
Puttur (Kar) 90 D6
Puttur (Tam) 93 F5
Puvar 98 C5
Pwinbyu (M) 75 G6
Pwinga (M) 75 G1
Pya (M) 75 G1
Pyapal 86 C6
Pyegan (M) 61 G6
Pyelongyi (M) 75 E5
Pyilongyaw (M) 75 G6
Pyingaing (M) 61 H5
Pynursla 42 B6

Qabula (P) 16 B6
Qadian 17 G2
Qadirabad (P) 16 C1
Qadiraganj 57 E1
Qadirbad (P) 20 A1
Qadirganj 23 G6
Qaimpur (P) 20 A2
Qasba Ao 34 C1
Qasba Naubug 13 F4
Qasimka (P) 20 B1
Qazi Baqar (P) 12 D6
Qazian (P) 12 C5
Qazigund 13 F4
Qila Dharm Singh (P) 16 C4
Qila Didar Singh (P) 16 D2
Qila Sobha Singh (P) 17 E1
Quepem 84 C6
Quilandi 94 C4
Quraish (P) 20 A3
Qutab Minar 22 C4
Qutabnagar 36 B1

Rabasar 31 E6
Rabda 63 E2
Rabiraipara 60 B4
Rabkavi 85 E4
Rabupura 22 C5
Rabwah (P) 16 B2
Rabyeiling Gompa (C)
  19 G2
Rachak Naru (C) 19 H1
Rachau (B) 41 F1
Racherla 87 F6
Radagaon 21 G6
Radampahar 71 E2
Radaur 22 B1
Radhanagar 57 H5
Radhanagart 84 C4
Radhanpur 49 G4
Radhapuram 99 E5
Radia 17 G2
Radui Khuathar (M) 75 E3
Rae Bareli 36 C2
Raemalwali 20 C4
Rafiabad 23 G6
Rafiganj 56 B2
Ragargad 19 H6
Ragauli 53 H2
Raghogarh 52 C2
Raghopur 38 D6
Raghopur 39 G4
Raghu Nathpura 20 C3
Raghunathbari 72 A1
Raghunathganj (Mad)
  54 D2
Raghunathganj (Wbg)
  58 A2
Raghunathgarh 21 F6

Raghunathpalli 79 G6
Raghunathpur (Ba) 59 E3
Raghunathpur (Raj) 34 B4
Raghunathpur (Bih) 38 B4
Raghunathpur (Wbg)
  57 G4
Raghunathpur (Ori) 71 E6
Raghunathpura 32 D5
Raghunatpur 38 B6
Raha (N) 25 E1
Raha (Ass) 41 G3
Raha (Ass) 42 C4
Raha (Guj) 49 G2
Raharmal 83 E2
Rahata 77 E2
Rahatganun 66 C2
Rahatgar 53 E4
Rahawa 34 A3
Raheri 78 A1
Rahim Hi Bazar (P) 48 B3
Rahimabad 41 E3
Rahimatpur 84 D1
Rahimgarh 51 G3
Rahlana 33 F3
Rahmunke (P) 16 C6
Rahon 17 H4
Rahu 66 C3
Rahui 38 D6
Rahumari (Ba) 41 E5
Rahuri 77 E3
Rahwali (P) 16 D1
Rai 22 B3
Raia 33 E5
Raiboga 70 C1
Raichur 86 C4
Raidih 56 B6
Raigadh 76 C5
Raiganj 40 B5
Raigaon (Mah) 78 B2
Raigaon (Mah) 84 D2
Raigarh (Mad) 69 H3
Raigarh (Ori) 81 E1
Raihara 56 A3
Raikal 79 F4
Raiked 78 D6
Raikera 56 A6
Raikheda 65 E3
Raikia 82 B1
Raikot 17 G5
Raimana 41 E3
Raimdra 20 C3
Raimoh 77 G4
Raing Hat (M) 75 E4
Rainsara 21 F3
Raipal 79 F6
Raipalli 78 D6
Raipur (Ba) 59 G6
Raipur (Ba) 59 H1
Raipur (Pun) 17 G5
Raipur (Him)18 A3
Raipur (Har) 18 B5
Raipur (Utt) 18 D6
Raipur (Utt) 19 E6
Raipur (Utt) 21 F1
Raipur (Pun) 32 D4
Raipur (Raj) 32 D6
Raipur (Raj) 51 H3
Raipur (Raj) 54 D2
Raipur (Wbg) 57 G6
Raipur (Mad) 68 D4
Raipur Khas 35 G1
Raipura (Ba) 59 G3
Raipura (Utt) 36 C6
Raipura (Mad) 53 H4
Rairangpur 71 E2
Raireshwar 76 C6
Raisar 33 H2
Raisen 52 D5

Raisghnagar 20 B2
Raisingpur 64 D3
Raison 18 B2
Raita (Ba) 58 C3
Raitalai 66 B4
Raivada (Guj) 50 C5
Raivada (And) 81 G6
Raiwind (P) 16 D4
Raj Gangpur 70 B2
Raj Kanika 71 G5
Raj Malk (P) 47 F2
Raj Nandgaon 68 C5
Raj Samand 50 D1
Raj Sitapur 49 F6
Raja Bazar 60 D1
Raja Hat (Ba) 74 B1
Raja Jang (P) 17 E4
Raja Ranpur 82 D1
Raja Sinsi 17 F3
Raja Takli 77 H3
Rajabari 43 H2
Rajabhat Khawa 41 E3
Rajabhita 57 F4
Rajagaon 81 E2
Rajahar (P) 30 B1
Rajahmundry 88 D2
Rajair (Ba) 59 F5
Rajakhera 35 E2
Rajale 77 E6
Rajamatam 96 D6
Rajamathai 31 G3
Rajampet (And) 79 E5
Rajampet (And) 93 E3
Rajanagaram 89 E2
Rajanvadi 84 C3
Rajapalaiyam 98 D2
Rajapokhar 57 G2
Rajapur (Ba) 59 H4
Rajapur (Ba) 59 H6
Rajapur (N) 24 C5
Rajapur (Utt) 36 C6
Rajapur (Ori) 82 C3
Rajapur (Mah) 84 B3
Rajapur Bay 84 A3
Rajar (P) 16 A1
Rajar (P) 30 B3
Rajaram (And) 79 G4
Rajaram (Mah) 80 A3
Rajasar (Raj) 20 B5
Rajasar (Raj) 20 D4
Rajashawar 78 B6
Rajasingamangalam 99 G2
Rajauli 56 D2
Rajaun 57 G1
Rajaund 22 A2
Rajauri 13 E5
Rajavolu 86 C5
Rajawala (P) 16 B2
Rajawaram 87 G3
Rajawas 21 E4
Rajbari (Ba) 59 E4
Rajbari (Ba) 59 G5
Rajbari 72 C1
Rajbiraj (N) 39 G3
Rajbpur 23 E4
Rajdhani 12 C5
Rajegaon (Mad) 68 A3
Rajegaon (Mah) 77 H3
Rajendraganj (Ba) 41 E6
Rajevadi 76 D5
Rajganj (Ba) 59 H6
Rajganj 40 C3
Rajgaon 78 B1
Rajgarh (Him) 18 C5
Rajgarh (Utt) 19 E5
Rajgarh (Raj) 21 F4
Rajgarh (Raj) 33 E4

Rajgarh (Raj) 34 B2
Rajgarh (Mad) 34 C6
Rajgarh (Mad) 52 B3
Rajgarh (Mad) 53 H2
Rajgarh (Utt) 55 G1
Rajgarh (Guj) 64 C1
Rajgarh (Mad) 65 F1
Rajgarhat (N) 40 A3
Rajgir 56 D1
Rajgoli 84 D5
Rajgur 87 F1
Rajhara Jharandalli 68 C6
Rajhat 60 D2
Rajiana (P) 16 A5
Rajisar 20 D3
Rajja 27 F5
Rajkot 63 E2
Rajmahal (Raj) 33 G5
Rajmahal (Bih) 58 A1
Rajnagar (Ba) 60 B2
Rajnagar (Bih) 39 F4
Rajnagar (Raj) 50 C1
Rajnagar (Mad) 53 H1
Rajnagar (Wbg) 57 H3
Rajnagar (Ori) 71 E3
Rajnagar (Ori) 71 G6
Rajnia (P) 12 B3
Rajo Khanani (P) 48 A1
Rajoa (P) 16 B3
Rajod 51 F6
Rajoda 81 F3
Rajoke (P) 16 A3
Rajoke (P) 17.E4
Rajoli 79 H1
Rajpainyan 12 C2
Rajpara 63 E2
Rajpipla 64 C3
Rajpur (Utt) 19 E6
Rajpur (Utt) 35 H4
Rajpur (Bih) 38 A6
Rajpur (Bih) 38 C4
Rajpur (Guj) 49 G6
Rajpur (Mad) 65 F3
Rajpur (Ori) 70 A3
Rajpur (Wbg) 72 B1
Rajpura (Har) 18 B5
Rajpura (Raj) 21 F4
Rajpura (Utt) 23 E5
Rajpura (Mad) 34 B6
Rajpura (Mad) 65 H3
Rajpura Hudan 20 D4
Rajrayal 31 F4
Rajshahi (Ba) 58 C2
Rajula 63 F5
Rajur (Mah) 76 C2
Rajur (Mah) 79 F1
Rajura 79 G2
Rajuri (Mah) 77 F5
Rajuri (Mah) 77 G4
Rajurvadi 79 E1
Rakehti 24 B5
Rakh 18 A1
Rakhabh Dev 50 C3
Rakhi 32 A5
Rakot 12 D3
Rakri 17 H2
Rakshasbhuwan 77 G3
Rakwar 54 B2
Ral 34 C1
Ralajung (C) 19 H1
Ralawal 21 H4
Ralawn (M) 61 F6
Ralegaon 67 E6
Ralol 63 G1
Ram Das 17 F2
Ram Dicherla 87 G4
Ram Sanehighat 36 D3
Ram Thamman (P) 17 E4

Ram Tirath Jaga 21 F1
Rama (Utt) 19 E4
Rama (Raj) 31 E3
Rama (Raj) 50 C2
Rama (Mad) 51 E6
Ramabhadrapuram 81 H5
Ramachandrapuram 89 E3
Ramagiri (Ori) 82 B3
Ramagiri (And) 92 A3
Ramagiri Udyagiri 82 B3
Ramakona 67 F3
Ramakuppam 92 C6
Ramallakota 86 D5
Ramampuram 93 E5
Raman 21 F1
Ramanagar 37 G6
Ramanagaram 91 H6
Ramanapeta 87 F2
Ramanathapuram 99 G2
Ramancheri 93 F5
Ramanguli 90 B2
Ramankkapeta 88 B3
Ramanuj Ganj 55 H4, 56 A4
Ramanujnagar 55 G5
Ramapuram (Kar) 95 G2
Ramapuram (Ker) 98 B2
Ramareddi 79 E5
Ramasamudram 92 C5
Ramavaram 89 E1
Ramayampet 79 E6
Ramayapatnam 93 G1
Rambagar 60 D2
Ramban 13 F5
Rambha 82 D2
Rambhapur 51 E6
Ramchandrapur 71 F4
Ramdeora 31 G2
Ramderia 31 F6
Ramdikhana (N) 24 D4
Ramdurg 85 F5
Ramdurga 86 B4
Ramechhap (N) 39 E1
Rameshwar (Utt) 24 A2
Rameshwar (Mad) 34 B5
Rameswaram 99 H3
Ramgad 91 G1
Ramganj (Ba) 59 G5
Ramganj 40 B4
Ramganj Mandi 51 H2
Ramgaon 66 C6
Ramgarh (Ba) 60 A6
Ramgarh (N) 24 B4
Ramgarh (P) 16 A6
Ramgarh (J&K) 17 F1
Ramgarh (Raj) 21 F3
Ramgarh (Raj) 21 F5
Ramgarh (Utt) 23 H2
Ramgarh (Raj) 30 D1
Ramgarh (Raj) 33 F2
Ramgarh (Raj) 34 B1
Ramgarh (Utt) 36 B2
Ramgarh (Bih) 37 H6
Ramgarh (Mad) 55 G6
Ramgarh (Bih) 55 H1
Ramgarh (Bih) 56 D4
Ramgarh (Bih) 57 H2
Ramgarh (Wbg) 57 H6
Ramgarh (Mah) 84 B4
Ramghat (Utt) 23 E5
Ramghat (Mah) 84 C5
Ramgiri 91 H3
Ramgura 54 C5
Ramjibanpur 58 A6
Ramkanda 56 A4
Ramkandu 13 F5
Ramki Chatta (P) 16 C1
Ramkola (Utt) 38 A2
Ramkola (Mad) 55 G4

Ramkola (Mad) 65 F3
Ramkot (J&K) 13 F6
Ramkot (Utt) 36 B1
Ramkrishnagram 100 B2
Ramlaitui 60 C5
Rammadagu 79 G4
Rammohan (Ba) 59 H5
Ramna 55 H3
Ramnagar (N) 38 D2
Ramnagar (J&K) 13 G6
Ramnagar (Raj) 20 C1
Ramnagar (Utt) 23 G2
Ramnagar (Utt) 23 G5
Ramnagar (Utt) 36 D2
Ramnagar (Utt) 37 G4
Ramnagar (Bih) 38 B2
Ramnagar (Mad) 54 C3
Ramnagar (Mad) 68 B1
Ramnagar (Wbg) 72 A3
Ramnagar (And) 100 B3
Ramnia (Ba) 59 H6
Rampaili 68 A3
Rampal (Ba) 73 E1
Ramparda 63 F1
Rampatti 39 F4
Rampella 70 A3
Rampur (N) 38 C2
Rampur (N) 39 F2
Rampur (J&K) 12 D3
Rampur (Him) 18 D3
Rampur (Raj) 22 A6
Rampur (Utt) 22 C1
Rampur (Utt) 23 G4
Rampur (Mad) 34 C4
Rampur (Utt) 37 F6
Rampur (Utt) 38 A3
Rampur (Bih) 38 C2
Rampur (Guj) 48 A5
Rampur (Guj) 50 C5
Rampur (Mad) 52 C1
Rampur (Mad) 52 C3
Rampur (Mad) 54 C2
Rampur (Mad) 54 D3
Rampur (Mad) 54 D5
Rampur (Bih) 56 D5
Rampur (Mad) 67 E1
Rampur (And) 80 A5
Rampur Hat 58 A3
Rampura (Raj) 20 D2
Rampura (Pun) 21 E1
Rampura 21 E2
Rampura (Har) 21 G4
Rampura (Utt) 23 G3
Rampura (Raj) 32 D6
Rampura (Mad) 51 G2
Rampura (Kar) 91 G1
Rampura Mandi 17 F6
Rampura Phul 17 F6
Rampuri (Mah) 77 H3
Rampuri (Mah) 78 A3
Ramra 20 A5
Ramrama Tola 67 H3
Ramri (P) 17 F1
Ramsan 49 G2
Ramsar (Raj) 20 B5
Ramsar (Raj) 31 E5
Ramsar (Raj) 33 F4
Ramsaratal 21 G4
Ramsen 50 A1
Ramshahr 18 B4
Ramshai 40 C3
Ramsia 33 E2
Ramsing 27 H4
Ramsu 13 F5
Ramtek (Mah) 67 G4
Ramtek (Mad) 69 G4
Ramu (Ba) 74 B4
Ramwao 48 D5

Ranagadh 49 G6
Ranaghat 58 C5
Ranahu (P) 30 C5
Ranakdhar (P) 30 C5
Ranakpur 50 C1
Ranao 30 D1
Ranasan 50 B5
Ranasar (Raj) 21 E4
Ranasar (Raj) 31 E5
Ranastralam 82 A5
Ranavav 62 C3
Ranbagha (Ba) 58 D2
Ranbirpura 14 D3
Ranchi 56 D5
Rander 64 A4
Randhia 63 F3
Randhikpur 50 D6
Randia 82 C2
Randisar 20 B5
Randrohi (P) 30 B3
Raneh 53 H3
Raner (Raj) 20 B4
Raner (Guj) 49 H3
Raneswar 57 H3
Rangagora 44 A1
Rangam 63 F4
Rangamati (Ba) 58 C1
Rangamati (Ba) 74 B1
Rangamati (Wbg) 41 E3
Rangamati (Ass) 42 B4
Rangampet (And) 79 E6
Rangampet (Kar) 86 A3
Rangapara 42 C2
Rangapuram 86 D6
Rangazumi 43 F5
Rangeli (N) 39 H3
Rangia 42 A3
Rangio 14 C6
Rangjuli 41 H5
Rangku 27 G5
Rangli 40 C2
Rangli Rangliot 40 B2
Ranglu Gompa (C) 28 D1
Rangpo 40 C2
Rangpur (Ba) 40 D5
Rangpur 49 E6
Rangse (M) 44 B3
Rangthong 42 A6
Rangunia (Ba) 74 B1
Rani (Raj) 32 B6
Rani (Ker) 98 C2
Rani Jot 37 F2
Rani Pokhri 19 E6
Rani Sawargaon 78 B4
Rani Unchegaon 77 H2
Rania (Har) 21 F2
Rania (Bih) 56 D6
Ranial (P) 12 B4
Ranibandh 57 G6
Ranibennur 91 E2
Ranibirta (N) 40 A3
Raniganj (Ba) 40 B4
Raniganj (Utt) 37 E2
Raniganj (Bih) 39 H4
Raniganj (Bih) 56 B2
Raniganj (Wbg) 57 H4
Ranigaon 33 E2
Ranigodam (Ass) 42 A4
Ranigodam (Meg) 42 A5
Raniguda 81 F4
Ranikhata 41 G3
Ranikhet 23 G2
Raninganj 37 E5
Ranipauwa (N) 25 H5
Ranipet 93 E6
Ranipur (Utt) 23 E1
Ranipur (Utt) 35 G6

Ranipur (Mad) 66 D2
Ranipur Jharial 69 H6
Ranipura 33 G5
Ranir Bazar 60 A4
Ranisankail (Ba) 40 B5
Ranisar 21 E3
Ranital (Him) 18 A2
Ranital (Utt) 55 G3
Ranitar (N) 39 G3
Raniwara 49 H2
Ranjangaon 77 E4
Ranjangudi 96 C4
Ranjani 77 H2
Ranka Kalan 56 A3
Ranod 52 D1
Ranotra (P) 12 B5
Ranpur (Guj) 62 B3
Ranpur (Guj) 63 G2
Ranpura 55 H3
Rantarodi 67 G6
Ranthambhor 34 A4
Ranuanaula 23 H2
Raogaon 77 F5
Raojan (Ba) 74 B1
Raoli (Him) 14 A6
Raoli (Har) 22 B6
Raota Kund 34 C1
Raoti 51 F5
Rapar 49 E5
Raphu 49 G4
Rapley (B) 40 D2
Rappakudi 96 D4
Rapri 35 F2
Rapur 93 F3
Rara (N) 25 E2
Rari 19 E4
Ras 32 D4
Rasafa (P) 20 A3
Rasegaon 76 C1
Rasela 69 E5
Rashil 14 B6
Rashivda 84 C3
Rashmi 51 E1
Rasi (N) 25 G3
Rasidpur 34 B2
Rasin 77 F5
Rasipuram 96 A4
Rasla 31 F3
Rasol 70 D5
Rasool 13 G4
Rasra 38 A5
Rasuan 57 H4
Rasul (P) 12 C6
Rasulabad (Utt) 35 H3
Rasulabad (Utt) 36 B3
Rasulnagar (P) 16 C1
Rasulpur Rohta 22 C3
Rasulpura 52 C2
Rasuwela 21 E1
Rata (P) 12 C5
Ratabari 60 C2
Ratadia 48 C6
Ratali (P) 16 D2
Ratangarh (Raj) 21 E5
Ratangarh (Mad) 51 F1
Ratannagar 21 F5
Ratanpur (Wbg) 57 G5
Ratanpur (Mad) 66 A1
Ratanpur (Mad) 69 E2
Ratanpur (Ori) 71 G6
Rath 35 H6
Rathedaung (M) 74 D6
Rathkuria 32 C3
Ratia 21 G2
Ratlam 51 F5
Ratnagiri (Ori) 71 F5
Ratnagiri (Mah) 84 B2
Ratnal 48 C5

Ratrahu (P) 30 A4
Ratria 31 H3
Ratsanr 38 A5
Rattasar 31 E6
Rattihalli 91 E2
Rattusar 21 E4
Ratu (Bih) 56 D5
Ratu (Miz) 60 D3
Ratua 40 A6
Ratwal (P) 12 A4
Rau (C) 28 D2
Rau Khanuana (P) 16 B4
Rauha (Ba) 59 F1
Raunapar 37 H4
Rauta 40 A4
Rautara 39 H5
Rauzagaon 36 D3
Rav 48 D4
Ravalgaon 65 E6
Ravangaon 77 E5
Raver 65 H4
Ravutulapudi 89 E1
Rawal 62 B3
Rawala Kot (P) 12 C3
Rawalpindi (P) 12 B4
Rawanwala (P) 20 A2
Rawapur 48 A5
Rawar 32 C4
Rawatsar (P) 49 E1
Rawatsar (Raj) 21 E3
Rawatsar (Raj) 31 G5
Rawwan (M) 75 F1
Raxaul 38 C2
Raya (P) 17 E2
Raya 34 D1
Raya Khas (P) 17 E2
Rayacholi 92 D3
Rayadrug 91 H2
Rayagada 81 H3
Rayakottai 96 A1
Rayalacheruvu 92 A1
Rayalapeta 92 D5
Rayalpadu 92 C4
Rayapalli 87 F1
Rayapeta 93 G2
Rayavaram 87 G5
Raybag 85 E4
Raygad (Guj) 64 D4
Raygad (Ori) 82 B3
Rayna 58 B5
Raypatan 84 B3
Razam 82 A5
Razephena 43 E5
Razole 88 D4
Razua (M) 75 E2
Rear (N) 25 F6
Rebai 35 H6
Rebra 79 H3
Redhakhol 70 B4
Redi 21 F4
Redivaripalle 92 C3
Reha 48 C5
Rehli 53 G4
Rehra (Utt) 23 E4
Rehra (Bih) 56 A3
Rehra Bazar 37 F2
Rehti 52 C6
Reiek 60 C4
Relangi 88 D3
Relawan 34 B6
Ren 32 D3
Renala Khurd (P) 16 C5
Renapur 78 A5
Rengakhar 68 C3
Rengalbera 70 C2
Rengali (Ori) 70 A3
Rengali (Ori) 70 C5
Rengazabal 13 E3

Rengdil 60 C3
Rengte 60 D2
Reni 21 F4
Renigunta 93 F4
Renlawara 50 C4
Renuka 18 C5
Renwal 33 G3
Reoti 38 B5
Reotipur 37 H6
Repalle 88 B4
Repanpalli 80 A3
Reru 14 B5
Rerwas 33 F6
Resho (C) 26 D4
Resubelpara 41 G5
Retachintala 87 G3
Revadanda 76 A5
Revdar 50 A2
Revelganj 38 C5
Rewa 54 D2
Rewad 56 B4
Rewari 22 B5
Rhatla 21 H3
Rhenok 40 C2
Rhilot 49 F4
Rhongo 15 F5
Rhonrasa 51 H6
Riagdango 14 B1
Riamal 70 B4
Rian 32 D3
Riang 42 D1
Riangdo 41 H5
Riasi 13 F5
Richabera 50 C3
Richha 23 H4
Richingpong 40 B2
Richubhutu 56 B4
Richwa 52 A2
Riddigang (C) 19 G3
Ridong (C) 29 F4
Ridwi (M) 75 F3
Riga (Aru) 27 H5
Riga (Bih) 38 D3
Rigauli 37 G2
Righagarh 71 G5
Rihabari 41 H3
Rijapur 58 B1
Rikinwas 13 G3
Rikor 27 H4
Ril 84 B2
Rilmilsar 20 C2
Rima (C) 29 E5
Rimbu (C) 27 E4
Rimi (N) 25 F3
Rinchenling (C) 26 B1
Rinchenpang (C) 28 A3
Rindukuri 42 C3
Ringkhap Songinong 41 F6
Ringnod (Mad) 51 F4
Ringnod (Mad) 65 F1
Ringus 33 G1
Riponpet 90 D3
Rir (P) 17 E3
Ririkot (N) 24 C3
Risaliya Khera 21 E2
Risgaon 81 E1
Rishikesh 19 E6, 23 E1
Rishivandiyam 96 C3
Risod 78 B1
Ritang (B) 41 F1
Rithi 54 A4
Rithora 35 E4
Rito Gompa (C) 26 C2
Ritu Ga (M) 44 B4
Riu 27 H5
Riwara 49 H2
Riwat (P) 12 B4
Rizong 14 C2

Ro (M) 75 F3
Roang 15 E4
Robertsganj 55 G2
Roda 17 F5
Roddam 92 A3
Rodhain 34 B4
Rodukoru (P) 16 B4
Roha (Guj) 48 B5
Roha (Mah) 76 B5
Rohana 22 D2
Rohangehari (Ba) 74 C2
Rohanglu 18 B3
Rohania 54 D5
Rohanpur (Ba) 58 B1
Rohat 32 B5
Rohina (Raj) 32 B1
Rohina (Raj) 32 D2
Rohini (Raj) 32 C1
Rohini (Wbg) 71 H2
Rohisa 63 F5
Rohitpur (Ba) 59 F4
Rohla 31 F6
Rohna 67 E5
Rohri (P) 30 A1
Rohru 18 D4
Rohtak 22 A4
Rohtas (P) 12 C6
Rohtasgarh 56 A2
Roing 28 B5
Roksum (C) 15 H5
Rol 21 F5
Rol Qazian 32 D2
Rolah (P) 16 A1
Rolla 91 H4
Rollapenta 87 F5
Ron (Mad) 35 F4
Ron (Kar) 85 G5
Rong (C) 26 B3
Rong 14 D4
Rongara 41 G6
Rongat 100 B4
Rongchugiri 41 F5
Rongdu 14 D2
Rongjenj 41 H5
Rongmachckgiri 41 F5
Rongra Asimgiri 41 G6
Rongsa (C) 26 B5
Rongyu (C) 28 A5
Ronipara (Ba) 74 C2
Ronvel 64 B6
Roorkee 22 D1
Ropahar (P) 30 B1
Ropar 18 B4
Rople 77 G5
Rorawad 34 B5
Rori 21 F2
Roriawan 32 D5
Roro 71 E1
Rosa 23 H6
Rosekadi 60 C2
Roshanganj 56 C2
Roshi (M) 61 E6
Rosia 32 A5
Rotung 28 A5
Rourkela 70 C2
Rowta 42 B3
Ruar 34 D4
Ruava (M) 75 F3
Rud 51 E1
Rudakota 81 F5
Rudarpur (Utt) 23 G2
Rudarpur (Utt) 37 G3
Rudarpur (Utt) 37 H4
Rudauli 36 D3
Rudhauli 37 G2
Rudrajupalle 88 B2
Rudrangi 79 F4
Rudraprayag 19 F6

Rudravaram 87 E6
Rudri 68 D6
Rudrur 78 D4
Rugi 85 H2
Ruhea (Ba) 40 C4
Rui 79 E1
Ruichattiai 77 E4
Ruju 20 B4
Rukanpur (P) 20 A1
Rukanpura 20 D1
Rukubi (B) 41 F1
Rukumkot (N) 25 F4
Rulagung 14 B4
Ruma (Ba) 74 C2
Rumbak 14 C3
Rumkhapalong (Ba) 74 B4
Run 32 C3
Rungarh 28 D6
Runija 51 F5
Runni 38 D4
Rupa 42 C2
Rupaheli 33 E5
Rupahihat 42 D3
Rupal 50 B4
Rupana 17 E6
Rupanagudi 91 H1
Rupawas 32 C4
Rupawati 49 H6
Rupbas 34 C2
Rupganj (Ba) 59 G4
Rupi 18 D3
Rupidiha 24 D5
Rupjhar 68 B3
Rupnagar 33 F3
Rupnayal 85 E3
Rupsa 71 H3
Rupshu 15 E5
Rupsi 31 E2
Rupwal (P) 12 A5
Rura 35 H3
Rurawan 53 G3
Rusera 39 E5
Rushyabari 60 B5
Russellkonda 82 B1
Rustam (P) 12 A2
Rutog 15 H4
Ruwo 21 H5

Sabaila (N) 39 F3
Sabalgarh 34 C4
Sabang 72 A2
Sabarimalai 98 C3
Sabathu 18 B4
Sabbavaram 81 G6
Sabedabar 60 B4
Sabhrai 48 A6
Sabla 50 D4
Sabri 100 B4
Sabrum 60 A6
Sabu 14 D3
Sabusi 60 C5
Sach Khas 14 A5
Sachandi 36 A3
Sachida 42 C2
Sachin 64 A4
Sachna (Ba) 59 H1
Sadabad 12 D5
Sadabad (Utt) 35 E1
Sadalgi 84 D3
Sadali 92 B4
Sadalpur 21 G3
Sadarpur (Ba) 59 F5
Sadarwala (P) 20 B3
Sadasar (Raj) 20 C6
Sadasar (Raj) 21 E4
Sadaseopet 86 D1
Sadashwarh 90 B1
Sadat 37 H5

Sade 77 F5
Sadepur 85 G1
Saderpur 36 C1
Sadhan 31 E1
Sadhaura 18 C6
Sadhli 64 B2
Sadhu ki Dhani 31 H6
Sadhuhati (Ba) 58 D4
Sadhuwala 20 C1
Sadianwala (P) 16 B5
Sadiya 28 B6
Sadolai 20 B4
Sadon (M) 45 F6
Sadr Gugera (P) 16 B5
Sadra 50 A5
Sadras 97 F1
Sadri 32 C6, 50 D1
Sadul Shahn 20 D1
Sadullahganj 23 G5
Sadullahnagar 37 F2
Sadullahpur (Ba) 41 E6
Sadullahpur (P) 16 D1
Saduna 32 C1
Safapur 13 F2
Safidon 22 B2
Safipur (Ba) 59 F6
Safipur 36 A3
Sagar (P) 12 A6
Sagar (Mad) 53 F4
Sagar (Kar) 86 A3
Sagar (Kar) 90 C3
Sagar Collectorganj 72 B3
Sagara 70 A5
Sagardighi 58 B3
Sagaria (Ba) 73 H2
Sagarpara 58 C3
Sagauli 38 C3
Sagbara 64 C3
Sagoda 81 H2
Sagolmang 61 F1
Sagong 27 H6
Sagoni 53 H4
Sagor 65 G1
Sagtala 64 C1
Sagthali 51 E4
Sagu (M) 75 H6
Sagwara 50 D4
Sah 36 B5
Saha 18 B6
Sahabad 23 G4
Sahajpur 53 F5
Sahamkawng (M) 29 F6
Sahanpur 23 E2
Sahar (Utt) 22 C6
Sahar (Bih) 38 B6
Sahar (Bih) 39 E3
Sahara 32 D6
Saharabedi 83 F1
Saharanpur 22 D1
Saharsa 39 F5
Sahaspur (Utt) 18 D6
Sahaspur (Utt) 23 F3
Sahaswan 23 F5
Sahatwar 38 B5
Sahawa 21 F4
Sahawar 23 F6
Sahawngte (M) 74 D2
Sahdar 38 D5
Sahg 14 A6
Sahibganj (Utt) 37 H2
Sahibganj (Bih) 40 A6
Sahiwal (P) 16 A2
Sahiwal (P) 16 B5
Sahiya 18 D5
Sahora 34 C1
Sahuka (P) 20 B1
Sahur 67 E4
Said Khan Lighari (P) 48 B1

Saidabad 37 E6
Saidapet 93 F6
Saidapuram 93 F3
Saidoke 17 E5
Saidpur (Ba) 40 D6
Saidpur (Utt) 22 D4
Saidpur (Utt) 37 G6
Saidu (P) 12 A1
Saidu (M) 75 E5
Saiha 74 D1
Saijarasar 20 C5
Saikede 76 D1
Saikhoa Ghat 28 B6
Saikul 61 F1
Saila 31 H6
Sailana 51 F5
Sailkupa (Ba) 58 D4
Sailu (Mah) 67 F5
Sailu (Mah) 78 A3
Saini 49 G4
Sainj 18 C3
Sainkheda 53 F6
Sainligunla 92 D6
Saintala 69 H6
Sainthia 58 A3
Sair 55 G6
Saira 50 C1
Sairang 60 C4
Sairep 60 D6
Saitlaw 60 C3
Saiyan 34 D2
Saiyda (P) 16 C1
Saiydan Shah (P) 12 B6
Saiyid (P) 12 B5
Saiyidan (P) 12 A3
Saiyidpur (P) 12 B4
Saiyidpur (P) 12 B6
Saiyidpur (P) 47 H1
Saiyidwala (P) 16 C4
Saizang (M) 61 E5
Saizawh 74 D1
Saja 68 C3
Sajeti 36 A4
Sajhauli 38 A6
Sajnekhali 72 D2
Sakaldiha 37 H6
Sakan (M) 75 F4
Sakarayinarkovil 98 D3
Sakardih 56 A6
Sakargarh 33 F6
Sakden (B) 42 B1
Sakengdan (M) 29 E5
Sakhai 43 G5
Sakhalu 43 G5
Sakhan 60 B4
Sakhari 67 G2
Sakhi 20 B3
Sakhi Gopal 83 E1
Sakhol 78 B5
Sakhpur 63 F3
Sakhun 33 F3
Sakhwan 17 F2
Sakit 35 F1
Sakkanurani 99 E1
Sakkarepatna 91 E5
Sakke 54 C6
Sakleshpur 91 E6
Sakli 65 G4
Sakna 33 G5
Sakoli 68 A4
Sakowa (Ba) 40 C4
Sakrai 34 B2
Sakrar 35 F6
Sakras 22 B6
Sakrauda 22 D1
Sakri (Bih) 39 E4
Sakri (Mah) 64 D5
Sakripur 58 B4

Sakta (M) 75 E1
Saktesgarh 55 F1
Sakti 69 G2
Sakur 76 D3
Sakyekang (C) 27 F3
Sala Gahtawng (M) 45 F2
Salagame 91 F5
Salahwas 22 A5
Salakpuram 79 G6
Salam (P) 16 B1
Salamatpur 52 C5
Salana 42 D3
Salanpur 57 F4
Salap (Ba) 59 E3
Salar 58 B4
Salara 50 D3
Salasar 21 E6
Salatua 56 A3
Salawas 32 B4
Salaya 62 B2
Salbaka 80 B5
Salbani 71 H1
Saldanggaon (N) 25 G3
Saldera (P) 20 A1
Sale (M) 75 H5
Salebhatta 69 H5
Salehji Wand (P) 30 C4
Salem 96 C3
Salema 60 B3
Salen (M) 61 E6
Salewara 68 C3
Salgar 85 E3
Salgran (P) 12 C4
Salgund 86 A5
Sali 13 G4
Salian (P) 12 C3
Saligrama 95 E1
Salikha (Ba) 59 E5
Salimagarh 51 E4
Salimi 81 E5
Salimpur (Utt) 38 A4
Salimpur (Bih) 38 C4
Salin (M) 75 H6
Salingyi (M) 75 H2
Salipur 71 H1
Saliwali 21 E2
Salkocha 41 F4
Sallaghat 18 B5
Sallopat 50 D5
Sallyana (N) 25 E5
Salmari 40 A5
Salo 21 F4
Salon 36 D4
Salonghkyet (M) 44 D3
Salotgi 85 G2
Salt Chauki (P) 48 A3
Saltora 57 G4
Salumbar 50 D3
Saluni 13 H6
Salur 81 H5
Salwa 32 C3
Salwan 22 B2
Sam 30 D3
Sama (C) 29 G4
Sama 24 A1
Samadh Bhai 17 F5
Samadhiala 63 G4
Samadiala 63 F5
Samaguri 42 D4
Samaiyapuram 96 B5
Samakhial 48 D5
Samalkha 22 B3
Samalkot 89 E2
Samalpatti 96 B2
Samalsar 17 F5
Samana 18 A6
Samanda 41 G5
Samani 12 D5

Samardarha 69 H4
Samaro (P) 30 B6
Samaruma 69 H2
Samastipur 39 E5
Samattur 95 F6
Samba 13 F6
Sambalpur (Mad) 68 C6
Sambalpur (Mad) 68 D3
Sambalpur (Ori) 70 A4
Sambhal 23 E4
Sambhar 33 F2
Sambhuganj 57 G1
Sambrani 85 E6
Sambrial (P) 17 E1
Samda 22 A6
Samdhiala 63 F3
Samdo (C) 29 G2
Samelia 32 D5
Samesra 31 G5
Samgam 13 E1
Sami (M) 74 D4
Sami Veri (P) 49 E2
Samjha 40 C6
Samla 63 G1
Samnapur 54 C6
Samoda 69 E4
Samot 13 E5
Samou Motawas 49 H3
Sampan 94 C1
Samparda 48 C5
Sampla 22 B4
Sampra 49 G4
Sampudruka (C) 29 G2
Sampurre 43 H5
Samra 70 A3
Samrala 18 A5
Samrau 32 A3
Samri 56 A5
Samsherpur 76 C2
Samta (Ba) 58 D6
Samtengang (B) 41 F1
Samthar 35 F5
Samuapur 68 A2
Samudaram 96 B5
Samuja 32 B5
Samundari (P) 16 B4
Samye (C) 26 A2
San 18 A1
San Gumma 81 F4
Sanacha 14 A2
Sanand 49 H6
Sanarpatti 96 A6
Sanasar 13 F5
Sanaur 18 A6
Sanawad 65 H2
Sanawara (Raj) 31 F6
Sanawara (Raj) 31 G3
Sanbala (M) 75 E6
Sanchi 52 D5
Sanchor 49 G2
Sanda (P) 30 A2
Sandalpur 66 B1
Sandawwa 21 H4
Sanderao 32 B6
Sandes 38 C6
Sandeshkhali 72 C1
Sandhan 48 A6
Sandhol 18 B2
Sandi 35 H2
Sandia 58 C6
Sandila 36 B2
Sando Bandar (P) 47 H3
Sandrapodu 87 F6
Sandur 91 G1
Sandurai 96 A6
Sanduria 37 H2
Sandwa (P) 12 A3
Sandwa 20 D6

Sandwip (Ba) 74 A1
Sanenya 101 F3
Sang (C) 27 G2
Sang 19 F3
Sang Jani (P) 12 A4
Sanga Choling (C) 26 D4
Sangacho Dzong (C) 29 E3
Sangakhera 53 E6
Sangali 93 F2
Sangam (J&K) 13 F2
Sangam (Kar) 85 G4
Sangameshwar 84 B2
Sangameswarpet 91 E5
Sangamner 76 D2
Sanganer 33 H3
Sangareddi 86 D1
Sangarhi 68 A5
Sangariya 21 E1
Sangarwain 13 F4
Sangau 60 D6
Sanghar (P) 30 A5
Sanghi 22 A3
Sanghoi (P) 12 C6
Sangla (P) 16 B3
Sangla 19 E3
Sangle 19 E3
Sangli 84 D3
Sangma 28 D5
Sangmai 61 F1
Sangod 52 A1
Sangola 85 E1
Sangramgarh 36 D5
Sangrampur (Bih) 38 C3
Sangrampur (Bih) 57 F1
Sangrar (P) 30 A1
Sangri (C) 26 B2
Sangrom 13 E3
Sangrur 17 H6
Sangsi (C) 26 D1
Sangtha 14 D5
Sangti (M) 44 B3
Sanguem 84 D6
Sangva (M) 75 F2
Sangvi 65 F4
Sanikosh (B) 41 F2
Sanis 43 G4
Sanivarsante 91 E6
Sanjak 14 A2
Sanjari 68 C5
Sanjeli 50 D6
Sanjit 51 F3
Sanju 32 D2
Sankal (Mad) 53 G6
Sankal (Guj) 64 C2
Sankanpalli 80 B4
Sankar 14 C3
Sankarada 81 H3
Sankarayalapeta 92 C5
Sankaridrug 95 H3
Sankdaha (Ba) 58 D4
Sankeshwar (Guj) 49 G5
Sankeshwar (Kar) 84 D4
Sankhatra (P) 17 F1
Sankheda (Guj) 64 C2
Sankheda (Mad) 67 E3
Sankher 78 C4
Sankhun 21 G5
Sankhwai 32 C2
Sanko 13 H2
Sankra (Utt) 23 E5
Sankra (Raj) 31 F3
Sankra (Guj) 49 G4
Sankra (Mad) 69 E6
Sankra (Mad) 69 F4
Sankrail 71 H2
Sankwali 32 A6
Sanna 56 A6
Sanosra 63 F2

Sanquelim 84 C5
Santa Kuni 49 G1
Santahar (Ba) 58 D2
Santajoturu 87 E5
Santaldih 57 F4
Santalpur 49 E4
Santaver 91 E4
Sante Bachahalli 91 G6
Sante Bennur 91 F3
Santemarahalli 95 F2
Santinagar 60 A3
Santipur (Mad) 68 D6
Santipur (A.I) 100 B4
Santpur (Kar) 78 C6
Santpur (Ori) 81 H1
Santrampur 50 D5
Santuri 57 G5
Sanu 31 E2
Sanu Kothi 13 H6
Sanvarde 84 B1
Sanwara 50 A2
Sanwer 51 G6
Sanwrad 33 E1
Sanya Manji 31 G5
Saoli 79 H1
Saondalga 84 D4
Saoner 67 F4
Saonli 67 F3
Saori 63 E1
Sapahar (Ba) 58 C1
Sapatgram 41 F4
Sapekhati 44 A2
Sapngmik 15 E3
Sapotra 34 B4
Saptashring 64 D6
Saputara 64 C5
Sar (Utt) 19 E4
Sar (Raj) 32 B4
Sar Banda (P) 12 A1
Sar ka Par 31 F5
Sar Qala (P) 12 A2
Sara (Ba) 58 D3
Sara (Guj) 49 F6
Sara 50 B3
Sarad 64 C6
Sarada 50 C3
Saradhna 33 E4
Saragaon 69 G2
Sarahan (Him) 18 C5
Sarahan (Him) 18 D3
Sarai 38 D5
Sarai 52 C2
Sarai Aghat 35 G1
Sarai Ajitmal 35 G3
Sarai Akil 36 D6
Sarai Alamgir (P) 12 C6
Sarai Ekdil 35 G3
Sarai jo Goth (P) 48 B3
Sarai Kheta 37 F5
Sarai Khwaja 37 F5
Sarai Rani 37 G5
Sarai Saleh (P) 12 B3
Sarai Tarin 23 F4
Saraidana 54 D6
Saraikela 57 E6
Sarail (Ba) 59 H3
Saraipali 69 G4
Saralgaon 76 C3
Saralpara 41 F2
Saran 32 C5
Sarana 31 H6
Sarangagada 70 A6
Sarangarh 69 G3
Sarangi 51 F6
Sarangkheda 65 E4
Sarangpur 52 A4
Saranguar 20 A4
Sarankhola (Ba) 73 E2

Sarankul 82 C1
Sarapal 70 C4
Sarapali 70 B4
Sarapgarh 70 A2
Saraskheri 52 D2
Sarath 57 G3
Sarauli 23 F4
Sarauth Pawayan 35 G1
Sarawan 57 G3
Sarbari 31 H4
Sarbhang 41 F2
Sarchipat 18 D3
Sarchu 14 C6
Sardagarh (Raj) 32 D6
Sardagarh (Guj) 62 D3
Sardah (Ba) 58 C3
Sardah (P) 12 A6
Sardargarh 20 C2
Sardarpur 65 F1
Sardarpura 20 D2
Sardarshahr 21 E5
Sardhana 22 C3
Sardhar 63 E2
Sardi 33 E1
Sardulgarh 21 F2
Sarendhi 34 D2
Sarenga 57 H6
Sareni 36 B4
Sareri 33 E5
Sareya 57 G2
Sargapur 86 B1
Sargaroin 19 F4
Sargigora'81 G1
Sargodha (P) 16 A2
Sargur 95 E2
Sarh 36 A4
Sarhed 43 E3
Saria (Bih) 38 C5
Saria (Mad) 69 H3
Sarila 35 H5
Sarira 36 D6
Sarishabari (Ba) 59 E2
Sarishad (Ba) 60 A6
Sariska 34 A1
Sarjakhanpet 86 C2
Sarjapur 92 B6
Sarjeko 84 B4
Sarkaghat 18 B3
Sarkal Kassar (P) 12 B5
Sarkhana 24 B5
Sarkhej 49 H6
Sarkher 42 D5
Sarla 49 F6
Sarli 31 G6
Sarmana 62 D2
Sarmast Lighari (P) 48 A1
Sarmera 39 E6
Sarnath 37 G6
Sami 21 E2
Sarod 64 A2
Sarola (Raj) 52 A2
Sarola (Mah) 77 E4
Sarona 68 D6
Sarotra 50 A3
Sarpataha 37 F4
Sarra 52 A3
Sarsai 63 E4
Sarsawa 22 C1
Sarsawah 12 C4
Sarseir 35 G6
Sarsha (Ba) 58 D5
Sarsiwa 69 G3
Sarswati (N) 39 F3
Sartal 13 H6
Sartam 27 F5
Sarthal 52 B2
Sartwan 17 E6
Saru Pathar 43 F4

Sarunda 32 B2
Sarupsar 20 C2
Sarurpur 22 C3
Sarva 63 F2
Sarvada 84 C4
Sarvakota 82 B4
Sarwa 51 E5
Sarwad 49 E6
Sarwai 36 B6
Sarwan (Raj) 50 C3
Sarwan (Mad) 51 E5
Sarwar (Raj) 21 E4
Sarwar (Raj) 33 F4
Sas Nagar 18 B5
Sasamusa 38 B3
Sasan Gir 62 D4
Sasaram 56 A1
Saser Brangsa 14 D1
Sasha 69 E4
Saskatta 84 D4
Saslu 92 A5
Sasni 23 E6
Saspul 14 C2
Sasthankkota 98 B3
Sasvad 76 D5
Satana 64 D6
Satangar 31 E4
Satapura 63 G4
Satara 84 C1
Satara Road 76 D6, 84 C1
Satbarwa 56 B4
Satbhaya 71 G5
Satgachia 58 B5
Satgawan 57 E2
Satghara (P) 16 C5
Sathamba 50 B5
Sathana 33 E5
Sathawng (M) 75 E2
Sathia 22 D3
Sathri 37 E3
Sathupalli 88 B2
Satiana (P) 16 A3
Satiana (P) 16 B4
Satidera (P) 49 E1
Satihal 85 H3
Satihalli 91 F6
Satjanda 20 C2
Satkania (Ba) 74 B2
Satkhira (Ba) 58 D6
Satkosia 71 E4
Satna 54 C2
Satnal 21 H5
Satnuru 95 G1
Satodad 62 D2
Satola 51 E3
Satpara (Mad) 52 D4
Satpara (Mad) 53 G3
Satpati 76 A2
Satra 21 E5
Satran (P) 17 E2
Satrikh 36 C3
Sattankulam 99 E5
Sattanur 96 C2
Sattavada 88 D1
Sattegalam 95 G2
Sattenapalle 88 A4
Satti (J&K) 14 D2
Satti (Kar) 85 E3
Sattigeri 85 E4
Satun 49 F4
Satuna 78 A3
Satur (Raj) 33 G6
Satur (Tam) 99 E2
Saturia (Ba) 59 F3
Satwai 13 F6
Satyamangalam 95 G3
Satyavedu 93 F5

Saukanwind (P) 17 E2
Saukatia (N) 24 B2
Saundari 55 H3
Saunk 34 C1
Saunshi 85 F6
Saur 19 F6
Saura 18 D4
Saurian 17 E3
Saurikh 35 G2
Sausar 67 F3
Savaikot 63 G3
Savalanga 91 E3
Savalgi 85 F3
Savangi 67 E6
Savantvadi 84 C5
Savanur 90 D1
Savar (Ba) 59 F4
Savar 67 E6
Savargaon 77 H6
Savarkundla 63 F4
Savda 65 H4
Savlaj 85 E2
Savli 64 B1
Savrat 84 C1
Saw (M) 75 G4
Sawaddi 17 G5
Sawai Madhopur 34 A5
Sawali 79 E1
Sawan Mahar (P) 30 A4
Sawangi Buzurg 78 B3
Sawar 33 F5
Sawargaon 78 C2
Sayalkudi 99 F3
Sayarpuram 99 E4
Sayatkharda 79 E1
Sayla 63 F1
Sayra (Ba) 40 D5
Saza 60 D6
Seb (C) 27 E1
Seba 34 B3
Secunderabad 87 E1
Sedam 86 C2
Sedan 13 E4
Sedarpalaiyam 95 H4
Sedaw (M) 61 H6
Segaon 65 G3
Sehar 34 B3
Sehore 52 C5
Sehot 33 F1
Sehra 12 D4
Sehramau 23 H6
Seikpyu (M) 75 H5
Sejakpur 63 F1
Seksih (M) 61 F4
Selari 49 E4
Selarpur 54 B4
Selbari 64 D5
Selgaon (Mah) 77 G2
Selgaon (Mah) 78 A3
Seling 60 D4
Selsella 41 F5
Selwasan 49 H1
Semapur 39 H6
Semaria 55 F4
Semariya 38 C5
Semarkhia 31 H4
Semarsot 55 H4
Semarwara 50 C4
Semathan 13 F2
Sembal 50 C1
Sembala 78 C2
Sembedeh 66 C3
Sembiyam 93 G5
Semiliguda 81 G4
Semli 34 B1
Semlia 51 E2
Semma 42 D2

Semradih 69 E3
Sena 32 A6, 50 A1
Senarijagaon 42 D4
Senbag (Ba) 59 H6
Sendamangalam 96 A4
Sendamaram 98 D3
Sendra 32 D4
Sendri 77 G5
Sendurai 96 C4
Sendurjan 66 C6
Sendurjana 67 E3
Sengaon (Mah) 78 B2
Sengaon (And) 79 G2
Senghe Dzong (B) 26 A6
Sengippatti 96 C5
Sengnam (M) 75 F4
Sengor (B) 41 H1
Seniku (M) 45 F5
Senjo Ga (M) 45 E5
Senthal 23 G4
Senvon 60 D3
Seogarh (Mad) 51 E6
Seogarh (Mad) 51 F5
Seohara 23 E3
Seona 65 H6
Seondara 23 F4
Seondha 35 F4
Seoni (Him) 18 C4
Seoni (Mad) 67 G2
Seoni Chhapara 67 G1
Seoni Malwa 66 C1
Seorinarayan 69 F3
Sepau 34 D3
Seppa 42 D1
Serai (Mad) 53 E2
Serai (Mad) 55 E3
Serajdikhan (Ba) 59 G4
Serampore 58 B6
Serchhip 60 D5
Serhmun 60 C4
Seri (*) 12 C2
Seri (*) 12 D5
Serkawr 74 D1
Sermadeva 98 D4
Serohi Nangal 21 H5
Serra 21 G3
Sershang (C) 15 G6
Seruna 20 C5
Seruvapu 80 A6
Sesai Buzurg 34 D6
Sesaipura 34 C6
Sesikhaliu 81 H3
Sethar 13 F3
Setigunta 93 E4
Setiyya 96 D4
Seturu 91 H2
Seulabang (N) 25 G5
Sevliya 50 B6
Sevur 95 G4
Sewa (Raj) 33 E1
Sewa (Raj) 33 G3
Sewar 34 C2
Sewara 49 H2
Sewari 50 B1
Shabzabi (P) 17 E1
Shacha Pebo (C) 27 F4
Shadaul 13 F4
Shadi 14 C4
Shadi Shahid (P) 30 A1
Shadipali (P) 30 B6
Shadipur 13 E3
Shadiwal (P) 12 D6
Shadiwal (P) 16 D1
Shadmand Lund (P) 48 A3
Shadnagar 86 D2
Shaduzup (M) 44 D5
Shafakhana 23 G3

Shafi (P) 16 B6
Shagbatta (Ba) 59 E1
Shagsar Dabla 20 C2
Shah (P) 12 B4
Shah Jiwana (P) 16 A3
Shah Kapur (P) 47 H2
Shah Paksiri (P) 30 A4
Shahabad (Har) 18 B6
Shahabad (Utt) 23 H6
Shahabad (Raj) 34 B6
Shahabad (Utt) 35 H1
Shahabad (Kar) 86 A2
Shahabad (And) 86 D2
Shahada 65 E3
Shahapur (Mah) 76 B3
Shahapur (Mah) 77 G2
Shaharwa 21 G3
Shahbad 64 B3
Shahbandar (P) 47 G3
Shahbaspur 17 F3
Shahbazgarhi (P) 12 A3
Shahdadpur (P) 30 A5
Shahdara (P) 17 E3
Shahdara (Utt) 22 C4
Shahdara (Mad) 52 D2
Shahderi (P) 12 A4
Shahdol 54 C5
Shahgadh 77 G3
Shahganj (Utt) 37 F4
Shahganj (Mad) 52 D6
Shahganj (Utt) 55 G2
Shahgarh (Raj) 30 C2
Shahgarh (Mad) 53 G2
Shahgarh (Utt) 53 G3
Shahi 23 G4
Shahibganj 38 C4
Shahjahanpur (Raj) 22 A6, 24 A6
Shahjahanpur (Utt) 23 H6
Shahkot (P) 16 C3
Shahkund (Bih) 39 G6
Shahkund (Bih) 57 G1
Shahnagar 54 A3
Shahpur (P) 16 A1
Shahpur (P) 16 D5
Shahpur (P) 30 B1
Shahpur (Pun) 17 F2
Shahpur (Pun) 17 G1
Shahpur (Utt) 22 C2
Shahpur (Del) 22 C6
Shahpur (Bih) 38 B5
Shahpur (Mad) 53 G4
Shahpur (Mad) 54 C6
Shahpur (Guj) 63 E2
Shahpur (Mah) 65 H4
Shahpur (Mad) 66 D2
Shahpur (And) 79 G6
Shahpur (Kar) 84 D5
Shahpur (Kar) 86 B3
Shahpur Chakar (P) 30 A4
Shahpur Patori 39 E5
Shahpura (Raj) 33 F5
Shahpura (Raj) 33 H1
Shahpura (Mad) 53 H5
Shahpura (Mad) 54 B5
Shahr Farid (P) 20 A1
Shahuwadi 84 C2
Shahzadpur (Ba) 59 E3
Shahzadpur 18 B6
Shaiai 18 D5
Shaikh Bhirkio (P) 30 A6
Shaikh Fazil (P) 16 B6
Shaistaganj (Ba) 60 A3
Shaji Ga (M) 45 E4
Shajpur 52 A5
Shakargarh (P) 17 F1
Shakti 26 B6
Shalayang (M) 45 E4

Shali (B) 42 A1
Shalkar 19 F2
Shalo (C) 26 B3
Sham (C) 26 D3
Sham Fattuwal (P) 16 A4
Shamalji 50 C4
Shambugarh 33 E5
Shamda (C) 26 C4
Shamgarh 51 G3
Shamhu 39 F6
Shamli 22 C2
Shampur (Mad) 34 B4
Shampur (Mad) 52 B5
Shampur (Mad) 81 E2
Shampura (Raj) 33 F6
Shampura (Raj) 34 A4
Shamsabad (Utt) 35 E2
Shamsabad (Mad) 52 C4
Shamshabad 87 E2
Shamsherganj (Ba) 60 A2
Shan Churasi 17 G3
Shandong 15 G4
Shangpung 42 C6
Shangtse (C) 19 H2
Shangwang (M) 45 F1
Shankargarh (*) 13 E1
Shankargarh (Utt) 36 D6
Shankarpalli 86 D1
Shankarpur 67 H5
Shankot 12 D2
Shankrampet 78 D6
Shanor 64 C2
Shansha 14 B6
Shantiniketan 58 A4
Shantipur 58 B5
Shapang (B) 26 A6
Shapur (Guj) 49 E6
Shapur (Guj) 52 D4
Sharagada 82 C2
Sharden (M) 45 G1
Shardi 13 E1
Shariakandi (Ba) 59 E1
Sharian 12 D3
Sharpur (P) 16 D3
Shatrana 21 H1
Shau Hkang (M) 44 D4
Shawngm Ga (M) 44 C2
Shazal 13 H5
Sheakhala 58 B6
Shebgaon 65 H5
Shebi Ga 44 C1
Shedbal 85 E3
Shedhumi 43 F5
Sheet (M) 75 F4
Shegaon (Mah) 66 B5
Shegaon (Mah) 67 G6
Shegaria (B) 41 F1
Shehera 50 C6
Sheikhupura (P) 16 D3
Sheikpura 39 E6
Shekapur 31 H1
Shelu 78 B1
Shenchottah 98 C3
Shendi 76 C2
Shendumi 65 G6
Shendurwara 77 F2
Shenkhor (P) 12 C1
Shenwa 76 C3
Sheodaspura 33 H3
Sheoganj 32 B6, 50 B1
Sheohar 38 D3
Sheokar 31 F5
Sheoli (Utt) 36 A3
Sheoli (Mah) 78 A2
Sheopur 34 B5
Sheopura 33 E4
Sheosagar 56 A1
Sher Bhatoria 67 E2

Sherad 77 F4
Sheradhon 77 H5
Sherah 22 B2
Sheran Chak 39 F6
Shergad 62 D4
Shergaon 42 C2
Shergarh (P) 12 B2
Shergarh (P) 16 C5
Shergarh (Utt) 22 C6
Shergarh (Raj) 31 H4
Shergarh (Raj) 50 D5
Shergarh (Raj) 52 A2
Shergarh Shera 20 D1
Sherghati 56 C2
Shergol 14 A2
Sheriala 20 C6
Sherkot 23 F2
Shermun 74 C1
Sherpur (Ba) 59 E2
Sherpur (Ba) 59 F1
Sherpur (J&K) 13 H6
Sherpur (Pun) 17 G6
Sherpur (Utt) 24 A4
Sherpur (Utt) 38 A6
Shertallai 98 A2
Sherwan (P) 12 B3
Shetphal 77 G6
Shetrawa 31 H3
Shevgaon 77 F3
Shi (C) 27 F1
Shianagar 63 G2
Shiani 63 G1
Shibganj (Ba) 40 B5
Shibganj (N) 39 H3
Shibkhola (N) 25 F3
Shibpuri 19 E6
Shidanwali (P) 17 E2
Shiggaon 90 D1
Shihmwe (M) 75 F4
Shihwuhsuan (C) 45 H5
Shikara 53 H6
Shikarpur (Utt) 23 E5
Shikarpur (Bih) 38 B2
Shikarpur (Wbg) 58 C3
Shikarpur (Kar) 90 D3
Shikhi 43 E2
Shikohabad 35 F2
Shikrapur 76 D4
Shilena 78 D2
Shilgarh 36 C3
Shillod 65 G6
Shillong 42 B5
Shim (M) 75 F4
Shimla (Him) 18 C4
Shimla (Raj) 21 E4
Shimoga 91 E4
Shimpi (M) 75 F1
Shinai Ga (M) 29 E6
Shinang (M) 44 B5
Shinde 76 C1
Shingbe (B) 26 A6
Shingbwiyang (M) 44 C3
Shingkarap (B) 40 D1
Shingkhor (B) 41 H1
Shingki Gompa (C) 28 B2
Shingnapur 77 E6, 85 E1
Shingwe 77 E3
Shingzhang 15 F4
Shinkiari (P) 12 C2
Shio (C) 26 C5
Shioni 64 B4
Shiradi 91 E6
Shirala 84 C2
Shirang (C) 27 H3
Shiraval 85 H1
Shirdi 77 E2
Shirgaon 84 B4
Shirguppi 85 F6

Shirhati 85 G6
Shiri (C) 27 E1
Shiriting (P) 14 A1
Shirkhed 66 D4
Shirnandgi 85 F2
Shirol 84 D3
Shiroshi 76 C3
Shirpur 65 E4
Shirsala 65 F5
Shirsoli 65 G5
Shirud 65 F5
Shirur 77 E4
Shirwal 76 D6
Shishgarh 23 G4
Shisongong (C) 29 H1
Shiuji (B) 40 D2
Shiv 31 F4
Shivalaung (M) 75 F3
Shivalli 90 C5
Shivanu (M) 75 E3
Shivna 85 E1
Shivner 76 C3
Shivni (Mah) 78 C2
Shivni (Mah) 79 E3
Shivpur 20 D1
Shivpur 34 C6
Shiwi (P) 12 B1
Sho 14 A5
Sho Gompa (C) 26 A1
Sho Kha Dzong (C) 27 F1
Shobo Shar (C) 26 C4
Shogi 18 B4
Shogran (P) 12 C2
Shohpur 66 C1
Shoka (C) 27 F3
Shokla 33 F4
Shol 27 G4
Sholapur 85 G1
Sholinghur 93 E6
Shongar Dzong (B) 41 H1
Shora 33 G3
Shoranur 95 E5
Shorapur 86 A3
Shorong (C) 28 A2
Showa (C) 28 A1
Shrigonda 77 E5
Shrirampur 77 E2
Shueiching (C) 45 G6
Shuganu 61 F3
Shugden Gompa (C) 28 D2
Shuhkishala 87 F3
Shujalpur 52 B5
Shujih (C) 29 F2
Shumo (C) 26 C2
Shuni (B) 41 G1
Shupiyan 13 F4
Shupkanjan 13 G3
Shurkhua (M) 75 E2
Shushot 14 C3
Shwedwin (M) 44 B6
Shwekondaing (M) 75 F3
Shwlebo (M) 61 G2
Shyamnagar 100 B2
Shyok 15 E3
Siago Samba (C) 27 F4
Siajuli 43 F1
Sial Sui 13 E5
Sialkot (N) 24 D4
Sialkot (P) 17 E1
Sialthaw (M) 61 F4
Siambar 30 D2
Siana 20 B6
Siang 69 G1
Siangngo (M) 75 E2
Siari (P) 14 B1
Siasar 20 B4
Siatlai (M) 75 E2
Sibalay (Ba) 59 E4

Sibchar (Ba) 59 F5
Sibganj (Ba) 58 D1
Sibnagar 59 H4
Sibpur (Ba) 59 G3
Sibsagar 43 H2
Sibuk (C) 26 B1
Sibukna (C) 26 B2
Sibutalung 60 D4
Sidapur 94 D2
Sidar Hat (Ba) 60 B6
Siddapur 90 C3
Siddapura 91 G2
Siddavanahalli 91 F3
Siddhaur 36 D3
Siddhavattam 92 D2
Siddhma 55 H5
Siddiganj 52 B6
Siddipet 79 F6
Sidhauli 36 C2
Sidhaw 38 A2
Sidhi 55 E2
Sidhnia Ghat (N) 24 D5
Sidhout 92 D2
Sidhpur 49 H4
Sidhpura 35 F1
Sidhwan Khas 17 G5
Sidi 54 D4
Sidlaghatta 92 B5
Sidli 41 G3
Sidmukh 21 G4
Sidnath 77 F2
Sidoktaya (M) 75 F6
Sidrias 33 E6
Sidsar 62 C3
Sigadam 82 A5
Sigalahalli 95 H2
Sigsari 62 D5
Sihai (P) 12 B5
Sihaung Ashe (M) 61 F6
Sihawal 55 F2
Sihod 64 C1
Sihoniya 35 E3
Sihor (Mad) 35 E5
Sihor (Guj) 49 E4
Sihora (Mad) 54 A5
Sihora (Mah) 67 H4
Sihori 49 G3
Sihunta 17 H1
Sika 62 C1
Sikandarabad 24 B6
Sikandarpur 38 A4
Sikandra (Utt) 34 D2
Sikandra (Utt) 35 H4
Sikandra (Bih) 57 E1
Sikandra Rao 23 E6
Sikandrabad 22 D4
Sikar 21 F6, 33 F1
Sikarapai 81 H3
Sikariall (P) 12 C6
Sikaripara 57 H3
Sikerkupa 81 H1
Sikkal (Tam) 97 H5
Sikkal (Tam) 99 G3
Siklangso Arda 42 C5
Sikosa 68 H5
Sikri 22 D2
Sikri Patti 34 C1
Sikta 38 C2
Sikti 39 H4
Sil 62 C4
Silana 22 B3
Silanwad 32 D1
Silao 56 D1
Silapi 14 B4
Silatpali 69 G5
Silaut 38 D4
Silawad 65 F3

Silchar 60 D1
Silda 71 G1
Silegaon 77 F2
Silgarhi Doti (N) 24 C3
Silghat 42 D3
Silheti 68 C3
Siliari 68 D4
Siliguri 40 C3
Silinda 81 G1
Silipur 34 B4
Siliserh 34 A1
Silkuri 60 D2
Sillanwali (P) 16 A2
Silli (Aru) 28 A5
Silli (Bih) 57 E5
Siloli 35 F4
Silon 53 H2
Silondi 54 B5
Silori 34 C5
Silpata 43 H1
Silpuri 34 B5
Silua 60 C2
Silvani 53 E5
Silvassa 64 B6
Silwai 56 D5
Simagaon (N) 25 F5
Simahaw (M) 45 F6
Simaltala 57 F2
Simaluguri 43 H2
Simanbadi 82 B1
Simaria (Mad) 54 C2
Simaria (Bih) 56 C3
Simbor 63 F5
Simdega 70 B1
Simengaon (N) 25 G2
Simga 68 D3
Simhadripuram 92 C2
Simikot (N) 24 D1
Similpalgarh 71 F3
Simla (Ba) 59 E2
Simoneri (C) 26 D4
Simplapal 57 H6
Simra (N) 38 C2
Simra 35 F6
Simrauta 36 D3
Simri 39 E4
Simri Bakhtiarpur 39 G5
Simrol 65 H1
Simu Dzong (B) 41 E1
Sinaingma (M) 61 G5
Sinbyugyun (M) 75 G5
Sinchaingbyin (M) 74 C5
Sindanur 86 A5
Sindaota 52 A4
Sindari 31 G6
Sindewahi 67 H6
Sindgi 85 H3
Sindhauli 23 H6
Sindhri (P) 30 B5
Sindhuli Garhi (N) 39 E2
Sindi 67 F5
Sindkheda 65 E4
Sindkher 79 E2
Sindri (Bih) 57 E6
Sindri (Bih) 57 F4
Sindughatta 91 G6
Sindukchhari (Ba) 60 B6
Sindurga 69 H6
Sindvani 65 E3
Sing 87 H6
Singabi 24 B5
Singad 78 D1
Singadavanahalli 86 B6
Singair (Ba) 59 F4
Singanallur 95 F5
Singanamala 92 B2
Singaperumalkoil 93 F6
Singar 32 C2

Singaraku Parbat 82 B3
Singarappettai 96 B2
Singarayakonda 88 A6
Singarbil (Ba) 59 H4
Singaung (M) 61 G5
Singgel (M) 61 E4
Singhana 21 G5
Singhanwala 17 F5
Singhara (P) 48 D2
Singhaur 18 B6
Singheswar 39 G5
Singhora 69 G4
Singhori 67 F2
Singhpur (Mad) 53 G6
Singhpur (Mad) 69 E6
Singia 39 F5
Singing 27 H3
Singkaling Hkamti (M)
  44 B4
Singmarigaon 42 C4
Singnghat 61 E3
Singoli 51 F1
Singpur (J&K) 13 G4
Singpur (Guj) 64 C4
Singpura 51 E1
Singra (Ba) 58 D2
Singramau 37 F5
Singraul 55 F4
Singrauli 55 F3
Singrimati 41 F5
Singtam 40 C2
Singu (M) 75 H5
Singwatam 87 E4
Sini 57 E6
Sinja (N) 25 E2
Sinjhoro (P) 30 A5
Sinkhed 77 H1
Sinli 31 H5
Sinlu (M) 75 G6
Sinnar 76 D2
Sinor 64 B3
Sinsa 79 H4
Sinwa 33 E1
Sippighat 100 B5
Sipra 51 H6
Sipur 70 D4
Sir 37 G1
Sir Muttra 34 C3
Sira 91 H4
Siraikoppa 90 D3
Sirali 66 B2
Sirampur 57 F3
Sirapdar 63 E2
Siran (P) 48 A2
Sirar 77 G3
Sirasmarga 77 G3
Sirathu 36 C5
Siravde 84 D2
Sird 32 A1
Sirdala 56 D2
Sirdang 24 B1
Sirdon 31 H2
Sirdukbari 60 A4
Sirgiri 69 F5
Sirha (N) 39 F3
Sirhali 17 F4
Sirhind 18 A5
Siriari 32 C5
Siriganj (Ba) 59 E2
Sirigeri 86 A6
Sirire 43 H5
Sirisadu 79 H5
Sirjagma 19 F2
Sirkazhi 97 E4
Sirkot (N) 24 D3
Sirmaur 54 D2
Sirohi 50 A1
Sironcha 80 A4

Sironj 52 D3
Sirpur (Mad) 66 A4
Sirpur (Mad) 69 E4
Sirpur (Mah) 78 B1
Sirpur (Mah) 79 H2
Sirpuram 88 B1
Sirsa (Har) 21 F2
Sirsa (Utt) 37 E6
Sirsaganj 35 F2
Sirsala 78 A4
Sirsi (Utt) 23 F4
Sirsi (Utt) 37 G3
Sirsi (Mad) 51 F4
Sirsi (Utt) 55 F2
Sirsi (Mah)85 F2
Sirsi (Kar) 90 C2
Sirsila 79 F5
Sirsod 34 C6
Sirsuphal 77 E5
Sirtiso 42 C5
Sirubal 69 H6
Siruguppa 86 B5
Sirumugai 95 F4
Sirupakkam 96 C3
Sirur 85 G4
Sirur Tajband 78 B4
Siruvallur (M) 61 G5
Sirvel 87 E6
Sirwa 49 E1
Sirwal 86 B3
Sirwar 86 B4
Sisagadh 48 B6
Sisai (Har) 21 H3
Sisai (Bih) 38 B4
Sisai (Bih) 56 C5
Sisaiya Thana 36 C1
Sisanah 22 B3
Sisang 62 D2
Sisauli 22 C2
Sisbani (N) 39 F3
Sisolar 36 A5
Sissu 18 C1
Siswa Bazar 37 H2
Siswali 34 A6
Sitai 40 D4
Sitakund (Ba) 74 A1
Sitalkuchi 40 D4
Sitalpati (N) 25 E5
Sitamarhi 38 D3
Sitamata 51 E3
Sitamau 51 G3
Sitanagaram (Ori) 81 H4
Sitanagaram (And) 88 D2
Sitapur (Utt) 36 B1
Sitapur (Guj) 49 G5
Sitarampuram 93 E1
Sitarganj 23 H3
Sithal (Ba) 59 E3
Sithra 69 G1
Sitlaha 54 D1
Sitlingyaung (M) 61 G6
Sito Ganne 21 E1
Sittaung (M) 61 G3
Sityin (M) 75 G2
Siuni 55 E6
Siurajpur 54 B2
Siuri 57 H4
Sivaganga (Kar) 91 H5
Sivaganga (Tam) 99 F1
Sivagiri (Tam) 95 H4
Sivagiri (Tam) 98 D3
Sivagunda 87 F2
Sivakasi 99 E2
Sivandippattai 98 D2
Sivane 91 F4
Sivasamudram 95 G1
Sivral 77 E1
Siwaith 37 E6

Siwala 78 C2
Siwalik Range 18 A4
Siwampet 79 E6
Siwan (Har) 22 A1
Siwan (Bih) 38 B4
Siwana 31 H5
Siwana Mal 22 B3
Siwani 21 G3
Siyana 23 E4
Siyuh 18 C5
Skiu 14 C3
Skirbuchan 14 B2
Sleemanabad 54 A4
Smaste (P) 12 B2
Sniebal 60 D4
Soa 20 C6
Sobasar 20 B5
Sobhapur 53 E6
Sodakor 31 F2
Sodaori 63 E4
Sodarpur 53 E5
Sode 56 D6
Sodhi (P) 12 A6
Sofale 76 A2
Sogam 13 E2
Soguru 81 F5
Sohagi 54 D1
Sohagpur (Mad) 53 E6
Sohagpur (Mad) 54 D5
Sohagpur (Mad) 69 F2
Sohagpura 51 E4
Sohal 17 E3
Sohan 34 D3
Sohana 18 B5
Sohawa (P) 12 C5
Sohawa Wariachan (P)
  16 C1
Sohawal 54 B2
Sohdra (P) 16 D1
Sohela 69 H4
Sohian 17 F3
Sohna 22 C5
Sohrarm 42 A6
Sohryogkham 42 B6
Sohuwala Chak Roln 21 F2
Sohwal 37 E3
Soila 32 C3
Soin 34 B5
Sointhra 31 H4
Sojat 32 C5
Sojat Road 32 C5
Sojitra 64 A1
Sojna 53 F2
Sokhniz 13 G3
Sokpao 61 G1
Solahpet 86 B1
Solan 18 C5
Solankuppam Mel 96 C1
Sollaguda 82 A1
Sollebail 90 D5
Solur 91 H6
Som 50 B3
Somala 92 D5
Somalsar 32 C1
Somanattapum 95 F2
Somanur 95 G5
Somar (C) 19 F2
Somaram 79 H4
Somasi 21 F5
Somavaram 89 E2
Sombe Dzong (B) 40 D2
Someshwar (Utt) 23 H1
Someshwar (Kar) 90 D5
Somna 22 D6
Somnath (N) 25 H6
Somnath (N) 37 H1
Somnath (Guj) 62 D5
Somnath (Guj) 63 F2

Sompeta 82 C4
Somra (M) 43 H6
Somran 32 D2
Somvarpet 94 D1
Son 69 F3
Sonabat (Ba) 41 E4
Sonabera 69 F6
Sonada 40 B2
Sonahatu 57 E5
Sonai 77 E3
Sonaili Bazar 40 A5
Sonaimuri (Ba) 59 H6
Sonala 66 B4
Sonam 59 H5
Sonamarg 13 G2
Sonamukh 60 D2
Sonamukhi (Ba) 59 E2
Sonamukhi 57 H5
Sonapur 70 A5
Sonari (Ass) 43 H2
Sonari (Mah) 77 G5
Sonaria 63 F4
Sonarigaon 43 H1
Sonarpur 72 B1
Sonatala (Ba) 59 E1
Sonath 86 B1
Sonaula 57 H1
Sonbarighat 60 D2
Sonbarsa 38 D3
Sonda (P) 47 G1
Sonda 90 C2
Sondad 68 A3
Sondar 13 H4
Sondo 79 G2
Sondwa 65 E2
Sone Ka Gurja 34 C3
Sonegaon (Mah) 67 F6
Sonegaon (Mah) 77 G5
Sonepat 22 B3
Sonepet 78 A4
Sonepur (Bih) 38 C5
Sonepur (Bih) 38 D5
Songarh 64 C4
Songhpe (M) 44 D5
Songir (Guj) 64 C2
Songir (Mah) 65 E5
Songsak 41 G5
Songsang 61 E2
Songting (C) 29 H4
Songurh 55 E3
Sonhat 55 F5
Soni 35 F3
Soniand 51 E2
Sonkach 52 A6
Sonnapurampeta 82 C3
Sono 57 F2
Sonpur 80 C2
Sonpuri 63 G3
Sonria 71 E4
Sontalai 66 B2
Sonthia 34 A5
Sonua 70 D1
Sonwan 24 D6
Sonwara 50 B1
Sopona 19 E2
Sopur 13 E2
Sorab 90 D3
Sorada 82 B2
Sorah (P) 30 A2
Soraon 37 E5
Sorbhog 41 H3
Soro 71 G4
Soron 23 F6
Sorukot (N) 25 E2
Sorung (N) 39 F2
Sorwa 64 D2
Sosale 95 F2

Sosing 40 B1
Sosonpal 81 E4
Sotha 17 E6
Sothri 48 A6
Sotipura 13 E3
Sotur 13 F3
Sour Bazar 39 G5
South Dum Dum 72 C1
South Salmara 41 F5
Southada 77 F4
Sowar 30 C3
Sowaran 13 G2
Soyet 51 H3
Soygaon 65 G6
Spitok 14 C3
Srang (C) 19 F3
Sravanabelagola 91 G6
Sri Bhadria 31 F2
Sri Chhatarpur 51 H2
Sri Dungargarh 20 D5
Sri Govindpur 17 G3
Sri Kalahasti 93 F4
Sri Karanpur 20 B1
Sri Madhopur 33 G1
Sri Mohangarh 31 F2
Sridharpur (Ba) 59 E6
Srigiripadu 87 G4
Srikakulam (And) 82 A5
Srikakulam (And) 88 B4
Srikhanda 58 B4
Srikonda 79 E5
Srikurman 82 B5
Srimangal (Ba) 60 B3
Srimangala 94 D2
Srimushnam 96 D4
Srinagar (Ba) 59 F4
Srinagar (J&K) 13 F3
Srinagar (Utt) 19 F6
Srinagar (Raj) 33 F3
Srinagar (Utt) 35 H6
Srinagar (Mad) 53 H6
Sringeri 90 D5
Srinivaspur 92 C5
Sriperumbudur 93 F6
Sripur (Ba) 59 G3
Sripur (Ba) 60 A5
Sripur (N) 39 E2
Sriram 69 G6
Sriramagiri 88 C1
Sriramapur 82 A2
Sriramapura 91 G4
Srirangam 96 B5
Srirangapatnam 95 F1
Srirangapur 86 D4
Srisailam 87 F4
Srivalkuntam 99 E4
Srivardhan 76 A6
Sriviliputur 98 D2
Srungavarapukota 81 G6
Stalkari 40 B6
Stok 14 C3
Stur 55 G2
Suadi (N) 24 B2
Suala 14 A6
Suar 23 G3
Suarmar 69 F5
Suatala 53 G5
Subakone (N) 25 F4
Subala 24 B1
Subalong (Ba) 60 C6
Subankhata 42 A3
Subarnagiri 82 A2
Subbuk 28 A5
Subil (Ba) 59 H4
Subrahmanya 91 E6
Subraved 87 H2
Suchetgarh 13 E6
Sudamda 63 F1

Sudasna 50 A3
Sudh Mahadev 13 G5
Sudhagad 76 B5
Sudi 85 G5
Sudimalle 88 A1
Sudrumkupa 70 B6
Sufali (B) 41 H2
Sufi Faqir (P) 30 B6
Sugrai 58 A5
Suguturu 92 B5
Sui 20 D4
Suigam 49 F3
Suisa 57 E5
Sujanagar (Ba) 59 E4
Sujanganj 37 F5
Sujangarh 21 E6
Sujanpur 17 G1
Sujauli 24 C5
Sujawal (P) 47 G2
Sujnipur 49 H4
Sukadhik (N) 24 D2
Sukal 83 E1
Sukcharer (Ba) 73 H1
Suke 51 H2
Sukhair (Ba) 59 H1
Sukhar (N) 24 C4
Sukhara 51 F4
Sukhban 38 A2
Sukhchainpura 20 C2
Sukheke (P) 16 C2
Sukhidhang 24 A3
Sukinda Khas 71 E5
Sukjoro 57 H2
Sukkur (P) 30 A1
Sukma 80 D5
Suktiyal 13 G2
Sulagiri 96 A1
Suldapara 80 D4
Sulgura 70 C2
Sulial 17 H1
Suliapada 71 G2
Sulibale 92 B5
Sulkia Tala 31 H3
Sultababad (Osmannagar)
   79 G5
Sultana 21 G5
Sultanganj (Utt) 35 F2
Sultanganj (Bih) 39 G6
Sultanpur (P) 12 C5
Sultanpur (Pun) 17 F4
Sultanpur (Utt) 23 E1
Sultanpur (Raj) 33 H6
Sultanpur (Utt) 37 E4
Sultanpur (Mad) 52 D5
Sultanpur (Guj) 63 E3
Sultanpur (Mah) 78 A1
Sultbhavi 85 G4
Sulur 95 G5
Suluru 93 F4
Sulya 94 C1
Sum Dzong (C) 28 C1
Sumar 52 A2
Sumar Gompa (C) 19 G2
Sumba 77 H5
Sumbal (J&K) 13 E3
Sumbal (J&K) 13 F3
Sumbar 13 F5
Sumbatse (C) 27 E3
Sumdeo 19 F3
Sumdo (C) 15 F1
Sumdo 19 F2
Sumondolo 82 C2
Sumpawng Mata (M) 45 F4
Sumprabum (M) 45 E3
Sumra 19 E2
Sumsen (M) 75 E2
Sumsi (M) 75 F1
Sumta (M) 45 F5

Sumtse (C) 26 C2
Sunag 85 G4
Sunakhala 82 D2
Sunakhalla 82 D1
Sunam 17 G6
Sunamganj (Ba) 60 A1
Sunauli (N) 37 H1
Sunda (P) 20 B1
Sundagarh 70 A2
Sundarapandiyam 99 E2
Sundarapandiyanpattam
   99 H1
Sundarganj (Ba) 41 E5
Sundarnagar 18 B3
Sundarpahar 57 H2
Sundarpur (Utt) 24 A5
Sundarpur (Mad) 66 B3
Sundarsi 52 A5
Sundra (Raj) 30 D4
Sundra (Mad) 80 B3
Sundrel 52 A6
Sunel 51 H3
Sungarpur 21 G4
Sunger 81 G2
Sungri 18 D4
Sungwa Katu (C) 29 H1
Suni 23 G2
Sunigram 79 G5
Sunksal 90 B2
Sunnambukkulam 93 G5
Sunpura 28 B6
Sunswara 34 B6
Suntikoppa 94 D1
Sunuru 88 D1
Sunwar 50 D1
Sunwara 67 H1
Sunye (M) 74 D6
Supa (Mah) 77 E5
Supa (Kar) 84 D6
Supaul 39 F4
Supe 77 E4
Supegaon 78 B4
Supka (M) 45 E4
Supkhar 68 C2
Sur Singh 17 E3
Suraj Tal 14 C6
Surajgarh 21 G5
Surajgarha 39 F6
Surajpur 55 G5
Suramangalam 96 A3
Surana 31 H6
Surandai 98 D3
Surangi 82 B3
Surapur 37 F3
Suraram 80 A4
Surareddipalem 88 A6
Surat 64 A4
Suratganj 36 D2
Suratgarh 20 C3
Suratkai 90 C6
Surendranagar 49 F6
Surgana 64 C6
Surgun 13 E1
Surgura 70 A2
Surianwan 37 F6
Suriapet 87 G2
Surihan 85 F5
Surir 22 D6
Surimagar 87 E2
Surjagarh 80 B2
Surjahsar 20 C3
Surjannagar 23 F3
Surjanwala 13 E1
Surkhet (N) 24 D4
Surkhi 53 F4
Surla 84 C5
Surngen (M) 75 E2
Suroth 34 B3

Surpalia 32 D1
Surpura 32 A5
Sursand 39 E3
Surtanahu (P) 30 C4
Suru 13 H3
Suruin 13 F6
Surul 76 D6
Surungia 70 A6
Surwaya 34 D6
Suryamal 76 B2
Susing Thach 19 E2
Susner 51 H4
Susnia 57 H2
Sutak 14 C5
Sutatha 72 B2
Suthalia 52 C3
Suthanbatheri 95 E3
Suti 58 B2
Sutlana 32 B5
Sutnga 42 C6
Sutrapara 62 D5
Suvali 64 A4
Suvi 48 D4
Suwasra 51 G3
Swabi (P) 12 A3
Swamihalli 91 G1
Swargdwar (N) 25 F5
Swarghat 18 B4
Swarupkati (Ba) 59 F6
Swarupnagar 58 D6
Swawai (P) 12 A2
Swebaukkan (M) 75 H5
Sya Gompa (N) 25 G3
Syamnagar (Ba) 72 D1
Syampur 72 B1
Syang (N) 25 H4
Syangbatang (C) 26 D1
Syedpur (Ba) 40 C5
Sylhet (Ba) 60 B1

Ta Chai (C) 45 G5
Ta-Nyaung (M) 75 G4
Tabo 19 E2
Tabwin (M) 75 F5
Tabya (M) 75 H4
Tabyin (M) 75 G3
Tachanallur 99 E4
Tachungkaru 15 E4
Tachupa (C) 45 H5
Tachupeng (C) 45 G6
Tada 93 G4
Tadach 63 G4
Tadali 79 G1
Tadana 31 F2
Tadas 90 D1
Tadcharla 79 H5
Tadepallegudem 88 D3
Tadikal 79 G5
Tadikelapudi 88 C3
Tadikonda 88 A4
Tadimari 92 B1
Tadivaripalle 87 G5
Tado 27 F6
Tadoba 67 G6
Tadpatri 92 B1
Tadubi 43 G6
Tadwalla 77 H5
Tafwap 101 H5
Taga Dzong (B) 41 E2
Tagtse Dzong (C) 26 A1
Taharabad 64 D5
Taharpur 76 B2
Tahawndam (M) 29 F5
Tahindesar 20 D6
Tahirpur (Ba) 58 C2
Tahkim (M) 45 G1
Tahli (P) 16 A3
Tahrauli 35 F6

Taihpa Ga (M) 44 D3
Taikri (M) 45 E4
Taimidong (Ba) 60 B6
Tain (P) 12 C3
Tainga (M) 61 H3
Taingapatam 98 C5
Taipudia 27 H6
Tairengpopki 61 E2
Tajipali Gompa (N) 25 G4
Tajjal (P) 30 A3
Tajpur (Ba) 60 A2
Tajpur (Utt) 23 F3
Tajpur (Bih) 38 B4
Tajpur (Bih) 38 B5
Tajpur (Bih) 39 E5
Tajpur (Bih) 40 C6
Tajpur (Mad) 51 H5
Takalghat 67 F5
Takarkhera 66 D5
Takashin 101 G4
Takh 14 C5
Takhatgarh 32 B6
Takhatpur 69 E2
Taki 72 D1
Takipur 58 B3
Takirambari 60 B3
Takkalai 98 D5
Takli (Mah) 77 E3
Takli (Mah) 77 F1
Takli (Mah) 78 B3
Takli (Mah) 78 D1
Takli Dhokeshwar 77 E3
Taktsang (C) 27 E4
Takum 27 E6
Takurgaon (Ba) 40 C4
Takwa 76 C4
Tal (P) 12 A1
Tal 32 D5
Tala (Ba) 58 D6
Tala (B) 41 E2
Tala (Mad) 54 C4
Tala (Mad) 69 G4
Tala (Mah) 76 B5
Talagadadivi 88 C5
Talagang (P) 12 A6
Talai 95 H1
Talainayar Agraharam
   97 E6
Talaivasal 96 B3
Talaja 63 G4
Talakalla 85 H6
Talala 62 D5
Talamanchipatnam 92 C1
Talamba (P) 16 A5
Talanda (Ba) 58 C2
Talang Ga (M) 44 D4
Talao 34 A5
Talarah 17 H1
Talasri 76 A1
Talati 50 B3
Talavada 84 B5
Talavadi 95 F3
Talbandh 71 F2
Talbehat 53 E1
Talbid 84 C2
Talcher 70 D5
Taldangra 57 H6
Talegaon (Mah) 67 E4
Talegaon (Mah) 67 E5
Talegaon (Mah) 76 D2
Talegaon Dabhade 76 C4
Talegaon Dhamdhere
   76 D4
Talekkod 94 D4
Talen 52 B4
Talera 84 B4
Talgaon 84 B4
Talgram 35 H2

Talguppa 90 C3
Talhar (P) 48 A1
Tali 27 F5
Talikota 85 H4
Talin (C) 28 D4
Taliparamba 94 C2
Taljhari 58 A1
Talkher 77 H3
Talkot (N) 24 D2
Tallak 91 G2
Tallapalem 89 F1
Tallaveru 89 E3
Tallui 43 G6
Talluru 88 A4
Talmamadi 86 C1
Talni 78 A2
Talod (Guj) 50 A5
Talod (Mad) 51 G4
Taloda 64 D3
Talodhi 67 H6
Talpada 71 G4
Talpaka (N) 24 B2
Talsana 49 G6
Talsara 70 B1
Talugai 96 B4
Talung Dzong 42 B2
Talupula 92 C3
Talvad 77 E1
Talvada 65 F5
Talwal 77 H3
Talwandi Bhai 17 F5
Talwandi Ghandhrain 17 F4
Talwandi Malak 17 H6
Talwandi Sabo 21 F1
Talwara (Him) 17 H2
Talwara (Raj) 50 D4
Talwara (Mad) 65 F2
Talya 91 F3
Tamantha (M) 74 C4
Tamanthi (M) 44 A6
Tamar 57 E6
Tamarhat 41 E4
Tamarkulam 98 B3
Tamaso 43 E2
Tamasvadi 65 F5
Tamba 85 G2
Tamballapalle 92 C4
Tambarahalli 85 H6
Tambaur 24 C6
Tambeibui 101 F1
Tambesra 51 E5
Tambre Rajuri 77 G4
Tamei 43 E6
Tamenglong 61 E1
Tamia 67 F1
Tamid Arung 27 G3
Tamkhor 21 G4
Tamkhung 43 H4
Tamkuhi 38 B3
Tamlor 30 D5
Tamlu 43 H3
Tamluk 72 A2
Tammampatti 96 B4
Tamoria 39 F4
Tamra 56 B6
Tamsa 78 D3
Tamu (M) 61 G3
Tamulpur 42 A3
Tana 50 D2
Tanakalla 92 B4
Tanakpur 24 A3
Tanda (P) 13 E6
Tanda (Pun) 17 G3
Tanda (Him) 18 B3
Tanda (Utt) 23 F3
Tanda (Utt) 37 F3
Tanda (Mad) 65 F1
Tanda Urmar 17 G3

Tandar 12 D5
Tandarambattu 96 C2
Tanden 28 B5
Tandi 14 B6
Tandianwala (P) 16 B4
Tandikkudi 95 H6
Tando Adam (P) 30 A5
Tando Allahyar (P) 30 A6
Tando Bago (P) 48 A2
Tando Fazil (P) 47 H1
Tando Ghulam Ali (P) 48 A1
Tando Ghulam Haidar (P) 47 H1
Tando Jan Muhammad (P) 48 A1
Tando Muhammad Khan (P) 47 H1
Tando Mittha Khan (P) 30 B5
Tandulvadi 77 H6
Tandur (Mah) 78 B5
Tandur (And) 79 H3
Tandur (And) 86 C2
Tandwa 56 C4
Tangadgi 85 H4
Tangail (Ba) 59 F3
Tangar 13 F5
Tangaturu 93 E3
Tangaturu 93 E3
Tangdhar 12 D2
Tangengs 43 E2
Tanghka (M) 45 F5
Tangi 82 D1
Tangibari (Ba) 59 G5
Tangkrau Ga (M) 44 C4
Tangla 42 B3
Tangmarg 13 E3
Tangsebi (B) 41 G1
Tanin 13 G3
Tanippadi 96 C2
Tankara 63 E1
Tankari 64 A2
Tankaria 64 B3
Tankla 32 C2
Tanko (M) 74 D6
Tankri 22 A5
Tankuppa 56 D2
Tanoria 51 H4
Tanrwa 56 B2
Tansa 63 H4
Tansing (N) 25 H6
Tantnagar 71 E1
Tantpur 34 C2
Tantse 15 E3
Tantwas 32 B2
Tanuku 88 D3
Tanur 94 D5
Tanze 14 C5
Taobat 13 E1
Taoh 22 C2
Taonra 21 E6
Taor Rajar (P) 30 B4
Taoru 22 B5
Tapa 17 G6
Tapaguda 87 E2
Tapan 40 C6
Taparia 69 H2
Tapatzu (C) 29 H5
Tapkara (Bih) 56 C6
Tapkara (Mad) 70 A1
Taplejung (N) 40 A1
Tapong 101 G4
Tappa 52 A6
Tappal 22 D5
Tapra 31 H5
Taptapani 82 B2
Tapukrah 22 B5

Tapun 44 C1
Tarabad 77 E3
Tarabari 41 H4
Tarabganj 37 E2
Taradehi 53 G5
Taradgaon 76 D6
Taragarh (P) 12 B5
Taragupal 79 G6
Tarahti 54 B1
Tarai (P) 47 H2
Tarai 52 D2
Taraia 38 C4
Tarail (Ba) 59 H2
Tarakanda (Ba) 59 F1
Tarakot (N) 25 G3
Tarana 51 H5
Taranga Hill 50 A3
Taranpur 58 A2
Tarapith 58 A3
Tarappi (P) 12 B2
Tarapur (Bih) 57 G1
Tarapur (Mah) 76 A2
Tarapur (Mah) 85 F1
Tarari 38 B6
Taras (Ba) 58 D2
Tarasinghbari (Ba) 60 B5
Tarawat 50 D2
Tarbela (P) 12 B3
Tarbha 69 H5
Tarbor 69 F6
Taregaon 68 C2
Tarenggaon (N) 25 H4
Tarepalli 88 B4
Targaon 84 D1
Taria Sujan 38 B3
Tarigonda 92 D4
Tarikere 91 E4
Tarkalas 78 B3
Tarkeshwar 64 B4
Tarki (P) 12 C5
Tarkulwa 38 A3
Tarla (Raj) 21 H6
Tarla (Mah) 84 C1
Tarla (Mah) 84 C3
Tarlakota 82 B4
Tarlupadu 87 G5
Tarn Taran (P) 16 A4
Tarn Taran 17 F3
Tarna 18 C5
Taro (M) 44 C4
Tarosingi 82 C1
Tarsa Khurd 79 H2
Tarwa 37 G5
Tasahku (M) 45 F1
Tasaing (M) 45 E6
Tasangki 43 F6
Tasgam 13 G2
Tasgaon 84 D2
Tashi Gang Dzong (B) 42 A1
Tashiding 40 B1
Tashigang (C) 26 C5
Tashigang 15 G6
Tashigong (C) 19 H1
Tashindongze 14 A3
Tashtanje (B) 42 B2
Tasrar Sharif 13 E3
Tasubum (M) 44 C4
Tatarpur 22 A6
Tatarsar 20 C1
Tathang (C) 26 A3
Tathni 86 A4
Taticherla 87 F6
Tatkon (M) 61 G4
Tato 27 G4
Tattakarai 95 G3
Tattamangalam 95 F5
Tattapani 55 H4

Tattayyangarpettai 96 B4
Taukkyan (M) 61 F5
Taulihawa (N) 37 G1
Taung Bazar (M) 74 C5
Taungbi (M) 75 H5
Taungbro (M) 74 C4
Taungdaung (M) 74 D5
Taunggyaung (M) 74 D5
Taungni (M) 44 D6
Taungteik (M) 61 F6
Taungtet (M) 75 F4
Taungzu (M) 75 G5
Taunzin (M) 75 H4
Tauria 54 A1
Tavakere 91 G4
Tavarikere 92 A6
Tawai 28 D5
Tawarg 85 H5
Tawipui 60 D6
Tawkzawl 60 D4
Tawmaw (M) 44 C5
Tawnggon (M) 75 F3
Tawngkalawng 74 D2
Tawsalun (M) 75 F4
Tawtaw 60 C3
Tawtha (M) 61 G4
Tawthalin (M) 75 G5
Taxila (P) 12 B4
Tayilar 92 C6
Tayyuru 93 E5
Tazan (M) 75 G2
Tazumuddin (Ba) 73 H1
Tazungdam (M) 29 F5
Tedwa 68 B3
Tegada 80 C6
Teghra 39 E6
Teharka 35 F6
Tehata 58 C4
Tehla 34 C4
Tehri 19 E6
Tehta 56 C1
Teidukhan 60 D3
Teinkaya (M) 61 G4
Teinnyo (M) 74 D5
Tejam 24 A1
Tejgarh 53 G4
Tejrawa 31 E4
Tekadhana 67 E2
Tekari 56 C1
Tekkalakote 86 B6
Tekkali 82 B4
Tekmal 79 E6
Teknaf (Ba) 74 C5
Tekra 31 G2
Telgaon 78 C3
Telhara 66 B5
Teligi 91 E2
Telkapalli 87 E4
Telkoi 70 D4
Tellamura 60 A4
Tellar 96 D1
Telpani (N) 24 D4
Telsang 85 F3
Tembhurni (Mah) 77 F6
Tembhurni (Mah) 77 H1
Temla 65 G3
Tenali 88 B4
Tendua 69 E2
Tendukheda (Mad) 53 F5
Tendukheda (Mad) 53 G5
Tengakhat 44 A1
Tengapania 43 G2
Tengnoupal 61 F3
Teni Allinagaram 98 D1
Tenkasi 98 D3
Tenlaa 101 H6
Tenmalai 98 C4
Tentra 34 C4

Tentulikhunti 81 G3
Teok 43 G3
Teonda 53 E4
Teonthar 54 D1
Teori 32 B3
Tera 48 A5
Terakanambi 95 F3
Terakhada (Ba) 59 E6
Terapur 61 F2
Terdal 85 E3
Terekhol 84 B5
Terevadi 76 B6
Terhagadh 40 A4
Terhatum (N) 39 H2
Terhi Ghat 37 H1
Terkhed 77 H5
Tervada 49 G3
Tetari 37 G2
Tetha 14 C5
Tethaliang 28 C5
Tettu 93 F1
Tetulbaria (Ba) 73 F2
Tevaram 98 D1
Tezgaon (Ba) 59 G4
Tezpur 42 D3
Tezu 28 C6
Thabyedaw (M) 74 C6
Thabyegan (M) 74 D6
Thadia 31 H3
Thadlaskein 42 C6
Thagwa 54 B4
Thaijuari 42 D5
Thair 77 H5
Thakkolam 93 F6
Thakle (N) 40 A3
Thakot (P) 12 B1
Thakurdwara 23 F3
Thakurganj 40 B3
Thakurgarh 70 B5
Thakurmunda 71 E3
Thakurtola 68 C3
Thala 49 F6
Thalara (N) 24 C2
Thalasseri 94 C3
Thalera 33 H6
Thalner 65 F4
Thalora 13 F6
Thamadaw (M) 75 H4
Thamayapeta 89 F2
Thamo 13 H3
Thana (J&K) 13 G5
Thana Bhawan 22 C2
Thana Galol 49 G5
Thana Ghazi 34 A1
Thanagaon 36 C1
Thanala 13 G6
Thanan (M) 61 H2
Thanbya Aing (M) 75 G3
Thandachhari (Ba) 74 B1
Thandar (N) 25 E4
Thandiani (P) 12 B3
Thandla 51 E6
Thane 76 A3
Thanela 13 H6
Thanesar 22 B1
Thang (P) 14 B1
Thangadh 63 F1
Thangaon 76 C2
Thangasseri 98 B4
Thangshu (C) 29 F3
Thangzang (M) 61 G6
Thaniyam 94 D6
Thanjavur 96 C5
Thanlon 61 E3
Thanna Mandi 13 E4
Thannamang 13 E4
Thaola 33 E3
Thara 49 G4

Tharad 49 G3
Tharakot (N) 25 G6
Tharali 19 G6
Tharbitia 39 F4
Tharet 35 F5
Thari (P) 30 A2
Thari Pauni 67 E4
Tharoch 18 D4
Tharochi 12 D4
Tharusar 20 B4
Tharuvana 94 D3
Thaska Miranji 18 A6
Thasra 50 B6
That 31 G3
Thati Kathur 19 F5
Thatri 13 G5
Thatta (P) 47 G2
Thatthi Bhai 17 F5
Thatti Bala Raja (P) 16 A3
Thattinur Ahmad Shah (P)
    12 A4
Thau (M) 61 E6
Thaungdut (M) 61 G2
Thayaung (M) 61 H2
Thayettabini (M) 74 D5
Thayettaw (M) 75 G5
Thaytkon (M) 75 H4
Thekkadi 98 C2
Thekman 37 G5
Then 17 G1
Thengode 64 D6
Thenzawl 60 D5
Theog 18 C4
Theri Sansi (P) 16 D2
Thesi (M) 75 F3
Thethaitangar 70 B1
Thethar 20 D3
Thetkegyin (M) 61 G5
Thetla (M) 61 H3
Theywa (M) 75 G5
Thiak 60 D5
Thichen (C) 28 B2
Thikarda 33 G6
Thikr 65 G2
Thilgaon 55 G5
Thimiri 93 E6
Thimphu (B) 41 E1
Thingfal 74 D1
Thingoang (M) 61 E5
Thingsai 60 D6
Thingsat 60 D3
Thirana 21 E3
Thirot 14 B6
Thirubuvanam 96 D5
Thirukkovilur 96 C2
Thirumatayhapaiem 87 H2
Thiruthuraipundi 96 D6
Thiruvaiyaru 96 C5
Thiruvananthapuram (Triv-
    andrum) 98 C5
Thiruvarur 96 D5
Thitpu (M) 61 H5
Thob 31 H4
Thode 40 C2
Thoha Khalsa (P) 12 B4
Thoi 33 G1
Thoise 14 C2
Thoiya 20 C4
Thol 49 H6
Thonde 14 B4
Those (N) 39 F1
Thotambadu 93 F4
Thoubal 61 F2
Thowbanga 42 D3
Thrissur 95 E6
Thruti 12 D4
Thuamal Rampur 81 G2

Thudialur 95 F4
Thugcha (C) 26 A2
Thuiangpara (Ba) 74 C3
Thunang 18 C3
Thur 50 C2
Thuthibari 37 H1
Tiak 19 F3
Tiamjipet 86 D3
Tiangzup (M) 45 E4
Tibbar 17 G2
Tibi 21 E2
Tibual (M) 61 E5
Tiddim (M) 61 E5
Tiden 101 G5
Tigaon 67 E3
Tiggur 14 D2
Tigiria 70 D6
Tigri 23 E4
Tihar 35 G4
Tijara 22 B6
Tikaitnagar 36 D2
Tikamgarh 53 F2
Tikar (Raj) 33 G5
Tikar (Guj) 49 F5
Tikaria 54 A6
Tikarpara (Ori) 69 G6
Tikarpara (Ori) 70 C6
Tikarpara (Ori) 81 H2
Tikkaballi 70 B6
Tiklik 18 D3
Tikondi 85 F2
Tikota 85 F3
Tikri (J&K) 13 F6
Tikri (Him) 17 H1
Tikri (Har) 22 C3
Tikri Khas 14 A6
Tikrikila 41 F5
Tikse 14 D3
Tikunia 24 C5
Tiladru 88 B2
Tilai 68 C4
Tilairawar 68 B5
Tilakwada 64 C2
Tilani 79 G3
Tilapara 41 H4
Tilara 82 B5
Tilarwan 50 B2
Tilasma 51 G1
Tilda 69 E4
Tildanga 58 A1
Tildega 70 A2
Tilhar 23 H6
Tilin (M) 75 F3
Tilin 19 E2
Tilonia 33 F3
Tilosingi 82 C1
Tilothu 56 A2
Tilvalli 90 D2
Tilwara 31 F5
Timana 63 H4
Timba 50 C6
Timen (C) 26 B2
Timli 18 D6
Timmanayanipet 92 C1
Timmanayudupeta 93 E2
Timmapur 79 F6
Timmapuram 89 E2
Timmaraipet 88 A2
Timmareddipalle 87 G6
Timmasamudram 93 F4
Timpa (C) 27 H2
Timurni 66 C2
Tinai 18 D4
Tindauli 35 F2
Tindivanam 96 D2
Tindu (M) 75 G5
Tindwari 36 B5
Tingawja Ga (M) 45 E5

Tingbu Tingsa (M) 45 G2
Tinghpang (M) 45 F2
Tingjegaon (N) 25 G3
Tingli 86 B2
Tingpa (M) 45 E4
Tiniteo (M) 75 E3
Tinkhang 44 A2
Tinkonia (Ba) 74 C1
Tinmaung (M) 44 A5
Tinsukia 44 A1
Tintilla (Ba) 60 C5
Tinzam Sampa (C) 19 F3
Tipamia 44 A1
Tipkai 41 F4
Tiplai 41 H4
Tipparti 87 G2
Tipri 18 A1
Tiptur 91 G5
Tira Sujanpur 18 A2
Tirap 44 B2
Tirawari 22 B1
Tiricha 14 C1
Tirido 15 E4
Tirkaulia 24 B4
Tirla 65 F1
Tirmalgiri 87 G1
Tirodi 67 H3
Tirora 68 A4
Tirpal 50 C1
Tirtamalai 96 B2
Tirth 85 G1
Tirthahalli 90 D4
Tirthpuri 77 H3
Tirtol 71 F6
Tiruchchendur 99 F5
Tiruchengodu 95 H4
Tiruchirappalli 96 B5
Tiruchuli 99 F2
Tirukkadaiyur 97 E4
Tirukkalikkunram 97 E1
Tirukkattuppalli 96 C5
Tirumakudal Narsipur
    95 F4
Tirumala 93 E4
Tirumalairayan Pattinam
    97 E5
Tirumangalam 99 E1
Tirumani 92 A3
Tirumayam 96 B6
Tirumullaivasal 97 E4
Tirunamanallur 96 D3
Tirunelveli 99 F4
Tiruparan Kundram 99 E1
Tirupathi 93 E4
Tiruppalaikkudi 99 G2
Tiruppanadai 96 D4
Tiruppattur (Tam) 96 B1
Tiruppattur (Tam) 99 F1
Tiruppurur 93 F6
Tiruppullam 99 G3
Tiruppundi 97 E5
Tiruppur 95 G4
Tirur 94 D5
Tirurangadi 94 D5
Tiruttangal 99 E2
Tiruttani 93 F5
Tiruvadanai 99 G2
Tiruvadur 99 F1
Tiruvalla 98 B2
Tiruvallam 93 E6
Tiruvallur 93 F5
Tiruvannamalai 96 C2
Tiruvengadam 99 E3
Tiruvengadu 97 E4
Tiruvennanallur 96 D3
Tiruvettipuram 96 D1
Tiruvidaimarudur 96 D5
Tiruvottiyur 93 G5

Tiruvuru 88 B2
Tisa 13 H6
Tisaiyanvilai 99 E5
Tisgaon 77 F3
Tisi (M) 75 E2
Titabar 43 G3
Titagarh 58 C6
Titalya 40 B3
Titara 38 B4
Tithal 64 A6
Tithwal 12 C2
Titimati 94 D2
Titlagarh 69 G6
Titoi 50 B4
Titron 22 C2
Tittagudi 96 C4
Titup 101 F2
Tiura Pipardhi 55 H2
Tivsa 67 E5
Toba Tek Singh (P) 16 A4
Tocham 79 F2
Toda 63 G3
Toda Bhim 34 B2
Toda Rai Singh 33 G4
Todgarh 32 D5
Todupulai 98 C1
Togamalai 96 A5
Togarakunta 92 A2
Togawas 21 F4
Tohana 21 H2
Tohogaon 79 H2
Tohurowas 13 G1
Toibalewe 101 E1
Toibuebe 101 E1
Tojobum 28 D5
Tokapalle 87 G5
Tokmid 19 F2
Toku 43 F1
Toli (N) 24 D3
Toliasar 20 D5
Tolingmatli (C) 19 H3
Tolo Humma 82 D3
Tolonga 69 H2
Toludur 96 C4
Tomia 56 A6
Tondangi 89 F2
Tondebhavi 92 A5
Tondi 99 H2
Tonduru 92 C2
Tongi (Ba) 59 F4
Tongkyuk (C) 27 H1
Tongpar (C) 29 F1
Tongsa Dzong (B) 41 G1
Tongul 13 H3
Tonhe (M) 61 H2
Tonk (Raj) 33 G4
Tonk (Mad) 51 H6
Tonnallur 98 B3
Tonnur 95 F1
Tonto 70 D1
Tonzang (M) 61 F4
Tonzi (M) 61 H2
Topa (P) 12 C3
Topangtoli 42 B4
Topi (P) 12 A3
Topke Gola (N) 39 H1
Topla (N) 25 E3
Topohanchi 57 F3
Toppur 96 A2
Topputturai 97 E6
Tora 62 D2
Torangallu 86 A6
Tordi 33 G4
Torgal 85 F5
Tori 56 C4
Tori Fatehpur 35 G6
Torkhed 65 E4
Torma Shong (B) 41 H1

Torpa 56 D6
Torpathar 55 F4
Tosbara 21 H4
Tosina 33 E2
Tota Am 23 G2
Totali (P) 12 A3
Totapalle Guduru 93 G3
Toti 13 G5
Totlabasti 42 C3
Tottiyam 96 B5
Tousem 61 E1
Tovarankurichchi 96 A6
Towang 26 B6
Tra (C) 26 A2
Tradum 92 D5
Tragbal 13 E2
Tragtse (C) 26 A4
Trailin 28 C4
Trakuda 63 E2
Tral 13 F3
Tranquabur 97 E4
Trap (C) 26 C3
Trapaj 63 H4
Trashi Rapden (C) 27 F3
Trashi Tongme (C) 26 C5
Trashiling (C) 26 D3
Tre (C) 26 B5
Treba (C) 29 E4
Tret (P) 12 C3
Tribani Ghat (N) 39 F2
Tribeni Ghat (N) 38 A1
Tribeniganj 39 G4
Trigu (C) 26 A4
Trijugi Narayan 19 F5
Triloknath 14 B6
Trimbak 76 C1
Trimo (C) 26 B6
Trimo (C) 26 C4
Trinder (C) 29 G2
Tripunitura 98 B1
Tripurantakam 87 G5
Trisal (Ba) 59 G2
Tro (C) 27 F1
Tromda (C) 26 D3
Trome (C) 27 E3
Truksum (C) 25 H1
Trupchuka (C) 26 D4
Tsadumu 92 B4
Tsale (C) 29 H3
Tsanagyi (C) 29 H1
Tsanang (C) 27 G3
Tsaplaw (M) 44 A4
Tse Kang (M) 26 A6
Tsegyu (C) 26 D2
Tsela Dzong (C) 27 G2
Tsemachi (C) 27 E4
Tseminyu 43 F5
Tshechogling (C) 26 A2
Tsogatsalu 15 F3
Tsogo (C) 27 G1
Tsomoro (C) 26 C1
Tsona Dzong (C) 26 B6
Tsonghai (C) 29 H1
Tsundupalle 92 D3
Tuan 14 B5
Tuensang 43 H4
Tufanganj 41 E4
Tugapur 100 B3
Tuggali 86 C6
Tuibangadam (Ba) 60 C6
Tuibel (M) 61 E5
Tuidang 74 D2
Tuimang (M) 61 E4
Tuipang 74 D2
Tuisen 61 E4
Tuishong 60 C6
Tukkath 60 C4
Tukotigaon (N) 25 G3

Tukrai 51 F1
Tuljapur 77 H6
Tulsihata 40 A6
Tulsipur (N) 25 E5
Tulsipur 37 F1
Tuman 52 D2
Tumba 56 B2
Tumbagad 82 B3
Tumbal 96 B3
Tumbatse (C) 27 H2
Tumbgi 85 H3
Tumbonghka (M) 44 D6
Tumdulvadi 77 H6
Tumgaon 69 E4
Tuminkatti 91 E2
Tumkur (Kar) 86 B3
Tumkur (Kar) 91 H5
Tumlingtan (N) 39 G2
Tummalapenta 93 G1
Tummurukota 87 G3
Tumner 80 D3
Tumpung 42 D4
Tumsar 67 H4
Tumudibandh 82 A1
Tuna 48 C6
Tundi 57 F3
Tundla 35 E2
Tunga 33 H3
Tungaturti 87 G1
Tungdur (C) 26 C5
Tungring 14 B4
Tunguna 13 H6
Tungzang (M) 61 E4
Tuni 89 F2
Tunkawng (M) 45 F5
Tunrikhel (N) 40 A2
Tuntili 33 G3
Tupran 79 F6
Tura 41 F6
Turade 76 B4
Turaiyur (Tam) 96 B4
Turaiyur (Tam) 99 E3
Turekela 69 G6
Turibari 43 H1
Turkapalli 87 E1
Turkaulia 38 B3
Turkauliya 38 C3
Turki 38 D4
Turkwal (P) 12 B5
Turtok (P) 14 B1
Turuvanur 91 G2
Turuvekere 91 G5
Turvihal 86 A5
Tushkadi (Ba) 73 E1
Tutan Banda (P) 12 A1
Tuticorin 99 F4
Tutilawa 56 C3
Tuting 27 H3
Twinlat (M) 75 H5
Tyaga Durgam 96 C3
Tyagli 90 C2
Tyamagondal 92 A5
Tzuchien (C) 29 H6
Tzupa (C) 45 H4

Ube (C) 26 B4
Ubhegaon 67 F3
Ubhrat 64 A5
Uchalon 58 A6
Uchana 21 H2
Uchchangidurgam 91 F2
Uchchhal 64 C4
Uchen 34 C2
Uchkagaon 38 B4
Udainagar 65 H1
Udaipur (Him) 14 B6
Udaipur (Raj) 50 C2
Udaipur (Tri) 60 A4

Udaipur Garhi (N) 39 F2
Udaipura 53 E6
Udaipurvati 21 G6
Udaiyarpalaiyam 96 C4
Udakatla 86 D3
Udala 71 F3
Udalbania (Ba) 74 C1
Udalguri 42 B3
Udampur 79 F3
Udankheri 52 A4
Udankudi 99 E5
Udarband 60 D1
Udawantnagar 38 B6
Udayagiri (Mad) 52 D4
Udayagiri (Ori) 82 B1
Udayagiri (And) 93 E1
Udayapur 53 E4
Udaynarayanpur 58 A6
Uddanapalli 95 H1
Uddhoke 17 F3
Udel 64 A2
Udesar 32 A4
Udgir 78 B5
Udhagamandalam 95 E4
Udhampur 13 F6
Udi 35 F5
Udianpur 13 G5
Udipi 90 C5
Udka 31 F5
Udmal 64 C5
Udoyogiri 80 D6
Udramsar 20 B6
Udrasar 20 D5
Udua 76 B1
Udumalaippettai 95 G5
Udumbanchola 98 C1
Udvada 64 A6
Ugargol 85 F5
Uggi (P) 16 A4
Ughi 17 G4
Ugli 68 A2
Ujalpur 70 A2
Ujhana 21 H2
Ujhani 23 F6
Ujiarpur 39 E5
Ujjain 51 H5
Ujjini 91 F2
Ujlan 31 G3
Ujni 78 B4
Uka Ga (M) 44 B5
Ukai 64 C4
Ukanwala (P) 16 A6
Ukdungle 15 F6
Uker 47 H5
Ukhia (Ba) 74 B4
Ukhrul 61 G1
Ukkali 85 G3
Ukkamba 82 A3
Uklanamandi 21 H2
Ukshi 84 B2
Ukynuoi (M) 45 F4
Ulans 18 A1
Ulapara (Ba) 59 E3
Ularia (Ba) 73 G2
Ulejula (N) 25 E4
Ulhasnagar 76 B3
Uli (C) 29 G5
Ulindakonda 86 D5
Ulipur (Ba) 41 E5
Ullah 79 E3
Ullal 90 C6
Ullapalem 88 A6
Ulubam 42 B4
Ulubaria 72 B1
Ulundurpettai 96 C3
Ulusara (Ba) 59 G3
Ulvi 90 B1
Umala 65 G5

Umanur 80 A3
Umarband 65 F2
Umarga 78 B6
Umargan 76 A1
Umari 50 A3
Umari pr Akola 66 C6
Umaria 54 C4
Umarkhed 78 D2
Umarkot (Mad) 51 H3
Umarkot (Ori) 81 E2
Umarkot (P) 30 C6
Umarte 51 E6
Umba 13 H2
Umbargaon 76 A1
Umbarpada 64 C4
Umbarthana 64 B6
Umberpada 76 B3
Umblibail 91 E4
Umbra 77 E6
Umbraj 84 C1
Umbrane 65 E6
Umdi 85 G2
Umednagar (Raj) 32 B3
Umednagar (Ass) 60 C2
Umedpur (Ba) 73 F1
Umedpur 23 H5
Umedpura 32 B6
Umeta 64 B1
Umia 48 A4
Umling 42 B4
Ummattur 95 F2
Umrad 77 G3
Umrala (Guj) 62 D2
Umrala (Guj) 63 G3
Umraonganj 52 D5
Umred 67 G5
Umreth (Guj) 50 B6
Umreth (Mad) 67 F2
Umri (Mad) 34 C5
Umri (Mad) 35 F3
Umri (Utt) 35 G4
Umri (Raj) 52 C2
Umri (Mah) 78 B3
Umri (Mah) 78 D3
Umri (And) 79 F2
Umsning 42 B5
Un (Utt) 22 C2
Un (Mad) 65 G3
Una (Him) 18 A3
Una (Guj) 63 E5
Unamaru 14 C1
Unanl 37 G3
Unao 35 F5
Unapani (N) 25 E1
Unarsi (Mad) 52 C3
Unarsi (Mad) 52 D3
Unchahra 54 B3
Unchaira 20 C4
Unchaulia 24 A6
Unchawad 52 A6
Undangaon 65 G6
Undi 88 D3
Undirgaon 77 E2
Undu 31 G4
Ungma 43 G4
Unhel 51 G5
Uniara (Raj) 33 F4
Uniara (Raj) 33 H5
Unjha 49 H4
Unnao 36 B3
Upalvai 79 E5
Upla 77 H5
Upleta 62 D3
Upni 20 D6
Uppada 89 E2
Uppal (And) 79 H5
Uppal (And) 86 C5
Uppalada 82 B4

Uppalaguptam 89 E3
Uppalapadu 87 H6
Uppalpadu 92 B1
Uppidamangalam 96 A5
Uppiliyapuram 96 B4
Uppinangadi 90 D6
Uppugunduru 88 A5
Upshi 14 D4
Urakam 95 E6
Uran 76 B4
Uravakonda 91 H1, 92 A1
Urdas 14 A2
Urdigere 91 H5
Urgam 95 H2
Urlana 22 B3
Urmal 81 F1
Urpear 17 H4
Ursar 21 E4
Uruli Kanchen 76 D5
Urun Islampur 84 D2
Usehat 23 G6
Usilampatti 99 E1
Uska 37 G2
Usrahar 35 G2
Ustapal 70 D6
Ustekayalapenta 93 E4
Usur (Mad) 80 C5
Usur (Tam) 93 E6
Utan 76 A3
Utarakosamangai 99 G3
Utaravilli 81 H5
Utami 31 G4
Utkela 81 G1
Utkur 86 C3
Utnur 79 F3
Utolo (C) 45 H3
Utraula 37 F2
Uttamapalaiyam 98 D2
Uttangarai 96 B2
Uttar Faridpur (Ba) 58 D2
Uttar Kashi 19 E5
Uttar Patiata (Ba) 58 D3
Uttar Sal 18 B3
Uttara 100 B4
Uttarpara (Ba) 41 E6
Uttiramerur 97 E1
Uttukkottai 93 F5
Uttur 84 D4
Utukuru 93 G2
Uwagaon (N) 25 F5
Uya (C) 29 F2
Uyushalan Ga (M) 44 C5
Uyyalavada 92 C1

Vada 76 B2
Vada Kalbadevi 84 A2
Vadakkanchery 95 E5
Vadakkevila 98 B4
Vadaku Valiyur 99 E5
Vadal 63 G4
Vadala Bhairoba 77 F3
Vadali 63 E2
Vadalibhu 64 D6
Vadamadurai 96 A6
Vadamala 93 F4
Vadangali 76 D1
Vaddadi 81 G6
Vaddanhal 91 F3
Vadi 76 B5
Vadipatti 99 E1
Vadiperiyar 98 C2
Vadiya 63 E3
Vadnagar 50 A4
Vadodara 64 B2
Vadoli 50 B4
Vadrupnagar 55 H4

Vaduj 84 D1
Vaed 32 B5
Vagaon 77 E2
Vagarpara 95 F2
Vaghotan 84 B3
Vagra 64 A3
Vagrol 49 H3
Vahai 74 D2
Vaikam 98 B2
Vaikkattur 94 D5
Vaimsur 88 B2
Vairag 77 H6
Vairowal 17 F3
Vaishali 38 C4
Vaishno Devi 13 F5
Vaithisvarankoil 97 E4
Vajapur 49 G3
Vajhur 78 B3
Vajiria 64 C2
Vajpur 64 C4
Vajreshwari 76 B2
Vakad 65 G5
Vakadu 93 G3
Vakal 64 B4
Vakav 77 G6
Vakkadar 96 D1
Valabhipur 63 G3
Valaiyapatti 96 A4
Valanadu 96 B6
Valangiman 96 D5
Valappadi 96 A3
Valasna 50 A4
Valatti 96 D2
Valaungpi (M) 75 E3
Valavanni 96 D3
Valha 76 D5
Valia 64 B3
Valigonda 87 F1
Valikandapuram 96 C4
Vallabhnagar 50 D2
Vallam (Tam) 93 E6
Vallam (Tam) 96 C5
Vallam (Tam) 96 D2
Valod 64 B5
Valparai 95 F6
Valpoi 84 C6
Valsa 77 H1
Valsad 64 B6
Valsang 85 F2
Valtoha 17 E4
Valva 84 D2
Vambori 77 E3
Vana 49 G6
Vanbawng 60 D3
Vandal 85 G4
Vandalur 93 F6
Vandheng 60 D5
Vandse 90 C4
Vangaon 76 A2
Vanghmun 60 C3
Vangi 85 G1
Vangte (M) 61 E5
Vani 64 D6
Vaniam (M) 61 E6
Vanike (P) 16 C1
Vanipenta 92 D2
Vanivalasapura 91 G4
Vaniyambadi 92 C6, 96 B1
Vankaner 64 B5
Vankas 76 A1
Vankeshwaram 87 F3
Vankia 63 F2
Vanlaiphai 60 D5
Vano 50 D2
Vanod 49 G5
Vansada 64 B5
Vanthli 62 D4

Vanur 97 E2
Vapi 64 A6
Varadayyapaliyam 93 F4
Varagam 50 B5
Varahi 49 F4
Varakallu 86 D5
Varanasi (Utt) 37 G6
Varanasi (And) 82 A4
Varandha 76 C6
Varangaon 65 H5
Varau Wandh 49 E5
Varavani 99 G2
Vardamankot 87 G1
Vardanapet 79 H6
Vari 77 E2
Variguntapadu 93 E1
Varkala 98 B4
Varkheda 64 D6
Varla 65 F4
Varse 64 D5
Vartej 63 H3
Varthara 62 B2
Varud 65 H6
Vasad 64 B1
Vasali 76 C2
Vasavad 63 E3
Vasco da Gama 84 C6
Vashi 76 B4
Vasind 76 B3
Vaso 64 A1
Vastara 91 E5
Vasurna 64 C5
Vatam 49 G3
Vatambra 85 E2
Vattaikundu 99 E1
Vattanam 99 H2
Vatul 84 B3
Vav 49 F3
Vavania Bandar 48 D6
Vavania 49 E6
Vavi 76 D2
Vawinthu (M) 75 F3
Vayalpad 92 D4
Vayittiri 94 D3
Ved 49 F4
Vedal 93 F6
Vedaranniyam 97 E6
Vedasandur 96 A6
Vedshir 77 H5
Vedullacheruvu 87 F6
Vegamallu 92 B5
Vejalpur 64 C1
Vekaria 63 E4
Velacha 64 B4
Velakavundanpatti 96 A4
Velanganni 97 E5
Velapur 77 F6
Velavadar 63 G3
Veldurti 86 D6
Vellakovil 95 H5
Vellaturu 92 D2
Vellore 93 E6
Vellur 96 A4
Velneshwar 84 A2
Veltur 67 H5
Veludavur 96 D2
Veluduru 87 G4
Velugodu 87 E5
Vemalwada 79 F5
Vembar 99 F3
Vempalle 92 C3
Venadu 93 G4
Vengal 93 F5
Vengannapalem 88 B1
Vengurla 84 B5
Venikatachelam 93 F3
Venkatagiri (And) 92 D5
Venkatagiri (And) 93 E4

Venkatagirikota 92 C6
Venkatapur 87 E2
Venkatapuram 80 B5
Venkatnagar 55 E6
Venur 90 D6
Vepanapalle 92 C6
Veparate 92 C3
Veppantattai 96 C4
Veppur 96 C3
Veraval 62 D5
Verayur 96 C2
Verinag 13 F4
Versara 63 F3
Versova 76 A3
Ves 77 E2
Vesma 64 B5
Vetapalem 88 A5
Vetawa (P) 49 F3
Vettavalam 96 C2
Vettur 98 B4
Vida 77 H4
Vidai 13 F3
Vidapanakallu 91 H1
Vidisha 52 D5
Vidul 78 D2
Vidyanagar 64 A1
Vihari (P) 20 A1
Vijainagar 20 C3
Vijalapuram 92 C6
Vijapur 50 A5
Vijayadurg 84 B3
Vijayanagar 50 B3
Vijayanarayanam 99 E5
Vijayapatti 99 E5
Vijayapuri North (Nagar-
  junakonda) 87 G3
Vijayapuri South 87 G3
Vijayapur 95 G4
Vijayarayi 88 C3
Vijayawada 88 B3
Vijaypur 77 E1
Vikarabad 86 D2
Vikramasingapuram 98 C4
Vikranpur 66 B3
Vikravandi 96 D2
Vilad 77 E3
Vilandai 96 D4
Vilattikulam 99 E3
Vilinjam 98 C5
Villarti 81 E6
Villianur 97 E3
Villupuram 96 D2
Vinchchavad 63 E4
Vinchia 63 F2
Vingur (P) 48 B3
Vinhera 76 B6
Vinjamur 93 F1
Vinjhan 48 A6
Vinnamangalam 96 D1
Vinukonda 87 H4
Viraganur 96 B3
Viraghattam 82 A4
Viralimalai 96 B6
Virambakkam 96 D1
Viramgam 49 H5
Virani 48 B5
Virapalle 92 D3
Virapandi 98 D1
Virapuram 86 B6
Virar 76 A2
Virarajendrapet 94 D2
Viravalli 88 C3
Viravanallur 98 D4
Viravdi 84 D2
Virawah (P) 49 E2
Virbhadra 23 E1
Virdel 65 E4
Virgaon 77 E2

Virichipuram 92 D6
Virpur 63 E3
Virudunagar 99 E2
Virupakelli 95 H6
Virwao 63 E1
Visakhapatnam 89 G1
Visapur (Mah) 77 E4
Visapur (Mah) 84 D2
Visarwari 64 D4
Visavadar 63 E4
Vishalgarh 84 B3
Vishamangalam 96 B1
Vishnupur 57 H5
Visnagar 50 A4
Visnur 87 G1
Vissannapeta 88 B3
Vita 84 D2
Vithalgadh 49 G6
Vithalpur 49 G5
Vittal 90 D6
Viyyampeta 81 H6
Vizianagaram 81 H5
Vommual (M) 61 F5
Vridachalam 96 C3
Vrindavan 34 D1
Vuilu (M) 75 E4
Vuyyuru 88 B4
Vyaparla 86 D4
Vyara 64 C5

Wabagai 61 F2
Wabyan (M) 74 D5
Wada 76 C4
Wadal 63 F4
Wadala (Guj) 48 C6
Wadala (Guj) 62 D2
Wadala Sanduan (P) 17 E2
Wadali 62 D2
Wadan (P) 48 C2
Wadapadhar 48 A5
Wadat Ga (M) 45 E2
Wadbhet 64 D1
Wadegaon (Mah) 66 B6
Wadegaon (Mah) 68 A5
Wadgaon (Mah) 76 D2
Wadgaon (Mah) 77 E6
Wadgaon (Mah) 77 H6
Wadgaon (Kar) 78 C6
Wadgaon (Mah) 84 D3
Wadgaon Sheri 76 C4
Wadgira 86 B3
Wadhi (P) 16 A2
Wadhiware 76 C2
Wadhona (Mah) 67 E5
Wadhona (Mah) 78 C5
Wadhwan 49 G6
Wadi 86 B2
Wadjhire 76 D4
Wadki 67 F6
Wadner 67 F6
Wadner Gangal 66 C5
Wadsar 47 H5, 48 A5
Wadwani 77 H4
Wafgaon 76 D4
Wagah (P) 17 E3
Wagan (M) 75 H3
Wagdari 85 H1
Waghai 64 C5
Waghnagar 63 G4
Wagholi 76 D6
Waghoriya 64 C2
Waghrul 77 H1
Wagrod 49 H4
Wah Cantonment (P) 12 B4
Wahegaon 77 G2
Wahndo (P) 17 E2
Wai 76 C6
Waidhan 55 F3

Waiku (M) 74 D4
Waingmaw (M) 45 E6
Wairagarh 68 A6
Wajidora 50 D5
Wakching 43 H3
Waki 76 C5
Wakri 79 G2
Wakro 28 C6
Wala (M) 44 D5
Walajabad 93 F6
Walajapet 93 E6
Walan 64 B2
Walandi 78 B5
Walawbum (M) 44 D4
Walayar 95 F5
Walgaon 66 D5
Walia (Ba) 58 D3
Walki 77 E4
Walong 28 D5
Walsang 85 H1
Waltair 81 H6, 89 G1
Walterganj 37 G2
Waluj 77 F2
Walunghung Gola (N)
  40 A1
Walur 78 A2
Walvad 77 F4
Walwad 77 G5
Wamanpalli 79 H2
Wamati (C) 45 H4
Wan Radhu Ram (P) 16 C4
Wandhia 49 E5
Wandoor 100 A6
Wandur 95 E4
Wangat 13 F2
Wangchindam (M) 29 F6
Wangda (C) 29 F2
Wangdu Phodrang (B)
  41 E1
Wangi 77 F5
Wangjing 61 F2
Wangla 43 H3
Wango (P) 48 B2
Wangom 13 G4
Wangtu 19 E3
Wanguta (M) 29 F6
Wani 79 F1
Wankal 64 B6
Wankaner 63 E1
Wanlah 14 B3
Wanparti 86 D4
Wansa 44 A2
Wansjalia 62 C3
Wanthali 62 D1
Wapsa Khani (N) 39 G1
War 56 B2
Warangal 79 H6
Waraseoni 68 A3
Warburton (P) 16 D3
Wardha (Mah) 67 F5
Wardha (Mah) 68 A6
Wargam 49 G5
Wargaon 68 A5
Warhona 78 D3
Wari Godri 77 G3
Waris Aliganj 57 E1
Waris 14 C1
Warisnagar 39 E5
Warman 50 A2
Warora 67 G6
Warsa 68 A6
Warsara 49 G3
Warshi (Mah) 78 C4
Warshi (J&K) 14 C1
Warud 67 E4
Warvad 77 F6
Warwala 62 A2
Warwania 65 E2

Waryam (P) 16 A4
Wasa 50 B2
Wasai 50 A4
Wasalmari 87 F1
Wasat (M) 45 F3
Washawng (M) 45 F6
Washim 78 B1
Wasi 77 G5
Wasirabad 87 G3
Waskui 64 B4
Wasna 64 C2
Wataman 63 H1
Watamkawng (M) 29 F6
Watgaon 67 E6
Wathar 76 D6
Wati 28 D5
Watnur 77 F1
Watrap 98 D2
Wawchon (M) 45 G6
Wayingyaing (M) 75 G3
Wazirabad (P) 16 D1
Wazirganj (Bih) 56 D2
Wazirganj (Utt) 23 G5
Wazirpur (Ba) 59 F2
Wazirpur 34 B3
Webula (M) 61 F6
Wedi 79 G2
Wegowal (P) 16 A1
Wehsi (M) 45 E5
Wekria 50 B2
Welaung (M) 75 F3
Welhe 76 C5
Wellington 95 F4
Wer 34 C2
Wetkva (M) 75 G2
Wetmasut (M) 75 H6
Whaikhyang (Ba) 74 C4
Whitefield 92 B6
Wihamandav 77 G2
Wijh (P) 16 A2
Williamnagar 41 G6
Wilsonpur (P) 16 B1
Winmaua (M) 75 H1
Wintong 44 C1
Wirur 79 G2
Wisawari 49 G5
Witung (M) 74 D2
Wodapatti 95 H2
Wokha 43 G4
Wolampalle 80 D6
Wondh 48 D5
Worhanpur 56 D1
Wosithang (C) 29 E2
Wrightmyo 100 B5
Wualu (C) 45 H3
Wuligang (C) 27 E1
Wunwa (M) 75 F6
Wura (M) 44 C6
Wynad 95 E3
Wyndhamganj 55 H3

Ya Nan (M) 61 G3
Yabin (M) 61 H5
Yadagiriguta 87 F1
Yadala 77 H6
Yadgir 86 B3
Yadgud 84 D4
Yadiki 92 B1
Yadiyur 91 H6
Yadvad 85 E4
Yagati 91 F4
Yagrung 28 A5
Yagyi (M) 75 F1
Yairipok 61 F2
Yakalo (C) 29 H3
Yalgaon 84 C2
Yalladabag 91 G5
Yalvigi 90 D1

Yamanpalli 79 H3
Yamgangpokpi 61 G1
Yamsing 27 H5
Yamunanagar 18 C6, 22 C1
Yamunotri 19 E4
Yan 90 B2
Yanam 89 E3
Yangar (N) 24 D1
Yanghel (N) 39 E1
Yankanmardi 84 D4
Yankenchi 85 H3
Yapkel (N) 24 D1
Yar Husan (P) 12 A3
Yargatti 85 E5
Yargol 86 B3
Yarlungto (C) 26 B3
Yarpur 23 H6
Yartak Gompa (C) 29 E2
Yasagyo (M) 61 F4
Yato (C) 26 D4
Yatung (C) 40 D1
Yaval 65 G4
Yavat 76 D5
Yavatmal 67 E6
Yavli 77 G6
Yavluj 84 C3
Yawpani (M) 43 H5
Yaytah 14 C5
Yebarhatti 85 E3
Yebawmi (M) 44 B6
Yechagam 13 E3
Yedapalli 78 D4
Yedatore 95 E1
Yediuk 44 B2
Yedrami 86 A3
Yegyanbyin (M) 74 D6
Yektin (N) 40 A2
Yelahanka 92 A5
Yelamb 77 G4
Yelandur 95 F2
Yelbara 67 E6
Yelbarga 85 H5
Yeldari 85 E2
Yelgonda 79 F4
Yeljal 87 E3
Yellaisharam 87 F3
Yellandu 88 A1
Yellapur 90 C1
Yellareddi 79 E5
Yellatturdibbe 88 C5
Yellur 85 E5
Yenan (M) 61 G3
Yenangyat (M) 75 H4
Yenangyaung (M) 75 H6
Yendigeri 85 F4
Yengji 42 D1
Yenkho (B) 41 F1
Yeola 77 E1
Yercaud 96 A3
Yergara 86 C4
Yerli 66 A5
Yermala 77 G5
Yerrapahad 87 G2
Yerukavale 92 C5
Yerupalem 88 B3
Yerur 93 G3
Yeshwantnagar 91 F1
Yestvantpur 92 A6
Yetagaon (M) 61 F6
Yethpa (M) 44 A6
Yezon (M) 75 H5
Yghtang (M) 29 G6
Yindam (M) 45 G6
Yindamyang (M) 45 E5
Yingku 27 H4
Yinmabin (M) 75 H2
Yipa (C) 29 F2
Yiyu 27 G4

Yoba 27 E6
Yol 18 A2
Yomcha 27 G5
Yomtain 27 E6
Yopong (M) 75 E4
Yortong (C) 28 A3
Yotarok (M) 74 D6
Yuksam 40 B1
Yunrang (M) 45 F4
Yurod 13 G4
Yusmarg 13 E4
Yusuf Badgaon 77 H4
Yuwa (M) 61 G4
Ywamondaung (M) 61 H5
Ywathit (M) 61 H6
Ywathit (M) 75 H4
Ywathitke (M) 74 D6

Zafarabad 37 F5
Zafarwal (P) 17 F1
Zagalnakchan 14 B1
Zagok 15 E4
Zahirabad 86 C1
Zaida (P) 12 A3
Zaidpur 36 D3
Zainabad 49 G5
Zaladanki 93 F1
Zam (C) 26 C3
Zamania 37 H6
Zampi (M) 61 E4
Zang-Imnu (M) 75 E4
Zangaredigudem 88 C2
Zangla 14 B4
Zawal 50 A1
Zawlpi (M) 61 F5
Zawngin 60 D4
Zawngling 74 D2
Zayat (M) 75 G1
Zayu (C) 29 E4
Zehlaung (M) 74 D5
Zeiotaung (M) 75 G2
Zephai (M) 75 E1
Zetang (C) 26 B3
Zibyubin (M) 75 G5
Zingrai 14 D3
Zira 17 F4
Zirapur 52 A3
Ziro 27 F6
Zobawk (Miz) 60 D4
Zobawk (Miz) 60 D6
Zokhua (M) 75 F1
Zong 15 F6
Zopui (Ba) 60 C4
Zorawarganj (Ba) 60 A6
Zozar 14 B4
Zulakallu 87 H4
Zulhami 43 G5
Zuljdor 14 A3
Zungsu (C) 26 B3
Zunheboto 43 G4

BEACHES
Aguada 84 B6
Anjuna 84 B6
Arambol 84 B5
Baga & Calangute 84 B6
Benaulim 84 C6, 90 A1
Betul 90 A1
Bogmalo 84 C6
Chapora & Vegator 84 B5
Chorwad 62 D5
Chowpatty 62 B3
Colva 84 C6
Dumas 64 A5
Hajira 64 A4
Kovalam 98 C5
Nagoa 63 E5
Samudra 63 E5

Tithal 64 A6
Ubhrat 64 A5

CAPES &
HEADLANDS
Cape Bluff 100 B4
Cape Comorin 98 D6
Cape Maud 101 G3
Cape Price 100 B2
Cape Winifred 101 G3
Colaba Point 76 A4
Dalhousie Point 72 C3
Divi Point 88 C5
False Divi Point 88 B5
Foul Point 101 F2
Godavari Point 89 F2
Hog Point 101 F2
Horace Point 101 G4
Jaigarh Head 84 A2
Keating Point 101 F2
Malabar Point 76 A4
Murray Point 101 H5
Narsapatnam Point 88 D4
Palmyras Point 71 G5
Point Stuart 100 B2
Pygmalion Point 101 G6
Ras Muari (Cape Monze)
   (P) 46 D2
Sombrero Point 101 H5

CAVES
Ajanta 65 G6
Amarnath 13 G3
Bedsa 76 C4
Bhaja 76 C4
Ellora 77 F1
Jogeshwari 76 A3
Kanheri 76 A3
Karla 76 C4
Pithalkara 65 F6, 77 F1
Udaigiri 52 D4
Udayagiri & Khandagiri
   71 E6

FORTS & HAVELIS
Agra 35 E2
Aguada 84 C6
Ahmedabad 50 A6
Ahmednagar 77 E3
Ajaigarh 54 A1
Allahabad 37 E6
Alwar 34 B1
Amber 33 H2
Bassein 76 A3
Bharuch 64 B3
Bhuj 48 C5
Bidar 78 C6
Bijapur 85 G3
Bikaner 20 B6
Bundi 33 G6
Champaner 64 C1
Chittorgarh 51 E1
Chunar 55 G1
Dabhoi 64 C2
Daman 64 A6
Daulatabad 77 F1
Deeg 34 C1
Dhar 65 G1
Fort St George 93 G6
Gingee 96 D2
Golconda 87 E2
Gulbarga 86 B2
Gwalior 35 E4
Jaipur 33 H2
Jaisalmer 31 E3
Jhansi 35 F6
Jodhpur 32 B4
Junagarh 62 D3

Kochi 98 A1
Kota 33 H6
Kumbhalgarh 50 C1
Madikeri 94 D1
Maheshwar 65 G2
Mandawar 33 H4
Mandla 68 B1
Mandu 65 G1
Munshiganj
Mysore 95 F2
Narwar 34 D5
Nawalgarh 21 G6
Nellore 93 G2
Orchha 35 F6
Padmanabhapuram 98 D5
Pokaran 31 G2
Pratapgarh 76 C6
Raisen 52 D5
Ramgarh 21 F5
Satara 84 C1
Srirangapatnam 95 F1
Surat 64 A4
Terekhol 84 B5
Thanjavur 96 C5
Tranquebar 97 E5
Udaipur 50 C2
Wankaner 63 E1
Warangal 79 H6

ISLANDS
Amala 76 A3
Andaman 100,101
Anderson 100 B3
Appa Tivu 99 G3
Balda 62 B1
Bangaduni 72 C3
Baratang 100 B4
Barren 100 D4
Batti Malv 101 F2
Bela 49 E4
Boat 100 A6
Bompoka 101 G3
Bulcherry 72 C3
Cabra 101 H5
Camorta 101 G4
Car Nicobar 101 F2
Chanch 63 G5
Churma (P) 46 D1
Cinque 100 B6
Colebrooke 100 B4
Dalhousie 72 C3
Defence 100 A5
Donmanick (Ba) 73 G2
East 100 B2
Elephanta 76 A4
Flat 100 B4
Gondhia 62 B1
Great Nicobar 101 H6
Great Coco 100 C1
Halliday 72 C3
Havelock 100 B5
Henry Lawrence 100 B4
Interview 100 A3
Island of Bet 62 B1
Isle of Man 101 H3
Jar 62 B1
Jegri 63 G5
John Lawrence 100 B5
Karumbhar 62 B1
Katchall 101 G4
Katubdia (Ba) 74 B3
Khadir 48 D4
Khanderi 76 A4
Kondul 101 G6
Kyd 100 B5
Lakshadweep 94 A3-C6
Landfall 100 B2
Little Andaman 101 E1

Little Coco 100 C1
Little Nicobar 101 G5
Long 100 B4
Lothian 72 B3
Maheskhali (Ba) 74 B3
Manpura (Ba) 73 H2
Meroe 101 G5
Middle Andaman 100 B4
Musal Tivu 99 H3
Nagaram 89 E4
Nallatanni Tivu 99 G3
Nancowry 101 G4
Neill 100 B5
New 72 B3
Nicholson 100 B5
Nicobar 101
Nora 62 B1
North Andaman 100 B2
North Brother 101 F1
North Button 100 B4
North Hatia (Ba) 73 H1
North Passage 100 B4
North Reef 100 B3
Outram 100 B4
Pachham 48 C4
Paget 100 B2
Panera 62 B2
Panikota 63 F5
Parlob 100 B4
Passage 100 B6
Peel 100 B5
Petman 100 B5
Piran 63 H3
Pirotan 62 C1
Putney (Ba) 73 E3
Rabnabad (Ba) 73 G2
Reef 100 B2
Ritchie's Archipelago
   100 C5
Rutland 100 A6
Sagar 72 B3
Sandwip (Ba) 74 A1
Sandy 100 A5
Shahbazpur (Ba) 73 G1
Shial 63 F5
Short's 71 H5
Sir Hugh Rose 100 B5
Smith 100 B2
Snark 100 B3
Sonadia (Ba) 74 B3
Sound 100 B3
South Andaman 100 B5
South Brother 101 F1
South Hatia (Ba) 73 H2
South Sentinel 101 E1
Spike 100 B4
Square Rocks 84 B5
St George's 84 B6
Stewart 100 B3
Table 100 B2
Talairi Tivu 99 G3
Tarmugli 100 A6
Tekra 48 D6
Teressa 101 F4
The Sisters 100 B6
Tillanchong 101 G3
Treis 101 G5
Trinkat 101 G4
Twins 100 A6
Uputtani Tivu 99 F3
Van Tivu 99 F4
Vengurla Rocks (Burnt Is)
   84 B5
Vilangu Shuli 99 F3
Vypin 98 A1
West 100 B2
Wheeler 71 H5
White Cliff 100 B2

Wilson 100 B4

MOSQUES
Ahmedabad 50 A6
Ajmer 33 E3
Ayodhya 37 E3
Bharuch 64 B3
Bhopal 52 C5
Bijapur 85 G3
Champaner 64 C1
Gaur 58 B1
Gulbarga 86 B2
Gwalior 35 E4
Hyderabad 87 F2
Jaunpur 37 F5
Mandu 65 G1
Nagore 97 F5
Pandua 57 C5
Sarkhej 50 A6
Sarnath 37 G6
Sonargaon 59 G4
Varanasi 37 G6

MOUNTAINS & PASSES
Abroka Pass 28 A4
Abu Hills 50 A2
Agastya Malai 98 C4
Ajanta Plateau 78 A1
Ajanta Range 66 A6
Akla 55 F4
Akrani Hills 64 D3
Albaka Hills 80 B5
Alech Hills 62 C3
Alwar Hills 22 A6
Ambagarh Hills 67 G4
Anamalai Hills 95 F6
Andipatti Hills 99 E1
Andra Pass 28 B3
Ane La 15 F3
Anginda 95 E4
Arakan Yoma (M) 75 E4
Argaon 65 G4
Armalang 40 B1
Ashang Kang Pass (C) 26 D2
Assam Shiwalik 42 D2
Astamba Dongar 64 D3
Ata Kang Pass 28 D3
Athara Mura Range 60 B3
Athmallik Hills 70 B5
Badami Hills 85 G5
Badrinath 19 G5
Bagalkot Hills 85 F4
Bagh Hills 65 E2
Baghelkhand Plateau 55 E4
Bailadila 80 D4
Bailadila Hills 80 C5
Baisha Pass 28 A5
Balaghat Range 77 G4, 78 B5
Bam Pass (C) 29 H2
Bamra Hills 70 B4
Bandarpunch 19 F4
Banihal Pass 13 F4
Banori 68 A1
Baorli Hills 32 A4
Barail Range 42 C6
Baralacha La 14 C6
Barda Hills 62 C3
Barkuar Dongar 55 G6
Barwani Hills 65 E3
Bastar Hills 80 C3
Bau La (C) 19 G2
Baudh Plain 70 A5
Bawangaja 65 F2

Bayana Hills 34 B2
Bazit Pass (C) 45 H1
Beda Pass (C) 29 G3
Bela Pass (C) 29 F3
Belak 19 F5
Belgaum Plateau 84 D5
Beshive Hill 100 B4
Betul Plateau 66 D2
Bhamangarh 54 D6
Bhander Range 54 A4
Bhiwani Bagar 21 G3
Bhopal Plateau 52 C5
Bichakhani Pahar 70 D3
Bija Pahar 54 D6
Bijawar Hills 53 G2
Biligri Rangan Hills 95 G3
Bimbi Pass (C) 27 E4
Bina Plateau 53 E3
Birmitrapur Hills 70 B1
Bison Hill 88 C1
Black Mountain (B) 41 G1
Black Mountain (P) 12 B1
Blue Mountain 74 D1
Bodamalai Betta 95 G3
Boizardin La 15 G6
Bomdi La 42 C2
Bonai Hills 70 C3
Bongru Pass (C) 19 H1
Brahmagiri 94 C1
Budil Pir Pass 13 E4
Buja Gutta 79 F5
Bulbul 56 B4
Bum La 26 B6
Bumhpa Bum (M) 45 E3
Burzil 13 F1
Camele Hump 94 D4
Chaduva Katrol Range 48 B5
Chaifil Tlang 60 D4
Chak Pass (C) 26 A1
Chakhure (N) 25 F3
Chamkang (C) 15 G2
Chandigarh Choalam 17 H3
Chandragiri 79 H6
Chang Chenmo 15 F3
Chang La 14 D3
Chang Pass 15 G5
Changlung La (C) 15 F2
Chappan Hills 50 D2
Chatchara 60 C3
Chaukan Pass (M) 45 E2
Chaundkai (P) 12 A1
Chaur 18 C5
Chenghehishon 43 E4
Cheru Konda 81 E6
Cheti Pass 28 D3
Chhapanka Pahar 31 H6
Chhuri Hills 69 G1
Chikodi Range 84 D4
Chilung La 14 A3
Chimur Hills 67 G6
Chin Hills (M) 75 E2
Chindwara Plateau 67 E2
Chitor Hills 51 E2
Chitroli Hills 80 B1
Chitteri Hills 96 B3
Chitung Bum (M) 44 D5
Chorbat Pass 14 B1
Chota Nagar Plateau 55 H5
Chota Nagpur 56 A4
Chota Udaipur Hills 64 C1
Chulam Pass 28 D6
Chungan La (C) 15 F3
Churen Himal (N) 25 G4
Churia Range (N) 24 C4, 38 D1
Chutupalu Ghat 56 C4

Coorg Plateau 94 D2
Dalma Range 57 F6
Dama Pass (C) 29 E2
Daman i koh 57 H2
Damoh Plateau 53 H4
Dandarmal 50 B3
Danta Hills 50 A3
Dantewara Plateau 80 D4
Darka La (B) 41 E2
Daru Pass (M) 45 E4
Dehra La (C) 15 F1
Deo Dongar 82 B4
Deo Tibba 18 C2
Deogarh 55 F5
Deogarh Hills 55 E5
Deogarh Upland 57 G2
Deosai 13 G1
Devar Malai 98 C3
Dhar 66 C4
Dhaulagiri (N) 25 H4
Dhinodhar 48 B5
Dhola Range 48 B5
Dhundi 63 E4
Dhupgarh 67 E1
Digar La 14 D3
Diphu Pass 29 E5
Do Pass (C) 29 G3
Doda Betta 95 F4
Domjor La (C) 15 G3
Dosheng Pass (C) 27 H2
Dre Pass (C) 29 F3
Dru Pass (C) 29 H1
Druk Pass (C) 26 C4
Dumka Upland 57 H2
Dunagiri 19 H5
Dundwa Range (N) 25 F6
Dzogu Pass (C) 28 D4
East Ladakh Plateau (C) 15 G1
East Manipur Hills 61 G3
Ellora Hills 77 G1
Erinpura Hills 50 B1
Erramala 86 C6
Fatu La 14 B2
Fenshuiling Pass (M) 45 H5
Gaikhuri Hills 68 A4
Gali Konda 81 G5
Galna Hills 64 D5
Gamalong Pass (M) 29 E5
Gandhamardan Parbat 69 G5
Ganga Ghat 57 E5
Gaurloir Baba Pass 25 F6
Gawilgarh Hills 66 C4
Gigi Pass (M) 45 H2
Giden Mata 32 D5
Gir Range 63 D4
Giridih Upland 57 F3
Girnar 62 D4
Girnar Hills 62 D4
Glei Pass 28 D5
Goaldes 70 C6
Gokak Hills 85 E4
Golapalle Plateau 80 C6
Golconda Plateau 86 D1
Gomokong Pass (C) 26 A5
Gondwara Hills 54 A6
Gongso Pass (C) 29 G1
Gopalswami Betta 95 E3
Gorakhnath 62 D3
Great Karakoram (C) 15 F1
Gulgupat 56 A4
Gundalamma Konda 89 E1
Guru Shikhar 50 A2
Gurusa Taung (Ba) 60 C6
Gwanagarh 19 F6
Gyala Lamp Pass (C) 26 D5
Gyala Peri (C) 27 H1

Gyandro Pass (C) 26 C5
Habo Hills 48 B5
Haramukh 13 F2
Harishandra Range 76 C3
Hathi Parbat 19 H5
Haunman 64 D5
Hazaribah Plateau 56 C3
Himalaya Range (N) 39 E1
Hingoli Hills 78 B2
Hiunchuli Patan (N) 25 F4
Hman Taung (M) 61 G4
Horlam La 15 E5
Horti Hills 85 G2
Hoshiarpur Choalan 17 H2
Hpungan Pass 44 D1
Hutti Plateau 86 A4
Impagat 86 C1
Indravati Plateau 81 F3
Irchik Dakhru 29 E5
Israna 32 A6
Jagtial Hills 79 F5
Jairaj 50 A2
Jalangpat 55 H5
Jalep La 40 C1
Jalori Pass 18 C3
Jamkhandi Hills 85 E4
Jampai Tlang 60 C4
Jantia Hills 42 C6
Japvo 43 F6
Jara Pass 15 H6
Jari Mura 60 B4
Jaswantpura Hills 49 H1
Jatang 100 B5
Javadi Hills 96 B1
Jhalawar Plateau 51 H3
Jhura 48 B5
Johgjit Pass (C) 45 H1
Juk Pass (C) 29 E3
Jyorong Pass (C) 29 H2
Kabaldurga 95 G1
Kabru 40 B1
Kadusam 28 D4
Kaimur Hills (Mad) 54 A5
Kaimur Hills (Utt) 55 H2
Kaimur Plateau 55 H2, 56 A2
Kaksel La 15 E4
Kalawali Rohi 21 F1
Kale Pass (C) 26 B4
Kalel (P) 12 A1
Kalianpur 52 D3
Kalibhit Hills 66 D2
Kaling Konda 81 F6
Kalrayan Hills 96 B3
Kalsubai 76 C2
Kalsuban Range 76 C2
Kamaiti Pass (C) 45 G6
Kambakkam Drug 93 F4
Kamet 19 G4
Kamri 13 F1
Kanaka Hills 70 D6
Kanara 62 D4
Kanchenjunga 40 B1
Kandenmarai 86 C1
Kangri Karpo 28 A3
Kangri Karpo Pass 28 C2
Kangto (C) 26 C6
Kanjarda Plateau 51 F2
Kanzam La 18 C1
Kaolikong Shan (C) 45 H6
Kappa Konda 81 F6
Kara Dongar 48 C4
Kargong Pass 27 G4
Karkang Pass (C) 26 B4
Karma Pass (C) 28 A1
Karu Pass (C) 26 A5
Karunjhar Hills (P) 49 E3
Kauntel Plateau 51 F3

Kaya Pass 28 D4
Kedarnath 19 G5
Kelingon 28 C4
Kennedy Peak (M) 61 F5
Keonjhar Plateau 70 D3
Ketamma Parvatam 81 G5
Kha Karpo Range (C) 29 G4
Khamar Pat 56 B4
Khammam Plateau 88 A2
Khan Tlang 60 C4
Khankhadaung (M) 74 C3
Kharagpur Hills 57 F1
Kharch (C) 26 A5
Khardung La 14 D2
Khasi Hills 42 A5
Kheri La (C) 19 G2
Khertri Hills 21 H5
Khichiwara Plateau 52 B1
Khondamal Hills 70 A6
Khondan Hills 81 F4
Khung (N) 25 G2
Kiagar La 15 E5
Kidarkanta 19 E4
Kinnaur Desh 19 F4
Kinnaur Kailash 19 E3
Kodarma Plateau 56 D2
Kokar Pass (C) 26 A2
Kolahoi 13 F3
Kolhan Upland 71 E2
Kollaimalai Hills 96 B4
Kondavidu 88 A4
Kongbo Pa Pass (C) 26 C1
Kongmo Pass (C) 26 D4
Konka La (C) 15 G1
Korea Hills 55 E5
Kottai Malai 98 D2
Koubru 61 F1
Kucha Pass (C) 27 G2
Kue Pass 28 C5
Kukrai Plateau 67 H2
Kumba Pass (C) 26 C2
Kumjawng Pass (M) 29 E5
Kumong Bum (M) 45 E5
Kun 14 A3
Kunda Hills 95 E4
Kungi La 14 A3
Kunu Valley 34 C5
Kunzang 14 D2
Kusumbani 71 F3
Kutch Hills 48 B5
Kya Pass (C) 29 H3
Kyet Taung (M) 61 G6
Kylas 41 G6
Kyung Pass 27 G4
Kyyur La (C) 19 H3
Lachalung La 14 D5
Laikot 43 F6
Lakhong Pass (C) 26 C3
Lakhpat Hills 48 A4
Lalsot Hills 34 A3
Lamar Pass (C) 29 G2
Lang Pass (C) 27 F3
Langtarai Range 60 B3
Langya Pass (C) 29 F4
Lenak La 15 F6
Lepa Pass 28 D3
Letha Range (M) 61 F5
Letha Taung (M) 61 H5
Lha Pass (C) 29 E3
Lohardaga Ghat 56 B5
Loiching 61 F2
Lokzhung Range (C) 15 G1
Lonak La (C) 15 G2
Loymye Bum (M) 44 C5
Lumbang La (C) 15 G2
Lung Pass (C) 26 C2
Lunghpa Bum 44 C1

Lungpon Chin 61 F3
Lusha Pass 27 H2
Madugula Kondas 81 F6
Mahaban (P) 12 A2
Mahabharat Range (N)
	38 D1
Mahadeo Hills 67 E2
Mahandra Giri 98 D5
Mahona 55 E5
Maikala Plateau 54 C6
Maikala Range 54 C5
Majala 84 D3
Makurti 95 E4
Malabar Uplands 94 D3
Malakanagiri Plateau 81 E5
Malandral (P) 12 A2
Malawar Plateau 52 B4
Malayagiri 70 D4
Mallavaram Hills 80 B6
Mana 19 H5
Mandav Hills 63 E2
Manirang 19 E2
Mankarnacha 70 D3
Maphitel 61 G1
Marang La 14 D5
Margor (N) 25 E1
Marpha 54 B1
Marsimik La 15 F3
Mata Pass (C) 26 B4
Matheran Hills 76 B3
Mathwar Hills 64 D3
Matsihku Bum (M) 45 E2
Medok Pass (C) 19 G1
Megasini 71 F3
Mewar Hills 50 B2
Miao Bum 44 C1
Mikir Hills 42 D4
Mira Pass (C) 27 F2
Miraj Hills 85 E2
Mirzapur Hills 55 F1
Mohadev 13 F3
Mohan 55 G5
Mol Len 43 H6
Moling 27 H4
Morena Plateau 34 B5
Mt Victoria (M) 75 F4
Mowdok Taung (Ba) 74 C3
Mt Diavolo 100 B3
Mt Thuillier 101 H6
Mudkhed Hills 78 D3
Muging La 19 F4
Mukandwara Hills 51 G1
Mukhalingam 82 A5
Mukut Himal (N) 25 H4
Mul Hills 79 H1
Murali Soru 82 B1
Mussoorie Range 18 D5
Myimo Chomo (C) 28 C2
Nag Tibba 19 E5
Nag Tisba Range 18 C5
Naga Hills 43 G5
Nagalpuram Hills 93 F4
Nagari Hills 93 F4
Nagarjuna Plateau 87 F4
Nalgonda Plateau 87 F2
Nallamala 87 F4
Namja (N) 25 F1
Namjagbarwa (C) 27 H2
Namni Pass (M) 29 F5
Namphu Pass (C) 27 G1
Nanaghat Pass 76 C3
Nand Kot 19 H6
Nanda Devi 19 H6
Nandivela 63 E5
Nauko Vum (M) 61 F4
Nauzuarzo Tlang 61 F4
Nayagarh Hills 82 D1
Nechen Kangri 28 D3

Nelliampathi Plateau 95 F6
Nila La 14 C2
Nilgiri Hills 95 E4
Nilgiri Range 71 F4
Nilua Hills 49 E4
Nishankonda 87 H6
Niti 19 H4
Niva Dongar 64 D6
Noepeji (M) 61 G5
Nokrek 41 F6
North Cachar Hills 42 C6
North Sahyadri 64 C6
Nun 14 A3
Nyenchen Kangri (C) 28 B2
Osam 62 D3
Pa Wa Pass (M) 45 G5
Pachamalai Hills 96 B4
Painlon Pass 28 C5
Pakhal Hills 80 A6
Palani Hills 95 H6
Palghat Hills 95 F5
Pali Plain 32 B5
Palni Hills 98 C1
Pangong Range 15 F4
Papikonda 88 C2
Parang Pass 19 E1
Parasgaon Plateau 80 C1
Parasnath 57 F3
Patkai Bum 44 C1
Pavagarh 64 C1
Payan Ghat 66 B5
Paze Pass (M) 29 F5
Pen La (C) 26 C6
Pendra Plateau 55 E6
Pensi La 14 A3
Periyar Plateau 98 C1
Phalut (N) 40 B2
Photi Pass 15 G6
Pir Panjal Pass 13 E4
Pir Panjal Range 14 A6
Pir Panjal Range 13 F4
Pir Parbati 18 D3
Poat La 14 B5
Pochamgat 86 D2
Polokongka La 15 E5
Ponnyadaung (M) 61 G5
Porahat Hills 56 D6
Potu 27 G6
Puba Pass (C) 29 E1
Punch-Riasi Hills 12 D4
Pungpung Pass 28 B2
Pungra Bum (M) 44 B3
Purabiya Plain 37 G5
Purandhar Hills 76 C5
Purulia Upland 57 E5
Pusad Hills 78 D2
Pushpagiri 94 C1
Qizil Dawan (C) 15 G1
Raichur Plateau 86 B4
Raigarh Plateau 68 B2
Raja Mayang 42 B4
Rajagarh Plain 21 G5
Rajgir Hills 56 D1
Rajmahal Hills 57 H2
Rajpipla Hills 64 C3
Ramgarh 55 G6
Rampa Hills 88 D1
Ranchi Plateau 56 C5
Ranthambhor Plateau
	34 A5
Ranwe Pass (M) 45 G2
Rasi La 14 A2
Rasibung 61 G1
Rati Gutta 79 E5
Ratong Pass (C) 29 G1
Rayalasima Plateau 86 B5
Rengma Hills 43 E4
Rewa Plateau 54 B2

Rewari Upland 21 H6,
	22 A5
Rirapphasi (C) 29 F4
Roberung 14 C4
Rohtang La 18 C1
Saddle Peak 100 B3
Sadura Giri 99 E2
Sagar Plateau 53 E4
Sagbara 64 C3
Sajum 15 F5
Sakhan Tlang 60 B3
Salher 64 D5
Salsal La 15 F6
Samla (N) 25 E3
Sanchi Hills 52 D4
Sangpang Bum (M) 44 B3
Sanjib Konda 89 F1
Sankha (N) 24 D1
Saramati 43 H5
Saranda Hills 70 C2
Sarkala 63 E4
Sasa 63 E4
Saser Kangri 14 D1
Saser Pass 14 D1
Sasser Muztagh 14 D1
Sasser Pass (C) 14 D1
Satmala Plateau 79 F2
Satopanth 19 G4
Se La 42 B1
Sechen Pass (C) 28 A1
Sehula (N) 25 G3
Sele La (B) 40 D2
Sersank Pass 14 B5
Shaboto Pass (C) 26 C4
Shahpur Hills 86 B3
Shamda Pass (C) 26 A3
Sharkhalep Pass (C) 26 A4
Sherpai 42 D6
Shetrunja 63 G4
Shilla 19 E1
Shillong Plateau 42 A5
Shilung La 15 F3
Shimla Hills 18 B4
Shingi 76 C4
Shingo La 14 B6
Shivalingapa 78 D4
Shivpuri Plateau 34 C5
Shiwalik Range 23 F2
Shoka Pass (C) 27 G3
Shukpa Kunchang 14 D1
Shuta Pass (M) 45 H3
Sibu Sharkong (C) 29 E1
Sikkim Himalaya 40 B1
Simdega Plateau 56 B6
Singi La 14 B3
Singingarh 54 D5
Singoli Plateau 51 F1
Sinthan Pass 13 G4
Sir Sir La 14 B3
Sirpur Hills 79 G2
Siruhi Kashong 43 G6
Siwana Hills 31 H5
Sojat Hills 32 D5
Sola Singhi Range 18 A3
Sonabera Plateau 69 F6
Sondwara Plateau 51 F4
Sonpar Hills 55 E3
Sonsagar 84 D6
South Brahmaputra Hills
	42 B5
Southern Ghats 98 C2
Srimant Gudda 85 G6
Srisailam Plateau 87 F4
Su Pass (C) 28 A1
Sudda Koppu 93 E3
Suket Hills 18 B4
Sunda 49 H2

Sundagarh Hills 70 A2
Sur Taung (M) 75 F6
Surantal 52 D3
Surjagarh Hills 80 B2
Tak Pass (C) 26 C4
Takmak 76 A2
Takpa Shiri 26 D5
Talpula Gutta 79 F4
Talu Pass 29 E5
Talung 40 B1
Tamunga (M) 61 G2
Tanglang La 14 D4
Tawang Bum (M) 44 D2
Telangana Plateau 79 F6
Telekon La 14 D5
Temo Pass (C) 27 G2
Teshkar Pass (C) 26 B2
Thana Hills 76 A2
Thangjing 61 E2
Thari Patan (N) 25 E3
Thatsong La 15 F3
Thepa La 40 C1
Tikarpara Range 70 C5
Tith Zarbo La 15 E5
Togtung Marpo La (C)
	15 G3
Tondu Pass (C) 29 G4
Tong Pass (C) 29 G4
Torgar Pass (C) 26 B5
Toridwari (N) 25 F4
Torna 76 C5
Trabgal Pass 13 E2
Trakge Pass (C) 29 E2
Trango Pass (C) 26 A2
Trikut Parvat 57 G2
Trisul 19 H6
Trome Pass (C) 27 E2
Tsaka La 15 F5
Tsang Chok La 19 F4
Tsang Kang Pass 28 C3
Tsema Pass (C) 29 G4
Tsong Pass (C) 29 F4
Tum Pass 27 G3
Tung Wang Pass (C) 29 G5
Tunga Pass 27 G3
Tunka La (B) 41 H2
Turer 56 A5
Udaipur Hills 69 H1
Umasi La 14 B4
Umatwara Plateau 52 A5
Umba Pass 13 H2
Vagad Hills 48 D5
Vaitarna Plateau 76 B2
Varar 48 B5
Varushanad Hills 98 D2
Velikonda Range 93 E1
Venu 62 C3
Vidisha Plateau 52 D3
Vijatanagar Plateau 85 G6
Vijayawada Hills 88 B3
Vindhyachal Range 54 B1
Vindhyan Scarpland 53 H3
Vinukonda 87 G4
Vorjing 27 G5
Wahao Pam (M) 45 G3
Warangal Plateau 79 G6
West Manipur Hills 61 E3
West Palamu Hills 55 H3
Yakko 43 H4
Yaksang Pass (C) 26 A4
Yavatmal Plateau 66 D6
Yonggyap Pass 28 B3
Yuko Pass (C) 29 E2
Zanskar Mountains 14 A3
Zanskar Range 13 H2
Zato Pass (C) 19 G1
Zhasha Pass (C) 29 F4
Zikyen Pass 28 A3

Zoji La 13 G2

**NATIONAL PARKS
& WILDLIFE
SANCTUARIES**
Anamalai 95 F6
Bandhavgarh 54 C4
Bandipur 95 F3
Bondla 84 C6
Chanraprabha 55 G1
Chhanga Manga Forest (P)
	16 D4
Corbett 23 F2
Cotigao 90 B1
Dachigam 13 F3
Darrah 51 H1
Gajner 20 B6
Guindy 93 G6
Hazaribagh 56 D3
Jaldhapara 40 D3
Kawal 79 F3
Kaziranga 43 E3
Keirul-Lamjao 61 F2
Keoladeo Ghana 34 C2
Kanha 68 B2
Khaptada (N) 24 C2
Little Rann of Kutch 49 F5
Madhav 34 D6
Manas 41 H3
Melghat 66 B4
Molen 84 D6
Mudanthurai 98 D4
Mudumalai 95 E3
Nagarhole 94 D2
Nar Sarovar 49 H6
Nawegaon 68 A4
Orang 42 C3
Pakhal 80 A6
Palamau 56 B4
Parambikulam 95 F6
Periyar 98 C2
Point Calimere 97 E6
Rajali 18 D6
Rajendrapur 59 G3
Ranganathitoo 95 E1
Ranthambhor 34 A4
Rara (N) 25 E2
Royal Chitwan (N) 38 B1
Royal Dharpatan (N) 25 G4
Royal Shukla Phat (N)
	24 A4
Sariska 34 A1
Sasan Gir 63 E5
She-Pholsundo (N) 25 F3
Similipal 71 F3
Sonai-Rupa 42 C2
Srisailam 87 F4
Sunderbans 72 C3
Sunderbans (Ba) 73 E2
Thattekkad 98 B1
Vedantangal 97 E1
Velavadar 63 G2
Wandoor 100 A5
Wynad 95 E3

**RIVERS, LAKES &
BAYS**
Achankovil 98 C3
Adh 55 F2
Adhwara (N) 39 E2
Adyar 93 F6
Adzom 28 B3
Agar 68 D2
Agashi Bay 76 A2
Aheli 34 B6
Ahneya 35 G3
Ahui 28 B4

Aiyar Reservoir 57 E4
Ajay 57 G2, 57 H4
Aji 63 E1
Alaknanda 19 F6
Alanka 71 F6
Aleru 87 F1
Alwara Tal 36 C6
Amanat 56 B3
Amaravati 95 H5, 95 G6
Amba 76 B4
Ambika 64 A5
Ami 37 G3
Anchar Lake 13 E3
Andhari 79 H2
Andheri 52 B2
Andhra Lake 76 C4
Ansar 51 G3
Aran 66 D6, 79 E1
Arani 93 G5
Arganglas 14 D1
Arial Khan (Ba) 59 F5
Arjuna 99 E2
Arna 78 D1, 79 E1
Arpa 69 E3
Arpangasu (Ba) 72 D2
Arrah (N) 25 F6
Arthur Hill Lake 76 C2
Arun (N) 39 H1
Arwari Tal 34 A2
Asan (Utt) 18 D6
Asan (Mad) 34 D4, 35 E3
Ashna 78 C3
Asoda 67 F6
Asola Mendha Tank 67 H6
Asthamudi Lake 98 B3
Atrai (Ba) 40 C5
Atrai (Ba) 58 C2
Attingal 98 C4
Auranga 56 B4
Awarja 86 A1
Ayeyarwady (M) 75 H5
Babai (N) 24 D5
Back Bay 76 A4
Badrahuan 37 G4
Badua 57 G1
Bagad 63 G4
Bagar 35 G1
Bagh 68 B4
Baghain 36 C6
Baghel Tal 36 D1
Baghmati (N) 38 D2
Baghmati 39 E4
Baghnadi 70 A6
Bahgul 23 H4
Baitarani 70 D2, 71 E3,
    71 F5
Bajaen 33 G5
Bakhar 55 F1
Bakhira Tal 37 G2
Bakra (N) 39 H3
Balasan 40 B3
Balimila Reservoir 81 F5
Bamani 51 G1
Bamni (Ba) 59 H6
Ban 23 F3
Banar (Ba) 59 F2
Banas 33 E6, 33 G5, 34 B4,
    50 A2, 54 D3, 54 D4, 49
    G4
Bandi 32 B5, 33 G3
Bandia 80 B2
Baneloi 58 A2
Bangaduni 72 C3
Banganga 34 A6, 34 B2,
    37 G1
Bangra (Ba) 73 E3
Banka (P) 12 C6

Baordhig 80 D2
Bar 42 B3
Barah 34 B1
Baraila Tal 38 D5
Barak 43 E6, 61 E1
Barakar 56 D3, 57 G3
Baramas (P) 12 A2
Baranai (Ba) 58 C2
Baranal 71 F6
Baratala 72 B3
Bardha ka Talao 33 G6
Barki 56 C4
Baryar 68 B1
Batane 56 B2
Baulai (Ba) 59 H2
Bawanthari 67 H3
Baya 38 C4
Baypore 94 D4
Bearma 53 H4
Beas 17 F3, 18 A2, 18 C2
Beas Dam 17 H2
Beda 65 G2
Bei 50 B2
Belan 55 E1
Belsiri 42 C2
Bemla 66 D5
Benithora 86 A1
Berach 33 F6, 51 E1
Besu 37 G5
Betwa 35 F5, 35 H5, 52 D4,
    53 E1
Bewas 53 F4
Bhadar 62 C4, 62 D3
Bhadra (Ba) 73 E1
Bhagirathi (Utt) 19 F4
Bhagirathi (Wbg) 58 B3
Bhagun 82 C2
Bhainsola Tal 37 G5
Bhaisal 76 B2
Bhakla 25 E6
Bhakra Dam 18 A3
Bhakru 23 G3
Bhargavi 83 E1
Bhaskal 81 F2
Bhavani 95 F4, 95 G3
Bhedan 70 A3
Bheri (N) 25 F4
Bhiga 13 G1
Bhigar 13 G1
Bhillangana 19 F6
Bhima 76 C4, 77 E5, 85 G1,
    86 A2
Bhogava 63 G1
Bhola (Ba) 73 F2
Bhota Kosi (N) 39 E1
Bhugai (Ba) 59 F1
Bibiyana (Ba) 60 A2
Bichom 42 C1
Bidya 72 C2
Bighai (Ba) 73 F2
Bihar 54 C2
Bijul 55 G2
Bina 53 E4
Bind 13 F3
Birma 35 H6
Birupa 71 F5
Bishkhali (Ba) 73 F2
Bisnali Tal 38 A5
Bisuhi 37 F2
Biswi 37 F3
Black Bein 17 F4
Boan (P) 12 A5
Bodalkasa Tank 68 A4
Boinu (M) 75 E2
Boinu 60 D6
Bokaro 56 D4
Bori 65 F5

Born 85 H1
Boma 37 G6
Bosau Tal 38 A5
Brahmani 57 H3, 70 D4,
    71 F5
Brahmaputra (Ba) 41 E5,
    59 E1, 59 G2
Brahmaputra 41 H4, 42 A4,
    43 H1
Brahmaputra (C) 25 H1
Bumtang (B) 41 H1
Buray 65 E4
Burhabalang 71 G3
Burhi (N) 39 H3
Burhi Dihing 44 A1
Burhi Gandak 38 D4, 39 F6
Burhi Ganga (Ba) 59 F4
Burhi Rapti 37 G1
Burhner 68 C1
Buriganga (N) 24 C3
Burishwar (Ba) 73 F2
Burtanga 70 C6
Castle Bay 101 G3
Casuarina Bay 100 B2
Cauvery Delta 96 D6
Cauvery 94 C1, 95 E1,
    95 H2, 95 H3, 96 A5
Chachla Creek 47 H5
Chako 56 C3
Chaliyar 95 E4
Chambal 34 A5, 35 E3,
    51 G1, 51 G6
Champamati 41 F3
Chanab 13 F5
Chandan (Mad) 68 A3
Chandan (Bih) 57 G1
Chandkapur Reservoir
    64 D6
Chando Tal 37 F3
Chandra 18 C1
Chandrabhaga 32 D6
Chang Chenmo 15 F2
Chankeshar 66 B1
Chapora 84 C5
Chautung 22 B1
Chayul Chu (C) 26 D5
Chem Tso (C) 26 B3
Chenab (P) 16 B2
Chenab 14 A5
Cheyyar 96 C1
Chhaporwawa Band 33 F3
Chhiramati 40 B6
Chhota Tawa 66 B2
Chhoti Kali Sindh 51 G4
Chhoti Sarju 37 H5
Chikanchara 41 G4
Chila Lake 82 D2
Chilwa Tal 37 H2
Chindru Chu (C) 28 B2
Chindwin (M) 44 A6, 61 G5,
    61 H2, 75 H1
Chingri (Ba) 60 B5
Chinnar 95 H2
Chinta 80 C5
Chintavagu 80 B4
Chitarewa 53 F6
Chitartala 71 F6
Chittar 99 E4
Cho Dzong Chu (C) 28 B1
Chulband 67 H5
Chungphari Tal (C) 25 H2
Chunlung (P) 14 B1
Coleroon 96 D4
Constance Bay 100 A5
Cuthbert Bay 100 B3
Daba (C) 19 H4
Dabra 38 C4
Dai 33 F4

Dakatia (Ba) 59 H5
Dakhin (Ba) 73 G1
Dal Lake 13 F3
Dalani 41 G4
Dalet (M) 75 F6
Damanganga 76 B1
Damodar 57 E4, 57 G4,
    57 H5, 72 B1
Dangma (B) 42 A2
Dangri 18 B5
Danr Ohhira (Ba) 73 G3
Dardha 38 D6
Daya 85 F1
Dayul or Nu Chu (C) 29 G2
Deg (P) 16 C4
Deh 60 C5
Dehar 53 F4
Denwa 67 E1
Deo 68 B3, 70 C1
Deoha 23 H4, 23 H5, 23 H6
Devgarh Bay 84 B4
Devi 83 F1
Dhadhar 64 A3, 64 B2
Dhalai 60 B3
Dhaleswari (Ba) 59 F4
Dhaleswari 60 C2, 60 C5
Dhamra 71 G5
Dhanai 82 C2
Dhanauti 38 C3
Dhansiri 43 E5
Dhap (Ba) 40 C5
Dharka (Ba) 41 G4
Dharlang 14 A5
Dharmauti 38 A6
Dhasan 35 G6, 53 F3,
    53 G2
Dhauliganga 19 H5
Dhawa 56 C2
Dhela 23 F3
Dhil 33 H4
Dhusan 39 G4
Dibang or Siang 27 H5
Dibang or Sikang 28 B5
Dibru 44 A1
Dihing 44 D1
Dikhu 43 H3
Dindi 87 E3
Diphlu 43 E3
Diple 41 F4
Disai 43 G3
Disang 44 A2
Dispur 42 A4
Diyung 42 D5
Diyung 43 F4
Dogi 85 E6
Dohan 21 H5, 21 H6
Don 85 G3
Dotu 68 D3
Dri 28 C3
Drukla Chu (C) 27 E1
Dubbo Creek (P) 47 E3
Dudh Kosi (N) 39 G1
Dudha 78 B3
Dudhari 41 H5
Dudhganga 84 D3
Dudhi 53 F6
Dudiya 40 D3
Dudna 77 G2
Duha 82 B1
Dukwan Reservoir 35 G2
Dungia Reservoir 55 G1
Durgauti 37 H6
Dwarka 58 A3
Dyap Tso (C) 15 H3
Ekiti Bay 101 E1
Ekruk Lake 77 H6
Eluru 89 E1
Emro 28 B4

Erra 88 D2
Fahuj Reservoir 35 E6
Fresh Water Bay 101 G3
Fuljar 62 C2
Gad 84 B4
Gadilam 96 D3
Galathea Bay 101 H6
Galwan (C) 15 F2
Gamar 40 B6
Gambhir 34 D2, 51 F2,
    51 G5
Gandak 38 A2, 38 C4
Gandhi Sagar 51 G2
Gangadhar 41 E4
Gangau Reservoir 53 H2
Ganges (Ba) 58 C3
Ganges 35 H2, 36 B4, 37
    G6, 37 H5, 38 B5, 39
    G6, 23 E1, 23 E4, 23 G6
Gangi 37 G5
Ganjal 66 C1
Garai (Ba) 58 D4
Garai 37 G6
Garaimara 41 H4
Garhvi 68 A6
Gartang (C) 19 H1
Gatwa 33 H5
Gaur 54 A5
Gaura 37 H3
Gautami Godavari 89 E3
Gayitri 95 E5
Ghaggar 21 G2
Ghaggor 18 A6
Ghaghar Reservoir 55 G2
Ghaghara 36 D1, 37 F3,
    38 B5
haghat (Ba) 41 E6
Ghagra 24 C6
Ghaiprabha 85 F4
Ghanpur Lake 79 H5
Ghela 63 G2
Ghi 62 B2
Ghod 76 D4, 77 E5
Ghodahada 82 C2
Ghorajhari Tank 67 H6
Ghugri 39 G6
Giamda Chu (C) 27 E1
Giri 18 C5
Girja 77 G1
Girna 65 E6, 65 G5
Girwa (N) 24 C4
Goda (M) 44 C2
Godavari 70 D1, 78 C4,
    79 G4, 80 A4, 80 C6
Godavari Delta 88 D3
Gohna Lake 19 G6
Gola 23 H3
Gomai 65 E3
Gomali 50 D3
Gomati 36 D3, 37 F5
Gomti Creek 62 A2
Gomukha 96 C3
Gona 72 D3
Gopat 55 E2, 55 E4
Gorewara Tank 67 F4
Gorha Tal 37 H5
Gosthani Reservoir 81 H5
Guasuba 72 C3
Gudra 80 D2
Guhiya 32 B5
Gulf of Cambay 63 H4
Gulur 60 C3
Gumani 58 A2
Gumbhir 34 B3
Gumti (Ba) 59 G4
Gumti 60 A4, 24 A6
Gundal 95 F2
Gundlakamma 87 G5

Gunjali 51 F2
Gureureo 81 F6
Gya Chu (C) 26 A1
Hail Haor (Ba) 60 A2
Hajamro Creek (P) 47 E3
Hakaluki Haor (Ba) 60 B2
Halali Reservoir 52 C4
Halan 68 B1
Haldi 79 E6, 72 B2
Haleji Lake (P) 47 F2
Hallia 87 G3
Hanle 15 F5
Hano 68 D3
Hansthal Creek 48 D6
Harankeshi 84 C4
Hariabhanga 72 D3
Haringhata (Ba) 73 F2
Hasdo 55 F5, 69 F2
Hathmati 50 B4
Hathras 22 D6
Hatia (Ba) 73 H1
Hatni 65 E2
Hatti 81 G2
Hemawas Tal 32 C5
Himayat Sagar 87 E2
Hindan 22 C3
Hindri 86 C5
Hirakud Dam 70 A3
Hiran 53 G5
Hirri 67 H2
Hoja (Ba) 58 C2
Hooghly 58 C5, 72 A3
Humla (N) 24 D2
Husain Sagar 87 E1
Hut Bay 101 E1
Ial Bakya (N) 38 D2
Ichamati (Ba) 58 D3
Ichamati 58 C5
Idar 51 F2
Imphal 61 F1
Inbaung (M) 61 H6
Indawgyi Lake (M) 44 C6
Indra 69 G6
Indravati 80 B4, 81 F3
Indus (P) 12 A3, 13 B2
Indus 14 B2, 15 E5, 47 G2
Irang 61 E1
Isan 35 H2
Jabunaswari (Ba) 40 D5
Jadukata 41 H6
Jagat Sagar 53 H1
Jahnari 19 G4
Jainti 57 F3
Jaisamand (Debhar Lake) 50 D3
Jalangi 58 C3, 58 C4
Jalaput Reservoir 81 F5
Jaldhaka 40 D3
Jaleswar 41 F4
Jam 67 F3
Jamira 72 C3
Jamner 52 B6
Jamni 53 F1
Jamuna (Ba) 59 E2, 59 E3, 72 D3
Jamuna 56 C2
Jamunia 57 F4
Jamwa Ramgarh Tal 33 H2
Jarghavati 81 H4
Jaugti 41 E3
Jawai Bandh 50 B1
Jharahi 38 B3
Jhelum (P) 16 A1
Jhelum 12 C2, 13 F3
Jhila 72 D2
Jiri 61 E1
Johilla 54 D6
Jojri 32 C4

Jokam 51 E3
Jonk 69 F3
Jorhilla 54 C5
Kabar Tal 39 F5
Kabbani 95 E2, 95 E3
Kabul (P) 12 A3
Kacha (Ba) 73 F1
Kaddam 79 F3
Kaddam Dam 79 F3
Kadogo 70 A6
Kadua 83 F1
Kagna 86 B2
Kahr Creek (P) 47 F4
Kahtna 24 B6
Kairi Lake (P) 47 G1
Kajhar Creek (P) 47 G4
Kajvi 84 B3
Kakki 98 C3
Kala (M) 74 D3
Kaladan (M) 74 D4, D6
Kaladan 60 D6
Kalang 42 B4
Kalaw Long (C) 29 G5
Kali 35 G2, 23 F6, 24 B1
Kali Gandak (N) 25 H6
Kali or Krishna Gandaki (N) 25 H1
Kali Sindh 34 A6, 51 H1, 52 A6
Kali West 22 C3
Kalinadi 84 D6
Kalindi (Ba) 72 D2
Kalindri 58 A1
Kaliveli Tank 97 E2
Kaljani 41 E3
Kallada 98 C3
Kallar 96 C4
Kalni (Ba) 59 H2
Kalyan 36 D2
Kalyani 36 A3
Kam Chu (C) 26 D1
Kamla (N) 39 E2
Kamla 27 E5, 27 G6, 39 E3
Kanak Sagar 33 G5
Kanar 65 H1
Kanchi 57 E5
Kandleru 87 G4, 93 G3
Kangsa (Ba) 59 H1
Kanhan 67 F4
Kanigiri Reservoir 93 F2
Kankai 40 A4
Kankawati 48 B5
Kanva 95 G1
Kanwa 34 C3
Kapra 78 B2
Kar Lake 15 E5
Karamnasa 37 H6
Karanja 78 C6
Karatoya (Ba) 40 C4, 40 D6, 59 E2
Kareha 39 F5
Kareli 34 A4
Karjan 64 C3
Karkari 57 E6
Karna 68 D3
Karnaphuli (Ba) 60 C6, 74 A2
Karnaphuli Reservoir (Ba) 60 B6
Karo 56 C6
Kasai 57 F5, 71 H1
Kata Purna 66 C6
Katha 22 C2
Kathani 68 A6
Katni 54 B4
Katli 21 G6
Kaubar (P) 12 C1
Kauriala (N) 24 C4

Kayankulam Lake 98 B3
Ken 36 A5, 54 A2, 54 B3
Keotan 53 E4
Kethan 52 D3
Khampa (M) 61 G3
Khanau 23 H5
Kharagoda Tank 49 G5
Kharak Creek (P) 47 G4
Kharakvasla Lake 76 C5
Khari 34 D2
Kharkai 71 E1
Kharlchara 68 C5
Kharnah (N) 25 E2
Kharo Creek 47 H5
Kharsua 71 F5
Kheri 48 A5
Kherkutia 43 G2
Khoprang 24 A1
Khowai (Ba) 60 A3
Khru 27 E6
Khuria Tank 68 D1
Kiadho 78 C2
Kiagar Tso 15 E5
Kichhu 23 G4
Kim 64 A4
Kinarsani 88 B1
Kindang Bum (M) 44 D2
Kinsha Kiang (C) 29 H1
Kishanganga 13 E1
Kisina 84 C1
Kobragarh 68 A6
Kodayar Lake 98 D5
Kohalia (Ba) 74 B3
Koila Tal 37 F4
Kolab 81 G4
Kolang 42 D4
Kolar 52 C6
Kolleru Lake 88 C3
Konar 57 E3
Konar Reservoir 57 E4
Kopil 42 C6
Kopili 42 C4
Kopra 53 G4
Kori Creek 47 H5
Korila 41 H3
Korttaliyar 93 F5
Kosi 39 F5, 23 G2, 23 G3
Kosi Reservoir (N) 39 G2
Kothari 33 F4
Kotri 80 B1, 80 B2, 80 C1
Koyna 84 C2
Koyna Reservoir 84 B1
Krishna Delta 88 B5
Krishna 85 F4, 86 D4, 88 A3, 87 E4, 88 B4
Krishnai 41 G5
Krishnaraja Sagara 95 E1
Kudaliar 79 F6
Kuinar (Ba) 59 F5
Kul 34 B6
Kulhan 69 E4
Kulong (B) 26 A6
Kulsi 41 H4
Kumar (Ba) 58 D4
Kumeng 26 D6
Kumhari Tank 69 E4
Kundalika 76 B5
Kundi 65 G3
Kunga (Ba) 73 E3
Kuni 79 F2
Kunwari 35 F3
Kur (B) 41 H1
Kurang 69 E2
Kurang Tank 69 F2
Kurnool 87 E6
Kusiyara 60 C1
Kuwal 33 H6

Kuwana 37 F2, 37 G3
Kyaw (M) 75 G3
Kyi Chu (C) 26 A1
Kynchinag 42 A6
Kyong (C) 25 G1
Kyun Tso 15 F5
Lachung 40 C1
Ladhiya 23 H3
Lakahmibai Tank 84 C4
Lakchmantirtha 94 D2
Lake Beale 76 C2
Lakhandai 38 D3
Lakhya (Ba) 59 G4
Laknavaram 80 A5
Laknavaram Cheruvu 80 A5
Lakundar 51 H4
Langai 60 C2
Laniye 43 G6
Lant 69 H6
Lemro (M) 75 E4
Lendi 78 C5
Lero Chu (C) 26 C5
Likhu Khola (N) 39 F1
Lilagar 69 F2
Lilri 32 D4
Ling Chu (C) 28 D1
Lingti 19 E3
Little Gandak 38 A3
Logtak Lake 61 F2
Lohandara (N) 39 H3
Lohit 28 B6
Loni 36 B4
Loro Nakpo Chu (C) 26 C5
Lubha 42 C6
Lung Kiang (C) 45 H1-6
Luni 32 A5, 32 D3, 31 G6, 31 H5
Luni Delta 49 F2
Machak 66 C2
Macharewa 53 G6
Machhu 49 E6
Machkund 81 F5
Machundri 63 E5
Madar 56 B1
Madha (N) 39 E2
Madhura 78 C6
Mahanadi 54 B4, 54 C3, 68 D6, 69 E5-H3, 70 A4-D6, 71 F6
Mahanada 40 A5, 40 B6
Mahanadi 69 F3
Mahawa 23 F5
Mahi 50 B6, 51 E5, 64 A2, 38 C4
Mahuar 35 E5
Maini 55 H6
Maipura 71 G5
Maithon Reservoir 57 G4
Majham 50 B5
Majhgawan Tank 35 H6
Majhoi 37 F4
Mala Tank 53 H4
Malampuzha Reservoir 95 F5
Malan 63 G4
Malancha (Ba) 72 D2, D3
Mali (M) 45 F4
Malin 23 E2
Malprabha 85 E5
Malprabha Reservoir 85 E5
Malung 14 D6
Malwan Bay 84 B4
Man 85 E1
Manar 78 C4
Manar Reservoir 79 F5
Manas 41 H3
Mand (N) 24 D5

Mand 55 H6, 69 H3
Mandakini 19 G5
Mandavi 84 C6
Mandira 70 B2
Maner 79 G5
Maneru 88 A3
Mangai 37 G5
Mangla Reservoir 12 C5
Maniari 69 E2
Manimala 98 B3
Manimukta 96 C3
Maninuttar 99 F1
Manipur (M) 61 F4, F6
Manjra 57 G4, 78 A5-D6, 79 E6, 86 D1
Manneru 93 F1
Manu 60 B3
Mara Manas 41 H3
Marakhi Reservoir 57 H3
Maramsilli Reservoir 68 D6
Markanda 18 B6
Masan 38 B1
Mashi 33 G3
Mat 60 D6
Matai 71 G5
Matamuhari (Ba) 74 C3
Matla 72 C2, 72 C3
Maukkadaw (M) 61 H6
Maw (M) 75 F3
Mayangdi (N) 25 H5
Mayu (M) 74 D6
Mechi 40 B3
Meda Creek 62 B3
Megal 62 D4
Meghna (Ba) 59 G4, G6
Mej 33 H5
Mekong (C) 29 G1
Mendha 33 G2
Meshwa 50 B5
Metoma (C) 26 B1
Mhasvad Tank 85 E1
Mi (M) 74 D3
Mipal Tso 15 F4
Miti 48 B5
Mitri 32 B6
Mogaung (M) 44 D6
Mogra (Ba) 59 G1
Mohala (N) 25 H3
Mohan 55 H5
Mohana 38 D6, 56 C2
Mohanada 40 B3
Mohedamada 79 G6
Moj 62 D3
Mon (M) 75 F5
Mor 57 H3, 58 A4
Moran Sagar 34 B3
Morand 66 D2
Morari Lake 15 E6
Morel 34 A4
Morhar 56 C2
Mormugao Bay 84 B6
Morne 55 G4
Mouths of the Ganges 72 B4
Mouths of the Godavari 89 E4
Mouths of the Indus 47 E3
Mouths of the Krishna 88 B5
Moyar 95 F3
Mugu Kamali (N) 25 F2
Mula 76 C3
Mullamari 86 B1
Mulni (P) 47 F3
Mulshi Lake 76 B5
Mun 66 B5
Muneru 80 A6

Munglam Tsangwa (C) 19 H4
Muma 66 B5
Musi 87 G2, 87 H6
Musi Reservoir 87 G2
Mutha Mula 76 D5
Muvatupula 98 B1
Muveru 80 B6
Myani (Ba) 60 B6
Myitha (M) 75 F2
Nabaganga (Ba) 58 D4
Nadanwara Tal 53 F1
Nag 67 G5
Nagar (Ba) 40 B4, 58 D2
Nagari 93 F5
Nagarjuna Sagar 87 F3
Nagavali 81 H2, 81 H4
Nahar Sagar 33 F5
Nahro 34 C3
Naigra 48 A6
Nakti Creek 48 D6
Nal Lake 49 G6
Nam Hkao (M) 44 A3
Nam Kiu (M) 45 F2
Nam Long (M) 45 E1
Nam Salein (M) 44 A4
Namai 42 B3
Nampuk (M) 44 B4
Namya (M) 61 G2
Nandhaur 23 H3
Nandiraj 80 C4
Nanganji 95 H6
Narayani (N) 38 B1
Narmada 52 C6, 53 E6, 53 H6, 54 A6, 54 C6, 64 A4, 65 E2
Navara Bay 101 G3
Nawegaon Lake 68 A5
Neran 13 G4
Neur 55 E4
Newaj 52 A2, 52 B4
Neyintaya (M) 61 F5
Ngagon Chu (C) 28 C2
Ngan Tso (C) 28 D2
Nibra 80 C2
Nim 23 E6
Nizam Sagar 78 D6
Nmai or Laung Pit (M) 45 G4
Noa Dihing 44 B1
Nogavali 82 B5
Noinai 38 D6
Non 36 A4
North Bay 101 G4
North Koel 56 A3
Noyil 95 G4
Nugu 95 E3
Nuna 71 F6
Nuni 83 E1
Nyak Tso 15 H4
Nyamjahg (C) 26 B6
Nye Chu (C) 26 C5
Ohar 52 A3
Ochito (P) 47 F3
Ojat 62 C4
Ong 69 G5, 69 H5
Ong Chu (C) 29 H1
Orsang 64 D1
Osman Sagar 87 E1
Pabar 18 D4
Padma 59 E4
Pagla 58 A2, 58 B1
Pagludiya 42 A3
Pahuj 35 F5
Paikat Bay 100 B3
Pairi 69 E6
Paisuni 36 C6
Paitiani Creek (P) 47 E3

Pakhal Lake 80 A6
Pakri Tal 37 H4
Palang (Ba) 59 F5
Palar 93 E6, 95 H2
Paleru 87 G6, 87 H6
Palleru Lake 87 H2
Palleru 87 H2
Palmar 56 D1
Pamban Channel 99 H3
Pambiyar 98 C2
Panam 50 C6
Panchet Reservoir 57 G4
Panchganga 84 D3
Pandu 35 H3
Pangali (Ba) 59 E1
Pangong Tso 15 F4
Panjhra 65 E5
Parambikolam Reservoir 95 F6
Parbati 18 D2, 34 A6, 34 D3, 52 B1, 52 C4
Parbati Tal 37 E2
Paringalkuthu Reservoir 95 E6
Paro (B) 40 D1
Parwan 52 A1
Pasum Tso (C) 27 F1
Patal 81 G5
Pathro 57 F3
Patialewali 18 A6
Patna 54 A3
Paunglin Lake (M) 75 H6
Payaswani 94 C1
Peddavagu 79 G2, 87 F3
Peechi Reservoir 95 E6
Pen (M) 75 H2
Pench 67 F2, 67 G4
Penganga 78 D2, 79 E2, 79 G2
Pennaiyar 96 C2
Penner 93 F2
Periyar Lake 98 C2
Perumal Eri 96 D3
Phairang 60 C6
Phalgu 56 C1
Phiti Creek (P) 47 E2
Phokswmdo Tal (N) 25 G3
Phulka 49 F6
Pi Chaung (M) 74 D4
Pilakhar 23 G4
Pin (M) 75 H6
Pindar 19 G6
Pinjal 76 B2
Po Tsangpo (C) 28 A1
Poini 93 E5
Ponnaiyar 96 A1, 96 D2
Ponnani 95 E5
Portman Bay 100 B6
Poto Chu (C) 28 B1
Pottaruvagu 81 E5
Pranhita 79 H2
Pravara 76 D2, 77 E2
Pulal Lake 93 G5
Pulantod 95 E5
Pulicat Lake 93 G4
Punch 12 D4
Punpun 56 B1
Puma 65 G6, 65 H5, 66 C5, 66 D4, 78 A2, 78 B3
Pumabhaba 40 C6
Pusur (Ba) 73 E1, E3
Putaimari 42 A3
Putama 82 B2
Qalandri (P) 47 F4
Rabnabad (Ba) 73 F3
Raidak (Ba) 41 E4
Raidak 41 E3
Raimanagal 72 D2

Raimangal (Ba) 72 D3
Raj Samand Lake 50 D1
Rakni 60 D2
Ramappa Lake 79 H5
Ramganga 23 F3, 23 G2, 35 H2
Ramgarh Tal 37 H3
Ramnagar Res. 23 F2
Ramtek Reservoir 67 G4
Rana Pratap Sagar 51 G2
Randi 49 H1
Ranga 43 F2
Rangmati 62 D2
Rani Sagar 34 C3
Rapti (N) 25 E5, 25 F6
Rapti 37 G2, 37 G2, 37 H3, 25 E6
Rara Daha (N) 25 E2
Ratoi Tal 37 H4
Ratua 40 A4
Raul 82 A1
Rawal 63 E5
Rehar 55 G6
Retam 51 F3
Retri 52 B2
Rihand 55 G2
Rihand Reservoir 55 G3
Rind 35 G2, 36 A4
Roberts Bay 100 B3
Rong Chu (C) 27 H1
Ronga 41 H5
Rongat Bay 100 B4
Rongtu Chu 28 D3
Rum Tso 15 G4
Rupen 49 H4, 50 A4
Rupin 19 E4
Rushikulya 82 C2
Sabari 80 D6, 88 C1
Sabarmati 50 A4, 63 H1
Sabi 33 H1, 21 H6
Sagar 67 F2
Sahibi 22 B6
Sai 36 B3, 36 C4, 37 F5
Sai Ti 29 E5
Saingdin (M) 74 C4
Sakhya Sagar 34 D6
Sakri 68 D3, 57 E2
Salandi 71 F4
Sali 57 H5
Salivagu 79 H5
Salona Tal 37 H4
Salween (C) 29 F2-G5, 45 H5
Sambhar Salt Lake 33 F2
Sami (M) 74 D4
Sandy Point 101 E1
Sangu (Ba) 74 B2, 74 C2
Sani Bhevi (N) 25 F4
Sani 62 B2
Sanjai 57 E6
Sankh 56 B5, 70 C2
Sankosh 41 E3
Sankosh or Mo (B) 41 F2
Sapt Kosi (N) 39 G3
Saptamukhi 72 B3
Sar Lake 83 E1
Sarada 81 G6
Saralbhanga 41 F3
Saraswati 33 E3, 22 A1, 49 H3, 63 E5
Sarayan 36 B1
Sarda 24 B4
Sarda or Chauka 36 C1
Sarigh Jilganang Kol (C) 15 H1
Sarju 36 D1, 23 H2, 24 A2, 24 D6

Sasoi 62 C1
Satna 54 B2
Satti 68 A6
Saura 39 H5
Savitri 76 B6
Sawi Bay 101 F2
Seaword Bay 100 B3
Sela (Ba) 73 E2
Sen (M) 75 E5
Sengar 35 F2
Seonath 68 C5, 69 E3
Seoni Tank 67 H5
Sesseri or Sessar 28 B5
Shahbazpur (Ba) 59 G6
Shahkar 53 G6
Shaldat Tso (C) 15 G5
Shanmukha 95 G6
Shastri 84 B2
Shedhi 50 B6
Shen 53 G6
Sheona 51 F3
Shetrunji 63 F4
Shimsha 95 G1
Shirawata Lake 76 B4
Shyok (P) 14 A1
Shyok 14 C1, 15 E1
Sib (Ba) 58 C2
Sibsa (Ba) 73 E2
Siddha 79 E3
Sike 27 H4
Sikrana 38 B2
Silai 57 H6
Sileru 81 E6
Silgi 56 A6
Siliserh Lake 34 A1
Sima 85 G1
Sina 77 F5, 77 G6
Sind 34 D6, 35 F4, 52 C2
Sindphana 77 G3
Singavada 63 E5
Singla 60 C2
Sipra 51 G4, 51 H6
Sir Creek (P) 47 G5
Sirsa 35 E1
Sisa Creek (P) 47 E3
Siyom 27 H5
Solani 22 D1
Someswari (Ba) 59 G1
Son 54 C4, 54 D3, 55 E2, 55 E5, 68 B3, 69 G2, 38 B6
Sonai 42 C4, 60 D3
Sonar 53 G4, 53 H3
Sonath 68 D4
Sondur 69 E6
Song 19 E6
Sot 23 G6
Sota 21 H6
South Bay 101 E1
South Koel 56 C5, 56 C6
Soyagi Sarovar 64 C1
Spanggur Tso 15 F4
Spiti 19 E2
Stanley Reservoir 95 H3
Subalong (Ba) 74 C1
Subansiri 27 F4, 27 G6
Subarnarekha 57 E5, 71 H3
Sukha 69 E5
Sukha Bhadar 63 H1
Sukhata 35 H1
Sukri 32 B6, 32 C5, 56 B4, 31 H6
Suktel 69 H5
Sulia 82 D2
Sulin (M) 75 G5
Sumna (C) 19 H3
Sun Kosi (N) 39 E1, 39 F2
Sundar 57 H1

Sura 55 H1
Suraha Tal 38 B5
Surangi 69 G4
Surma (Ba) 60 B1
Sursar 39 G4
Suruli 98 D1
Sutlej (P) 20 A1
Sutlej 17 G4, 18 D3
Sutlej or Lanchen Khambab (C) 19 G3
Suvarnamukhi 81 H4
Sweta 96 B4
Tadima Bay 100 B5
Talpavu 80 C4
Tamai (M) 29 F6
Tambraparni 98 D4, 99 F4
Tammileru 88 C3
Tamur (M) 39 H2
Tan 55 F6
Tanai (M) 44 C4, 44 D4
Tandadori Tal 55 F1
Tandava 89 F1
Tandula 68 C5
Tandula Tank 68 C6
Tangan 40 C5
Tansa Lake 76 B2
Tapti 64 A5, 65 E4, 66 C3
Taralait Bay 100 B3
Taron (C) 29 G6
Tarung (M) 44 D2
Tashi Yang-tsi (B) 26 A6
Taungdicin (M) 75 G1
Tawa 52 D6, 67 E2
Tawa Reservoir 66 D1
Tawang (M) 44 D3
Tazon Wang (M) 29 F5
Tel 81 G1
Telhu 28 D5
Temur 53 H6
Tendoni 53 E5
Tetulia (Ba) 73 G1
Thala Wang (M) 29 F5
Thega 74 C1
Ther 43 G6
Thoubal 61 F2
Tighara Reservoir 34 D4
Tikra 70 C4
Tilabeh 39 G4
Tilaiya Reservoir 56 D2
Tiljuga 39 G4
Tin Va (M) 74 D2
Tirap 44 B2
Tirna 78 A6
Tiru 78 C5
Tirunanimuttar 96 A3
Tisang (M) 43 F1
Tista (Ba) 40 D5
Tista 40 C1
Titas (Ba) 59 H3
Tixu 43 G5
Tixu Nantaleik (M) 44 A4
Tongsa (B) 41 G2
Tons 18 D4, 18 D5, 37 E6, 37 G4, 54 C2
Torsa 40 D3
Towang 42 B1
Trape (C) 19 H2
Trigo Tso (C) 26 B4
Tril 61 F1
Trulung Chu (C) 26 D3
Tsangpo (C) 26 B2, 27 G2
Tsarap Lingti 14 B4
Tso Bunang (C) 27 E4
Tsuri Chu (C) 27 E4
Tuichang 60 D5
Tuichong 74 C1
Tuilianpui 60 C5
Tuimang (M) 61 E4

Tuirai 61 E3
Tuivai 60 D3
Tuivaw 60 D4
Tung (Ba) 59 G3
Tungabhadra 86 B5, 86 D5
Tungabhadra Reservoir
    85 G6
Tupari 85 F5
Tuyungbi 61 G1
Tyao (M) 61 E5
Ubon 62 D3
Udai Katan 34 B3
Udai Sagar 50 C2
Uiar 52 A2
Ul 24 C6
Ulh 18 B2
Ulhas 76 B3
Umed Sagar 33 F6
Umiam 42 B5
Umran Lake 34 B1
Umran Tal 37 E5
Und 62 D1
Uran 57 F3
Urmal 53 H1, 54 A1
Urpad 41 G4
Utai 69 H6
Utangan 35 E2
Uyu (M) 44 C5
Vaghotan 84 B3
Vaidarbha 79 F1
Vaigai 99 F2
Vaippar 99 E3, 99 F3
Vaisali 35 F4
Vaitarna 76 A2
Vamsadhara 82 A2, 82 B5
Vardha 81 F6, 98 D1
Varna 84 C3
Varshalai 99 G1
Vashishti 84 B1
Vasishta Godavari 88 D4
Vatrak 50 B5
Vedaranaiam 97 E6
Vegavati 81 H5
Vellar 96 C6, 96 D4, 97 E5
Vembanad Lake 98 B2
Vettar 96 D5
Victoria Tank 77 E5
Viranam Eri 96 D4
Vishnuganga 19 G5
Vogarivagu 87 H4
Wa Chu (C) 29 E1
Waddi Khuddi Creek (P)
    47 E2

Waghari 79 E1
Wainganga 67 H1, 67 H6,
    68 A3, 68 A6, 79 H1
Wak (M) 75 E6
Wakai 50 B2
Wan 78 A4
Wardha 67 E4, 67 F6,
    79 G1
Wartu 62 B3
West Bay 101 E1
Wetthigan Lake (M) 75 G6
White Bein 17 G4
Willingdon Reservoir 96 C4
Wira Lake 88 A2
Wira 88 A2
Wong (B) 41 E1
Woodmason Bay 100 A6
Wular Lake 13 E2
Wunna 67 F6
Ya Tso (C) 26 B5
Yamne 28 A5
Yamuna 18 D6, 35 E2, 35
    H4, 36 A4, 36 B5, 22 C1,
    22 C5, 22 D6
Yarlung Chu (C) 26 B3
Yaw (M) 75 G4, 75 H4
Yerla 84 D1
Yeshwant Sagar 51 G6
Yu (M) 61 G3
Yume Chu (C) 27 E4
Yung Song Chu 27 H3
Zahaw (M) 75 F2
Zamunang Co 15 G4
Zanskar 14 C3
Zayul Chu (C) 29 E3
Zayul Ngu Chu (C) 28 C2
Zungla 43 H5
Zuvari 84 C6

RUINS
Chanderi 53 E2
Chaul 76 A5
Gaur 58 B1
Lothal 63 H1
Mahasthangarh 58 D1
Mainamati 59 H5
Old Goa 84 C6
Paharpur 58 D1

TEMPLES
Aihole 85 G5
Allahabad 37 E6
Amaravathi 88 A3

Amritsar 17 F3
Auroville 97 E2
Ayodhya 37 E3
Badami 85 G5
Baijnath 18 B2
Basaralu 95 F1
Belur 91 E5
Bharuch 64 C1
Bhopal 52 C5
Bhubaneswar 71 E6
Bodhgaya 56 C2
Chidambaram 97 E4
Darjeeling 40 B2
Dharamsala 18 A1
Dharmastala 90 D6
Eklingji 50 C2
Dwarka 62 A2
Fatehpur Sikri 34 D2
Gangtok 40 C1
Gawahati 42 B4
Gaya 56 C2
Gwalior 35 E4
Halebid 91 F5
Haridwar 23 E1
Hemis 14 D3
Hyderabad 87 E2
Island of Bet 62 B1
Jagannath 83 E2
Jaisalmer 31 E2
Junagadh 62 D3
Kalimpong 40 C2
Kanchipuram 93 F6
Karaikal 97 E5
Karkal 90 C5
Khajuraho 53 H1, 54 A2
Konark 83 F1
Krishnaraipet 95 E1
Kulu 18 C2
Kumbakonam 96 D5
Kushinagar 38 A3
Leh 14 C2
Madurai 99 F1
Mahabalipuram 97 F1
Maheshwar 65 G2
Mathura 34 D1
Melukote 91 F2
Modhera 49 H4
Mount Abu 50 A2
Mudabidri 90 C6
Mysore 95 F2
Nagarmangala 91 G6

Nagarjunakonda 87 G3
Nalanda 56 D1
Nasik 76 C1
Nathdwara 50 C1
Onkaresh 66 A1
Onkareshwar 65 H2, 66 A2
Orchha 35 F6
Palitana 63 G4
Parasnath 57 F3
Patan 49 H4
Patna 38 D5
Pattadakal 85 G5
Pemayangtse 40 B1
Ponda 84 C6
Pushkar 33 E3
Qutab Minar 22 C4
Rajgir 56 D1
Rameswaram 99 H3
Ramtek 67 G4
Ranakpur 50 C1
Ratnagiri 71 F5
Rishikesh 23 E1
Sanchi 52 D5
Sarnath 37 G6
Somnath 62 D5
Somnathpur 95 F2
Spitok 14 C3
Sravanbelagola 91 G6
Srinagar 13 E3
Sringeri 90 D5
Srirangam 96 B5
Srirangapatnam 95 F1
Sudh Mahadev 13 G5
Tashiding 40 B1
Thanjavur 96 C5
Thiruvananthapuram 98 C5
Thiruvarar 96 D5
Thrissur 95 E6
Tikse 14 D3
Tirchchendur 99 F5
Tiruchirapalli 96 B5
Tirukkalikundram 97 F1
Tirumala 93 E4
Tiruvannamalai 96 C2
Udaipur 50 C2
Udayapur 53 E4
Ujjain 51 H5
Varanasi 37 G6
Venur 90 D6
Vijayawada 88 B3
Vishnupur 57 H6
Vrindavan 34 D1
Warangal 79 H6

Yamunotri 19 E4

VALLEYS
Adilabad 79 F2
Asifabad 79 G3
Banas 50 A2
Baspa 19 E4
Bobbili Basin 81 H4
Dibang 28 B6
Indus 14 B2
Kabaw (M) 61 G4
Kamban 98 D2
Kangra 18 A3
Kanhan 67 F3
Kashmir 13 F3
Krishna 86 D4
Kulu 18 C2
Lahaul 18 C1
Lower Assam 42 B4
Lower Bhima 85 H2, 86 B2
Mahasu 18 B4
Middle Godavari Basin
    80 B5
Middle Krishna 85 F3
Murwara Basin 54 A5
Nandyal 87 E5
Narainpur Basin 80 C2
Narmada 66 B1
Rampur 18 D3
Sabari 80 D6
Samodar 57 G4
Spiti 18 D1
Upper Assam 43 G2
Upper Bhima 77 E5
Upper Gudavari 77 F3
Upper Krishna 84 C1
Vamsadhara 82 B4
Zanskar 14 B3

WATERFALLS
Cauvery 95 G2
Dandeli 85 E6, 90 C1
Deo Dhari 55 G1
Dudhsagar 84 D6
Gokak 85 E4
Hogenekkal 95 H2
Jog 90 C3
Kevati Kunt 54 D1
Magod 90 C2
Sivasamudram 95 E2